I0113309

Just Do It !

Manifesto for the New Age

JUST DO IT ! Manifesto

for the New Age

© All rights reserved Cyril Belshaw 2012

Front cover image: Humans are still far from maturity and their real potential, *Raven and the First Men* —MOA # Nb1.481 by Bill Reid (1980) Photographed by Bill McLennan Courtesy University of British Columbia Museum of Anthropology, Vancouver, Canada Back cover: Humankind searches for the promised land. Detail from Bill Reid's Advancing Canoe, YVR Vancouver International Airport international departure lounge author's photograph.

ISBN: 978-1-926820-24-8 Hard cover Library Edition. 2013 printing.

This text is re-written from those published as *From Youth Maturity to Global Government, Where is Utopia?* and *Fixing the World.* With the exception of the first (Stockholm. Raketa Press) these have been withdrawn from distribution.

Printed and retailed by Lulu.com Distributed by Lulu and Ingram Books

Webzines of Vancouver 2012

Suite 2901 – 969 Richards Street Vancouver BC Canada V6B1A8

JUST DO IT !

Manifesto

for the New Age

Cyril Belshaw

Webzines of Vancouver

2012

Let a Global Spring create the Rainbow
Revolution !

Contents

Manifesto for the New Age

I – The Point of View

Few would disagree with the thought that the global society is in a shambles especially fom the perspective of human satisfaction.. It can be argued that our world is a much better place than it was two hundred years ago. But it falls far short of what we would like.

There are still millions of malnourished mothers and children. Armies and armed gangs still devestate populations and countryside's, tyrants still hold power in countries without freedom of expression or action. Great cities have populations of homeless the destitute and youthful unemployed who have less and less hope, families where violence is the norm and children are abused.

The Manifesto is not a catalogue of ills. Each one of us can make up his or her own.

Instead it takes a positive stand to work out what needs to be done to clean up the mess. This is no easy task or we would already have rallied around the solutions. I will refer to studies and arguments which address specific issues. Such a slice by slice approach is not enough and sidesteps the reality – the reality that every aspect of life bears upon every other. Thus I attempt a holistic view, one in which each dimension of society is interpreted as having ramifications for all the others.

Everyone who lives anywhere in this world, of whatever culture, religion, or political persuasion, other than babes in arms, very young children or hermits, feels that what goes on with humanity in this world is disastrous and should be fixed if only one could do so. Those who are given the authority to do something about it, from politicians and CEOs to philosophers and religious leaders have been and are ineffective.

The most obvious reason is vested interest and special pleading in which the immediate satisfactions derived from possible action take precedence over global interests. Not many people, except in the field of environmental cleanliness, take the global consequences of their actions into account. As we shall see this is built into our system of nation states and of business ethics. Scholarship has divided the world into little bits – specific studies of this or that institution, this country and that country.

Is it time for an anthropologist to show his hand? We'll see. He is not so foolish as to believe he has all the answers but he will have a stab at re-starting the debate in a systemic way.

In attempting to find out what we need to do I adopt an approach which is a kind of applied anthropology. There are several principles which run through the argument[1].

The first is that there is only one "natural" society, namely the global one. All the others which we describe in anthropology and similar disciplines are artefacts of our sciences which require us to simplify our models in order to handle them. All those things we call "societies" "polities" or "economies" have cross boundary relationships and institutions which are an integral aspect of their functioning, nature, their culture and their social organisation. The global society is bounded by the nature of its globe – a situation which may not last forever if we discover life elsewhere in the universe, or create lasting settlements somewhere else in our galaxy.

Anthropology is known for its holistic approach to society and culture. That means to say that each functioning element relates to the others; religion to agriculture, kinship to property, child rearing to ethics, and so on and on. Since the global society is a single unit I apply that anthropological technique to its understanding as best I can. One perhaps obvious discovery I make by using this method is that the education of youth is fundamental to the operation of global government and the nation state; and of course that the nation state and global government in their present forms affect and restrict what we can do by way of educational change.

Stated like that the holistic links are obvious but this principle needs further and deliberate application.

The second principle I use is about the nature of innovation and its presence in the global society[2]. It would

11

be pointless to talk of a successful evolution of the global world if innovation did not take place or were in some way dysfunctional. In the next chapter I argue that invention, which is the precursor of innovation, is not only present functionally but is universal in the lives of every individual in all sub-cultures. The processes of innovation can be rapid and we should think of harnessing it to our objectives. To avoid needless repetition, once examined in the next chapter, the potential speed f innovation is assumed throughout.

The third principle is that society and culture are the expression of, in the case of the globe, billions of what Talcott Parsons once called "unit acts". They are what we as individuals do from day to day in our private and our public lives which result in the structures and regularities of culture and social relationships which we reify as nation states, and, yes, the global society, culture, economy and polity.

The fourth principle is embodied in my title. This essay uses objective information but it is in essence subjective and strongly normative. As individuals we must choose our destiny, where we want future generations to go. We must name those goals and direct our actions towards achieving them. You may have different ideas from mine. But I am exhortatory. *This is a manifesto setting out ideas for action.* At present what we do is to let everyone else decide through their individual actions how global society is evolving. Most of us don't realise that what we do is the foundation for the result[3].

We have considered ourselves to be impotent bystanders as the globe changes. Of course this does not apply to all of us. We have leaders, thinkers and activists of all stripes and an increasing occurrence of popular uprisings. They usually act within limited practical arenas but we now know of their potential revolutionary effects. If we are really to choose our destiny instead of merely allowing it to happen it will require conscious debate and decision on the part of the global citizenry giving life to what is, even now, speeded up innovation, both material and in behaviour and thinking.

We have most of the knowledge to proceed though it may be shredded into disorganised chunks. On aspect of this knowledge will be so show where we need research, identifying what is important to know. Our increasing knowledge makes it easier to identify what it is we *don't* know and to take steps to find out. More than ever before, if we identify a problem we can usually find the way to produce an answer.

Finally I try to make use of the principle that it requires cold hard logic with no ideological influences and taking the argument wherever it may lead. This is not totally possible if one is a human being with a passion for the world. I will do my best. You will find flaws in my logic and disagreements about value statements. So I challenge you. As you read this book *make your disagreements conscious and express them in debate.*

Remember also that this is a holistic treatise. If you disagree on one point it will have implications for others. You will need to work out the total ramifications. And if you have the energy, write another book with an alternative scenario. By such actions you will be moving the enterprise forward.

That perspective relates to another principle. A good anthropologist shares his or her findings with the people studied. I am studying *you* so I want to know how you react to my conclusions. This is a global fieldwork ethnographic report as much as anything.

I intend to analyse the great problems of the contemporary world, get down to the fundamental reasons why these are worrying and work from there ass logically as I can to convert them into viable solutions which represent what I believe most of us desperately want. And then show what we must do to fix things up.

You may think of this as some kind of Utopian dream[4]. If by Utopia you mean some kind of unrealistic model of an ideal society you would be wrong. There is nothing in what I have to say that cannot be achieved – if we want to do it. For the most part we already have a great deal of the knowledge and technology. The question for each of us to answer is: "Do we want it? Are we willing to pay the price in individual effort? Can we persuade our leaders – who are supposed to be in the forefront of reforms but who are usually standing way behind their citizens – to think outside the box?" I believe the answer should be and is a resounding "Yes". My conclusion will be *"Yes, we will."*

There are multiple ways of arriving at the goal we choose, and billions of value-laden decisions to formulate along the way. Here the premise is that we, as *peoples*, must take steps to examine, evaluate, and discuss the intermediary objectives – the ones to be defined as we move forward to our ultimate goals. However definitive I may seem in my ideas, they are just that - ideas. I believe in them at this moment. But they need to be discussed, amended, and replaced.

Cultural ideas, whether local, professional or global are dynamic. The changes which took place in the twentieth century – little more than one lifetime – were fundamental to all societies in the world[5]. Some would argue, persuasively, that the rate of change increased exponentially, leading to inequities and anxieties about our ability to absorb the innovations. What is more, the changes have not been limited to technology or commercial practice or instruments designed to kill. In a very uneven way, they have included the most basic elements of human culture, from religious belief to marriage and sexual practice, and to the accountability of authority.

One major comment on the human condition is that it is a result of tension between Krishna's idealisation of duty and Arjuna's belief that our actions will be judged rather on their consequences. Krisha wins the argument in practice, with violence and disaster for his victims. As Amartya Sen points out, the *Bhagavad Gita*, where this drama classically unfolds, may be interpreted as a warning about the blind devotion to duty, for its consequences may be successful in the short term, but dire in the long term. Indeed it is the autocratic, rule from above, philosophy of many political systems – including "democracies". This essay comes down firmly on the side of the primacy of consequences, but also argues that duty in fact implies precisely that – duty to humankind means being aware of and respectful of consequences.[6] Note that the duty is to humankind, not to a junta or necessarily one's own country.

Up to the present, despite the existence of pressure groups, powerful politicians and CEOs, the changes have been blind. There is one relevant rule of human life. However much we plan, scheme, and rationalize policies, the results of any action, public or private, contain unforeseen elements. Sometimes these are trivial, sometimes they completely frustrate the given objective. In all cases they require re-thinking about what we do. The move ahead must be dynamic in its ideas, *not* bounded by ideological precepts. To successfully follow the threads in this book, the reader must be critically alert to such issues in my thoughts if we are to move forward from them.

Thus we cannot be 100% certain about what we do. This is not a plea for more research. It is important to *accept* uncertainty and, its concomitant, the learning

16

experience of making mistakes along the way. We cannot wait for the completion of a major study – too often an excuse for inaction; while searching for, and using, knowledge we must act in good faith, with the best knowledge and sensitivity we can muster.

The cliché has it that the movement of a butterfly's wings in the Amazon will influence the state of mind of a hermit in the Himalayas. We cannot detect that tiny influence. What the cliché says is that what we do has ramifying effects on the thoughts, actions, emotions, planning, of others both near and far. We do not normally extrapolate the consequences of our individual acts to the analysis of the nature of the world order. Yet the pond ripples, and it would be good to judge the effects of our own actions, however humble, in terms of their rippling results.

At an intimate level, there is much that can be done. We can judge our own actions in terms of what we know about their effects. This is already being done. Husbands and wives ponder the effect of their words and behaviour on their partners. Sincere environmentalists amend their private actions, consciously working if not to improve, at least not to further damage, the environment as they know it. Parents use theories and ideas about what works best for their children, and in doing so have at least some wider respect for social responsibility. The exercises will be the more effective the more they become spontaneous, as natural results of attitudes towards life. To handle this is of course a prime goal of activities which create maturity in youth to which I give a fundamental chapter.

The vast differences between the rich countries and the poor, not only in commercial wealth but in the opportunities presented to the human spirit, create obvious targets for action. Too often, this takes the form of "Let them be like us". Put baldly, the gross flaws in such an argument are obvious to all except the proselytizers of U.S. style capitalism or religious fanatics. I have claimed elsewhere[7] that the more centralized and detached a political entity, the more humans value small scale associations of great variety (from Churches to carnavals and cultural associations) within which they may find an identity.

Thus what we may call global values (e.g. embodied in international law, behaviour and policy) both emerge from and impinge upon systems of significant *localized* values. Adaptation, resistance, judgement, positive excitement and anger are part of the dialectic. No great work can emerge which can take into account all the variations. But principles, such as those of understanding the nature and ramifications of change, the implications of reform, may be applied and respected.

I base my hope and optimism on several features.

The first is that we are already arguing, not following the structure of this book, but in our daily lives and politics. The second is that intimate and global societal changes have taken place in the past sixty years with a speed that perhaps is not as great as with technology, but is nevertheless mind boggling, chaotic, and needing popular and rational choices. The third is the rise of people power in the first years of this century, often indicating that the popular will is in advance of the political (though it is sometimes reactionary). Another phenomenon is the effect of growing education and enquiry for a higher and higher proportion of the globe's citizens.

I owe it to you to begin by explaining how change occurs, and showing that it is not a great mystery but is a part of everyday life. This I hope will give you some confidence in understanding that this century could be the one in which we achieve our current goals – and imagine further ones.

<u>2012Postscript</u>

- We are already moving into the subject of the next chapter – innovation. A book like this is useless if it is not somewhat innovative itself. In this sort of context it used to be called "thinking outside the box". It can be deliberate by noticing what the accepted model is and then manipulating the variables to see if something equally or more functional appears. I am not consciously doing it this way but the process here may be unconsciously similar. It would be helpful in the long run if readers might do the same, that is by finding points of disagreement in my arguments and then figuring out what the preferred alternative could be. (And then tracing the consequences for other elements in the global structure.) The value of alternative thinking is expressed in a book entitled "The Art of Being Unreasonable."[8]

II – How Society Works The Bedrock of Innovation.[9]

Reaching forth to create a better world, even just living in the present, requires innovation writ large. It seems that as the world changes, the speed and volume of innovation rise astronomically, some would say exponentially. Yet even so we seldom consider what innovation consists of, how it works, and ultimately how we can maximise its functional effects while minimising its dysfunctional one. Since I will be demanding change, often of fundamental habits and procedures, it is well to take note of innovation's characteristics and dynamics.

There are some general principles which underlie my optimism and belief that a practical utopian world is achievable and may be possible by the time this century closes. These are the principles which govern and account for innovation and change. The recognition of them demonstrates that Utopia has moved from science fiction and fairy tales to potentiality. It is now a matter of will.

First a couple of definitions or we will be misunderstood. *Everyone* invents, throughout the their whole lives. Invention is simply to do something not done before – washing the dishes in a different way, disposing of garbage using procedures not done before. We *invent* for ourselves all the time. No culture is immune. The difference between individuals is not that some invent and others do not – it is rather in the focus and substance of the inventions.

Often we teach our family to follow suit, to copy what we have just done. This is the beginning of much *innovation* as the new methods are taken up by others. There are thus differing strengths with which innovation percolates from the individual inventor through institutions, enterprises and eventually perhaps global culture. Many inventions go unnoticed. Individuals do something new but nobody else takes note or copies. The action remains an invention, but does not become an innovation, common to elements in the culture.

How does societal change, social innovation, occur? As a boy with left wing ideals my critics often said to me "But human nature will never change". Biologically there are limits. Yet culturally there are few such limits with one exception. This is that where we go is dependent on where we are and have been before. We build the future on our past history and our present situation. In the past, that has put serious limits on our imagination of where we *can* go. But today so many options are open to us that such a limit is now of minimal importance.

If we wish to play our part, as individuals, in the movement of society to a more satisfactory state we may preach to influence others (as perhaps I am doing now) or, to the extent that it is in our ability, to *live* our beliefs. Not many of us can be political leaders of countries, let alone of world "government". But in family, business, or creative life we can do indeed lead insofar as the world around us permits. As more and more are doing, we can, if it suits our temperaments, exercise influence in associations and in whatever political process is open to us and in the day to day operations of our work and recreation. We can become activists for pushing toward the achievement of the world we want. As I shall show we can do much of this simply by adapting our own individual, even family, behaviour.

Since in this discussion we are working toward change it is not going to be easy. It is hard to think of changes in ourselves -- managing the control of depression, working fewer hours, dealing with conflict -- that will not be noticed by others, thus giving rise to comments and judgement. We put ourselves on the line, we are stating who we are, exposing our identities to the evaluation of others.

Those who run the gauntlet of possible criticism, however, can be comforted by the phenomenon that *any* action or belief, at least in industrialised society, will be criticised by some, open to the charge that it is mistaken, immoral or evil. (The obverse is not true: Murder, child abuse, rape, are not likely to be approved by anyone. Though killing is often condoned, as in a "just" war, ethnocide is often advocated, and some may excuse sexual assault as a war time instrument.) A good football player, idolised by crowds, is condemned as a macho bonehead by others. Mother Theresa had her critics, as did Albert Schweitzer. A computer whiz or brilliant mathematician is scorned for being outside the real world. Giving to charity is blessed to some and tabbed as posturing by others. Discipline a child in the family circle, and neighbours will comment - when does it become abuse? A manager who promotes an able woman attracts gossip and jealousy. How many are they who have been hurt and disappointed when they find that their well-meaning, generous, or innocent actions have attracted derision, hostility or suspicion?

In many small societies in which I have worked, success is both highly sought after and dangerous. A successful person is one of power, manipulating the ties of kin, friends, or compadres to create obligations. The reciprocal bonds of indebtedness ensure that the successful person is one who is owed much by others, ensuring that he or she gets material, moral or political support when it is needed. It is the generosity that makes this possible, for to give creates an obligation. But too much success attracts competition, envy, hostility, so that it must continually be managed sensitively. The successful person must speak in the idiom of family, tribe, community, ancestors, not of himself alone. If generosity falters, then it can be seen to be blatant, self-serving, and selfish. Dislike of aspects of behaviour -- failure to perform a ritual properly, slighting a relative, the failure of a crop -- leads to resentment that masks envy. Of a sudden, success is dangerous. There is illness or a string of bad luck attributed to sorcery or the success of competitors. The mana, the power, is gone. The high are toppled.

Complex societies have not evolved very far from reciprocal dependencies and the levelling influence of envy. We sometimes mistakenly think this to be so because of the ideology of individualism, and the perception that "simpler" societies were somehow non-competitive because they had ideologies of kinship, family, clan, tribe. We must address this issue, the way in which *ideologies mask the empirical realities*, the way in which they can disguise the realities of the system they represent. Until I raise that question more systematically later it must be reserved as part of the background to some of my arguments, held as a continuous modifier to interpretations.

Anthropologists do not have much difficulty in demonstrating this. The public pretends reciprocity is not there. Yet ceremonial events -- birthdays, weddings, Christmas -- tie in dramatically with each other. The intensity, or lack of it, in personal and family relations, by which is meant personal interactions, create networks of giving that are dynamic, and in which what happened before influences what happens now. That the giving is generous does not remove the fact that it recognises past obligations, and creates new moral ones too. And the proportion of consumer spending that can be attributed to ceremony and friendship is enormous.

The impersonal market system of commerce and industry is not impersonal. Yes, contracts may be up for bidding. Yes, they are usually awarded on price and quality. The strict rules that apply to governmental contracts demonstrate, by the very "need" for them that something other than "objectivity" is significant. Of course it is. Reliability, the return of a favour, security based on personal knowledge, are of key significance. Entrepreneurs want to *know* their clients and suppliers, both to favour them and to exploit their weaknesses. Why else should there be business clubs, entertainment accounts, golf, exchange of gits, horse racing, networking........ and corruption?

I see pros and cons as I make judgements about such features. As a "scientist" my orientation is to understand without judging, to try to elucidate *how* it is that societies and cultures work the way they do, *how* did present conditions arise, *what* makes phenomena functional or dysfunctional within the system that is presented to me. By attempting to understand what goes on in one society and culture I may be able to arrive at principles or intuitions which can be applied to the interpretation of others. Some principles may be extended to apply to numerous, even all, "societies", that is to global society.

Indeed it has happened already. The study of the classical prestatory (gift-obligation) societies -- North West Coast Indians engaged in potlatch, Trobriand Islanders, then many others throughout the world -- enabled anthropologists to hypothesise, in fact predict, the occurrence of such dynamics in as yet undescribed cultures, and, as mentioned above, in a re-interpretation of what goes on in the "individualistic" West. Clearly, because so many things are otherwise different, prestatory dynamics will not, empirically, be identical or even similar in different contexts. But they will be there, in some form or another, in all "societies", because giving (not only in material forms, but in emotions and communication) and receiving, and the psychological demands and moralities of the exchanges, are the essential bricks out of which the regularities of social organisation and of social predictability are built. One of the most noticeable applications of this theory is in the observation of negotiations between nation states on trade or military policies.

Let us continue, bearing in mind that we are leading up to thoughts about the nature of innovation, for we have determined that the necessity for change is pretty well axiomatic, and change rests upon just that. Innovation in the context of reciprocity..

The dynamics of prestation suggest that individuals pursue their goals through the creation of networks of social exchange with others. In some societies the networks may be hierarchical or kin-oriented. In the industrialised world the networks are far more open, although hierarchy and kinship are still very much there.

It seems difficult for many, including some of those in the intellectual community, to apply the concept of social exchange that underlies prestation. Most economists, with the exception of those who follow Gary

27

Becker, have escaped from their ancestors into narrower concepts of exchange, confined to goods and (commercialised) services, or to market, that is monetised, transactions. Even many of my fellow anthropologists still speak of "the economy" or "the economic" as being related to material things, relegating services such as the provision of ritual to some other domain. The concept can be not only confining, but mistaken and ethnocentric and undermines our holistic principles.

It is mistaken, from the point of view of the subject matter of this argument, because such separations are artificial rather than real, because the material and the non-material are inextricably blended together by webs of value and meaning, and because ideas, values, concepts, emotions, spiritual thoughts, philanthropy, the search for power, are all there, in competition, both as instruments for a satisfying life (resources) and as competing goals for our actions – and hence for where we want the globe to go.

It is ethnocentric, for the ideas of money and the market are used to separate "market economies" from the rest, a separation that denies continuities between the two categories, postulates the near impossibility of the one evolving naturally into the other, and obscures analytical similarities. I have argued elsewhere that "money" is a matter of degree of acceptance, not of kind[10]. It is not coinage and bank balances, but the *degree* to which whatever it is (materially) serves such functions as medium of exchange, store of value, and so on, in which other elements such as liquidity and confidence are embedded. There is nothing new in this; indeed it is old-fashioned. It is mistakenly ignored.

So, as it were, we must turn things on their head. In the context of innovation, we talk of *exchange* not market, and we recognise that the things that are exchanged are not simply commercialised goods and services but all those other things that link one person to another, the immaterial, the intangibles, power and love, altruism as a goal, those other things that are never "equal".

Almost by definition, human beings cannot be totally in isolation from one another. Some groups such as some monasteries can separate themselves more or less, and some individuals may opt to be hermits. These are decisions which result from previous histories of social interaction. Furthermore, , supplies are almost always, if minimally, required from elsewhere. A completely localised and bounded exchange system is impossible to sustain. Those who advocate reducing consumption, especially of foods, to those produced within a hundred mile radius are advocating a social and psychological consumer impossibility (which also falls foul of one of the most significant precepts of economic knowledge: that development is based on "taking in each other's washing" or, in anthropological terms, some form o reciprocity). In other words we always need things from elsewhere and our prosperity depends on trading to and for them.

The desire of individuals to link with groups is among their decision-making goals, and as such will be a subject of later discussion. Here it is sufficient to note the tension between the individual and the group, whether that group be a family, an association, a church, an ethnos or whatever. At one end of the spectrum, the group in question may succeed in subduing the individual and creating authoritarian conformity. (Even here individuals are not carbon copies of each other, so that some degree of tension is present.) At the other end the individual attempts to reject a group, to find his own path, to seek isolation, to be a total rebel -- or to find another association.

For by far the majority of persons, linkage with one or more groups is an essential element in the construction of personal identity. We cannot live alone; the choice of whom we associate with, in varying contexts, is part of our self-expression. This is true of even abstract communication, such as my writing this book.

At present it is almost an accepted truism in therapeutic ideology that it is not an appropriate goal for an individual to be so surrounded by inescapable group influences that he or she has lost his or her identity. Such individuals must seek their identities from a renewed consciousness of what lies within -- especially if the pressuring group has been a dominating family. Early family influences, once regarded as almost the inescapable creators of the persona, are now often seen as the enemy, to be rejected in order to find one's self. The specifics of such an argument are for later chapters. Here, let us simply note that this is an example of the tension to which I refer. Moreover, the individual is in fact often replacing one group with another -- the family (which he or she has probably already lost) with the cultural group constituted by therapists and their clients and like-minded others or by other groups which appear to offer the chance of remedy..

III Innovation is the Bedrock of Society – But What is it?

Tensions taken to degree we have described above can be horrendously destructive. Yet some degree of tension is the source of creativity and hence innovation, since tension implies that there is a problem to solve. It might be in social relationships, politics, domestic living, or industrial technology. Awareness of a problem, and its desirable solution, is part of the process of innovation, of change[11]. An alertness comes with reasonable tension, an alertness in which the mind identifies ranges of problems.

Problem solving, that is creativity, however modest, can draw its ideas from within the identified group, for this is where the idioms of communication will be fairly clear. In such groups there are shared languages. Mostly, a modicum of security is needed for the innovator to take the risky step of not only thinking, but of doing, something new. That security comes from group membership. And the innovation comes from mixing the ideas that lie within the group in new ways, and is extended when ideas enter the group from the neighbouring cultures. We can see the tensions, opportunities and restrictions at work very clearly in immigrant groups -- not only now, but over the centuries. Overseas Chinese constitute the most well-known and marked example, reinforced by immense international networks of friends and persons who can be called kin. But almost every migration has had its stimulating effects -- Huguenots, the nineteenth century movement of Swiss,

English, Scots, and German; Cantonese, Lebanese, Punjabi, Bengali, Polish, Ismaili, the list goes on.

Of course, the group can be self-limiting and inward-turning. If it is not open to outside influences while retaining the central core of values, absorbing and using them, the capacity to innovate will be limited to the mix of ideas already present, and that limitation will be reinforced if there is an isolationist ideology. This is particularly true of some religious groups, who place an emphasis on their uniqueness, and the superiority of their ideology and ethics. The current phenomenon of extreme Christianity and Islam is an example.

Another significant aspect of group identification is the use of innovation to reinforce that very identity. We must be careful not to confuse innovation with only so-called "utilitarian" considerations. Spectacular ceremonies and extravagant festivals are the most cogent examples of other kinds of pervasive innovation. Note the widespread extensions of carnival and similar group festivities since World War II, especially as communities have more wealth to spend on them.

In a world where so much of our living is related to the anonymity of functionaries, where we interact with people of whom we know very little, when we must make meanings for ourselves as tiny particles in an infinite universe of others, where we are lumped together as being of a certain age, or sex, or tax bracket, we must, the therapists tell us, know ourselves. What better way than to see ourselves not as part of the whole world, but as a member of an association, an individual who can make a creative contribution in a cultural group -- while "out there" we pass almost unnoticed?

When western developers first pondered the potential of Third World communities to "grow", they almost unanimously decried the existence of "wasteful" ceremonial. It took time before they could understand the anthropological truism that such ceremonial was often a way of re-distributing wealth and socio-political power; that it created dynamics of social exchange without which the economic system would be dead; that it embodied positive goals, part of the economists' "competing ends" to which "scarce resources" would be allocated.

Surprise, surprise. As income increased, so did the amount of resources devoted to ceremonial -- even to the extent of re-inventing activities that had been apparently gone, as with the famous medieval football game of Florence, proscribed under Mussolini.

And most such activities are still further segmented. In Florence and Siena the activities are organised -- over months -- in parishes of the city, to which loyalties are addressed. In Rio and Basle the competing carnival enterprises are handled by long term associations. Throughout the world there are events of a similar kind, let alone weddings, funerals, and Christmas giving. Embedded in them are values of power, fame, pride in the group, self-identity (look at me, I belong

34

here), companionship -- and often spectacular innovation. Are the competitions of sports, both professional and amateur, not similar -- for athletes, "owners", coaches, advertisers, and the home fans?

But wait. Competition is dangerous. Associations have their own charters, their own rules, the procedures that set themselves apart from others. Like professions, which are restrictive by definition, they set boundaries to acceptable activities. An innovator may get away with enormous power; or by contrast the very fact of being too ambitious may lead to him being dragged down by envious rivals. To be successful, he must work within cultural rules and norms. Go too far beyond them and the power slips away. Nowhere is this more clear than in Industrialised political parties -- both internally, and externally as the electorate expresses envy at perks and the symbols of power, and stretches out claws to tear down the "improperly" powerful. It is everywhere.

An innovator, then, must often express a different kind of personality from his fellows to give expression to his ideas. He must often break with his group; his creativity is perhaps first expressed by doing just that. He may even be expelled or excluded by suspicion as to his motives, his intellectual nature, even his strange powers. He may find that the group with which he is associating simply does not have the imagination, the resources, the drive, or the interest, to support him when he needs to work with them to start up his new methods.

His risk taking assumes a new dimension. It is not only the risk of failure in the eyes of those who have trusted him, but the risk of self-failure. It is not only the risk of bankruptcy or that his ideas are not functional or are ahead of their time, that they won't work, that others won't recognise them. His own self is on the line. Can he fight through the reverses and disappointments? Can he find the niche in society that will allow his talents to flourish?

So many innovators discover themselves to be different, must live with those differences, become outcasts at least for the moment. In this age when we study almost everything, writers have drawn attention to two kinds of individuals who, except for a few perceptive observers, are somewhat like this. One set consists of those many differing individuals who have brain damage or sensory handicaps. The fact that "normally" equipped people have difficulty communicating sensitively with them hides their interior lives from all but the closest companion-observers. Those who do communicate find enormous resources of intellectual activity, artistic sensitivity, and creativity that comes from the narrower but more intense focus of their perceptions, which, when expressed, may be highly compulsive, yet innovative and valuable when made known to the rest of society. Autism is the major example of this and may have been present in, for example, some of the great philosophers and mathematicians.

And there are the "eccentrics", people who in effect say to the world "I'm me. I shall concentrate on behaving the way I like. If you wish to learn to live with my foibles, good. If not, I'm sorry, but I laugh." Britain was once renowned as a country that valued its eccentrics, turned them into the subject of warm satire and playful cartoons. Britain defended to the hilt their right to be eccentric. The most recent small example I ran into was at a pedestrian crosswalk in London. A tweedy gentleman with a cane stepped forth. The oncoming car kept moving at the crosswalk. The gentleman stepped into its path, waved his cane angrily, went to the driver's window and gave him a dressing down.

Take that little incident for a moment. Trivial? Not at all. To an observer like myself it was a warmingly welcome incident, with which I identified, but perceived as unusual, hence eccentric, probably part of a personality that would express many other similar actions. In some parts of the world, doing that would have been a high risk matter. Here, in this part of London, it seemed to carry little risk, denoting the thought that such behaviour was still tolerated. But it carried another thought, namely that if there were a growing number of incidents of that kind, if it were on the rise, so to speak, then drivers would begin to realise that infractions of this kind, the inherent threat of danger within them, was no longer a matter to be taken for granted. In other words, the eccentric act of one individual at one time, if repeated and taken up by others, could become the norm. Is this why, now, I do whatever I can to make my anger known to drivers of rowdy motorcycles, unsuppressed car mufflers, and heavy metal emerging from 4 x 4s. Carried further, if adopted by others, there would be innovation.

Individual actions *are* significant. It is through them that norms become established.

"Eureka" he shouts in the bath tub, "I have it!" The dramatic flash of insight that in a moment changes the world..... Coming from nowhere, into a brilliant mind.

Not so fast. There are many components to innovation. An innovation is, by definition, a new cultural artefact. Innovations flower in a thousand ways. But they all have one characteristic.

They make use of *already* known cultural components. The components must be *recognised* by the innovator, they must have meaning for him. Even in dreams, in the wildest imagination, the elements that combine to make the fantasy are each, if taken apart one by one, already known. The angels do not send down a flash of lightning with the message here is something, dear innovator, for you to use, something that is beyond the comprehension of your culture. Even if that were so, the innovator could not be expected to understand its significance unless he were mentally ready, unless the novelty were composed of elements he recognised, unless he had some understanding of how it fitted into already established life or thought. An innovation may be revolutionary, may have uncomprehended consequences, but in itself it combines in a new way characteristics that are already there. The novelty may come from accidental observation, the insight of a dream awakening, but the components of what is observed must have meaning; or it may come from painfully elaborated abstract logic.

Whoever first used fire to cook something, maybe meat, already knew that fire burned, already knew that meat was good to eat. Perhaps he dropped the meat in, but his senses were ready for the result.

Obversely, it is no use preaching the value of platinum to a culture which does not yet recognise the uses of the substance, directly or in trade. And the outcome of mathematical logic depends on the elaboration and manipulation of concepts that have already been developed, doing so in new combinations, creating more substantial or simpler concepts. Each concept, once established, adds to what is there, expands it, becomes a stepping stone for the next stride.

That axiom is at the root of what follows.

For it follows that if you have very few components in your culture the likelihood of recombination will be slim, the changes slow. But if you have limitless components, then the possibility of recombination is also limitless, and the pace of innovation is fast.

It used to be argued that "traditional" societies were "innately" conservative, lacking an "achievement orientation". Not so. In the first place, *all* societies value achievement -- where they differ is in the objectives of the achievement. It may be good hunting, producing children, warfare, riches, spiritual attainment, leisure, or of course in combination. It is true also that some societies, or social groups, value the security of stability or unchanging continuity; but so strong is the appeal of innovation that they can only do so by attempting to place strict boundaries around themselves, trying to prevent the enlargement of their cultures. And there, of course, in this modern world at least, they fail, with the result of change, of schism, or of loss of population.

In a previous work I wrote, confusingly, of an "orientation" toward innovation. It is probable that it would be more useful to place innovation within the list of culturally valued goals as a variable. This is most easily illustrated with art. In some cultures new pieces of work are valued for their continuity with past forms; in others they are valued for their "originality", their change from the past. Such goals have to be balanced with, and to compete with, other goals -- perhaps some aesthetic principle -- to become effective. The explosion of the art of the Northwest Coast Canadian Indians would provide a beautiful case study – incorporating new materials and presentations on a basis of new arrangements of old continuing symbols. Brilliant artistic inventions were taken up by others with large innovative results.

Certainly, *individuals* differ the one from the other in their ability to create the recombinations, to invent, that is they differ in their creativity. In the simplest of societies there are those who think, who tell stories imaginatively, who philosophise, who tinker, who adventure, who explore, and thus stand out as different.

As I have pointed out earlier a new idea or artefact is not in itself an innovation. It must somehow spread beyond the individual's own world, be communicated to others, and embraced into the cultural world of others. If it stays privately with the individual, it is lost to culture. It is the individual's private toy.

The individuals to whom a new idea or artefact is presented judge it from the point of view of their own thoughts, interests and goals. That is, does it somehow fit into their conceptual framework? A proposal that is "ahead of its time" may simply not fit well; it must wait until the rest of culture has changed to make the fit more aptly, more usefully, more acceptably.

The impact does not have to be acceptable to everyone. On the contrary, its value may be in stimulating further debate, further change. The point is that it has entered the pool of ideas, become part of the capital stock of culture, available for yet further recombination, known to other minds.

There must be hundreds if not thousands of material inventions which are in themselves inherently sound, but which have not been recognized, or have been rejected because their creation does not fit into the mind set of those to whom it may be targeted[12]. One current example is that of the Skegway. This is a battery operated device which transports the human body making use of the body's own inherent attributes of balance and adjustment which come into play when we walk. Its foundation is a platform on two specially tired wheels which the user's body manipulates by linking the body to the device through a rigid handle. It replaces the single occupancy car, is environmentally safe and energy efficient and, with adaptations, can be used on all terrain. The inventor could not get financiers, policy makers, and certainly not vehicle manufacturers to take up its production and distribution. Despite this, through his own efforts, the device has been successfully demonstrated in many contexts, is now in manufacture, and is being adopted in numerous industrial contexts (such as the Vancouver International Airport and several warehouses) to move people around expeditiously. For that use it was ready. It has had some but limited use by private individuals, many of whom were not ready for it, or were facing bureaucratic licensing obstacles. The innovation has been limited by cultural perceptions.

In other words it is more likely than not that initial inventions will meet nay-sayers who have vested interests in reducing competition, or who, unlike the inventor, are still thinking blindly within a dark box.

If this is true of material inventions, how much more true it can be of non-material and policy innovations. Don't rock the boat, there are too many unknown risks and uncertainties, are common objections to the most innocent of proposals, let alone those which have world changing attributes. Indeed, inventive ideas in this book are bound to attract opposition as a matter of blind principle as well as a matter of genuine thinking. It will be a task of what follows to show that such objections are open to challenge and that they can have consequences which are often dire as well as obstructive. Nevertheless it behoves the innovator to consider the socio-cultural context in which he or she is working, and to bring the ideas and proposals into touch with those elements of culture and knowledge which are already in place to be tapped and recognised.

To sum up so far, the rate of innovation in a culture is a function of the size of the cultural stock, that is the pool of ideas, knowledge and material resources, interpreted widely, plus another factor I will introduce shortly..

Material resources are included for two reasons. The obvious one is that material resources provide some of the raw materials for inventors to play with, to help them communicate their ideas, and to put them into effect.

For this to happen the resource must be recognised in some form. When a resource crosses from one culture to another, it is frequently the case that its meaning, and therefore its function, will also change. Guitars will be used for different purposes in Nova Scotia and Pernambuco -- the outflows in music and in the social context are not identical. The aluminium and wires of an abandoned aircraft in Kenya will not go to a recycling depot, but will be turned into articles of bodily adornment. To sell the benefits of oil production to a culture that does not know the concept "oil" as it applies to underground liquids and industrial use or consumption requires conversation and persuasion to introduce the relevant notions, that is to add to the stock of cultural capital.

In other words the material is never just the material. It does not consist of objects isolated from cultural linkages. Whether it be coins or a chair or women's adornments, or a rock by the side of a road, or a road itself, it is irrelevant except insofar as it has meaning, can be interpreted, and unless it communicates that meaning, which may have utilitarian, aesthetic, personal, or even spiritual overtones. It is with the manipulation of such meanings that material innovation takes place. Hence, from an innovative point of view, the elements of the material that are significant are those that are immaterial. Remove the legs of a table and replace them with rollers; change the shape of the table; replace the wood with glass; etch the glass; place flowers on it; put a Japanese screen behind it; place food on it; put your feet on it; all these changes take place through the use of concepts. Put the table in a Melanesian thatch hut and it may be out of place, not wanted -- unless another idea comes into play, that of prestige, one-upping the neighbours. The material consists of concepts, then, and those concepts are available to the inventor in the same way as are the ideas translated into a book or a painting.

I have already pointed out that the size of the cultural stock affects the chances of innovation taking place, that is the quantity of innovation which results. Let us do a bit of innovation ourselves along the lines of the principles I have been enunciating. From economics we know the concept that the size of the money supply consists of the quantity of money modified by its *velocity of circulation*. It seems sensible to borrow the concept here.

For surely if two men sit side by side, each with differing ideas, but don't talk to each other, i.e. with a velocity of circulation of ideas of zero, the size of the sum of ideas of each of them will be minimal if not zero. Minimal rather than zero because mew thought combinations may be occurring in their brains. Zero velocity, minimal innovation. Even if one of the men has enough ideas in his head to think up something new, he is not communicating by talk, hence minimising the potential innovatory impact.

Once they start talking, the chances increase. Expand the conversation to others, they increase further. Circulation is happening within the pool of ideas. And so it goes on. It is no accident that the exponential innovation growth of the twentieth century was founded on profound changes in communication. And it is no accident, either, that mediaeval scholars, often quite isolated in their own communities, placed enormous emphasis on travel to scholarly centres to expand the limits of their communication. Was not the need for communication, for disputation, for the interacting of minds, in times when travel was inefficient, a most powerful impetus for the founding of universities? And did not a lingua franca, Latin, contribute to that possibility?

It is obvious to all that the world wide adoption of smart phones and social networks has increased the velocity of circulation of ideas exponentially for the 21st century with innovatory effects in Asia and Africa and political innovation which authorities can no longer control effectively.

So, the rate of innovation is a result of the size of the pool of ideas modified by the velocity of communication.

In later argument I will be writing of cultures as imagined entities, that is as being in some sense bounded, a concept that raises many issues. For the moment, however, let us assume that this is so, despite what I have written about the global culture being the only "natural" one.

In this model we can conceive of culture as something like a liquid containing millions of moving cells -- not people, but ideas, concepts, values, moving through talk, gestures, facial expressions, the internet and embodied in recognised institutions and items of man-made material culture. To conduct empirical research on culture, in connection, say, with my theses, it would be ideal to be able to quantify the number of those cells. To do that one would have to break down everything --ideas, elements of material items -- into both their smallest parts that can conceptually stand alone and into those combinations (a table, a table leg, a table top, a mathematical equation, each of the concepts which make up that equation) which also have meaning. An enormous and impractical task.

Failing that, and failing the ability to conduct hypothesis testing on the basic of such a necessity, a major conclusion stands out nevertheless, which will have an impact on later chapters. We have come across one of many limitations to the certainty of knowledge. Our knowledge about the kinds of matters we are discussing cannot be perfect. It can be indicative, approximate, subjective. As individuals facing the future we must reconcile ourselves to *the certainty of imperfect knowledge*.

To return, however, to the concept. If a cultural boundary is tight, with no movement over it (almost an impossibility as is the economist's "perfect competition") the number of cultural cells contained within the boundary is finite at any given time. But there are more of some than of others. There may be ten mathematicians and a hundred boat builders and five thousand lovers. The number of cells related to these conceptual domains will be affected by the complexity of the thoughts in each domain (let us say 1,000 cells mathematics, 500 boat building, and 50,000 lovemaking -- not very realistic, but illustrative), by the number of individuals sharing those thoughts, and by the velocity of circulation, that is communication.

To draw up an account of what is going on, one would in fact be drawing up an inventory of the cultural stock, and analysing modes, patterns and intensities of communication (which would have to allow for the possibility that the receiver did not absorb the communication in precisely the way it was sent -- that is, filtered it). This inventory I call a *profile of culture.*

Profiles of culture do, approximately, exist. They are called thick ethnographies. Most of them, for the non-specialist, are terribly dull to read, because they describe in minute detail elements of the daily life of a people, as completely as possible, preferably based on participant observation, a technique in which the observer merges as closely as he or she can within the daily life, using the language as the medium of talk. They are indeed inventory-like, and they produce interpretations and generalisations based upon the way in which elements in the inventories relate to each other, that is, communicate.

Because such profiles describe the here and now of the observation, they are also the *only* data that approximate what the economist calls effective demand, that is what people actually do with their resources at any given time, whether that be of a material or non-material nature. In practice, economists deal with only little bits of effective demand, treating some of the most important wants (or goals in life) as outside their models, or as "other things being equal". Not many of them read ethnographies, even of modern communities.

In fact the ethnographies also fall far short of the objective. The writers do not have, at least in these decades, the scientific objectives that would be implied in the questions of this chapter. Paradoxically, once upon a time the objectives would not have seemed so strange, for anthropologists in the early part of the 20th century were obsessed by what they called "cultural traits" that correspond very roughly to the cells, and they were guided in doing so by a search for the influence of cultural traits upon each other within and across cultural boundaries. Many of them did so out of sociological content, that is with inadequate attention to context.

Studies of profiles of culture are also hampered by manpower, its training and its distribution. Doctoral candidates are seldom given the finances to employ research assistants to gather data in ways that permit quantification. Their theoretical orientation suggests, anyway, that this is less worthwhile than the creation of a range of studies, each focusing on a theoretical problem which does not require such minute quantification. In most cases, discussion is by way of *example*, minutely dissected. If there were enough of these examples, the data would be there, but there cannot be through these methods.

I myself, in looking at the interlinkages between ceremonies in parts of Fiji, in which scores of individuals were involved, with the massive exchange of goods, and large feasting, and me working alone, could not cover all the significant detail of any one marriage, for example. I had to attend several, and combine the observations. And then do the same with funerals and other events for they were all interlinked. But I did not count the *number* of such ceremonies in the observation period. It could have been done, quite simply. But other things.....the number of first fruits ceremonies performed? I would have had to redirect my four Fijian part-time assistants, who were very busy doing household budgets and tracking cargoes on the trucks going to market......

We can improve, if the questions are deemed important enough. We are not likely to improve enough to give certainty, even in the quantification mad 21st century. I have argued before, and state again, that in the absence of appropriate techniques we can never truly know the operable values in a culture or predict its movement. We can only approximate.

I think the questions *are* important, because I believe there are significant generalisations about the way in which innovation translates into societal change, which are capable of being investigated more closely. Begin with the notion that the profile of culture is not a random hodge podge of cells accidentally linked to each other. The cells are linked by communication, which is the electricity that attracts or repels them, and by the power of thought that binds those that are attracted into conceptual nuclei. Add to this the notion that societal change takes place not when a single nucleus is altered, but only when it spreads within the system to some degree. The system is just that, a system, its parts influencing each other.

A changed nucleus can bring about ramifying consequences. For example, the introduction of reading skills can bring about a demand for reading materials, newspapers, books, libraries; can lead to changes in other ideas as a result of the fusing of concepts contained in the written word with ideas already in place, and so on and on. It can also have multiplying effects, that is for more reading instruction given to other persons, children or adult. However, such effects may be no more than potentials, if the means of satisfying them are not there, or are too onerous to be used. When I was in the Solomon Islands in the 'forties the ramifying effects were primarily limited to religious literature and the writing of letters which sometimes had almost mystical connotations of power, for there was almost no other reading material. (Paperbacks from the U.S. forces were snapped up, and a typewritten "newspaper" I created engendered a flow of story and article contributions which totally surprised me.) After the war the resource base changed, and the potential demand was translated into a vigorous and effective search for high school and university learning.

To disentangle a viable *potential* profile of culture, in precise terms, is almost impossible, but in approximate terms it must be attempted. If asked, individuals will certainly express their hopes, fears, goals, values. But when it comes to the point, when actually confronted with the possibility of achievement, many of the thoughts fall by the wayside. The precise costs, the alternatives that have to be downplayed or given up, the price in terms of time, emotion, or material things, turn out to have a reality that differs from the fantasy. Such conundrums are the bane of social workers, community developers, political activists, reformers of all kinds. Many of the suggestions that come later in this book will be wrecked, at least in the short term, on this sharp rock. [13]

Assertions about the future, and about what is *likely* in fact to happen, whether by politicians, by pundits or by preachers, must be taken with mountains of salt. *The harsh truth is that they do not know what the total consequences of their actions will be, and nor do I.*

We must live with approximation. We cannot stand back from the world or fail to act because our informed guesses about the future are just that. Further, the limitations of predictability increase the desirability of normative analysis. **We *can* articulate where we *think* we want to go**. We *can* change our minds if we find the costs too high, or the satisfactions of achieving the goal are less than we had anticipated. We can and do live with uncertainty, and that does not and should not prevent us from doing things that we imagine, anticipate, will bring about a better world. Dealing with uncertainty is an adventure, an emotional challenge, a value in itself. Uncertainty is no excuse for sitting on one's butt.

We all learn to live with our inconsistencies. We handle them, tell ourselves they don't matter, or we follow one idea at one time and another at the next. There may be objective inconsistencies that observers could agree are manifest in our expressions or behaviour. We can ignore them, and are usually unaware of them.

Sometimes, though, they become uncomfortable, to the point of interfering with our actions, rising to obsessive dominance in our thoughts, and arguments with our fellows. The inconsistencies demand resolution. We seek to amend our thoughts and our world until our internal peace is reconstituted; we are in equilibrium again. *Incompatibilities* are once again reduced to compatibility, by some adjustment in the cultural nuclei. This is a constructive path to societal change, one that, ideally, we would all like to follow, since it posits an outcome, a psychological resolution. Peace and well-being return. There is a sense of having achieved something. There are some of us who innovate in this way continuously, thriving on the succession of problems, resolution, problem, resolution -- and sometimes other related rewards, such as the respect and prestige it can bring. (Don't forget the costs: failure, envy.)

Here we are on the very edge of *dysfunction.* There is no law that states that a cultural system has to be perfectly adjusted. If it were, there would be no demand for change whatsoever. Functional (and its offshoot structural) anthropology reacted to the popular conception that many cultural traits were irrational, strange, inexplicable, savage. It was and is a major tool of understanding to actively seek the explanations, the rationalities that underlay the apparently irrational, the common sense of what was being done in the light of the total context, the damage that systems would suffer if one such significant trait were to be destroyed by outside thoughtlessness. The sources of change to functional or structurally sound systems did not come from stresses within. They came from without, and caused pain and problem-solving as the outside influences ramified through the culture, creating inconsistencies and incompatibilities that cried to be resolved.

In the modern world, there is still much to be said for the humanistic values of such an approach. But it needs to be amended. As analysts were quick to show, what came from outside did not descend on an inert body waiting for injections of new nuclei. The body of culture had its own immune systems, and chose from the invading viruses those they could handle and those they rejected. (Not literally: individuals did not have the power to resist biological viruses.....) Of course, power played a part, the power of the outsider to use force and blandishments; and the power the insider sought to gain by adopting new strengths. And while this was happening, the functional systems had their own problems to handle, and were involved in the ongoing adaptations of their cultures. Invading ideas had to fit the dynamic, force the dynamic into another path, or be adapted to fit the dynamic.

When competitive nuclei refuse to accommodate in such ways, when individuals hold to them as precious, as so highly valued that they will pay high costs to keep them, and the accommodations can be resolved only by a clash, often of titans, sometimes of dwarfs, we are led straight into *dysfunction.* In individuals it manifests itself in depression, alienation and the like, which, if treated, can return to the functionality of solutions. But as a manifestation of a cultural system, or two in a clash, we have measures of adjustment which aim at control, an inability to compromise, and often force in one form or another. Divorce, violence, anti-social behaviour, war, totalitarianism, racism, family violence, the attempt by groups to *impose* their will on others, the list goes on.

The processes I have mentioned in this summary form all imply that one can abstract a culture, talk about it as an entity, and think of it as being composed of a multitude of interacting parts, which not merely gear together in some mechanical way, but rather influence and change each other. The conceived culture is *articulated* insofar as rules can be discovered which guide the effects of nuclei upon each other. One such theme is that the powers of nuclei to adapt and to change others are based on their psychological component, manifested most significantly in perceptions. It is the *perception* of compatibility or incompatibility that counts, not some outside idea of functionality. Would-be reformers must constantly be reminded of this. An idea is much more likely to move into the system, or through it, if the persons involved *perceive that it fits*, and, based on that perception, judge that it will be good for them. Good for them usually means that it brings a benefit to their thought or behaviour that is worth the costs and sacrifice involved.

Here we are close to the ends-means relationship that is essential to the thinking of economists and some other social scientists. I adhere to the use of this relationship in the form I understood it to mean among the *pioneer* economists. That is, what is an end and what a means is not an objective external definition, but depends upon the personal evaluations and concepts of the actor. Influenced by their need to measure and to manipulate quantities, economists have largely dropped this notion, and they themselves attempt to define what is a means and what an end, what is productive capital and what is a consumption good.

There are signs of trends back to what I regard as basics. This is coming about because economists have been forced to become interested in factors of production and social objectives that link with finance but have non-material components -- health, social policy, education to take the most obvious. Once seen as social objectives and thus calculated as "ends", they are now recognised to have effects on "production", must be picked apart as "factors of production" *as well as* ends in themselves.

The circumstance that education has both characteristics, that is as a valuable end in itself, and as a means to greater productivity, should give us pause for thought. It impinges on arguments in various sections of these essays. But more profoundly, it raises the hypothesis that **all** *behaviour and objects contain* **mixtures** *of means and ends.*

A grand cathedral is a means to spirituality, but it is also a direct provider of awe and aesthetic satisfaction in itself. Tourists are shown Gaudi's buildings in Barcelona, not because they are functional but because they challenge the eye. A craftsman carves or builds a boat to make money for his family; but the activities are chosen because he loves them, he is prepared even to take a loss or a pittance of profit because he values the work in itself.

Once again, reform has often stalled because the element of satisfaction in something the reformers define as having only pain can so easily be overlooked, or put down to "innate conservatism". Why should shifting cultivators give up their forest digging sticks for "more effective" spades and shovels, and their clearings for fields, when they *like* the way their bodies move in traditional agriculture, enjoy the leaves around them, are happy with the schedules of work and rest in their present system? There can be good reasons, but reformers need to be absolutely sure that the benefits they dream up are real ones, do not have hidden unexpressed costs, and above all fit well into the perceptions of the cultivators about what they want from the world.

If there is confusion about ends and means, there is equivalent confusion about the material and non-material. The distinction seems so straight-forward: the material is something I can touch. If I can't touch it, it is non-material..

Material objects are, though, a collection of symbols put together in material form. In that, they are at one with non-material symbols like language and thought. They are in fact composed of thoughts, of the recognition of meanings. Buildings are libraries of concepts, so are coal mines, so are piles of grain waiting to be shipped, so is a pavement. Without their embodied concepts they are meaningless, they do not exist, they rot away.

And the meanings and concepts are subject to change according to the same rules we have been discussing. All the things we think about them, all the recognitions, ambiguities and puzzles, are nuclei in the profiles of culture. At one time a building is ripe for demolition; at another a historical treasure. At one time it is a school, another a warehouse. Coal is something dirty for domestic fires; or an alternative source of energy. The mine is dangerous and dirty, or a work place with perhaps high wages, or a source of tourist dollars, or something to be closed down. The pavement is hard on the feet and needs replacing, it is the route to the nearest good restaurant, it is composed of ugly stones, it is the embodiment of the history of the feet which have passed over it. The house on the corner is environmentally destructive, to some its staircase is beautiful and functional, to others it is something to be taken away to an antique market, what happened to the trees?,it accommodates too many people, it interferes with my view, I don't like the idea it is a half-way house.....

Material innovation and cultural innovation are one and the same. Cultural and social changes arise from the dynamics contained in the profiles of culture. The move to, or from, Utopia, is a cultural event. Within that context, politics and economics are not even sub-divisions. They do not exist except as part of the changing cultural whole.

You may of course be wondering why I have used the word "innovation" instead of "creation" or "creativity".. One reason is pragmatic. The word "innovation" focuses on a process which results in something new. Much of creation does too. But in my view quite significant creation does not. A woodworker may turn out chair after chair of quite skilled handcraft. His original concept may have been innovative, but thereafter it is repetitive. Yet he is a creator of good things.

The other reason is that much confusion surrounds the analysis of creation, so that there is good reason to break away from it. One of the most recent compilations of perspectives and analysis, with the words "Theory and practice" in the title is almost encyclopaedic in its range of examples[14]. It even suggests that the religious stories of "Creation" are part of the subject, not because they are creative fables, but because the subject they deal with is one form of creation – that is not due to human hand. This is going too far, but the author correctly notices that the approaches of creative individuals differ widely according to subject matter – in literature, music, engineering, for example. Then the matter is left up in the air – there are many creativities and no over-arching theory[15] A set of propositions which accounts for the process? Considering innovation in all domains of human endeavour enables us to approach understanding in a theoretical way. And having undertaken such an approach, we can use it to inform ourselves or our own innovative behaviour, and that of the institutions of which we are a part.

There is also a psychology of innovation. Studies of innovative individuals have revealed that for the greatest of them psychological props help. My favourite example is that of writers or composers who must settle to their work at a particular time of day, must have their pen or keyboard just so, with a cup of favourite coffee of just the right blend and strength, and the page open at the end of an unfinished sentence or musical phrase which gets them back in the mental swing. If any of these items is missing, it takes time to get settled perhaps with confusion. Thinkers are noted for their walks in the woods. A sculptor or a painter must have the work space arranged (however chaotic it may seem to an outsider) to their satisfaction, and maybe spend some moments reflecting on how his creation meets his ambitions in the new morning. And should we speak of chefs with their *batterie de cuisine*. So it goes on.

An understanding and an application of a theory of innovation gives us the opportunity to be more effective in changing our world towards that of a magnificent place in which to live late in the 21st century.

Which raises the question, can innovation be taught?

Invention certainly can be. The principles of invention as made evident in our daily lives, can and should be part of the awareness of students in our revised approach to education, outlined in the next chapter. From there it is but a step to show how invention becomes - or does not become – socially accepted innovation. Part of such a process of learning needs to relate to the non-material. Innovation takes place in our spiritual, domestic lives and in the ways we behave towards other persons. Knowledge that our relationships are not set in stone, but change and evolve, often deliberately, is a significant part of our movement towards a better future.

Manifesto for the New Age

IV – Reformed Education is Imperative[16]

Education is the foundation of reforms in every sphere. The reorganisation of the approach to engendering maturity in youths is interwoven with the concerns of every other chapter in this book. We must try to tackle it alongside all other reforms, which will be weak without it. It will minimally take a generation to experience maximum results in other spheres as time is needed for youths to become adults, put precepts into practice and generate other children to grow in maturity.. So we had better get on with it.

You think this is not necessary? Examine the state of education in the most advanced countries and you will find it necessary to think again. This is where we begin.

Take a moment to examine critically the ways in which official policies relate to the maturation of youth, primarily through the educational system, primarily but not only, in richer countries. More and more frequently schools are being confronted by manifestations of societal ills – violence, depression *et al*. This is not new. But schools have not been equipped to remedy the problems they face, and there are bureaucratic and communication difficulties bringing other community resources to bear on the issues.

Once we identify the tasks and challenges necessary to optimize the ways in which youths mature into responsible citizens, we may then design appropriate institutions to do the job. That design will be a major goal to achieve well prior to 2100 – in my view it should be achievable fifty years before that - indeed very soon - in much of the world. Special adjustments will be required to modify the institutions and ensure that they are effective when feasible in the poorer countries. In all instances the interaction of these ideas with indigenous values and systems will need careful culture-specific appraisal.

I start with youth suicide in its several forms.

In many parts of the industrial world, high school (and university) age youths are committing suicide in increasing numbers. As their age group rises as a cohort in the demographic scale, so the general figures of attempted suicide rise. In other words, the tendency toward suicide carries on into higher age groups.

Recently -- I do not know for how long -- the elderly had the highest suicide rates in such countries. Now the rates among the youth cohorts match those for the elderly. Unless there are fundamental transformations, the changing attitudes towards euthanasia coupled with the entry of present youth cohorts into the ranks of the elderly could produce a suicide explosion in forty years or so.[17] that could shake the capabilities of society to respond.

I accept and advocate the right of the elderly to take their own lives, though I would prefer it to be in the context of psychological peace rather than age-induced depression. I do not accept it as a necessity in other age groups such as youths, for which the future is still an open possibility. That would not be my idea of the world toward which we strive.

In Japan and other countries suicides take place as the young take their lives for fear of failing examinations or similar tests. Family and peer pressure play a role: so do induced or real feelings of self-worthlessness in a demanding society.

A further form of suicide is ideological. This is particularly the case in Arab society, where young, well-educated people, notably including women, undertake acts of terrorism in which their own deaths are virtually certain – acts of martyrdom. Many are the ideologically prepared tee-age suicide bombers.

Then there are those whose alienation is not that of the body, but of the mind and its spirit. These include the habitual criminals, so often and so long behind bars that they are seriously unable to function outside of prison, and who, when freed, commit acts so that they can return. They do not kill their bodies, but their way of life has become virtually suicidal – often, at a young age, because of experiences "inside" prison, that breeding ground of anti-social behaviour.[18]

The first step in tackling the issue *throughout all age groups* lies with education.

Suicide is part of the nexus of concerns that include violence, bullying and harassment in schools, truancy, youth prostitution, youth homelessness, the recourse of youth to violence and gangs on the streets, abuse in the family, and drugs. These are not just urban problems. Until the idealisation of rural life in the second half of the last century, it was well known that sexual abuse, family instability, incest, and violence were typical phenomena of **rural** living. They are more dramatic, more concentrated, less hidden, more newsworthy, and more frequently observed because the populations are higher, in cities. Although this is so, it is doubtful whether the statistical incidence is higher than in earlier centuries, and it is certain that there have been periods in modern history, for example the nineteenth century, when the situation was much worse.

That is, though, beside the point. It doesn't matter what the trends are, except insofar as wrong publicity over-creates immoderate anxieties and backlashes. What *is* to the point is that there should be *zero* tolerance of any of these phenomena in a civilised society. I am not referring to the superficial remedies of authoritarian crackdown. I mean getting to the remedial basics.

The basics consist in the *positive* upbringing of youth, presently a disjointed responsibility of family, schools, youth organisations, religions and the state.

Families are having great difficulty. It has *always* had great difficulty, among rich *and* poor. Let us be freed from "traditional family values" which have done such a poor job, and been the cover up for abuse. That does not mean throwing everything out. It means re-thinking responsibilities and dynamics.

Unnecessary and dysfunctional guilt. Inhibiting anxiety. Confidence destroying hopelessness. From time to time these strike at all parents who take their responsibilities seriously. What, oh what, am I doing wrong?

What parents tend to do is to bring forward the learning that they acquired in their family of origin, and as they acquired a philosophy of parenting in their twenties and thirties. Parents themselves survived troubled times, in the late 'sixties and 'seventies, for example, battling authority with the assertion of permissiveness. When adults become responsible for loved children themselves, the two themes fight for dominance and balance. Parents blame themselves for not getting the balance right, for not foreseeing. Unprepared for separation they usually relieved when the offspring make it clear that they themselves are in charge of their own destinies, having definitively left the nest.

Parents cannot get the balance "right" by themselves. Nobody knows what that balance is, for any individual child and there is the law of unintended consequences in the background. The outside influences

67

are so powerful. Parents must count themselves fortunate and extraordinarily sensitive if their offspring make the transition to adulthood reasonably well as most but not all do. Quite frequently, the path is first one of natural rebellion which can take extremely dangerous turns beside the abyss of drugs and alienation. Quite frequently, parents find that the children, now "friendren", have survived, matured, found new solid roads out of their own personal strengths.

This is not to argue that, if parents do not *know* they should not try. Of course they will. Their efforts, whether misguided or highly sensitive, *will* have an effect, a positive one, when guided by love and support, come what may. It is almost the only principle that counts for sure. Parents, after all, are not the only variables.

There is the child itself. Life never will be a cakewalk. Despite the incidence of trouble, by far the majority of children become reliable adults. Even when they have inner pains, they function well, even creatively.

And they live in a challenging environment in which they are led by a myriad of influences toward a myriad of choices. In individual instances the influence of the parents can be exaggerated pr countervailed.

In what follows I am somewhat neglecting the influence of religion. This is a pity, but I can't do everything at this moment especially since the world contains so many differing religious philosophies and values. Despite refusing the concept of a God or gods in human form, I am not one of those who believes that religion, or at least the search for spirituality, is insignificant. On the contrary, the search for spirituality, within or without the churches, is a major preoccupation, a resource, an intellectual and emotional drive, that has a major part to play in the lives of an increasing number of men and women, especially youths, even traditionally dominating in some cultures. On the other hand, the influence of formal religion and the spiritual beliefs of parents on children is a part of family life, determined by parents. Further, the range and variety of belief and of the types of searching are now so great as a result of increased global communication as to defy summary. For the growing young, seeking their own paths as they enter the enquiring teens, the range and variety are part of the almost infinity of choice with which they are confronted. It is that infinity of choice which evokes creativity, thoughtfulness, anxiety and despair, an infinity that continues well beyond school into adulthood. As each decade passes, the conscious part of that infinity expands, life juxtaposing simplicity and resounding chaos, in which the ears as well as our other senses defend themselves against both aggression and se, often not being able to distinguish this from that.

The school is the place in which family influence confronts the perspectives of other families through the filter of other children's presence. It is the place where the influences of the media, of adult role models, of professional teachers, the contributions of churches and voluntary youth organisations, and the policies of the state, come together, working out their pressures and contradictions in the minds and behaviour of children.

It is inevitable that education should thus be the focus of power rivalry, conflict and co-operation, demands and compromise. Ideally, the state should be in a position to take a detached view, to consider the meaning, objectives, philosophies and methods of education. This is not the case. The state is governed by men and women whose basic philosophies are *a priori*, joined with those of political allies in a mostly confrontational competition with oppositions. The state is strongly advised by bureaucracies who control data and implementation, who are a force for conservative continuity which is fortunately somewhat counterbalances the potential swings of elected political opinion. Theocratic states are additionally dominated by clerics and religious authorities. Powers are variously filtered through intermediary bodies down to the school, or in some instances tightly controlled by the central government or a recognized religious hierarchy. Powers relate to the official objectives and philosophy of education (sometimes ideology), the curriculum, and budgetary influences on school practice.

Teachers, like any other professional corpus, have the responsibility for the direct contact with their client-pupils, and to a lesser extent with the semi-client-parents. It is this responsibility, together with their common experience of professional training, that binds them together, and constitutes the reality of their power base. Furthermore, the most significant reality in the exercise of educational policy is what teachers do with it. A fiat from above is useless if it does not fit well with the perceptions that the teachers themselves have of their realities, their philosophy, their responsibilities, and, increasingly, their material conditions. Even unintentionally teachers internalise their beliefs and practices in ways that are difficult to change, and of course sometimes they don't want to change, because what they do is a sacred pursuit.

It might be said that the way to change teaching is to change teacher training. Indeed, without this, change would be even more difficult. If serious changes are to be contemplated -- and I have not yet made my case for them -- we must recognise that young newly trained teachers have limited influence and, perhaps, none at all within the educational hierarchy. It is not only that time must pass before they rise in seniority and their proportions increase -- with the consequence that even newer ideas must enter the system with the young cohorts now the conservatives. It is that they are posted to schools as individuals, surrounded by those whose training belongs to an earlier period. They meet in committees, socialise, discuss issues, are rewarded, with and by those who belong to an earlier generation. Inevitably, most of them will unintentionally modify their positions to conform to those of their peer group. Their impact is reduced. (They could have greater impact if posted *en bloc* to specific schools, more or less taking them over, at the expense of experience.)[19]

Some of this can be modified by major refresher training. This is not readily achieved by North American style "professional days", or by uncontrolled sabbaticals. It would require periodic freedom from classroom activities for substantial blocks of *required* refresher education.

There are other difficulties in teacher formation. What is to be taught to them? Subject matter? Pedagogical philosophy? The state's requirements? In these matters, wherein lies the "academic freedom" of the teacher? Does the teacher in fact have "academic freedom" that a university professor is supposed to have? I think not. The teacher has a responsibility for the vulnerable children of parents, and is thus morally responsible to those parents, whereas university faculty are supposedly guiding young mature adults questioning and focussing on ever-changing knowledge. The teacher interprets responsibility by using skills the best way possible to influence young minds. In my view, those skills have technical components that can be taught, and personal, human components that training can influence but not control. Because of the latter limitation, the effectiveness of the classroom has, ultimately, to depend on the individual teacher who makes the institutional framework operate through personal qualities which technical skills support but do not suffocate. The freedom of the teacher lies in his or her application of those skills, *not in deciding what the ultimate classroom goals should be.*

Ultimately, then, I argue that innovation in the school system is the same as in any other context. It comes through the interplay of ideas and concepts that can come in all forms, formally and informally, which the individual teacher rejects or accepts. The rate of acceptance will be proportional to the degree to which the concept or practice "fits" the profile of culture of individual teachers, and can be incorporated into that profile.

You will find only a few small countries -- some Pacific Islands, perhaps -- where the main corpus of teachers individually share more or less identical cultural profiles. In all others, there is considerable variety. Within that variation, individuals who approximate each other in ideas and point of view may be grouped, more or less categorised. If one wished to do so, one could identify such groups. Educational innovation would have differing impacts on each such group. This is one potential influence towards diversity in the school system. Teachers with differing philosophies and methods can, conceptually, operate schools with differing philosophies and methods. This observation will make the idea of diversified schooling more practical.

If there is truth in this, how much more is it relevant for another power group, the parents. Whereas teachers, despite their differences, have some common ground derived from occupational considerations, parents do not. Their variability is much greater, except in rural tribal communities. And in developed and developing countries they increasingly demand more variation in education. States, and teachers, confront increasingly multi-faceted parental cultures.

Some argue that the more varied and complex a society, the more important it is to use schooling as a cohesive force. (In some times and places, compulsory army service was justified in this way as it partially is in Switzerland.) I confess to doubts about this, if the objective is an ideally progressive system., for we have seen that diversity adds to the size of the profile of culture, and hence to innovation, and because, as I shall argue in a later context the state is not, fundamentally and as we know it, holy. Yet in the shorter term, this is a practical consideration. Do we want the cohesiveness of the state to be weakened? The issue is being modified by demographic changes. In most mature countries it is more and more likely to be the case that schools will be attended by children of differing cultural backgrounds. The emphasis then changes to influencing such children to understand each other within the larger society.

Let us keep this in mind.

What should be the functional objectives of the school? Do they imply major innovation? In approaching these questions I am not implying that, for any function, the school is the only influence that is relevant or that is needed. The school, however, works with children for long hours, day after day. Its potential influence, through both teaching and the influence of peers, is as great as that of parents and it may be identified as the primary institution which exposes children to non-family society in a coordinated way[20].

Such influences embody major ethical problems. If state schools were fully effective in carrying out their mandate, they would be imposing a single universal philosophy on children. The authoritarian and centralising dangers are modified by the essential individuality of both teachers and children, the existence of programme choices, and the counterbalancing effects of family and other outside influences. Yet a single, universal, little modified, state system could move in the universalising direction and is contrary to my sense of the ultimate goal of a diverse creative culture[21].

There is also an incipient conflict between the goals of particular schools and the goals of parents, individually or collectively. One of the most dramatic illustrations came from special Indian schools in British Columbia in the nineteenth and early twentieth centuries. A now discontinued type of school, known as "residential schools", deliberately removed young children from their parents and communities (considered to be retrograde influences), transferring them to boarding schools. Later, in more subtle ways, Indian community day schools were sometimes staffed by dedicated, earnest and responsible non-Indian teachers who, as individuals, considered it their duty and mandate to be agents of change. In itself, this indeed might have been a legitimate mandate -- it would in effect have been impossible for a school to have operated *without* engendering change of some sort. The issue here, though, is that, at least to begin with, many of the teachers did not have the skills or incentives to match their ideas about the goals of change to those of the Indian parents. The child, unintentionally, became the location of a battleground between two sets of adults, overt or unseen. Even teachers in village schools were drawn into such conflicts. In extreme cases the tensions and misplaced mandates brought despair, neurosis in both teacher and pupil, and revolting abuse in the residential schools.

This is an extreme form of a tension which is frequent, teachers consideringsome parents to be irresponsible, uncaring, harmful to their offspring, ignorant about the educational needs and strengths of their children, causing anti-social behaviour; parents considering teachers to be using wrong methods, presenting irreligious values, encouraging laziness or pushing children too far. The obverse of this is the rote and ideological learning of schools in extreme religious contexts.

To advocate no tension at all would be unrealistic and false. A major part of learning, as I shall reinforce, is to deal with tension and to work out the implications of inconsistency and conflict. It is from such bases that innovation takes place. However, whatever I may suggest by way of resolving issues, I am in no doubt that differences will continue in the ultimate world, and that, in reasonable ways, they should. When I set forth ideas about objectives for ultimate achievement I know I shall be establishing a battleground or, I would rather hope, a platform for debate.

By way of opening the subject, I once had ideas about an ideal base curriculum for a modern world. It was oriented toward mobility and the growth of the individual. The underlying theme was to maximise the child's potential for communication as an adult. Thus the three r's were essential -- few disagree about that today. To literacy, numeracy and communication skills (including logic and rhetoric) were added those languages which worked as *linguae francae* across major segments of the world -- English, German and Russian (for much of eastern Europe), Arabic, Spanish, French (for parts of Africa and Asia), written Mandarin, Malay, and Swahili (for East Africa). To this would be added comparative anthropology, world social and political history and geography, medical diagnosis,data searching and processing, and, for real mobility, basic motor mechanics, horse riding, sailing (with navigation) and outdoor skills. Such a curriculum was predicated on one specific goal -- making it possible for young adults to move through the world anywhere with confidence and to move forward (with specialised advanced education) into their professions anywhere.

While such a model programme may be teasing to some, ***all it does*** is to demonstrate that current curricula are not writ in stone; that what is taught depends entirely on objectives. The major limitation of the above imagined programme was that the objective was narrow for widespread use, though perhaps appropriate for specialised variability in schools. But the limitations of the above extreme case are also present, if to a lesser degree, in *all* curriculum models. The very idea that one curriculum serves the needs of all students in all parts of society is and should be a non-starter. The major thread running through all good curricula is that they establish standards of rigour, mental discipline, clear thinking, and the processes of continuously acquiring and using knowledge, old and new. In view of my later arguments to give priority to engendering empathy and eliminating violence pedagogy needs to discover ways of emphasizing these in practice, and not just in words and moral precepts.[22] Almost all educational institutions in the world must deal with children affected by multi-cultural and religious tensions, psychological disorders and distractions competing with the priorities of the school itself.

If the above is not currently satisfactory, then what should most, if not all, schools do, in principle? There is a great deal.

Particularly in the second half of the twentieth century and into the twenty-first, schools have been experimenting with our children, often in the light of general theories which can be misinterpreted when put into practice, theories which, in the nature of things, have not been properly tested in terms of results. What I write now is of the same order. It is opinion, linked to some observation, some experience, and, I hope, some logic. In particular, *it is linked to ideas about what the end results should be*. Recall one of my foundation statements. There is no complete knowledge; anything put into practice will lead to unexpected results. What we do in schools will have profound effects on the future. The cautions of this paragraph will have major implications for the organisation and dynamics of future schools.

In 'fifties Canada I saw schools in which uniforms had been abandoned as a matter of theory. Uniforms were felt to be authoritarian, representing an expense for those not so well off. At the same time schools emphasised the skills of social interaction, the ability to get on with one's fellows. The solitary pupil was an anachronism. The children themselves stepped into the gap. Peer pressure dictated clothing, both boys and girls decided that what they wore had to be what youthful fashion dictated. Those who wore different clothing were open to derision. Within the peer dictates, some of the better off were seen to be better off by the expense of the clothes, the cars driven, the hair-dos and makeup of the girls. The concern for the visible aspects of group personality seemed to take priority over the content of school work, where conformity emerged naturally.

By the 'nineties more individuality was expressed. But the use of externals and clothing is still an identifier. This time it identifies group *difference* as well as juvenile peer-conformity. Gangs have their markers. Certain conformist schools mistakenly attempt to enforce clothing standards which reduce ethnic or religious identification. They are kinds of uniforms without the admission that this is so.[23] The attempt to ban religious symbols in dress, as in France, is surely mistaken, for surely an element in school goals should be to make cultural difference natural and understood, rather than attempting to deny them[24].

The most marked change in school ethos in many industrialised countries since the late 'sixties has been the formal redefinition of the appropriate tension between conformity and individuality, a redefinition which affects major changes in adult perceptions. In one sense, the group is re-asserted. Group projects frequently take the place of individual ones. Seating arrangements create eye-to-eye contact in the classroom, emphasising interactions, and hence peer control, in place of the more individualistic lines of desks.

On the other hand, the self is re-asserted. Therapies dealing with relationships in adult society often emphasise self-awareness, self-knowledge, the discovery of the past and of the child within; and self-assertion. Mishandled, as therapy often is, the "other" becomes secondary. The right kind of concern for the "other" will emerge only after the "self" has been discovered. Introspection and selfishness can result.

In both schools and universities there have been times, teachers, and classes for which self-expression is valued simply because it is the expression of self, with little or no regard to the quality of the expression. The fact that I thought it is quite sufficient to give me top marks. Indeed, since everyone in the class thought something, let's give them *all* top marks. Such caricatures have been realities.

However, even where such naive extremes have been in place, it is interesting to see both teachers and the public striving to establish something else, "standards". And it is more interesting to see children discovering that there is more to creativity than simple effort; discovering, as they step into the world, that they have been betrayed because they were not prepared for "standards"; that much of peer pressure "out there" is indeed about standards and performance rather than superficialities; and that there is excitement to be obtained from meeting intellectual challenges. The cliché has it: if there are rigorous and demanding standards in sports, why not in thinking?

Both themes need expression, and never will either disappear. To equip children for a world in which there is extensive adult non-work that I envisage for the better world[25], it is essential that they know themselves. It is a fundamental part of creative education that children learn how to explore, out of their own interests. They will not fully discover themselves in high school. Currently, most children do not discover their creative capacities until well into young adulthood. No school can place before a young person the whole total richness of the world and what the human capacity is capable of; no school can provide the total basis for choice[26]. But all schools can aim at encouraging intellectual -- in which I include artistic and psychological -- exploration, the discovery that one is capable of entering undreamed-of realms of creativity, the knowledge that the search for self-fulfilment is never-ending and wondrous.

Beyond these issues the whole question of creating maturity has been pushed into the background. Old fashioned ways of "building character" do not work for the modern scene, and in some instances produced distorted adults. It cannot be dismissed because of that: we must strive to modernise our methods and create new kinds of mature characters who can handle both each other and the contemporary and future world. The challenge is by no means unknown. There are numerous studies which have the underlying theme: maturity is deficient in young people. Most of these relate to boys – are they men? The conclusion in most of them is that maturity, if it arrives at all, usually comes well after schooling as young people face the real world and are confused by what they face there. A few even return to the family nest. The massive unemployment, especially among the young, in the first decades of the 21st century is devastating not just in material earning but even more seriously in self esteem, boredom, and he temptations of crime or drugs. In what follows we must bear this phenomenon clearly in mind.[27]

The emphasis on the mind and spirit implied in my last sentences does not reduce the significance of the bio-physical.

The truism that healthy minds emerge from healthy bodies is only partly true. Many great minds belong to those who are or have been physically and emotionally warped. Touch a great philosopher and you will find a troubled soul. What *is* true, on the other hand, is that *all* thought and self-expression arrives through the senses, is filtered internally as a result of sensory experience. Especially in the puritanical parts of the world, where the creative uses of some senses are denied, the ability of teachers to encourage sensory experience is strictly limited -- and rightly so, since maturing children are especially vulnerable to sensory abuse and dysfunctional influence. Yet a balance can surely be attained in which sensory experience is valued, and individually encouraged, and the links between experience, creativity, and innovation are made known.

Furthermore, the world of physical activity intersects directly with the mind, its expression, and its choices. The physical and the mental are not opposites; they are part of one state. The choice of physical activity over desk activity is not a choice of body over mind. It is a choice in which body and mind unite to go in a specific direction. The application of thought and knowledge to sport and recreation makes this clear. Some children will make physical activity a greater part of their lives than others; almost all children should understand that this is not a separate, classified as different, part of life, but an integrated aspect. It will, like every other aspect, be used creatively by some and less by others, just as is music or scientific experimentation. But the bio-physical and the mental are fundamental, part of every single one of us, in a way that music or scientific experimentation is not.

In parts of North America today some teachers are directly integrating exercise and thinking. They recognise that as high pulse rate gives energy to the mind and increases powers of concentration and perception. Exercise bicycles are installed directly in the classroom. Students work on them to get their pulse rate to say 120 per minute. They then go to their desks. Positive results, even on "problem" pupils is outstandingly high.

To start the process of knowing one's self, then, is a primary goal of school education. The search for that knowledge will never end if properly engendered.

At the same time, it is of utmost significance to limit that search for self. This will be done by placing it in context. Without balance and context an over-emphasis on the ego is likely to be hurtful, to the child, and to others. It will engender the continuous life-long question, the dominance of Who-am-I? Anxiety because I do not know myself, perpetual introspection, inhibition from action because it might not be right for me. In this field, even more than in all others, it is of major necessity to indicate also that I will *never* fully know who I am; that *why* I am who I think I am doesn't matter so much -- it can't be changed retrospectively -- as *who* I am. I must learn when to think about it and when to stop thinking about it. The importance of the search is to find out what my values are, what I would like to do in living my life, how I can get on with others, how I can communicate myself to others, and how to make some reasonable choices for myself.

Education is replete with paradoxes, contradictions, and oppositions. Successful education does not allow one theme to dominate, balances the contradictions in ways that alert the child without creating improper anxiety, that make use of the paradoxes for creativity, and that meet the needs of different children in different ways.

Thus self-expression is counter-balanced by awareness of and concern for others. I personally feel that *the primary underlying issue is courtesy, understanding and respect for others*. And I feel that somehow, all over the world, schools have limited success in conveying this message, and that very frequently the concern is treated as peripheral rather than fundamental. Indeed as we know only too well, schools in some places specifically engender distaste for the other, even to the point of preaching the merits of violence and martyrdom. If there is no courtesy and respect for others a school simply cannot function adequately in the ideal world. A functioning adult society cannot exist.[28] We will have more to say on this subject when we discuss terrorism and freedom. The issue links to so many other aspects of society -- violence, crime, autocracy, self-interest pressure groups, attitudes to work are rather obvious. I shall identify others.

Hence self-expression should not be confused with selfishness and egoism.

In my elderly superficial observations I see small examples of the confusion. Young people at all times and places have difficulty in defining their personal space. Anyone who encounters young people on public transport, in shopping areas, in souks, anywhere where there is a strong possibility of physical contact, is bound to get an elbow in the ribs, toes stepped on, the sensation of being pushed aside as the energetic young, in groups, steam ahead. One remarks on the natural courtesy of a youth who gives his, or more usually her, seat to an elderly person of no matter what ethnic community. One often feels that in such a case it is parental, not school, influence that has been responsible; and that peer pressure is against it through derision, especially amongst boys.

Trivial. Not at all. Fundamental. Which is why I repeat the point.

If courtesy is not taught in little ways, the large ones, when there, are hypocritical.

Some schools, of course, do in fact stress courteous behaviour. All should. How?

I do not like the word "tolerance" in multi-ethnic or cross-religion contexts.[29] It implies that there is something about another's behaviour that I don't particularly like, but will tolerate. Yes, indeed, we often do run across behaviour which we dislike and tolerate. Often when we run across behaviour that we dislike and should ***not*** tolerate; we should do something about it.

What I object to is the easy way in which we can think of tolerance of, rather than respect for, ***or understanding*** of, others. It is not tolerance that should be emphasised in schools, but respect and understanding. Tolerance implies "Real weird he digs classical music. Who cares?" or "They have such weird customs. I don't mind, though, that's for them". Patronising.

On the contrary, respect for others implies "I wonder what he gets out of classical music? Makes him interesting." or "What they do makes considerable sense for them. Even though it's not for me, I'd like to know about it." And understanding means just that, figuring out the reasons behind the behaviour in question and placing them in cultural and "philosophical" context.

One of the results of the late 'sixties was the re-emphasis of the idea that discipline, however valued in sports, was unnatural in mental activity, and that "failure" was an assault on the persona. On the contrary, both discipline and failure are essential experiences for a truly civilised person who wishes to be capable of the fullest self-expression and the fullest contribution to total well-being. Blaming others, or circumstances, or upbringing, can too easily slide over into excuses for failures which should be faced up to and learned from. The "culture of complaint" as one writer perceptively put it, is very far from our global goals, fort both adults and children.

However much a creative person enjoys the outcome of his chosen activity, there will be costs involved. To commit to the chosen outcome requires the payment of those costs. They include not only the material, but the psychological. If you are not prepared to pay the costs, you do not value the activity as highly as you thought. To summon the resources, internal and objective, to pursue a goal, it is necessary to have the discipline to pay, in effort, in materiel, in mental concentration, and, quite often, in going through boring and seemingly pointless stages and bits of training. You may have to suffer through boring instructors. To get to the fullest enjoyment of achievement it is necessary to be prepared to go through times when you ask yourself, is this all worthwhile?

You do not simply get an answer out of the air. There has been groundwork laid for those flashes of insight, of intuition, of bodily achievement, of controlled logic.

As I have said, and will repeat, there is no greater betrayal of a child's capabilities that to pretend to him or her that whatever they think is objectively as good as what someone else thinks, just because it is thought. That any thought is as good as another. That what matters is to do the thinking without regard for its significance, and that the skills of communicating that thinking are insignificant. This sort of betrayal is not to be confused with the genuine attempt to encourage the emergence of the child's thoughts -- and then, skilfully and gently, to show that those thoughts can be extended by the application of discipline -- even by going through disliked procedures.

The betrayal I have mentioned is matched by another equal treachery, -- the denial of "failure", the belief that the term "failure" has to mean the denigration of the individual, that it is somehow shocking and should never occur. It is true that in the past, and still in the present, failure has been used as a punishing stick in that way; it has discouraged and destroyed individual talents.

The word "failure" should be brought back into current dialogue. It should be used with understanding as a positive element in life. To "fail" means that you have *tried*, that you have attempted something that is for some reason at this point beyond you. To fail gives you guidance. It tells you what to work on -- it may even be lassitude or lack of discipline, but it can also be lack of a technical mastery, of understanding. It may even tell you that the subject matter will not, eventually, be for you. You might even have to look elsewhere. Or by persisting and solving the problem you break through a fog and see your goal brightly ahead.

Placed in a positive context, failure should be a challenge. It should alert both teacher and child that something requires attention. As a child I failed in both mathematics and French. My teachers dealt with the other pupils who understood and were not so mentally lazy. My father bought me a French tutor and in a couple of months I was second in the city's schools. I wish he had thought to do that in mathematics, for in later life I found, without knowing any math, that symbolic logic has an extraordinary appeal and value that my laziness[30] undermines.

In my case the teachers did not have the will or the interest to advise someone who, to them, was a bit of an idiot and lazy to boot. Literature recounts many tales of dedicated teachers whose avocation is to find and nurture the wandering child, to bring him or her through the tests of discipline and failure. It is also full of accounts of harsh disciplinarians who have little interest but to give vent to their own internal problems, and in doing so stifle the growth of others. For many talented men and women the suffering of school is something to eventually be put behind them, for adult life is their real school, the place where they find an outlet for their skills and even achieve fame. True. But many others fall by the wayside. And what a waste of school resources and energy to let the opportunity slip by.

Embrace failure. Let teachers resurrect it as a positive force. It will be there throughout life; it is a step on the path to achievement; it must be understood, not fled from. He who does not fail does not try; indeed is not alive.

The question of sex education is fraught and highly controversial. It needs serious addressing because, as I shall be arguing in connection with the family, and with health and the law, sexual ills are at the source of many or most of personal dysfunctions and inter-personal troubles. Far from being a subject addressed on tip toe it should be front and centre in the concerns of Youth Maturity Institutes which I advocate later to replace schools. We choose to downplay or hide such facts as that the relationship between mother and child at the breast is highly sexual; that babies are tactile; that young children are curious and interested in the body, experimenting with it and investigating. Add to that the perception, perhaps the fact, that sexual experiment is going on amongst teens and in pre-teen friendships.

Our attitudes to sex are cultural, and we need cultural adjustments to handle them. Except for some of the potential medical consequences and the psychological effects of repression, there is little biological about our thoughts about sex. What indeed is a sex act? Voyeurism? Playing with one's own genitals? Intimate caressing? On a small island in the southern Solomons I witnessed young girls below the age of ten dancing a hissing dance, in which the rhythms and hisses coincided – as did the rubbing of genitals on genitals and genitals on thighs. Sex act or fun? The licentious ribaldry of cross cousins of opposite genders in some parts o Fiji would get close to sexual harassment if performed in a Canadian bureaucracy – yet they are designed to say "no copulation allowed" and to emphasize the delightful but forbidden danger. A Western phenomenon emerging as I write is that of the daisy chain, in which young pre-teens of both sexes join their naked bodies in a circle and play with the one next in the chain.

Repression makes behaviour with sexual content seriously damaging. It often removes the highly desirable supportive and warm touching that should exist between appropriate adults and unhappy children who need comfort. It turns sensuous or insecure children into dysfunctional adults in many psychological areas. And I will be asserting later that it is a prime mover in crime and hatred.

So Youth Maturity Institutes must do something about it. They will focus on parents (see Chapter IV on the family). But they will also investigate and innovate in sexual education.

Sex education today is primarily biological – how the reproductive system functions – medical – for example, the dangers of sexually transmitted diseases and unprotected sex – the moral, psychological and social implications, and how to get help. It is inescapable that the emphasis is on danger and discomfort rather than pleasure and joy. Is it any wonder that searching teens, discovering more positive pleasures, ignore the warnings and take risks.[31]

The problem is that the truths about sex as joy are ignored, and young people are too often experiencing the fumblings, discomforts and ignorances of sexual adventure as they try their hands at it. Guilt, fear and ignorance turn the experiences into distaste and repeated searching for something better. Pity the young girl faced with a would be lover who doesn't know how to stimulate her before he satisfies himself. And pity the self-confidence of the young boy who discovers his inadequacy, or the arrogant young man who thinks that dominance is what it is all about. The guilty atmosphere of hush hush secrecy/ For that read, at least for a while, almost 100% of young intercourse.

What to do? Don't raise your eyebrows. I'm serious because the implications are serious. People engage in sex for enjoyment. That characteristic is given to us so that as we engage in sex we can also procreate – but don't have tp.

It is not even certain that the evolutionary function of sex is limited to procreation. For example, various theories of female orgasm are rooted in the assumption that that is what sex is about. But studies have shown that the biological theorems underlying such a postulate are quite mistaken and that the female orgasm has no bearing on the power to conceive. And while male orgasm and ejaculation go, shall we say, hand in hand, once again there is little of any relationship between its physical manifestation and the rate of conception.[32]

While sexual activity has a bearing on procreation it is also there, deeply embedded, for its own sake. It is an activity which can be, should be, joyous and wholesomely rewarding, engendering compassion, love, delight, and the renewal of the body and the senses. It can go seriously wrong, become nasty, evidence of sickness, fumbling and crude. To keep it in balance and to gain the most from it, young people *need to be coached in sex as an art form*, just as they are taught the essence of aesthetics in art or the beauties in mathematics. Vestal Virgins and other priestesses undertook this task for young men as a religious duty. In numerous cultures young men were and are initiated by engaging prostitutes. Neither of these institutions engenders more than some technical knowledge for the satisfaction of the male. Rarely does it educate the male in the desires of the woman.

Girls are marginally better off. Self experimentation and playfulness with other girls can create considerable sensual satisfaction, so that lesbianism may be a pleasing outcome. On the other hand many grow into women who are overcome by guilt, dry dissatisfaction and "frigidity" so that even sex for procreation becomes an unpleasant chore.

So how can Youth Maturity Institutes undertake appropriate coaching and education? Get with it, pedagogues. The blackboard alone will not do. And it needs to completely avoid exploitation by and the perversion of instructors. It must be entirely sensitive to the individual child, yet skin to skin, body to body teaching of ways to satisfy the other partner and retain one's own integrity.

One must inset an obvious warning. If adults are to teach younger adults the arts of sex, is there not a risk of perversion and abuse? Most certainly there is. But remember we are dealing with such matters within the context not of present day schools but of yet to be analysed Youth Maturity Institutes which will replace them and have many more professional and parental resources to deal with such matters. And we are working with the expectation that there will, in time, be fundamental changes in the behavioural ethics of youths becoming in their turn adults.

Even then there are certain principles to be observed, rigorously and sensitively. Biologically, young people become pubescent at different ages. There are some who, for whatever reason, resist and dislike sensual touching. It would be disastrous if sexual education, in the sense in which I am using it, became a classroom exercise to be administered mechanically to a specific age group. At the very least, this has to be something in which the individual child's readiness is assessed accurately For some it may be not until the late teens or not at all.

Below I shall be opening the challenges for pedagogy. This is clearly one of them. Should instruction be given in clinical surroundings, as if it were an extension of hygiene? Should there be and to what degree, an enhancement of sensuous atmosphere –

lighting, music, scent. How far should group instruction be desirable, effective? Is it possible that for some sexual activity will be repulsive, and for what reasons, and with what consequences? Should homosexuality be included and under what conditions if any? Should instructors/instructresses be given a special *cachet* and perhaps privileged and circumscribed status?

Whatever your, the reader's, views, this is not a matter to be ignored. Give it deep, constructive thought.

For it is fundamental to many aspects of a future world, well beyond the confines of the sex act itself – family life, equanimity, peace with one's self and the world, self-confidence, anger control, even crime. We must face up to it, and follow through with determination.

At present we are going through what I hope is a blip on a hidden screen. We are, up to a point quite properly, tying education to social goals; but the blip on the screen tells us that the primary goal is to train young people for employment. Vocational and/or practical education is, will be, and should be of as much concern as the so-called academic, for this is the path that many will choose in life, and it is significant for the full life and recreation of many whose primary occupation will be less definable.

So here I address a problem of pedagogy. Let me illustrate. Many years ago I administered an educational programme for the United Nations which consisted of extending the horizons and knowledge of senior civil servants from developing countries, in almost all substantive fields, from social work to hydraulic engineering. The previous director of the centre, with great perspicacity, set in place a system in which he talked with each of the fellows to determine what, in their *theoretical* understanding they were lacking. At first the fellows resisted. What they wanted were the latest practical techniques and gimmicks. Each individually tailored programme, however, was designed to reinforce the *principles* from which the practical techniques emerged, to create professional on-going contacts with the world of advanced knowledge and innovation, and to help the candidate to control, throughout his or her life, the flow of *new* information, techniques and ideas. He or she faced the issue that the "latest" today is the "out-dated" tomorrow; that education in the "latest" will be démodé by the time the student returns home. In other words, the student aimed instead at broadening capabilities for life-long development, individually, instead of making the experience a one-shot, classroom kind of quickly out-dated and ephemeral instruction. In that context the experiment, for that was what it was, was "too expensive" to last, yet it was in truth a most efficient and long-lasting expenditure of resources.

Similar principles apply to "practical" instruction in high schools.

The reasoning is simple. If you train children with employment in mind, what precisely is that employment to be? You begin educating in that manner in the teens, but it will be four years (more if tertiary education follows) before the child is offering his or her services. In the present and future world, changes in the work place, in both technique and distribution of tasks, move so fast and unpredictably that you may be training for dead ends. Furthermore, unless there is a very close liaison with the *whole range* of employers, it will be inevitable that the skills represent only a portion of what is needed. How many schools train butchers in sushi techniques? (Some do.) How far behind were schools in adapting auto mechanics courses to the electronic age?

Furthermore, it is obvious that the work place itself will change many times during the career of the employee, and that an employee is likely to change jobs more frequently than at present. How can schools keep up with the fast changes and movements in occupation? They can't, unless they specialise as technical high schools, which is not always to be recommended, and also may not be what employment needs require.

What the school can best do is to educate, not train. Even for those whose major aptitude is practical, it is still the mind that counts. Skilled tradesmen and secretaries can adapt. They understand what lies behind the practice, they play with alternatives in their minds, they are not shocked but challenged if there is a technological revolution, and they have psychological command of what is needed to go through the adaptation. Schools that build programmes on the concept of a survey of employer-specific needs are doomed to fall short as out of date

This is not to say that school and the work-place should be separated. Children should *know* what the workplace entails -- not as a fixed static entity, but one that is always in fluctuation. Since time is limited, not all careers can be demonstrated by class activities. The notion of dynamics needs to be extended by indications that there are other worlds out there, other kinds of industry and commerce. And, especially for the more academically inclined, that boring subjects are sometimes of great advantage, from languages to abstract mathematics.

If the school is to combine practice and theory in generalizable ways, employers will still fret about the lack of trained applicants to do immediate tasks. As most Europeans have known -- but maybe are losing sight of -- that is the task for the employer himself. For that kind of training, there is no substitute for it being on the job, linked precisely to the issue of earning a living. A modernised concept of apprenticeships -- which will have to be followed time and again by refresher training -- still makes sense. Some large industries may be able to support class activities, either in-house or in association with training or technical post-high schools. It is their responsibility.

Don't dump this on secondary schools. They have too much to do to create the dynamic fundamentals and to nurture creative aptitudes and youth maturity.

One of the concomitants of undisciplined self-expression is the inability to communicate effectively and to discriminate between incoming messages. Disturbingly, many adults take manipulatory advantage of this.

Before World War II ideology was linked to political propaganda. Both the left but especially the right honed the skills of communicating falsity and manipulating half-truth. Crowd behaviour, mass rallies, manipulation of mass theatrical devices, endless repetition, slogans instead of thought -- all these were common. Mostly, educators could see them for what they were. As a youth and young man I found that classes in logic and books which showed the nature of the techniques and the logical *Léger-de-main* quite fascinating -- of course using what I had learned to support my own prejudices!

It is difficult to find such classes and books today, especially for high schools.. States still manipulate with propaganda, but, save for those which are ideologically founded, their positions are usually more subtle. They make use of PR firms and techniques, with communication models derived from advertising, but now being cynically distrusted as "spin". In the industrialised world the techniques of propaganda have been taken over by a kaleidoscope of pressure groups. Pressure groups organised around particular points of view and philosophies are a natural outcome of democratic life and the new technologies. It behoves the citizen to see clearly the relationship between argument and data, to know the empirical base of points of view, the logic and assumptions with which it is upheld. Youth is particularly vulnerable to the power of repeated assertions, the mis-use of emotion, and loud slogans – yes, even when teachers use them.

And this applies, even more, to nurturing the ability to appraise critically the numerous ideologies and unsupported "scientific" and folk claims with which all of us are confronted today. Without sacrificing independence of thought and respect for mavericks, youth needs to be able to make judgements about balderdash, mumbo-jumbo, "obscurantist bunkum, swirling hogwash, mendacious codswallop" and to be guided to simple expressions in their own language, avoiding the obscure language which is nowadays typical of corporations, politicians and academics[33].

Ideally, a citizen society equipped to judge and think and appraise would, by its own standards and criticisms, reveal the strengths and weaknesses of arguments, and hence punish by scepticism those who try to win by playing tricks on the mind.

There is evidence that the public senses much of this. There is widespread cynicism about political statements, derision about the way the media fasten on a limited aspect of a "story" and repeat it *ad infinitum* until it goes away, neglecting the balancing data. While many fasten upon visual scenes of horror and distress, others know that this is manipulative, replacing thought and balance with blood and tears.

A few recognise that, while it is proper for children to know what demonstrations are about, what lies behind them, it is exploitative to include very young children in those demonstrations; it is abusive and brain-washing, especially at primary school age. By the secondary level, lessons in logic and rhetoric become essential for the formation of critical citizens, and teachers must be prepared to have their values and perspectives openly challenged and debated.

I am disturbed about other phenomena. The movements of the late 'sixties in the "West" properly shook up received ideas in almost all public fields, from sex to the environment. In part they did so by affirming the significance of the emotions, of feelings, of the subjective, and did indeed provide a much-needed corrective to the idea that logic is detached from the senses and is the only path to understanding[34]. Paradoxically, however, one result was to create group tyrannies, ideologies that built dogma and used emotion, particularly anxiety, alienation and anger, to bind adherents together.

Out of that came positions that held certain beliefs to be absolutely right, positions shared by some, not all, parents and teachers. Schools become the loci for the transmission of such beliefs, whether they were about the dangers of nuclear catastrophe, global warming, over-population, depletion of non-renewable resources, crime, sexual harassment, and much more.

Here enters a matter of difficult judgement. Such issues are indeed a matter for study and education. They will not be understood in their complexity and balance at very young ages. They must be approached at later ages. By the end of high school, pupils should be in a position to approach such topics *independently* from the teacher and with an ability to work out their position after having looked at argument and data – they should be becoming adept at finding and thinking about both.

My problems are two-fold.

Many of the issues are presented in a highly charged emotional context in which adults transmit their own fears, *creating* anxieties, fears and even emotional upset in personae who are not ready for it. If this matter is not dealt with, goes the message, the apocalypse will arrive. And it is going to be *your* task to deal with it. It will be on *your* consciences. Can anyone forget the strained faces of *primary school* children in the 'fifties and 'sixties as they expressed fears of nuclear catastrophe? Now the fear that strikes home most immediately is fear of sex=AIDS, of poverty; of violence on the street, of terrorism, of unemployment, even, in some parts of the world, of the possibility that the United

States will destroy our religion and culture.. Fear and reactive thoughts of violence and even revenge permeate the schools. Somehow we must replace it, not with over-confidence, but with balance, thought, belief that we *can* and *will* make a difference, by playing thoughtful roles where our capabilities count.

The second problem is that even well-meaning and just positions are frequently tainted by dogma; and slogans replace thought. Time and again I see high school students praised in public when they trot out the latest fashionable position on a complicated issue, repeating *ad nauseam* already-tired clichés. We do not expect world-shattering innovation from high school students. But by the end of high school clear individual, even original, statements of position, which are not simply the regurgitation of a teacher's or parent's ideology, should be the norm. This is even more serious an issue in those parts of the world where the basis of learning is by rote, and based on fundamentalist religious beliefs.

My own statements here are condensed and hence somewhat simplistic. I must go further, although even then the legitimate debate will only be opened up, by no means concluded. I would like to see schools consciously and clearly organise their approach to teaching and engendering thought around the following kinds of ideas.

Children can be helped to comprehend that understanding can be achieved through two alternative but interlinked processes. The one is subjective, intuitional and aesthetic, making use of words *and other signs* (harmonies, shapes) characteristic of "the arts". The other is rational, logical and communicable through words or similar (mathematical) signs. In making judgements about the efficacy of what is revealed, ideally the nature of the mix of the modes should be assessed. In dealing with the more subjective, it is of course interesting to pursue the influence of the creator's history and personality. This, though, is a part of knowledge itself, as revealing how it came to be, *not* part of the judgement of the significance or otherwise of the ideas themselves. Youth must understand that *ad hominem* arguments are not arguments. Whatever the nature of the communicator, it is his or her statements that count, in themselves. (It is nevertheless legitimate to interpret the *meaning* of the statements, where they are ambiguous, in terms of other signals the communicator may have given by his or her other statements and behaviour. Behaviour is then identified as a part of the statement.)

Both methods deal with ideas which consist of logical relationships, though differing in how they go about presenting them. Music consists of types of sound, notes, tones, movement, rhythm, harmonies, volume, all knit together into relationships which are the obverse of chaotic. Natural science includes the teasing out of explanations, that is relationships between this and that variable. So do the social sciences. Painting and architecture involve form. So it goes on. The horror of Hiroshima or 7-11 can be approached through art, communicating through visual form, the connotations of music, poems which link the act to feeling and experience, statements that show the relationship between nuclear action and catastrophe. It can also be placed in the context of, that is it can be related to, total war, generalisations about the dynamics ofwar and international politics, the state of the world society at the time, the linkage between that and the present, the proximal and fundamental causes of the events. All these and many more relationships are there to be explored, and full understanding needs them all. Although it is a statement of a relationship, it is superficial indeed for children to be encouraged simply to say "I think it was horrible". They must know there are other relationships involved, other generalisations to think about, approached through well constructed modes of thought and expression which we call disciplines. Disciplines are tools, tools that the young need to learn to use.

Within that mastery they may learn to criticise, be dissatisfied, with what the disciplines can do. There may here be the seeds of creative endeavour. But most of us cannot create, cannot innovate, unless we have the kinds of building blocks that schools can provide. Remember that invention and creativity are based on re-ordering what is know, that is the building blocks. (Yes, it is true that some creators and innovators find their building blocks away from school, even rejecting the institution. But disciplinary building blocks they do find, nevertheless.)

Even subjective assessments involve statements about more or less, that is about quantity, whether or not the quantities can be enumerated. There is more or less beauty, subjectively speaking. Ugliness is negative beauty.

When explanations are involved there is an inherent significance in the quantities. The arts deal with single representations, unique cases -- the original painting is not more or less interesting because it is replicated in prints; it is *unique* in its statements. The same applies to a theatrical or musical performance, a sculpture, a book. That is, the single case has a certain validity, which is *dependent upon its success in communicating*. The communication may be contemporaneously ineffective, but received at some future time, which makes immediate judgement problematic. Popular approval may be ephemeral, yet the relationships involved, for example in "hard metal", are in communication, and are thus there to be teased out, examined, as a part of "knowledge", both subjectively and objectively. Youth needs to know these things as part of the fundamental basis of what they are "learning".

Matters of equal importance are not frequently addressed. We have already noticed the value of the single case, the unique and non-replicated statement. It is important to relate this to and distinguish it from, *explanation* in the more formal sense, not because of the nature of the revealed assertions, but because of the demands of the methodology.

This morning I was reading a front page story in a well respected and carefully presented newspaper. It dealt with ozone thinning for the coming summer, a matter of great concern and certainly a matter for school discussion. The main space in the story was contained in a full column on the front page. That consisted of repeated statements of concern, linked to such phrases as "It has been shown that". The identification of who had done the showing and how it was done was not mentioned until a very short column concluding the story on an inside page. There was not the slightest attempt to communicate any reason for accepting or rejecting the findings by representing the pros and cons of the methodology and its locus in general scientific knowledge. The implication was that the results should be accepted because they came from a reputable scientific organisation – and because the newspaper presented them. One assumes the results to be valid until someone comes along later with another story. This is unacceptable. It is as *ad hominem* as the dismissal of a politician's ideas because of his sexual peccadilloes. It is difficult but necessary for teachers to inform their pupils of such thinking traps and reinforce the maturity of their judgements.

Even where data *are* presented quite fully, citizen-children need to learn how to evaluate them. This applies especially to anecdotal and statistical material. Is the anecdotal to be considered as a unique work of art? Quite possibly. No more and no less. Since it is unique one can draw legitimate conclusions *subjectively*. Within the media anecdotal evidence does not have the same seriousness or sincerity of purpose as a major work of art. Most frequently the portrayal of an incident communicates to the emotions on subjects -- for example crime -- that are open to consideration from the other, more logical, more enumerative methods. A citizen-youth must be aware of the values and emotional impact of the unique instance; but also to be able to place that in the context of knowledge obtained by other methods.

Doubt. Uncertainty. Scepticism. Yet we must act on the basis of what we know now without waiting for the ultimate truth. These are major conundrums that youth have to be prepared for, have to understand if they are to live with the huge changes in knowledge that are being thrust at them.

Youth need that understanding, *and the acceptance of it* more than ever for psychological reasons. The unknown has always been a threat. Deep within ourselves, in primitive, perhaps irrational, fear, we do not know how to deal with it. It impinges on our personal lives every day, it is thrust upon us as a characteristic of the world, indeed of the universe. We correctly discuss the possibility of annihilation by projectiles from outer space.

What is troublesome is the serious anxiety and stress that comes from fear of the unknown. I am not concerned here with the modes of dealing with it, from religion to witchcraft, alternative therapies or fatalism, many of which at least have the possibility of relieving stress. What are more serious are the inhibiting features, the negative pessimism, inhibition of activity, chronic anxiety and depression, which flow. Suicide among youth. Alienation.

It is fundamental to serious education that children learn to deal with the unknown, especially before a personal crisis hits them. They must examine the validity and limitations of unique experience, learning from it but not turning it into dogma. A teacher who is sick may be ill because of the effects of a new detergent in the washroom. That is a matter for investigation. But if it turns into a dogma it can dangerously deflect investigation from some other causative possibility -- even one that is at present not identified.

It is a primary responsibility of school education to engender clear individual judgements about the presentation of information, and to show how youths can get to the sources of information themselves and at least be sceptical about inadequate materials, however persuasive the cause. What I have argued for is complex. In its sources, like everything else taught in school, it is embedded in subject matter which belongs in universities and beyond, which high school students cannot normally be expected to fully master. That in itself is not a reason for dismissing it. The principles *can* be (and often have been) taught directly in high school. And, with good pedagogical attention, they can be communicated indirectly as an aspect of normal studies.

To move toward the informed citizenship that is necessary in our goals we must re-emphasise, especially in high school, the arts of logic, discourse, debate and rhetoric; the relationship between data, theory and judgement; the ability to search for, assess, and use data; the positive force of constructive criticism, both logical and aesthetic; the role of sensory experience in arriving at observations and judgements; and the ability both to speak and to write about well-marshalled ideas. School children should be able to test the statements of teachers with confidence and skill, but on the basis of reasoned argument and data, and mutual respect. Challenge simply for the sake of challenge is not good enough.

We want our children (grandchildren) to be educated in such a way that they utterly reject slogans, false jargon, and improperly communicated data.

The social purpose of the school links, as I have said, with other objectives than the vocational. I will be discussing the distress of the elderly who find themselves unstimulated, bored, and alienated. We know of the unemployment of youth. We know that most countries have high steady rates of unemployment and that one of the major difficulties in developing countries is linked to chronic under-employment. In other words, perhaps fifty per cent of the world's population has *unwanted* time on its hands[35]. To the extent that this is true -- I ask you to suspend judgement on that issue for the meantime -- the primary institution for properly handling the situation is, once again, the school. To be stated bluntly, schools must

111

be able to help children to find ways to stimulate their leisure time and to obviate *boredom*, one of the most depressing characteristics of old age, unemployment, and youthful crime.

For this reason the educational system has a major responsibility, at least equal to the others I have outlined, to assist children in the task of discovering their self-directed creative and recreational capacities. Modern schools do some of this, by including courses in the arts, from music to theatre, and practical skills such as carpentry and metal-working. However, when such activities are simply slotted into the timetable problems arise. They inevitably compete with one another for rare time slots, which include what most consider to be the basics, and the artistic courses become the target of parents who see them as "frills". The "practical" courses are almost always justified by vocational rather than avocational considerations. Furthermore it is impossible for schools as they are now to bring students in touch with the whole variety of possible pursuits one of which may be precisely what the student finds stimulating.

To remedy this schools would have to be able to plan and justify the activities in terms of the principles I have outlined before. Most adults will have a hard time agreeing, since the underlying argument runs counter to the philosophy, which I shall continue to dispute throughout my theses, that Work is King. Hence those responsible for educational policy will have an uphill struggle to make those policies clear, consciously advocated, and fully planned. Creative Leisure is Queen. And here we have the beginning of the thought that school as known at present are inadequate. We need something better.

Lying behind the discovery of the creative self is the challenge to learn to occupy oneself when not being supervised. A number of cultures deliberately used isolation in stressful conditions as a rite of passage. Self-reliance, even in highly interdependent communities, was necessary for survival. Isolation forced the young candidate for adulthood to know his inner being, and to know that being in its relationship to a potentially threatening nature, a nature with which the candidate learned also to be at peace. It was an exercise in being, and in spirituality. Such procedures could well be studied. So too could modes of meditation, relaxation, and emotional control.

Similar exercises can expose the values and dangers of living with small groups, mutual dependencies under stress, the uselessness of making a habit of ascribing blame to others or giving dysfunctional expressions of aggression, and learning the ways of small group diplomacy. For some young people will find their creativity not in the private actions of solitude but in the co-operation of acting with others toward a common outcome or sharing resources and skills.

It will be for the pedagogues to work out such possibilities. The objective of drawing out self-reliance and spontaneous creativity carries the additional benefit of improving self-knowledge and becoming sensitised to small group interactions which have implications for family life and the workplace as well as for unpaid positive activity.

The issues lead to the conclusion that the school course-ridden day is insufficient. Good schools already intrude into family life through the demands of home study. Perhaps more of that should be done in current school class time, moving some of the avocational activities -- as is done with sports -- outside the conventional structure. Carrying this theme to its ultimate conclusion will require major changes in the organisation and operation of what we now call schools in our 21st century society.

Since the school has children in its care for such an enormous proportion of their time, and since those children are subjected to so many confusing, worrying and contradictory influences in their lives, the school cannot avoid being in a position of ***nurturing***. It may not want to do so, it may not be mandated to do so, and it is almost certainly not equipped to do so. Yet in this responsibility it is almost equal to that of the family.

What I have written so far has dealt mostly with the mind. But the mind is inseparable from the body, the senses, the emotions, the influences, the interactions, and the memories. *Pace* some forms of psychoanalysis, the child is far from completely formed in infancy. What happens in school will be a major influence in creating the ever-dynamic or statically-confined persona.

A great deal of this cannot be *controlled* by the individual teacher, for it is a result of the complexities of the institutional *ambience*, peers and other teachers. Individual teachers do, frequently, detect problems of concern which range from attention disorders to malnutrition and the possibility of crime. They give of themselves through advice, discipline, listening and referral. By role definition they must give priority to the effects of what they detect to the operation of the classroom and the formal work of teaching itself. Very commonly the child's personal problems can show through surly indiscipline, avoidance of work, theft, obscenity, anger, nonchalant insolence, gang behaviour, bullying and violence -- all the problems, in fact, that are found in the adult world, but in more vulnerable forms.

Consultation with parents may, but mostly are unlikely to, help, since teachers are not in a position to enter into family therapy. Teachers by themselves cannot create the remedies. Yet schools have to deal with concerns, just as they are now learning to deal with the "physically and mentally challenged" -- oh, what wonderful and inadequate jargon to obscure the reality that the child, deprived or contorted with respect to his or her capabilities may or may not feel "challenged" but certainly needs attention and help. It is an inescapable responsibility that has serious consequences for revised school mandates and organisation.

All of which intersects with the issue of behavioural discipline. There has been a school of socialisation that asserts that the only legitimate form of control is that of argument and discussion. The problem is that it doesn't always work.... And when it does it can sometimes breed conformity rather than courtesy.

Hit 'em and learn 'em in righteous anger and its sadistic extremes has gone by the board in many parts of the world. There, teachers must control their reactions, however provoked. On the other hand some parents encourage their children to express their angers, which can mean placing the self before others with insolence, refusal to heed, and rejection of what the school is trying to do -- just as disruptive reactions as the surly introversion of unexpressed problems. More frequently than not, minor irritants of these kinds move through the classroom, as peers delightedly cheer the culprit on. Then follows open defiance, the use of appeal procedures to undermine the teacher, and the intervention of angry parents convinced they are not themselves responsible, or frustrated ones who do not know how to deal with situations that are out of control.

Indeed, in some areas I know of the school has no effective powers of discipline and control, and would be totally lost if it were not for the decency of the majority of the children. There are, it is true, possibilities of assigning extra work or detentions, which the hard core can simply refuse to honour. When that happens, when violence breaks out, when there is habitual absence from the classroom, when there are drugs or weapons, the ultimate threat is there. Exile, banishment from the school. What a game! A game that tempts others who are toying with the lure of dropping out. To be officially pronounced unwelcome in the school, no longer hassled by authority, officially able to roam the streets -- exactly what such delinquents want......

We do not want this in our world. Not only does it represent the loss of an individual from the common good, but it is an example to the half-alienated and is disruptive of those who have other ideals. It is an instance, potentially, of the spread of an anti-school innovation. Since parental responsibility is either not there or is insufficient, the school itself must develop other tools, even though, without outside help, it cannot get at root problems such as dysfunctional family life.

There are two methods at least which might help. As I write this I read of an experiment in Toronto. Youths expelled for violence are identified as such and transferred to another specialist programme for them only. Instead of roaming the streets each student works (expensively) with a psychiatrist and a programme co-ordinator. In the pilot programme, fifty per cent of the students have been judged ready to return to regular schooling. At least for the others some education is achieved. My information does not reveal what happens if the youths refuse to cooperate, nor what kind of family involvement is in place. Nevertheless the thought behind such approaches deserves attention.

This is to involve the children themselves in peer responsibility, and to give them some of the tools to do so. As in so many other cases, older methods which have gone out of psychological fashion (such as the use of prefects) have been ridiculed on the basis of extreme caricature. All methods, old or new, have their defects. Perhaps one should look again, and tease out the positive from the negative.

Many schools nowadays have some form of student council, a useful way of enabling, usually the better, pupils to voice difficulties and to organise events. There are also emergent student-teacher initiatives, such as plays and discussions, which aim at demonstrating such topics as the handling of violence when it occurs, the difficulties of sex, or the release of anger. Even in primary schools selected children are trained in mediation, intervening in quarrels to persuade quarrellers to look at each others' points of view, to find ways out of the situation before it explodes.

Experiments of these kinds however helpful cannot deal effectively with every situation, and cannot always be on top of day to day incidents. We shall see part of the remedy in the replacement of schools by proposed Youth Maturity Institutes below.

It seems that the old idea of a "school spirit" based on identification with the school, pride in what it attempts to do, rivalry with others, and internal pupil-based discipline, is worth another look. As with any other type of cultural or sub-cultural identity, it can go too far, with autocracy emerging, too much interference in private acts, too much peer pressure, and, in extreme instances, schools becoming rivalrous gangs. What is different nowadays, and even more we hope in the future, is that in the developed world the teachers who have the ultimate responsibility are better informed about such dangers and are likely to be more sensitive to their emergence.

Let us then consider re-inventing (where it has to be re-invented) the system of prefects for day schools. Let there be chosen leaders at various levels in the school, with responsibilities according to the degree of maturity that their age can handle. Senior prefects might very well act as disciplinary agents and interveners under policies formulated by, or with the assistance of, the student council. Let them have the authority to discipline for designated infractions -- giving detentions for example; to maintain order and respect on school premises and at school functions; to report serious infractions; to present constructive ideas to council and staff; in short to supervise, *on behalf of the student body,* standards of good order and courtesy.

One of the primary tools that street gangs use to reinforce solidarity and identity, is dress and body decoration. They do so naturally, out of spontaneous recognition of principles that are as old as human groups. Schools in many parts of the world, and especially North America, deliberately gave away this reinforcing tool. In some form, whether through simple uniforms or badges, it needs to return. It is one way of enhancing pride. I am on my mettle because I can be seen to be a *member* of the school that has a great team, organises volunteers for a social cause, puts on an exciting art show, or perhaps, even, is the place where academic achievement gets us going. At least when I'm wearing that uniform outside of school I behave; I'm noticeable and proud of it.

I'm well aware that the wearing of uniforms at schools where state schools do *not* wear them is an identifier of difference that is often not acceptable and is even embarrassing to the wearers. Acceptance changes when the custom is *general*.

The easiest part of this discussion is to write the words; the most difficult to interpret the principles in specific contexts, to give them pedagogical content and reality, to make them work. None of my statements can be considered as an absolute.

First and foremost it is the teachers who have the responsibility for method and content, for the specifics of classroom and school. They claim to be, and are, and should be, the professionals. It is what they have learned, their experience, their skills, that makes the difference. But those skills, as with any profession, must work in context, the context of societal aims, immediate culture, and changing knowledge.

One of the realities is that henceforth they will be working in a society that changes ever more rapidly, and that they must second-guess what the needs of the future may be. Is that to be toward some vision of Utopia, a world in which we wish ourselves to live, even though we may never see it in our lifetimes? Some vision of a better world? I hope so. But if so that kind of ultimate purpose needs discussion, needs teacher attention, needs definition, even though that definition is bound to change over the decades.

This is an area that lies beyond the horizons of teachers alone. Teachers are in a position to be arbiters of society, communicating (deliberately or without noticing it) their own values. But they do not have the mandate to *decide* where society should go. In that they are simply one set of citizens. Who then does? The interplay of parents, non-parent voters, political and community leaders, teachers, other professionals who, as we shall see, are involved with the same objectives.

Teachers then interpret the objectives. The trouble is that the objectives, at this stage in our evolution, are not spelled out for society as a whole (except, for example, in fundamentalist religious schools or autocratic state systems), and can only be defined in simplistic and programmatic terms, tinged with political ideology. Just the same, some observations can be made.

One is that in a future world society and culture not only *will* consist of varying groups, cultures or sub-cultures, with non-uniform ideas, but *should* do so. The reality of the statement for contemporary societies is beyond dispute. Look within your country. It is there[36].

To the extent that this is so, it follows that schools **must** themselves vary. The concept that each State school must have an identical, centrally determined, philosophy, curriculum, and pedagogy is now revealed for what it is, an ideology based upon a false socio-cultural premise, upon a false objective that we should all be the same, an anachronism.

Ideally, varying schools should match variations in child response to varying methods, varying parental philosophies, and variations in cultural realities, at least. Such clear matching is seldom practicable, but close approximations are possible. Perhaps the following principle is worthy of thought: schools and teachers within schools should have the utmost flexibility to exercise their ideas in directions which link with a recognised dream and educational philosophy; but no child should be forced into a particular variety of school. Choice that is now available to some (the better off) should be available to all.

Such a principle implies that variation should not merely be between state schools and private schools, religious schools, schools for the rich and the not so rich. State systems themselves need to abandon the assignment of children to schools on the sole criterion of geographical proximity, a policy which derives from the false notion that equity and equality of opportunity imply pushing every child into the same cauldron. Equity and equality of opportunity imply the opposite, that every child should be in the school that suits him or her best. The identification of what is "best" will not be accurate. It involves parents' ideals and parents' knowledge both of the child and of the nature of each possible school, a knowledge that will undoubtedly change with time and experience.

Hence movement of pupils between schools must be possible. And schools must provide parents with information -- documentation, for example, about its educational philosophy and goals, its methods, its achievements, what it is trying to do better. *Every school in the system should be required to formulate and enunciate its point of view.* Every piece of data that bears on the parents' potential evaluation of the school should be public.

One specious argument against this principle is that once it is known that one or two schools meet needs better than others they will become elite, based on restricted entry. Of course that is possible, but it reveals inflexibility in the school system. (It may also involve prejudice and lack of knowledge of the alternatives.) It may encourage some other schools to emulate. But in addition it will be the case that there will be no single definition of "better". Parents will not be like lemmings, moving in one single direction. Schools that meet children's varied educational needs best require replication; others require down-sizing.

The two most difficult sources of inflexibility are teachers and buildings. If choice reveals that certain wanted types of teaching are not reflected in the distribution of teacher skills, then, at least in an adjustment period, some individual teachers will be in difficulty. The implications are that in the long run teacher education itself should teach less dogma and more adaptability; that there should be maximum support for teacher re-education; and that unadaptable teachers will have to go or be assigned elsewhere to a school where their skills fit better.

At present the conditions under which teachers do their work are highly variable, country to country, sometimes responding to bargaining conditions, sometimes to social status, sometimes to poverty, sometimes to religious ideology. However I do not know of any countries in which the conditions of work and education, except in some of the most expensive private schools, correspond to the need. Sometimes good principles have been subverted by union action and bargaining into privileged "rights". This is not professional.

Days off for professional education, in which the school closes; long summer vacations, originally to permit children to undertake agricultural tasks -- such arrangements, fiercely union protected, become inflexible, inefficient, rule-bound, subject to abuse, and archaic. Professional days, for example, are often boring, not attended by individual teachers, and, while sometimes useful, are not administered to face up to improving and updating the skills of *individual* teachers. That requires more than the occasional discussion or lecture, but weeks of analysis and education. Teaching, especially in high school, is an ever-moving profession, in the roles required, and in the subject matter. Educational updating requires much more, with longer term refresher courses and opportunities for serious debate.

It is a normal fact of employment that teachers in most systems take their classes home with them, figuratively and also literally. Much of their work consists of out-of-class paper work, including marking and preparation. When classes take place throughout the day, either teachers stay very late at school, or work at home, with effects not only on their own domestic arrangements but on overworked stress. The short breaks between classes, or class time off, are seldom adequate to do serious work. Despite what the public regards as soft and privileged work time, teachers in most advanced systems are typically stressed out, under constant emotional and psychological pressure, especially when dealing with under-motivated, tumultuous children; to say nothing of those pupils with severe personal problems. Moves in several systems to mix "special needs" children into conventional classes, while highly desirable in theory, add to teacher stress (especially when the teacher has no education in the specialty of the needs) and divert him or her from attention given to the ordinary, who, in their own ways, are just as needy. Unless very special measures are taken, such moves are typical of the ways in which principles can come to grief because the material and organisational resources are not adjusted sufficiently.

If to these present difficulties we add the requirements of striving for our ideal world, without other adjustments, mayhem and breakdown could destroy what little is left of the high school system. Any reforms must be built around the capacities, physical and mental, of the staff -- teachers *and others* -- whose task it is to deliver.

In many systems the school year is built around terms divided by short breaks -- one, two, or three weeks -- instead of a concentration of holidays on a long two month summer break typical of others, during which the dynamic of school progress can be threatened. A number of breaks of around two weeks enables the progression of teaching with little interruption of the dynamic, especially if some of the breaks are designated for projects, independent study, alternative creative activities. Such breaks provide an opportunity for teacher refresher courses as well.

Teachers are not only over-worked but also inefficiently directed. Some systems provide teachers with, not just the occasional class off during the week, but up to an equivalent of classroom time for study and preparation. Initially, in systems where teachers are not accustomed to that, the provision of such time could be significantly abused. Many teachers are simply not used to the idea that handling the subject matter requires continual research and reading. Such teachers would not know what to do with their time, except paper work, until guided into its effective use. (Are there still teachers who have the time, the drive, the energy, the knowledge, to *contribute* to the growth of knowledge, to undertake research, however modest; even perhaps to involve their classes in that activity? Yes there are. They should be among the role models, though it is too much to make that a formal requirement until our brave new world is here.)

An efficient educational system requires a surplus of resources beyond those immediately used in the classroom. Contrary to the drives of budget-minded administrators, if you show me an educational institution of serious intent in which all classrooms are being used at every minute of the day, and in which there are no teachers outside the classroom, I will show you a static, unresponsive, bureaucratised, anti-educational operation, unable to meet society's needs.

Why? When considering the distribution of teachers, it should be obvious that they should be pedagogically sound and know their subject matter. In secondary schools particularly, it is not good enough to say, as some have, "Give me a class and I'll teach it anything." That is the sure way to superficiality. But teachers take ill, the ideal system would require them to take time off for formal re-education, and they must have an opportunity to take real holidays that would involve being absent for terms. Redistribution among existing teachers, re-posting, now often means assigning teachers to subject areas of which they know little or nothing.

Short term replacements are often temporary substitute teachers, which may often be effective in individual cases. But as a *system* it cannot be efficient. Such substitutes usually have to have other sources of income and cannot afford to place themselves in a one-line teaching career position; their standards and updating cannot therefore be rigorously controlled. Both these situations *require a pool* of subject-oriented teachers in the career stream available for replacement allocation. Members of the pool would not be in the classroom until called upon, but would be salaried.

I have been referring to refresher education. The movement of school responsibilities into non-vocational and therapeutic fields, as I am about to propose, will increase the range of required specialties, of differing combinations of skills. School professionals, just like health professionals, will in some instances be stimulated to re-combine their skills: a combination of language teaching and family therapy might be a case in point. And just like health professionals, or university professors in North America who are seeking promotion, they will require formal certification, from time to time, of their continued pedagogic and coexistent subject area skills.

As I write I am living in an urban area in which the distribution of the population is changing fast. Immigrants are arriving in substantial numbers, finding living space in new areas, and needing educational courses (such as language) which differ from those of the past. Some locations are no longer affordable for new growing families in the same numbers. Changing technology requires new subject matter which is unevenly developed and which requires altered forms of teaching and working space. New interactive multi-media teaching tools again require new forms of space to be effective -- even bringing the home into the classroom (especially with web based distance learning). Old school buildings are sometimes emptying, and some cannot be adapted easily to new teaching needs.

Demographic forecasts are notoriously affected by value and political judgements and are seldom reliable in detail. Educational authorities are thus reluctant to spend large capital sums on new buildings when the trend that demands them may be applicable only, say, for six or seven years. They meet the need by throwing up temporary port-a-classrooms, which parents immediately identify as sub-standard and discriminatory.

Yet the flexibility afforded by mobile classrooms is clearly more desirable than the inflexibility of monuments hewed in stone. The unresolved problem suggests that the expenditure of money, efficiency of operation, and educational flexibility and quality will be best where buildings can respond to differing needs from decade to decade instead of dominating and freezing the delivery of service. If this is so, then there is a major architectural challenge to design school buildings which can easily be moved from one location to another, which consist of modules of differing functions which can be combined and recombined to fit changing educational needs, and which, probably, are less expensive than conventional structures. Paradoxically, this may be more easily achievable in developing tropical countries, making use of traditional structures which can be removed and rebuilt with less cost. Here is a field for UNESCO innovation.

Someone has to take decisions and to provide resources in an environment in which, at least in the short term, resources are getting scarcer. The desirable specifics will vary so much from one system to another that I can only write in generalities. But it should be clear by now that we need to re-think the structure and operation of what we now call schools, if they are to properly educate, nurture and create cohorts of well-adjusted future citizens.

The initiative to establish and design variable schools will come mostly from parents, from some teachers, and from some citizens. Since it is the community providing the funds, it is likely that what I will call the Youth Maturity Institute management authority will be vested in an overall area board which allocates funds and authorises establishments. The board will need to represent the taxpayers and those who elect the political authority; it should also have representatives of parents and teachers (not in their self-seeking but in their professional capacities); and it might be beneficial to have representatives from senior high school classes. The danger in such a board is that each of these constituencies will provide members, elected or chosen, whose debates will result in some sort of majority opinion. The danger then is that the majority will be seen as having a political mandate to exercise that opinion throughout the system, giving no voice to alternative philosophies and styles. This is the opposite of what we are endeavouring to achieve. Hence it seems essential that the terms of reference for such a board require as a matter of law that the board recognises the principles of school, now Youth Maturity Institute, variation.[37]

As I have said, each individual Institute should be required to establish and publicise its philosophy and methods, paying special attention to its unique character. The initiative for doing this should come from both parents and teachers *and other professional contributors* acting in concert. Until our world becomes less confrontational there will undoubtedly be conflict between opposing philosophies; someone will lose out. The area supervisory board needs to ensure that the Institute management council losers will be accommodated, that there is another school for them to join, or that one can be organised. Considerable initial adjustment is likely to take place, a necessary price for the achievement of the ultimate goals.

I deliberately placed the phrase "other professional contributors" in this context. There are now in fact examples not only of private schools in the conventional sense but of schools established by large industrial firms. Such schools are in response to two drives. One is the improvement in working conditions when working parents have on-premise schools (especially for younger

131

children) with recreational as well as classroom space. Parents can visit in their breaks, and their children will be occupied instead of returning home to an empty house.

Another motivation, for upper year youth, is vocational training. It is very doubtful if adequate applied training for the workplace can be conducted effectively in conventional schools. It is often best done on site. Large firms can do this with either narrowly focused classes, in association with and supplementing Institutes, leading to apprenticeships or by actually locating and financing upper year broad education on their premises.

The feasibility of such schemes does not have to be limited to commerce and industry. The civil service, hospitals, universities, large public service and charitable organisations also have roles. Education affects us all; it percolates throughout; the barriers should be of malleable rubber.

A similar principle works in reverse. The objectives of the proposed Institutes run far beyond the capacity of conventional schools to honour. This implies not that the objectives are wrong but that school capabilities must be altered to meet them. The most ineffective way of doing this is to throw money at schools and teachers. For most teachers are not educated to carry out many of the tasks (such as therapy for a suicidal youth), and do not have the time or energy even if they were equipped to do so. And school management would have to undergo a revolution to assess and address the broadened role; managers notoriously find this difficult although there are many innovative school heads and principals trying new approaches which have to be dubbed "experimental".

We are dealing with the "whole" child. We are seeking a holistic education. The state of knowledge and professionalization of society create more and more specialists who are dealing with various parts of that whole. Their perspectives need to be brought together, and *the use of their manpower optimised*. There is dreadful duplication, waste, uncoordination, and confusion, not in the best interests of the child.

In order to achieve our vision, the concept of "school" as an institution with a narrow mandate needs to be jettisoned. Schools should be replaced by organisations which are mandated and equipped to nurture children and youths in a holistic manner toward the objectives of individual maturation. Maturity is the new goal.

As I have hinted, let us call these, until a better term is devised, **"Youth Maturity Institutes**."

First, each Youth Maturity Institute should have a management committee in which teachers, parents and representatives of youths from the final class should be represented. The task of the management committee should be to ensure that the teachers and staff in their day to day operation, act in accordance with the approved school philosophy, and to organise the operation of the Institute.

Second, each Youth Maturity Institute should have an advisory committee consisting of members appointed by the various bodies in the community concerned with the welfare of youth. To the extent that they bear upon the philosophy of the Institute and the needs of its operation, there could be included, for example, representatives of churches, youth organisations, social services, the media (not for "stories" but as being perceived as partly "responsible" for what goes on), police, medical services, employers, unions, and high school pupils. It would consider identified problems (such as drugs, violence, for example), the bearing of all of the services on each of those problems, possible co-ordination and changes of policy, not only in the Youth Maturity Institute but in the institutions which surround it.

Third, there would need to be a fundamental reappraisal of financing, the conception of "school hours", and personnel. We are dealing not only with the classroom where the teacher is paramount, but with recreation, and individual and family counselling (not in the vocational but in the psychological sense) with wide ramifications.

What has to come is the re-direction of appropriate outside services into the Youth Maturity Institute itself. Social service youth and family counsellors should move their offices and operations into the Institute, be seconded into the Institute from their bureaucracies, and have their budgets identified as part of the Institute budget, subject to Institute management.

Other organisations which have a bearing on Institute programmes need to be brought more formally into the Institute budget and field of responsibility. For example, the Youth Maturity Institute, in the running of its theatre programmes, might contract with a theatre company or organisation to do part or all of it, to the benefit of both. Many organisations concerned with the culture of creativity, or the creativity of culture should be more intimately involved with Youth Maturity Institutes, both on premises and off. Such contact would have the additional advantage of introducing children to the hard reality of creation (without putting them off), giving the starry eyes something to focus upon[38].

Since we are proposing an institution which has a holistic view of youth development, it follows that therapeutic and judicial functions[39] should be removed from *external* organizations and integrated with the Youth Maturity Institutes. This gives the Institutes opportunities to adopt therapeutic and restitutional procedures in the case of violence and delinquency. It enables them, in each case, to focus on the troubled youth and to work as long as it takes, and by whatever means, to reintegrate the youth into peer society. The use of therapy, even of medical knowledge, and of alternative ways of dealing with crime come together in one set of coordinated actions which in a formal judicial system is limited by professional bureaucracies and often stymied by the state of the law[40]. Healing circles, psychotherapy, peer group and parental influences will all be part of the considerations as the youth is challenged to recognize the damage he or she has caused, and to make restitution to those who have been hurt. Incarceration or expulsion will not be part of the answer, although indigenous methods of spiritual isolation may well be in some instances. The issue is made more complex by the discovery that there is a gene which influences anti-social behaviour, though it can be over-ridden by appropriate environmental and therapeutic circumstances.[41] Restitution, recognition, reintegration are the three 'r's. Such an approach will relate to major reforms in the judicial and legal systems which I will be proposing in a later chapter.

Clearly parents are intimately involved. Frequently they react defensively, protecting the family boundary, or from the shame of guilt and perplexity. If a child acts aggressively or criminally the cause may not be in the family. Or it may be. We need medical and therapeutic analysis. Parents should not be fingered immediately as the culprits. But they must be brought to understand, helped to deal with the issues and change their habits, and given support, together with the child. Not even "special needs" teachers can do this by themselves. There has to be team work in the Institutes, another reason for stressing the need to use them to replace schools.

Paradoxically, the more such methods succeed the more inner tensions may arise, unless another theme is addressed. For underlying a certain percentage of delinquency is the attraction and excitement of taking risks[42]. Car racing, experimenting with drugs and sex, toting an hand gun or knife, using machetes in moments of hysteria and involvement in political or religious terrorism. Logical argument will have only a small effect when such youth drives are paramount. Recognitions of consequences in dramatic form, the experience of devastation, will. But it requires a more widespread policy.

Bronislaw Malinowski's dictum "Let cricket replace warfare" has become a cliché, but deserves attention for all that. Many – not all – boys and an increasing number of girls want risky challenges, both mental and physical, without which they cannot move knowledgeably into adulthood. Show me a road racer and I will show you a school that is too bland in its challenges. This is an essential part of education, which cannot be completed in the classroom. Youth Maturity Institutes, as do a number of schools, for example in the Duke of Edinburgh's network, need to plan to encourage and support appropriate risk taking.

Recently a Canadian private school decided to drop challenging winter skiing because of tragic deaths from an avalanche. On the assumption that all reasonable precautions were taken, the cancellation was a mistake. Risk taking implies just that, risk taking. Mollycoddling so that there are no risks defeats the purpose – and there will be accidents along the way, or the risk will not be there.

The positive role of soccer in Africa and cricket in South Asia and the Caribbean cannot be over-stressed (especially when associated with material ambitions).

Schools are in fact better at devising intellectual risk taking tests - mathematical or chess challenges and competitions for example. But these reach only the elite. Professionals must devise ways in which the youth at whatever level, feels challenged, excited by even small accomplishments, prompted to risk the next stage.

Fear and anxiety are the concomitants of risk taking. Both are normal states even when risk is not at the forefront. Over the decades there have been enormous fears, communicated to school children, about atomic bombs, nuclear war, ecological disaster, poisonous foods. These have been communicated by teachers, parents and the media. There is no moral justification for this kind of adult fear transfer to children. On the other hand fear and anxiety are a normal part of risk and should be accepted as a normal state. Youth must learn to deal with them constructively in order to reach maturity and the Institutes have a major role in developing ways for this to happen constructively.

At the same time there are those for whom various forms of fears and anxieties, phobias, invade ordinary life in circumstances which may be deemed unwarranted, leading to the serious inhibition of appropriate behaviour. Again, the Institutes will have a pivotal role, not so much through teachers, though they may draw attention to the issue, but for therapists and parents.

Youth Maturity Institutes would accumulate an immense amount of experience and knowledge of direct interest to those dealing with social issues outside the Institutes themselves. Schools in my part of the world seem to have an almost nil impact on the fatally growing use of methadone and other drugs. They are not equipped to do so. But Youth Maturity Institutes would be. I would find it very difficult to believe that such Institutes, operating effectively, would not know the sources of the drug. They could combine an attack on crystal methadone with risk taking – for example assigning young at-risk victims to accompany police on inner city drug beats. Show them what doctors and nurses have to go through to deal with extreme cases. Remember that therapists, doctors and police are involved directly in the Institutes. The synergy that comes from the juxtaposition of professionals with quite different perspectives will lead to many innovative ideas. And it is one thing to lecture and to show a documentary but quite another to visit the live scene, prisons and hospitals.

The needs of poor countries require special comment. In many of the poor countries' rural areas, despite the trauma of war, and migration disruptions, and the ever present threat of famine, floods, and the depredations of both nature and man, the absence of a sophisticated therapeutic and institutional structure need not hold back a movement to reform. In some societies there are already male age-specific initiation rituals which can be adapted to go the youth maturity route. This is seldom the case for girls, other than, say, the declaration of puberty. Closely knit communities and kinship bonds do not mean the absence of internal strife, and they are sometimes the very sources of dissatisfaction and emigration. Nevertheless, skilled attention to their positive elements can aid the process.

Despite this, poverty and a natural emphasis on the less personal processes of development create national priorities in which youth maturity may take a back seat. Thus the capability to establish functioning Youth Maturity Institutes will depend on the success of developing countries to gain reasonable levels of living – and hence upon other aspects of the globe which I approach in later Chapters. In countries such as Kenya and India there is a smattering of innovative schools which suggests that there may be more opportunities for wider change.

Much the same concerns relate to possible resistances from conservative religions, such as, perhaps, forms of Islam or autocratic Christianity. It is *not* the intention of my discussion to advocate the forcible imposition of a particular form of Youth Maturity Institutes on specific cultures, where a Western model may not be appropriate. It would however be demeaning to assume the contrary, that modern Islam is somehow contrary to the principles of such Institutes. There are many educational practices in some parts of Islam which are contrary to the precepts of the Institutes – in some instances, for political reasons, violence is advocated; in others learning is by submission and rote. But no one can accuse reformist Turkey, pre-Saddam Iraq, or Iran, at least in the cities, of not having educational values and achievements which would be entirely compatible with their own variants on Youth Maturity Institutes.

There is no time to lose. We urgently need the generations which Youth Maturity Institutes will create. Without those generations, the rest of the task of creating our desirable world by say 2100 will be a rough ride. We expect the Institutes will minimize human tendencies to violence against and disrespect for others. This is needed to give us the risk taking courage to reform the totality of society. Fortunately, if we have the will, the replacement of schools with Youth Maturity Institutes need not be a long drawn out affair. It could be accomplished in many parts of the world by 2050. Globally, UNESCO (pending the United Nations changes I recommend later in this book) could take a lead role in nudging States to take action, and spreading the word and the message. In order to remove violence from the world and to create mature citizens there will need to be policies of an effective new kind of global government. Education and global government depend directly upon each other.

That having been said, there are no quick automatic results. There will be trial, error, mistakes. After the introduction of Youth Maturity Institutes, critics and nay-sayers point out "But there has been no reduction in violence". Of course not, in the short term. It will take a minimum of twelve years for those entering the new system to mature out of it. It will take longer for them to parent new intakes and to find their roles in society. We must learn to be patient and not give in to short term desperation.

2012Postscript

Papers considering the anthropology of childhood education in December 2011, resulting from conference on the subject organised by the Centre for Anthropological Research on Childhood, Youth and Education Brunel University, are available at www.brunel.edu.uk/sss/reserch/research-centres/centre-for-child-focussed-anthropological-research.

Manifesto for the New Age

V – The Family in Context

There is no such thing as THE family, nor is there a dominant set of "family values". Anthropologists have analysed scores of variants. The Western model of the nuclear family – parents and children cohabiting – is famous for variants in practice and its moral force has major limitations. Families are noted as the locus of love – and hate; unity – and divisiveness; support – and unwanted dominance; property unity – and argumentative tensions; social integration – and criminality.

The family has as one of its major roles the bringing up of children. Thus what it does affects the success or failure in the creation of maturity, one of the major goals of a worthwhile society. For schools to succeed in this role themselves they need to be strictly in tune with the family so that both work together in some sort of unity. A failure of schools dealing with minorities is that they have often been at cross purposes with the relevant parents with teachers attempting to use the schools for unwanted social reforms. The structure of Youth Maturity Institutes would modify that particular defect.

We have seen that a problem with schools is often that they exhibit boundaries, with teachers on one side and parents on the other. Children cross the boundaries daily, each time experiencing a little bit of a culture shock. Youth Maturity Institutes, with strong parental interactions, will not succeed if the world is to be made up of dysfunctional families. Dysfunctional families dominate in the richer world and often in traditional societies. Not only do they affect schooling but clearly have a major impact on crime and illness and the values which pervade political and monetary conditions.

Today there is a strong tendency in some parts of the West to bemoan the passing of the nuclear family. After the children grow up it consists just of mother and father until one of them dies; and then the survivor until he or she dies or has to be placed in a charity home. By contrast, Carol James, the Native Indian leader of a political party in British Columbia, openly celebrates her childhood life, during which, because of extended family connections both maternal and paternal. She could never quite predict who was going to be in the house at any one time, a situation which established mobility and flexibility in family relationships, with elders always respected, and which gave children a sense of well-being, comfort when needed, and security. "Family was never just immediate family, it was whoever was in the house at the time". By comparison with other types of family around the world, there is something rather bleak, arid, and sterile about the much vaunted nuclear family. This is not to decry the warmth which can exist; it is simply to pint our that the warmth has to be achieved and that when it is it becomes the envy of those who do not have it.

Those who remark on the apparent breakup of the nuclear family do so thinking of such matters as divorce and what anthropologists now call serial monogamy.

A few years ago there was exactly the same bemoaning of the passing of various forms of extended family, in particular the one most common in the West in which grandparents lived in a three-generational house. There is often a call to reinstate such a model, which remains significant in many Asian communities in the West and which may be returning as the proportion of the elderly increases and as the young face difficulties in paying for their independence.. The resultant warmth is by no means universal so that young people often resent their situation and escape from it if they can.

We often also regret the passing of wider extended families -- largely under the influence of migration, the example of industrialised societies, and the urbanisation and commercialisation of the poorer world. The variety of family structures is still enormous, and the bonds sometimes continue and have utility across oceans, and between town and countryside. To simplify grossly, links in such families frequently involve the common or nearby residence of siblings with their children. Because of rules of exogamy and property, the siblings may be sisters, or they may be brothers, less commonly both. For years analysts linked industrialisation, modernisation, and secularisation with the conversion of extended into nuclear families. Quite often, as in working class East London or the Caribbean, such trends did NOT create nuclear families, but matrilocal and matriarchal families, in which mothers lived in proximity to *their* mothers and to their sisters, gaining support thereby, with perhaps a succession of males producing a family of children with different fathers. Anathema to social workers dedicated to the ideology of the nuclear family, yet under the circumstances it could be highly functional. In technical terms, such structures resemble polyandry (in which a woman has several husbands), except that the males are serial. Just as we have serial monogamy, here we have serial polyandry.

The nuclear family, with which many right wing politicians so fervently identify, is almost entirely the invention of urban commercial middle classes, with significant differences in aristocracies and both urban and rural working poor. Those social workers who use the nuclear family as the operating model - indeed those therapists who do so - miss significant realities and place a limitation on their potential success.

Idealised family structures, whatever they may be, are supported by elaborate cultural statements, from myth and religion to rational ideology. Anthropologists are usually trained to look behind such statements to discover what might be described as the empirical or statistical reality - what actually goes on in life. The myths have a jural, normative, moral function designed to regulate interactions between the partners, and for the socialisation of children and the continuity of culture, and for pressure when aberrations become too obvious and out-of-hand for the rest of society or its laws to handle. The myths, the stated norms, constitute texts around which arguments about proper behaviour, and indeed about property, are built. Just as proper church-goers abjure extra-marital sex, but actually do it, it is quite common for the behavioural reality to be substantially different from the verbal norms, which often become operative only when crisis looms. This was clearly the case for example when the mainstream golfer, Tiger Woods, had an accident which led to the public discovery that he had sexual relations with women other than his wife. The myth of "we don't do that, you have let us down, you cannot now be squeaky clean" dominated the press and the commentary. Here we have revealed the sheer hypocrisy to which morality myths can lead. No one looked into the private lives of the critics. But the incident served to reinforce the notion that sex outside of marriage was improper, despite its almost universal presence in practice. Do we want the continuation of such hypocrisies in the world we are striving to fix?

One example from my own fieldwork will illustrate further. The Fijian societies I worked among (there are many differences between them) presented to the world a strong ideology of a patrilineage, in which men were representative of their lineages and seemed to perform all the primary ceremonial and political functions in the name of their lineages. Ownership of land was invested in such male-dominated lineages. With the coming of formal administration, the system was incorporated into colonial law.

Over time, lineages segmented as there was schism or they grew too large. Or they formed political and military alliances, which sometimes resulted in a form of merger. By contrast to such dynamism, the formal law was static.

Behind the law was a reality, which played havoc, for example, with the system of land registration. The realities were of self-interest and above all the power of women. Whatever the appearance of male domination -- and sometimes its stark truth -- there is always the possibility of women's power.

Because of the rules of exogamy in Fiji, married women came from different lineages and usually different villages than did their husbands. Frequently lineages grouped together with significant differences from others in their languages, tabooed behaviour, manner of living, rules of courtesy -- all those things that are significant in the rearing of children. While men were close to their children, it was the women who bore most of the responsibility of early rearing, and thus of ensuring cultural continuity by teaching children how they should behave.

But most of the women were foreigners to the culture they had married into. Hence at the time of marriage, elaborate women's ceremonies took place, in which the new bride was inducted into the sisterhood, as it were, of foreign wives. Here she found a vigorous and proud support group.

In any society, whatever the norms may appear to be, it is essential to look, as it were, for the opposites and for significantly different parallels. Hence, in Fiji, it became apparent that, despite the patrilinearity, matrilineal and affinal linkages (through the wives) played fundamental roles. The mother's brother (usually living elsewhere) played a real part in the upbringing of teen-age male children, complementing the father; and was in a situation in which a young man could demand from him whatever he needed to support his enterprises. Throughout the life cycle there were numerous occasions in which the wife's kindred would support her emotionally, materially and ceremonially, and massively complex and reinforcing exchanges took place between her kin and those of her husband.

There is no doubt that, right up to the most high levels of Fijian chieftainship, women exercised, through such linkages, major powers of influence, often becoming overt in the woman's right. If this were so, how much more it was in more mundane matters. I traced scores of instances in which a wife, for agricultural, commercial or emotional reasons, decided to move husband and children back to *her* family location. By agreement with her lineage, land would be made available. Over time, the pair's descendants would constitute a new, allied lineage.

Such moves were not formally registered with the government as a change in family land title, so that the official Fijian land registry has little bearing on the facts of land use.

Without such practical departures from the strict rules, the system would find it difficult to function. At least, it would have much less flexibility. I have grave suspicion of those descriptions of culture and society which are presented as rigid, on the basis of enunciated rules. And what is unorthodox at one time becomes orthodox at another.

The Fijian case should alert us to the realities in Western society as well. Behind the theoretical, religious, mythical norms lie the realities of actual behaviour. These realities provide the rules by which society actually lives.

Family structures are subject to considerable *de facto* change. Policies which seek to enforce "stability" are doomed and have no place in a reformed world, which requires dynamism and flexibility.

Similar considerations suggest that the very definition of what is a marriage is fraught, and, being so, complicates and confuses jural policies based on some abstract legal definition of "marriage". Is it a union, whatever that is, between a man and a woman? Does "union" imply a common household and/or the procreation of children? Does the "union" imply that only within it is there sexual congress? Is there a necessity for cohabitation, and does that have t to be between a man and a woman? If we look at the world comparatively, searching for *functioning* forms of union, the answer to each of these questions is "No".[43] [44]

A few examples. The Cathars until suppressed by a vicious French crusade, believed that sex was a sin. *Ipso facto* a union between a man and a woman, a marriage, was sinful. But sinning is human. Only church elders had the holy strength to be without sexual sin. Other people's sexual activity within AND WITHOUT marriage was indulged as a natural weakness. It was open to women as well as to men, to husbands as well as to wives. But not to the holy. What was happening in any case became recognised in theology.

In mediaeval times there was another institution identified as *celibate* marriage, in which sex and procreation were not to take place.

Numerous societies such as the Ndumba and Sambia in Papua New Guinea, the Mundurucu of the Amazon, and the Hopi in their winter *kiva*, men and women lived apart, the women in individual houses, the men in what some have called club houses.

Islamic societies permit men to take a limited number of wives who cohabit. Polygynous societies[45] abound, in some of which wives live in individual houses, in others cohabiting. The IIRC Human Relations Ethnographic Survey estimates that 75% of human societies practise or tolerate polygyny.[46] Early Chinese concubinage approximated polygyny.

In several societies it was/is incumbent on the husband's brother to marry and care for the husband's widow.

In aristocratic circles as far apart as Hawai'i and Pharaonic Egypt there was brother-sister union and the marriage of a husband to his wife's sister.

There is some thought that the in-breeding of the royal houses of Europe had detrimental generational effects. Apart from that, all the above instances relate to socially healthy, stable, and well functioning societies.

In North America, after the legal decline of polygyny among orthodox Mormons there has been a rash of prosecutions of males in polygynous communities. It has been asserted that such systems inherently involve child abuse *ipso facto*. It does not. There is no doubt in my mind that should there be provable cases of abuse they should be handled in terms of the law, according to the principles I shall describe in the next chapter.

However the equation "Polygamy[47] (a.k.a. polygyny) equals the suppression and exploitation of women and the abuse of the young" as a proposition is nonsense, both empirically and theoretically. There are no comparative data whatsoever that show abuse to be more prevalent in polygynous communities and families than in monogamous ones. Indeed, there are reasons to believe that children in such families have more protection and flexibility than they do in standard nuclear families.

There is a major brake on the expansion of polygyny in a community. Only "strong" men, as the community identifies them, can maintain multiple wives, many of whom are comparatively young, since it requires a modicum of wealth and senior's ability to handle interpersonal relations. Evolutionary principles have been adduced to suggest the attraction of a polygynous male lies in his success, and that this tendency to success will be genetically and/or socially transmitted. (At a time when it seems that the necessity to have male partners is, for women, slowly eroding, this argument may be due for a revival.)

From a normal woman's point of view, polygyny has some clear advantages. The marital "duty" of being in the husband's bed is no longer a monogamous routine, but shared out. The same remark holds for the tasks of the household, which may in fact become something like a small enterprise with division of labour. There are of course instances of jealousies, rivalries and angers just as there are in monogamous households. As far as children are concerned, there are many psychological and supportive advantages in having a bevy of aunts and their progeny toward whom to turn for variety and in case of need.

Part of the idealisation of the nuclear family is a reaction to the growth of single-parent families since the 'sixties. In some parts of the world, the phenomenon is borne out by statistics, which identify mothers who are single by choice, and young people living alone or with non-familial friends. In my city, Vancouver, there are major sections in which the housing is constructed with residential units for such situations, and those in which two single persons live together with separate bathrooms and bedrooms, sharing expenses and cooking facilities.[48] Alarmists raise serious questions, thinking of such a trend as an anomaly, and harmful to children.[49]

On these and similar questions, more perspective is useful. There are in social history many instances in which families have been disrupted by the forced departure of the husband, or of the young, mostly males. One may think of the mines of South Africa, slavery, current illegal international human trafficking, the forced use of child soldiers, the indentured labour systems of the South Pacific and elsewhere. Effects on children there must have been, though the existence of wider kinsfolk would mitigate them, unless the adult male population was almost totally absent, as it often was. Extended families however take care. And the role of the mothers is increasingly important

I am reminded of my family arriving at a tiny island off the coast of Papua to camp with the people for a few weeks. The thatch houses were on stilts, next to a very deep channel which separated the house and beach from a reef. My daughter was in her crawling and beginning walking stage. We quickly learned to have no fear. The moment she, or any other child, wormed her way in the direction of the danger of the water, loving brown arms from some hitherto unseen person swept her up.

In the same community I carried out two household censuses, a few weeks apart. *Almost none of the children*, toddlers or not, were sheltering in the same house in each period. They were cross with their parents, liked the food at the other place, wanted to spend time with someone there, wanted to hear stories -- whatever it was, if they felt like it, they upped and moved.

If that happened in a large industrialised city, I can hear the tut-tuts. No discipline. Irresponsible parenting. Certainly no stability. What risks they run. Call in social services quickly.

Yet under certain circumstances this may be precisely the sort of flexibility and experience that both parents and children need and are denied. Though nannies and kindergartens do something institutionally, it is not at all the same. And I have seen instances in which a child of separated parents gained both power and an enlarged horizon by interacting with both households.

Let us return to the structure of the family itself. I have called in question the norms of the nuclear family structure and residence. What about its monogamous base?[50]

There seem to have been two contradictory evolutionary paths at work.

The first probably grew with early hominid division of labour as humans with upright posture were still hunters and gatherers. The human child has a long drawn out non-ambient helplessness, during which time it has to be carried and nurtured by a mother who has herself gone through a restricting pregnancy. The male provided nurture through his freedom of action, his strength, and his continued hunting ability. There was no capital accumulation to give advantage to the amassing of wives. Thus there is a strong emphasis in our bio-cultural heritage towards monogamy as a partnership though there might be opportunities for polyandry..

On the other hand, the accumulation of capital, on however modest a scale, made it advantageous to use marriage as part of the creation and maintenance of riches. Settlement, land, agriculture, pastoral herds, trade and the growth of concomitant political powers and structures, all contributed. Marriage created political and property alliances. The woman, while maintaining the family and administering the hearth, opened networks of co-dependency with her relatives. Men went about their business earning and increasing wealth and power.

Under these circumstances it became possible and advantageous to engage in plural marriage. Men could start to afford more wives, and the more they did, on the whole, the more they had of both women and riches. Furthermore, plural marriage epitomised social status and power.

The phenomenon was mostly in the cultural, rather than the biological domain. Other circumstances arose in which the consolidation of capital was as important as its growth. Here the advantages of polygyny and the choice of brides from "outside" could be cancelled by dangers to the passing on of the estate at inheritance. It became advantageous to seek brides closer to home, and one at a time -- even in some ranks of some societies to marry a sister or a brother's widow.

Being cultural, the tendency toward polygyny was affected by ideology and religion. After all, if widespread, it could leave young men unmarried, with disruptive consequences.

The tendency, though, was not simply cultural; it had bio-evolutionary support. Men have a need to make use of their sperm and could not always do so with a single wife. Contraception was there, but difficult. Abstinence after pregnancy was common. There was and is a drive to seek other sexual partners.

For women, who better to couple with than an older man, proven to be successful? An older man had (or had not) shown that he had the power to survive, significant until recent centuries. If he were in a position to marry more than one wife, he had status based on personal action -- acumen, physical power -- or family inheritance. For the survival of society, the marriage of young women to older men had a distinct advantage. Older men continue to beget, and pass on whatever it is in their genes and their social heritage that helped in their success. There are many continuities in this stream of evolution today, as younger women and older men sometimes attract each other, though the specific biological advantages are harder to discern.

The danger, as I mentioned above, was in the sexual tensions of younger men who did not have legal access to wives. Usually the incidence of polygyny was not high enough to threaten the social fabric in such a way. But also in practice there were a variety of mechanisms to release sexual energy -- pre-marital intercourse, homosexuality, illicit assignations, prostitution, the induction of young men into active "age regiments" for purposes of warfare and political control. As long as the property aspect of marriage was not threatened, the world went on its sex-driven way.

In present-day industrialised society monogamy is the ideological norm which masks the verities. In the 'fifties, men were said to have a forty year itch, and for both women and men "life began at forty". The 'sixties broke open many of the taboos among the young, although most returned to monogamous ideals as they reached adulthood, in or out of formal marriage. Formal marriage became a matter of sacrament or of regulating a property contract, or indeed a ceremony of fun and self-directed thought that publicised a relationship. Maurice Godelier, in his Chapter "What future for what relationships" (my translation) sums up the situation in Western society pithily and accurately – "*Le marriage n'est plus l'acte fondateur du couple"* (Marriage is no longer the founding act of couples – again, my translation). ....[51].

It has never been a secret that general extra-marital sex has been common over the centuries. Because it breaks the formal rules and involves sex, always a topic of delighted gossip and titillation, it has always been a subject for publicity when public figures are involved, exacerbated nowadays by intense media coverage and twittering. Biographies almost always examine sexual behaviour, and usually find something to write about. A novel without some such theme is hardly a novel. We often know what is going on amongst our colleagues, but seldom in our own marriages.

We sneer at the hypocrisy of the Victorians, but even today the phenomenon continues to be surrounded by an inadequate and censorious vocabulary. "Extramarital sex" is so clinical. "Affair" (sometimes with an "e" to make it oh so French, not English at all, you know); "infidelity", "unfaithful", "disloyal", are terms that get thrown about. All, including "affair", which carries the implication that it might be a tough business proposition, carry with them the suggestion of a *property right* in one's partner.

When the terms do arise in a marriage, when emotions get charged by the breach of rights, the consequences are painful, angry and hurtful. Children are caught up in the atmosphere. There may be divorce. Joint property has to be disentangled, a wonderful focus for revenge and passion.

Comparative empirical studies reveal that we are not talking really about a "forty year itch". The behaviour is much more deeply embedded. Helen Fisher has gone so far as to claim that there is a natural cycle from infatuation to seeking another sexual partner in as little as four years. For every man who enjoys sexual revival there is a woman whose own sexual freedom is discovered.[52]

Is it not possible to release ourselves and our spouses from the hypocritical angry passion that is too often the result of a multiple sexual partnership? Can we not admit that at the root is a misplaced and intolerable property right? Can we not see with our own generosity that multiple intimacy can be enriching for all concerned? Can we not recognise that our passionate reactions are the result of insecurity and the need we have for a lie to cover up the truth?

If, as I believe they are, multiple intimacies are the empirical norm, why add to that the sin of lies? If the original intimacy is worth its salt, honesty and the sharing of experience is part of it. *Why should sexual intimacy be the **only** domain of **normal** conduct that has to be lied about?* Why?[53] It should be the lies which hurt, not the broadening of understanding which additional intimacy can bring about.

It is not necessary and it is uncivilised. It poisons the most precious element in the lives of men and women. It puts the right to one's partner as property, as something owned above the strength of love or even lesser emotions.

To move on toward a civilised family life is certainly not easy. Yet it is not only possible, but, in many individual famous cases, has been lived. It is lived today by many individuals throughout the industrialised world, and elsewhere. But the idealisation and valuation of such generosity toward and respect for one's partner is far from being admitted into the dominant ideologies. Only the recognition that it is possible and rewarding, incorporated into our own personal behaviour, will eventually bring about the appropriate change. Where one partner is generous and open, and the other possessive and closed, there will be either break-up, or the sacrifice of each persona, most likely by the reduction in generosity and openness.

Unfortunately, that is not the end of the story. Part of the drive toward multiple intimacies derives from the fact that individuals who decide to cohabit change into different personae later in life; and also that the stresses of living together turn out to be intrusive to the sense of personal privacy and integrity.

The world we live in cannot be restricted to family walls. During infatuation we cannot know all there is to know about the object of our emotions. The hormones drive us. They do so with good reason, for the

162

characteristics of the time stay in our memories and emotions. As we get to know more about our partner, we are most likely to adapt, but also sometimes to resent.

Our outside worlds pull us apart. There is no help for it. Each of us finds workplace colleagues who irritate or inspire us for at least a third of our time, with another third engaged in sleeping...... Artists, writers, become absorbed in what they are doing, often excluding families from those times. We correct for these influences by sharing experiences, talking about them, complaining, expressing enthusiasm (for everything except sex......). Quite often it works, to the enrichment of both.

But sometimes it turns out that the growing experiences of one partner reveal that he or she is a different person from the one initially imagined. Always, when there is growth, there is change. It may not be the kind of change that you want in a partner. You yourself may not be growing comparably, and may feel inadequate. All of a sudden there is the realisation that the partnership is not there any more, or is minimized.

So either you move away and try again; or you resign yourself to the intolerable loneliness[54] that marriage can drift into, seeking, if not sex, at least those outside marriage to whom you can talk. This is happening more and more. It is partly that we are a little bit more honest about our feelings, partly that we search for something better. So frequent is it nowadays that anthropologists have coined the term "serial monogamy", though usually there has been some multiple intimacy during the stage of growing disillusion.

There is no way that partners can remain the same during the duration of a lifetime. Whether they can, or want to, or should, adjust to those changes is for individuals to work out. If there are children, what is for the best? Tension or honesty?

The issue of children is complex. Pretty well throughout the Western world and frequently in other parts of the globe, as children get older they seek activity outside the family. It varies, but is everywhere significant. In England 45% of *fifteen year old* boys spent their evenings out with friends, in Scotland 59% and in France 17%. This is what monogamy does. Would serial monogamy change this? We don't know. And should it be changed? Again we don't know.

There is at least one institutionalized example (apart from polygyny and polyandry) of a method of dealing with the possible loneliness of marriage. In Italy there was (is?) a fellow called the *cavaliere intime*. He was known to all and recognized as the wife's boon companion. He was not, as some might think, a toy boy – that was a different game altogether, though I imagine the two roles might merge. In any event he looked after the wife and spoiled her while the husband went about his business, including, no doubt, a mistress. He helped her in her bath, ensured that she had flowers and delicacies, took her to the opera and social functions. In this most

Catholic country, marriage, in these circumstances, turned out to be for child bearing and property considerations. Other essential functions in a partnership were outsourced. (Of course it was only for the rich.)

Much disillusion is exacerbated by living arrangements. We are finding more and more that the intimate sharing of living space is both richly rewarding and damnably difficult. A greater proportion of adults in the industrialised world are making use of their aesthetic and intellectual capabilities in their home lives, a tendency that has to be reinforced if we are to survive the changes of the present technical revolution. With the advent of TV, multimedia and Internet on the one hand, and the reinforcement of recreational pursuits from handicraft to sport on the other, the possibilities of conflict of interests abound. This is not merely that one partner does one thing while the other does another, which has always been the case, but that the interests compete for space, noise, and attention. Technology may soften the competition, but the Sound of Music can stifle the attempt to write a novel. On a more mundane level, one person's tidiness is another's irritating obsessiveness. Should there not be a space where one can be tidy, and another where junk can prevail?

In theory yes. Although when children come on the scene, one set of conventions seems to have to predominate.

There is another way. It is mostly practised by divorced or separated couples who share children, or when the demands of a profession involve separate locations, or in polygynous societies where individual wives have their own homes.

It is to live separately. There is nothing written in stone which says that a man and a woman living in intimacy have to live under the same roof. By living separately each creates his or her own space without interference. Many of the young individuals who enter the statistics as "one person or one parent households" in fact have "significant others" with whom they sleep and share children.

There are marked advantages to this. The excuse for daily disagreement is reduced. Intimacy is renewed as desire, less as habit or duty. My guess is that the relationship, though in an evolving form, is longer lasting on average. If not two residences, at least adjust the residency to provide a modicum of separate space. It is an expression of generosity and respect.[55]

Of course this is not for everyone. But it appears to be a convention that more are thinking about, or adopting without thought, as natural to them.

I have written about residence as something involving men and women. Nowadays the openness of homosexuality permits the residence of same sex couples, for whom the same considerations apply. But are same sex couples married? The concept of same-sex unions is not as unusual in history as attitudes towards the issue nowadays would make out. They have existed, often openly, throughout European history, sometimes requiring their formal sanctioning. The 1990's were by no means the first period in which the question demanded answers. Note ancient Greece and Rome.

Such matters are increasingly the subject of legislation and political and ideological policy. They are thoroughly confused by the ambiguity of the word "marriage" itself. We have already shown that it has no agreed universal cultural meaning whatsoever. And we could add that if individuals do the things that are to be done in whatever relationship they choose, but decide not to assert that it is "marriage", nobody, least of all the State, really cares.[56]

The Judeo-Christian formal concept of marriage requires the ceremonial recognition of the union. Nowadays unions which are not ceremonially celebrated tend to be treated civilly in Western countries in the same manner as marriage. Yet in any jurisdiction there is usually a requirement of recognition and registration in some form, for example that the couple represents themselves as cohabiting over a reasonable period, and that their associates recognise this also. The cohabitation requirement usually implies common residence, whereas a formally married couple do not have to reside together. Such recognition establishes social boundaries against interference, and may result in public entitlements, and in particular access to property law should there be a break-up. So far it seems that there should be no grounds for opposition to single sex unions, since all that is involved is jural recognition of a partnership, and of the fact that property in partnerships gets intermingled.

Why does the State bother about the regulation of marriage at all? Any rules about marriage can be avoided by people just cohabiting or doing what they want without involving the law. The State gets involved because it needs, or thinks it needs, statistics, and also to regulate the wellbeing of children and the issues of property which arise when a relationship breaks up. A major social purpose of marriage, and the recognition of unrecognized unions, is to legitimise children, allow them to acquire rights in the family, and to allow rules to be applied with respect to the welfare of children within the family. But surely those issues apply to *any* relationship, whether termed marriage or not. Property rules and child welfare policies should surely apply whether there is formal marriage or not.

The next step is more tricky. We are led to the question, in the ideal society, should same-sex unions be thought to have the same relationship to child-bearing as bi-sexual unions?

I think not quite. At the very least, the issue should be addressed in terms of the goals of the culture. If the culture does not care about its continuity and the creation of future generations, there will be one answer. If the culture values that continuity, there will be another.

I shall assume that the culture values its continuity: it is not embarked on a path of self-inflicted ethnocide. In that context the care of children by single sex unions is not to be encouraged or supported. Why?[57]

It is one thing to encourage understanding of single sex unions as a matter of personal choice in a humanist environment. It is another to encourage their spread to become a larger proportion of unions, if not the norm. I think the evidence shows that the example of homosexual teachers in schools and the welcome creation of sympathetic discussion in classes, together with the more open environment, have resulted in increased known homosexuality -- although much of the increase is undoubtedly a function of more open living and reporting.

The sources of homosexuality are two-fold: a biologically induced disposition, and the control of one's dispositions by thought and emotions that lead toward homosexuality. In other words, there is both nature and nurture. (Some recent biographies have shown that some individuals who embraced homosexuality through the English public school system turned in later life to vigorous heterosexuality -- the dynamics can go in both directions.)

It seems unreasonable to expect same-sex unions to be neutral in such matters in the course of bringing up children. However hard the adoptive parents may try, their example must have a major influence -- turning some towards and some against homosexuality. And whether children "need" both men *and* women in their intimate lives is still a matter of debate. In any event it seems highly probable that the caretaking of children in same-sex households is likely to increase the incidence of homosexuality. At first, this may be of little consequence. But in the long run it is surely not to be encouraged by a culture interested in continuity, because procreation is a necessity for that.

I do not consider this to be an argument for *forbidding* same sex couples to have adopted children. But a culture that values its continued existence should be very cautious.

However, when two people of whatever sex intermingle their daily living, this inevitably involves intermingling property. Little problem – until a break-up or re-arrangement occurs. Then the State is called in to regulate the disentanglement and to take care of progeny, *whether or not there is a formal marriage.*

Similarly, the fact that someone is married or not should have little if any impact on social services. It is the human who counts, not the marital status. Such matters are relevant to my discussion of poverty, and of the universal minimum income concept. Forget about marriage as a State concept, and let it lie in the realm of religion, personal belief and practice, and maybe ideology. So it follows – let the State be concerned with *any* relationships and their consequences. Forget the secular use of the term marriage in State law. Leave that to the usage of the Churches and individual beliefs.

It may turn out that in our new world it is decided that artificial procreation is a "good thing". There can be no holding back the advance of artificial procreation. It has many strong humanistically supported advantages, allowing, for example, infertile women to have children. It *may* be a "good thing" more generally to separate sex from procreation.

Procreation is not, culturally speaking, the primary objective of sex, although biologically speaking that is where it all began. Humans in most cultures enjoy sex for its own sake, for the sensations and intimacies it brings, for its ability to create profound communication. In this respect, humans have evolved along a path in which they take measures to *stop* the procreative elements in sex.

The issue of artificial procreation does not end there. I am preaching choice, the deliberate control of our future. Artificial procreation[58] offers the ultimate in choice.[59] Choice of the sex of offspring now, choice of their biological characteristics soon. Because those choices have been exercised in other domains in horrendously inhumane contexts, we are naturally and rightly suspicious of anything that carries the name eugenics. I do not know how to control these forces, which cannot be ignored. Could it be sufficient to rule that the choices be exercised by the individuals involved, and not ever by the State or any external authority? Could this be part of the global morality that comes with reformed global government (see a ;later Chapter).

Despite the rapidity of social change and the use of invention, cultures by their very nature stress conformity. It has already been noticed in India and other places that there can be a marked unpopularity of girl children since boys are perceived to be better able to contribute to family fortunes. The ability to know the sex of the foetus leads to the abortion of girls with unfortunate demographic and other results.

We are already in the era of designer babies. We should resist any intervention of the State or of religious ideology in such matters. In the first case it would be a fruitless attempt to put the clock back, or an unwholesome move toward eugenics. In the second, religions are simply not equipped to handle such issues for total populations. Any such regulation contains the inevitability of creating substantially uniform populations destroying the gene pool and creating an almost robotic society.

On the other hand if individuals, not necessarily in marriage, can choose a child, including its sex, filters for handicaps, and the like,

Although it is an error to assume that potential fathers have, or should have, little or less say than potential mothers in the choice to have children, the fact remains that the sudden enormous increase in the choices available to women is revolutionising their lives. At first the dilemma was restricted to the issue, to work or to have a child? All young women in my experience over the past twenty years or more have had to confront that choice, their answers being as varied as the individuals themselves.

Now the choice is even wider. It is when, if at all, how, and with whose sperm? It is no longer improbable that women will have children, themselves or through surrogates, at age sixty; they no longer have to be linked permanently or at all with the sperm donor; they may choose a father and choose not to live with him; they may choose to have a child through a sperm bank without a known father at all; they may choose the sex of the child; they may of course adopt. These new facts of life, and many more still to come, are causing much controversy, much of it misplaced.

If a significant number of older women join the small numbers of older men who have new children, the concept of parenting will change. I hope the older parents will be wiser. They will need to make clear arrangements for child care should they die. There may be an evolutionary advantage to having a trend towards older parents, since many very young parents, like first lovers, do not know how to do it properly.

I opt for individuals to determine the course of evolution. The State, as I shall affirm later time and again, does not have superior powers of prescience. My thought is reinforced by the fact that each State will order matters differently, so that the wealthy will be able to find loopholes in any event -- at least until we reach a world of Global Government.

In some countries, debates are continuing about whether to give social assistance to adoptive same sex parents. Unless the matter gets out of hand -- which is a long way off -- the criteria should surely be the welfare of the children. If they are within such a family, the needs of that family should be met. The way of countering such adoptions is not by withholding needed support, but through education and discussion in terms of the public interest.

When I was in my teens and an enthusiastic, idealistic Marxist I tried unsuccessfully to organise youth in my city to stand up and be counted and to express views about what they wanted their lives to be. Not only did I promote the dissolution of marriage, but also advocated its concomitant, the State care of children.

I shudder to think of that now, in the sense that I cannot imagine a worse fate for children. Later experience of the inanities of governments, horrendous bureaucratic chaos in social welfare agencies despite individual officials who are purposeful, well-meaning and sensitive, and the knowledge that State policies are unpredictable in their results, pulls me back from that abyss. And how my parents must have taken my arrogance to heart, for they were caring and supportive and my childhood was in no way painful.

I have to admit that, despite all the studies as to what happens in child rearing, all the more systematic knowledge that exists about child abuse, the field is chaotic and indeterminate, with public awareness based largely on idiosyncratic and sensationalist information. The ability to disentangle complex strands of influence, let alone causality, is minimal. Perhaps that is as it should be. For both parents and children are individuals, among whom the variety is infinite. Children, as were their parents before them, are genetically programmed (itself a hugely complex consideration), affected in the womb and at the breast, and subject not only to family but external influences such as peer pressure, school interactions, and the media. No one line of causality is dominant -- which, thank goodness, is probably why children survive as well as they do. Some children succumb within an ideal family, some survive famously and creatively out of disaster.

The family, writ large, has its happy, jolly times. But it is not over-all a happy jolly place. I doubt if it is meant to be. The socialisation of children is into a tough world where there is no easy ride, and never will be, even if all the reforms dealt with in this book were achieved. Parents do not normally become sadists in order to prepare children for future life; far from it. They are rightfully intending to be protective and caring, and in the best examples, which don't create newspaper headlines or

TV documentaries, show their love directly. Today there is stress upon the arts of communicating that love. In the ordinary life of the family, the recurrence of crises and stresses involving the children, directly or through osmosis, are part of positive upbringing. It is also one of the paths toward ultimate separation, the desire to move away from the family.

We tend to stress the difficulties of the modern age, the problems that confront us immediately, and in so doing perhaps idealise the past. Let us be clear about this.

The past was not ideal. At no time and in no place was the family without its stress and suffering. The common people of rural and urban Britain, and rural Switzerland, in the early nineteenth century had levels of material living that were far below those of the South Seas or many parts of Africa and Asia, to say nothing of North American Indians (at least those beyond the full impact of European invasion), during the same period. In such places as what was recently called the Third World there was nevertheless the threat of violence, famine, militarism, sorcery. The life of children and the destitution of families in much of Europe would be, to our eyes if we were to visit, as shocking as are the televised scenes of Darfur or the documentaries about inner city ghettos. Such pains and stresses were much more widespread than they are today.[60] Let us not go backwards. Let us recognise that our concerns about the present are in themselves an improvement over the past, and that if we take hold of ourselves we can do more about them.

We now recognise as never before that child abuse and marital violence are not only vicious but are matters for public intervention. Indeed, that awareness has allowed adults to identify to themselves abuse and violence that under other circumstances they might well not admit. Almost paradoxically, the recognition does not always have positive results. Some men and women dealt with it by ignoring or suppressing it and getting on with their own lives. Being forced to face up to it can create fierce pain and self-doubt, increasing the ranks of those who need counselling. We have been given the capacity to repress memories for a biological purpose – our own behavioural management. Like all biological factors there are complicating side effects, so that the resulting management can fall short of the ideal person concept, and since most of us want to approximate the ideal we identify the self-management as demonstrating imperfection, and seek alternatives, probably through therapy.

The openness and recognition, however, allows us to examine the issues more fully and pragmatically, as long as we do not jump into ideological traps. There has been a major value change, not, I agree, accepted by everyone, and far from even beginning in many parts of the world. Abuse of children, of fathers and of mothers, is no longer tolerated, and sexual harassment between adults is moving fast to the same state, the movement supported by legal procedures in many countries.

There can be no dispute where pain, emotional trauma, and in the case of harassment, fear, anxiety and interference with private lives, are concerned. In the case of adults, even cohabiting adults, no has to mean no. But matters of definition, and impact of ideological wars in place of pragmatic enquiry, are troublesome and suggest that we have not yet put matters in appropriate perspective.

We are sexual animals, in the best sense, with cultures to focus, control, and use, our sexuality. At the same time as we are attacking abuse and trying to get rid of it, we are correctly told that the absence of physical love in a home, of touching, holding, hugging, familial kissing, leads to emotional deprivation, confusion and anger toward parents or spouses in later life, to something that has to be dealt with as, even, a form of abuse! As a grandparent, I would resent it very much indeed if I and my grand-daughters were not sufficiently well-balanced for us to hug, to put our arms around each other, or I to stroke their hair. There are many families who, I think rightly, believe that over-puritanical hiding of the body is not only uneducative but leads to unnecessary prudishness in later life: to varying degrees members of such families do not unnecessarily hide their bodies one from another. I think that is the families' right, and expression of what I would regard as a healthy lack of inhibition, just as I would support Scandinavian values on nudity in public places. It is true that in inhibited societies the sight of nudity becomes gross stimulation. It is just this kind of inhibitory result that a civilised society would aim at destroying -- by openness. It is inhibition that is the problem, not openness.

What I do feel confident about is that our present political correctness on these issues is far from the last word. I want not some puritanical *a priori* inhibiting ideology but the healthy functioning of the relationships between men and women and parents and children. By healthy, I mean relationships that operate in the best possible way to reduce neurosis and provide warmth and confidence in each person.

Children are born, to varying degrees, with marked tactile and sexual drives. When they are infants, we tend to allow these, though we may, wrongly, try to inhibit the self-touching of genitalia. As they get older we introduce the notion of guilt. That varies considerably from culture to culture, and period to period. The very definitions of what is abuse, incest, parental love, individual responsibility for actions, are often indeterminate. Examples.

I should not have been surprised at a documentary aired by ABC television in the United States (on 10th May, 1995). A producer discovered that a certain amount of aggressive sexual activity was going on in grade (primary and kindergarten) school, the clearest example being that of a young boy who made a habit of pinning little girls to the floor under his desk and attempting intercourse. The producer worked with colleagues to test the sexual knowledge and attitudes of young children, from, if my memory serves me correctly, age five to ten or so. They set up a room with television and one way mirrors, and onlookers who consisted, separately, of parents and therapy professionals. The children were shown raunchy advertisements using super-models, and parts of programmes that had torrid love scenes.

Parents and professionals were totally shocked at the children's attitudes and conversations. *Both* boys and girls enjoyed the shows, laughed in titillated excitement, described clothing or the lack of it as "sexy", used phrases such as "they're having sex", (boys) "I'd like to have sex with her". Some boys were stimulated to touch their genitalia. Girls said they wanted to dress "sexy".

The observers took the word "sex" as having literal meaning, but that was not always true. Sometimes it was little more than repeating what the advertisement said, without further knowledge. However, at the end of the experiment the children were questioned about what the concept meant. Some did indeed have ideas: "When they're naked", "When they're in bed they do things", "When he gets on top of her".

That was what shocked the observers, even the so-called therapists. (I don't know how the latter were chosen.....)

As far as I could see, the children were totally "normal" happy youngsters. True, the programme was stimulated by the grossly aberrant and aggressive behaviour of a young boy who was not being controlled by his teacher, and by unsubstantiated idiosyncratic external reports of an increase in unacceptable sexual behaviour in grade schools.

What was shocking was that the children had "a little knowledge", were interested in matters that adults were interested in, and felt free to express themselves amongst each other, but not to their parents. The show told me more about parental attitudes than about troubled children.

In 2009 a study sponsored by Symantec[61] monitored the search engine keywords favoured by young people under the age of 18. For boys sex was the fourth favoured (coming in after entering the name of search engines like Google, YouTube and Facebook), porn was fifth. For girls sex was fifth and porn was 24th. For youths closer to the cut off age this may be as much a search for titillating information as anything else, but the interest is clearly there and natural.

In a previous chapter I mentioned the way young girls danced in a Solomon Islands community, masturbating their genitalia. And note the following from an anthropological discussion group:

"Sexual activity directed towards and carried out among pre-pubescent children is tolerated and even encouraged in some societies. The Sambia, with their male initiation rituals, come immediately to mind, as does the practice of masturbating infants to calm them in some societies. This does raise the issue --- of how widely to define "sexual relations". I doubt we'd describe a Hopi mother quieting a fussing child as having sexual relations with him; likewise, the Sambia ritual"[62]

Many of these things go on privately in Western societies, let alone others throughout the world. I know of no studies whatsoever which even hint that such practices create sexually disturbed adults. There is indeed much thought along the lines that minor sexual contact enhances the bonds between parents and children in wholesome ways.

Problems occur, but should not, when such behaviour becomes overt or is discovered in societies embracing Judeo-Christian-Islamic values and is then politically correctly defined as abuse, with surrounding guilt trips, not so much on the adults, as on the children themselves. Then indeed serious disturbances and breakdowns occur. If churches, synagogues and mosques have the health and well being of humanity at heart, it is time they reconsidered their theological, ritualistic, and ethical positions on these matters.

None of this is to excuse in the least the sexual exploitation of minors – or anyone else for that matter - submitted to aggressive sexual practices, often painful and against their will, often by figures who use authority to demand sexual services, and sometimes through the literal enslavement of victims. Our new society will not tolerate that for one second, and it will be dealt with in accord with the juridical precepts outlined in the next chapter.

There is simply no way of escaping the communication of sexual knowledge. The more it is hidden, the more it creates damaging inhibitions, neurosis and crime. It becomes an object of obsessive search instead of a description of a natural world. The problem has been with parents trying to hide that which was real, leaving children with half-baked distorted ideas.

The swings of culture on such matters are the stuff of legends. Remember Michel Angelo's David? A great celebration of the nude body, complete with substantial penis, it was also a metaphor for Florence's then need to stand up to and defeat the larger tyrants which threatened it with death. The followers of Savonarola desecrated a copy of the statue, it was then hidden away, then re-emerged with a fig leaf, and is only now on show in its original form. What, we may ask, is wrong with admitting that the male form has a penis????????????????????? (Images of naked women, even being raped, have been exhibited for centuries.)

We will learn not to play such tricks with nature, and it will revere the aesthetics and truth in both the male and the female form, both in art and nature. That is done as a matter of course in parts of Scandinavia, and was and is done in many parts of Oceania and Africa, save when "Western" culture in its puritan form intervenes. As I asserted earlier, children in Youth Maturity Institutes – and therefore even doubly more in families – will learn to celebrate sex, and therefore the body. Sex will not be a tabooed subject, but a matter of creative, wholesome, joy –and in some cases boredom.

More and more we are discovering the widespread existence of sexual abuse. The phenomenon was improperly hidden until it started coming out of the closet two or three decades ago. Now it is so fashionable a matter for discussion that almost every aberration of the human psyche is being traced to it; the moment a human problem emerges, analysts start looking for abuse. And low and behold they find it. When they find it they stipulate that it was causative.

Of course in a tremendous number of cases they are likely to be right. Yet wait a moment, be cautious.

What happened before abuse became an issue? Many men and women had their lives distorted. They decided they were themselves somehow to blame, and lived with severe guilt instructed by priests who were themselves not blameless and manifested sexual problems of their own. It was a secret. Others lived happy normal lives.

Now the tables have turned. One of the cruellest consequences of the extreme pursuit of cases of abuse is that those who are now made to remember it, to find it in their past, do not in fact escape the anger and guilt. Men and women who did not bother about it suddenly find they must do so, they are expected to do so. Many in fact learn, by public pronouncements amounting almost to propaganda, that if the troubles in their personae cannot be traced to abuse there must be something *really* wrong with them. I need not enter the debates about false memory syndrome. The pressures are real.

The fact of the matter is that some of what may now be called sexual abuse is not necessarily harmful in itself. Some of it is harmful *only* because of the attitudes that surround it in the culture. There is no doubt that sexual abuse is *always* harmful when it is accompanied by pain, exploitation, the use of the child as object, and above all guilt, the knowledge that something was not right.

But some behaviour that now goes by the name of sexual abuse does not have the same characteristics. Consider a child who *enjoys* a light caressing form of sexual contact, even if it involves genitalia, who does not even have guilt until later in life religious or social communication suggests that guilt is appropriate. It is not the caresses that cause the abuse, it is transmitted guilt.

185

When such a child, now an adult, accepts that he or she engaged in guilty behaviour, he or she seeks to identify other aspects of later adult behaviour as also wrong. The two have to be linked. This has the effect of (1) identifying other behaviour (perhaps attitudes toward the other sex) as aberrant when it is perfectly natural, (2) identifying a causative explanation which is quite possibly false and misleading.

The reason child-hood abuse is so significant is clearly that the results can be unknown at the time and nasty in the future. We have made a major advance toward a civilised society in the public recognition of just that. The other reason is that children are defenceless, often not yet aware of judgements about incest and sexual taboo, and are in no position to judge what the experience will mean to them in later life. Some children, enjoying and seeking, needing, the emotional results of physical warmth, often not getting it from parents, may see nothing wrong in the milder forms of sexual contact with non-relatives, may enjoy it and even seek it. Indeed, at a minimal level there may indeed be nothing wrong. The point is the child is not in a position either to know or to control. The child needs protection from the excesses and the disturbances which may result in later life. Yet those problems often arise less from sexual contact than from the culturally imposed guilts that surround it.

In the future guilt about sexual expression in families or between young people would be removed, and the concept of "abuse" limited to those instances where aggression, pain exploitation and/or suffering resulted. But until the wiser world is around the corner, it is necessary to protect children from the damaging consequences of guilt and censure and the road of therapy down the line. We are caught between the rock of withdrawing manifestations of natural love and the hard place of implacable social interference.

It is also a paradox that while we seek an end to abuse, at the same time there is a strong school of thought that intimates should not merely say what they think openly, but should let their angers out, shouting the verbal abuse, and hitting, punching and breaking *things* which are sometimes not easily differentiated from the partner! I happen not to believe in this, except as a last resort. It leaves an inevitable bitter taste, can socialise children toward violence or make them cynical about adults just as does viewing violence on TV. Counselling should aim at handling our angers better, not concealing them, but as a reinforcement of self-control.

Just the same, it is inevitable that humans are at times angered or irritated to the point of slapping. Unless it becomes habitual or is used with damaging strength or is a tool of deliberate humiliation, to legislate it out of existence is phoney. We must be self-controlled, but a person who does not lose his or her cool from time to time is hardly human. Furthermore it serves a most significant social purpose. It indicates as in almost no other way that a breaking point has arrived, so severe that it cannot for the moment be put into words. Gesture is communication, and a slap tells an immediate story. In families where that sort of action is almost unknown, it becomes the statement of a boundary, a wake-up call to all parties. It teaches children in particular that other people have breaking points. It carries an unstated implication that if the offence occurred outside the family there could be an aggressive reaction.

We are walking a fine line between love and abuse, between discipline and abuse, and, while we are on the subject, between verbal criticism and verbal abuse. This is not black and white, and wherever an abuse charge is laid, not only must the evidence be squeaky clean, but the general context of family life must be understood.

The case against violence in the family is that it is a nasty part of violence in general since it may be one of the psychological foundations for other violent contexts which constitute perhaps the major manageable challenge for the removal of fear and the acquisition of peace. We must find ways of pursuing peace (NOT the absence of tension) in the family relentlessly until it is totally removed from conduct.

The family is no longer the sole agency devoted to the socialisation of children, and is possibly not even the predominant one. In the long run, that may be useful; it is inevitable as society becomes more and more complex and communication wider. Families themselves are under scrutiny, from social work agencies, from teachers, from public policy makers. Parents often feel threatened and inhibited by the possible limelight into which an act, justified to them -- such as a well placed slap on the buttocks, or a desire to control medical therapy -- can reveal and cast shadows upon their behaviour and their "rights". Parents should indeed be put on the defensive against abuses; far too many still regard abuse as normal. But too much reaction to outside norms can relieve parents of their own thinking, their own judgements, their own ideals.

Should it be well intentioned bureaucracies and professionals who create the norms, or parents? Who should be the primary guardians of the continuity of culture, and of democratically, responsibly oriented citizens? At the moment, influenced by many accounts of bureaucratic interventions which have resulted in disaster, I believe that the balance nowadays is tipped in favour of statism and the cop-out of rules and regulations. There are signs of parental revolt, more especially with regard to the educational system, but also in a determination that it is they who are ultimately responsible. Too often professionals move beyond their role as helpers and advisers, as conveyors of knowledge, to become rulers of lives.

Authorities do not "know" perfectly. Those who pretend to do so, whether official, professional, or voluntary, and who translate their knowledge into rules, prescriptions and proscriptions, need to be treated with the utmost caution. While governments can sometimes legislate effectively, the effectiveness depends on the correspondence between the legislation and individual beliefs and behaviour. Legislation in advance of its time may have an educative role: it may set a standard toward which individuals may decide to aspire. Other organisations are most effective (though not necessarily within their own stated goals) when they indicate options from amongst which individuals may choose in an educated manner. Education, example, discussion, yes. Ready ears in times of crises. Conversations between friends uninhibited by "what others may think". The sum total of individual choices, rather than legislation, will eventually make the difference.

It is a truism that is not necessarily true that "children are not what they were". Of course children in this century exhibit some differences in persona from those in the fifteenth. Further, they are imperfect. They are growing up, seeking their way in a world in which their parents' anxieties are only too readily communicated to them. They can be rude, aggressive especially amongst themselves, lacking in politeness toward their elders, provocative, bullying. Adults in contact with children moving around town see much of this frequently. They are pushed aside as children jostle with sharp elbows in stores, on buses. They do not give up their seats to the elderly on public transport. They shout invective and wrestle in your way. They don't seem to know anything. You see bullying, trampling on gardens, and when you tell them off, and perhaps grab one by the sleeve, your are told that their father will get you. A neighbour's seven year old girl, prompted by an eleven year old in the background, came up to me in the courtyard and oh so innocently said "Would you like to stroke my pussy; we'll let you if you give us your balls to play with....." Ten year olds (and younger), walking home from school, chaperoned by adults, shout to each other "Fuck off", "You dirty mother fucker", "Shithead", "Arsehole". This in a well-off, bourgeois, genteel, yuppy, area of cultivated adults.......

Once again, a corrective. Most of the time, and for most children, this does not happen. It strikes the observer because it is more noticeable than good behaviour, which is predominant. And rowdyism has always been there. As children grow older, most of them become aware, and conduct themselves accordingly[63]. Especially with younger children and teen males, the children's sense of space does not forbid body contact, and still needs considerable adjustment. What is different is not its occurrence, but its tolerance. As a boy in short pants I presume I was as rowdy as anybody else, especially in a group on trams. But adults would have had no hesitation about intervening if things got a bit too much. Later as a school prefect (in a state school) I was charged, with others, in maintaining courtesy and discipline, outside school (uniforms helped with that) as well as in, handing out detentions right and left.

For almost 100 per cent of my present experience in a situation when I am obviously old and noticeably sight deprived I am in fact continually reminded of the courtesy of the young *when they notice* and it warms my heart and gives me confidence in the future.

Parents themselves have never been perfect. There were several sadistic delinquents in my school, some of whom came from families who didn't care. Parents who do care are full of anxieties and frequently feel they cannot cope. I suspect, without proof, that such feelings were not common in past centuries and other civilizations.

On balance, many of the anxieties are probably with little foundation. There is no one to one relation between childhood experience and the future adult. Even abused children can end up well balanced and caring. Children go through many "stages" in which difficult behaviour is part of growing up. Parents who feel an interior despair but who can maintain a difficult even keel, are justifiably proud of the characters who emerge, their sudden maturity and balance, even when the paths chosen may be alien to an older generation. Children are transformed into what I call "friendren", for they are friends within the family, cannot be called children any longer.

The need for adventure, for self-assertion, for the active discovery of self has to be tested against the positive results or the dysfunctional anti-social ones. Involvement in discourtesy, and its ultimate form, violence, simply cannot be tolerated in a civilised society. Without courtesy, such a society is a nothing, and is likely to be a threat to neighbours. So that whether current discourtesy and violence amongst youth is greater or less than it was previously; whether it is sufficiently great to cause fear objectively or with paranoia is irrelevant. ***Because it must not exist at all.***

Zero tolerance of discourtesy.

I do not want to prejudge that parents, and teachers, can create zero tolerance. I doubt it. In any event they need the support and help of those of us who are not parents and teachers. This does not have to be organised, though Youth Maturity Institutes can go a long long way to help. It needs to be part of our cultural response as individuals. It means not turning a blind eye. It means that if I see churlish behaviour I must be prepared to say so, make my opinion clear. Yes, it can be or can get out of hand. In which case authority has to be called upon.

Adults have considerable difficulty at times in being both responsibly caring and non-patronising. They might start by avoiding the word "kids". The connotations of the word -- little goats -- have largely disappeared, as have the affectionately patronising overtones. When I was in my childhood it was associated with the wonderful children's matinee programmes, short films that have disappeared as a genre from our screens and cultures, for along with Laurel and Hardy and Charlie Chaplin and wild westerns we had the fun politically incorrect Katzenjammer Kids, children who were alive and laughing in semi-ghetto conditions and up to truant like mischievous activities. My mother was horrified. Don't ever use that word "kids" to apply to children. She was right. I am so socialized to this perspective that I have difficulty accepting the word even now.

The other patronisingly false phrase that adults used to use with great frequency, and which can still be heard, is to pontificate to teens: "Stop complaining. You will never have it so good. This is the best time of your life.

It isn't. Certainly, there are wonderful features. The glandular emotions of sexual attraction, of falling in love. The deliciously naive certainties that you know better than your parents and other adults, whom you can criticise for the state of the world. The discovery of demanding physical activity and intellectual discipline. The ability to talk wonderingly for the first time about the nature of the universe, God, love. Rolling on the grass, feeling the leaves of the forest and the sand on a beach. All new and fresh. Under ideal conditions, these result in experiences that cannot be repeated. There is only one time for that kind of self-discovery.

Self-discovery continues well into adulthood. In my own life I have had so many good and totally stimulating times I cannot regret the passing of my childhood. Even the times of intense pain cannot erase the resulting growth. Children must know that their positive lives lie ahead of them, not just in the present. They must understand the mystery of the future, ignoring hints that the best is all over -- if it were, why not, then suicide?

Underlying all the positive features of young adulthood are the disturbances and pains. Sexual discovery is accompanied by sexual doubt, fumbling, emotional hurt, which seems to be arriving earlier and earlier, before children seem to be emotionally or physically ready. Formal teaching puts it into a clinical context, and other kinds of teaching are verboten. There are parent and teacher induced anxieties about the state of the world in which simplicities are turned into, in many instances, paranoia. There are conflicts between learned notions of success criteria, and the likelihood of achievement, as places in universities become tighter and rates of unemployment seem here to stay. There is the continual battering of noise and short attention span entertainment creating artificial highs without which life is a bore. There is the threat of drugs and violence, and the force of peer estimation. None of this is new. But the intensity is increased via the media, visual and digital, and the content changes from one decade to another and one country to another.

Present day parents and some teachers have been through much of this themselves during the permissive 'sixties and 'seventies. Many find it hard to cope, for they are feeling responsible and more conservative, and find the content has moved away into dimensions that are more extreme and threatening. They are more aware of the dangers. They must wrestle with their past ideals as problems emerge.

The advent of the nuclear family and its parallels, and the dispersal of siblings throughout the world, where it has occurred, have dealt a serious blow to inter-generational solidarity. (It is useful to note that the continued weight given to extended family, clan, inter-generational and similar ties by globally widespread cultures, such as Cantonese, Punjabi and Ismaili, have given those families and cultures a major advantage in dealing with issues of present and future, especially when it comes to commerce and travel[64].

There are two notable effects. One is that a force for cultural continuity is threatened by the lack of contact between children and grandparents. Parents, even those who had little contact with grandparents themselves, often place weight on this, and try to make up for it in various ways -- recording of the past, diaries, visiting when funds and space allow, stressing family history. At present there is also a vogue for the fashions of the past, and in a deeper sense, young people who come from immigrant families seek to visit their ancestral homes and kin, re-learn half-forgotten languages from their past. It is almost inevitable that other sources must at least partially replace grandparents.

This has to be, at least until attitudes and the realities of work change. It may be that we are looking at the ultimate individualisation of families. My manta though is that, realising this, we must as individuals decide consciously instead of just letting it happen. Only extended families can cope with the elderly in the home.

196

Otherwise the burden of care and occupying one's self with the fact of elderly boredom is far too much for families who must give priority to work and their children in order to survive.[65] It is seldom now that the elderly and the middle-aged in industrialised society can live together in the kind of harmony and joint usefulness that makes a workable arrangement. Add to that the likelihood of large distances being involved, and major financial burdens can arise. The provision of homes, nursing homes, hospices, is now a major industry, with the best giving thoughtful attention to well-being. I also know of no country that, as of now, totally avoids the financial, material, psychological and sadistic exploitation of the aged in the worst of such homes, a major scandal in which the lonely have little voice.

The issue is associated with the second effect, just plain boredom. During our adult lives, few of us think of being old. Some years after my retirement I was living in a high rise apartment, the building occupied by a mix of young people and old. When I mentioned my plans of extended travel and writing to the manager, she said, more or less, "I'm so glad to see it. Do you know that hardly any of the retired people here have any interests at all? They sit around in front of the TV, bored to tears, or take a motor-home to a trailer site and sit around for a holiday."

I am sure that these people didn't think of retirement like that when they were working adults. They thought of a happy, peaceful life, occasionally linked to grand-children, with minimal financial needs and worries. At the moment of retirement they were classified. They were dubbed "seniors", and because they did not have thoughts of a future, or of creativity, they were patronised, jollied along. Those who care try to do something, "seniors caring for seniors", *animateurs* getting the more active to play golf, others square-dancing, learning handcrafts, going on bus tours, going in groups to plays which carry sociological themes with which they are unsympathetic -- *anything* for goodness' sake, to keep them occupied.

I am not putting down such activities. I am, rather, horrified at the necessity for them on such a scale. Nothing is more indicative of the fact that the aged (in very general terms) are a burden on the world's finances and consciences. Some of this will always be necessary and desirable; it is important for the elderly to be occupied, and, for some, that they socialise.[66]

This is tinkering with symptoms, not getting at the root problem. The sources of boredom go far far back, to childhood and adulthood, to the near disappearance of the extended family, to good health which makes us last longer, to the loss of adult initiatives in the work place, and especially to schooling which failed to identify and build on innate creativity.. We do not want to reinvent the extended family for the sake of relieving our consciences, or to cut off medical services. We have to get on with what we are doing and improve this part of our lives.

We have already discovered the solution. It will be in the way Youth Maturity Institutes take care to discover the creative impulses in maturing youth, encouraging them in activities outside of employed work throughout their lives and into retirement. We must begin at the beginning – and save remedial financing at the same time.

For those who do not fit into the category of the elderly as I have both described and resisted it, there are already major advances. For many, old age is a time to explore, and the increase in travel and demanding educational, even university courses, is becoming widespread. Too often the demands on the mind are not enough: a one-week course at a British university on English Art is good for a Canadian tourist, but there is little else to follow up with except another dilettante course. I have ideas for hotels that cater to the retired *who want to think and do.* Hotels which have links to libraries, sources of knowledge, reading rooms, combined study-bedrooms, in places where there are major themes to be explored, and with not too expensive long-term stays to permit exploration in depth, and occasionally to make original contributions.

For most of the elderly, such solutions are not feasible if they involve expense and costly travel. They must dig into themselves for their resources. They do not know the interior resources they have, those which have not yet developed. (They are still growing!) The solution for future phalanxes of the elderly starts in childhood, as it does for us all. It continues and changes through adulthood as they nurture their potentialities. In short, it relates to education. It is also similar to the problems of unemployed youth. I say again Youth Maturity Institutes hold the long term keys.

The use of the term "seniors" which puts us all together for certain purposes, is ghettoising. The aged should live together, is the incipient message, then we can handle them. Speaking for myself, I resist, I won't have it. I demand more than seniors' discounts, and will force the world, I arrogantly imagine, to give it to me. I have been fortunate, in that being in contact with students for so many years made it possible to imagine I was not in an elderly ghetto; it was true that contact with younger people was revivifying. It still is. (The thoughts in this book could not have emerged had it not been for their stimulus.) I like to be with friends of my own age though there are few left. We have much to discuss and laugh about. But younger people, from their teens to their 'sixties, teach me more. It is still possible to dine and converse with them, one on one, to flirt and spend time, as friend to friend. Not all younger people accept that. The right has to be earned.

The kind of disadvantaged old age that I have mentioned is, for many of us, the signal that life has ended. Looking around us, we see the State, through our children's taxation, paying for our coming decrepitude. We see kindly volunteers being kind. We see harassed nursing home staff expressing their distaste, irritability and patronisation.[67] We feel it is time to go.

And why shouldn't we, if we feel like it? If we feel that our lives have been lived, that we have done what we could mostly the best we could? If we feel at peace with ourselves? Is this not a good time to go? Why on earth hold on until self-contempt occurs, amid depression? Is it not better to go when we can look upon ourselves with dignity, if not pride? Don't make of us an instrument that salves your consciences.

Then stop putting the law in our way. Allow elderly assisted life termination as open as humanly, not juridically possible.

There needs to be a much more open, flexible, and understanding approach to the family and relationships, removing dysfunctional elements such as jealousies and arguments over jural terms which bear little resemblance to realities. The State should get out of the relationship business as far as possible and be open to every kind of permutation and combination of relationships consistent with the relevant culture. And the more that culture can be flexible and open, finding ways to stop hiding behind the hypocrisies of terminology and forbidden subjects, the better.

2012Postscript

- Modern technology is creating more choices when it comes to deciding whether or not to abort a foetus. This is not merely a question of birth control *per se* – the decision whether or not to reproduce as for example has been a matter of state policy in China for decades – but also whether to bring a defective child to tem, which all the consequences of caring. In India and elsewhere there is often a strong cultural and economic preference for boys over girls which the result that if technology determines that the foetus is that of a girl, abortion can result. And the prevalence of female infanticide is a major social issue. With implications for education, employment of women, the pursuit of crime, political agendas, and global ethics[68]. As multiculturalism spreads so too do immigrant cultures, such as those in Canada, bring their preferences with them, spreading them globally.

•   When one is set in a particular place and time it is difficult to determine the long term evolutionary trends that one is in the midst of. Such an observation applies particularly o trends in marriage patterns in the West. It has been clearly observable that there has been an increase in unions without the formalities of official marriage, whether religious or secular. Some like Maurice Godelier have predicted the demise of this sort of union. That does not however, mean the necessary demise of the nuclear family. Immigration introduces other models of extended family, yet the nuclear core remains intact, for practical reasons, in Europe and the Americas,

•   Much has been made of assertions that particular forms of family structure lead to move violence than others. Such assertions usually take place in highly charged political or religious contexts with evidence and arguments based on limited data rather than global examinations of the type of family in question. As far as I know there is *no* evidence to back up any assertion whatsoever that a particular form of family or marriage such as polygyny[69] has a built in propensity to violence, and particularly not child or marital abuse. Examples to the contrary based on the examination of a single community do not at all *ipso facto* carry over to global conditions.[70]

- If immigration and multiculturalism results in the introduction of new family and marriage forms into the West. Thus the *Economist* August 20 2011 p.21-3 with data from India and SE Asia.

- Underemployment, costs of child bearing, expensive housing is making living with parents increasingly acceptable and thus re-introduces extended family life. The pressures on youth throughout the world, discussed in the next chapter, is leading to a multiplicity of family organisations, so that political ideas of "family values" as something desirably universal are no longer objectively persuasive.

- Many women are fearful that the Arab spring may bring about a resurrection of male dominance. *Economist* October 15 2011 pp. 29-32

- U S Census Bureau reports in 2011 that for the first time married cupules are less than 50% of households. *Economist* June 25th 2011

Manifesto for the New Age

VI – Of Youth and Time

(All2011Postscript)

Throughout the globe the improvement of medical facilities and in levels of living have brought about a sharp increase in the proportion of the aged in the population and a comparative dearth in the numbers of and attention given to the well being of youth. As a ninety year old myself I can only deplore the resulting imbalance.

In many European countries unemployment of young adults is out of hand, rising to as much as fifty per cent[71]. The social and political consequences are obvious. The underlying themes are despair, boredom, disillusion, anger, distrust of and hostility to authority and where the energy is still present, mass protest.

Time and again we hear that it is underemployed and well educated youths who have led the Arab Spring[72], or in extreme cases have chosen the path of Islamic martyrdom as suicide bombers. At least the last gives meaning to death. The association of some youth with gangs with the dangers of drug manipulation provides an occupation, a much needed sense of risk in life, an income, and self worthiness through the approval of other gang members.

In assessing the balance of concern between that for the aged and that for the young adults a major consideration should be that it is the young adults of today who will be guiding the future of the globe.

A prime example of short sighted public policy is the trend in richer countries to extend the age of retirement. This is justified as a matter of accountancy, theoretically reducing the sums spent on retirement benefits (which will anyway be swallowed up as the aged population continues to grow). An immediate effect is to reduce the number of employment openings, i.e. to punish the young and to some extent to skew production methods in favour of the old fashioned instead of the innovative.

In its core the Occupy[73] movement is an expression of such feelings although in some parts of the world it has been unfocussed and confused. In its more rational essence it blames the situation on the decision makers sand especially bankers and other high executives making use of an otherwise faceless capitalism.

It is ironic that some of the very achievements which are a technical expression of this new age fit well as tools which make the organisation of protest more feasible and more difficult to ignore.

The root issues are threaded throughout this manifesto for they are systemic, cannot effectively be dealt with in isolation from each other, in other words emphasize the holistic nature of the forces which bind and separate us.

Growing up in the teens has always been a tough period of discovery complicated by its sexual dimensions. At various times in world history it seems that youths entered adult culture at earlier ages, taking on adult responsibilities before their twenties. The harshness of life had much to do with this, with adult deaths requiring early succession responsibilities. It was by no means only that. There was little opportunity for alternative activity (by comparison with today) so that youths were drawn early into adult work.

Today youths are confronted with a myriad of choices and it can be as late as the twenties before they feel settled into their life's destiny. These can be years of serious anxiety and self doubt. It is not surprising that some seek escape or reinforcement in drugs and gangs. Perhaps the miracle is that most manage to keep their balance[74].

Where should we look for answers?

The so-called Blackberry riots in England in 2011 provide some indicators. Major gatherings of otherwise unorganised people, especially youth, happen with some degree of spontaneity within minutes of a call to arms[75]. It is clear that the youths involved were mostly unemployed, bored and disillusioned with life, with pent up anger at the authority and society which had let them down. They turned to the crowd activity of violence and vengeful anti-social behaviour. They were the product of schools which were not organised, equipped or even understanding of the notion of Youth Maturity education[76], despite dedicated staffing with much knowledge of the social dystopia. In the schools, despite extra programmes, there was little emphasis for lack of resources on the engendering of creative time use. Family involvement and the involvement of other youth-oriented institutions in school design and government was not present. Families which can be supportive of functional social behaviour were themselves in disarray, often broken, hobbled by poverty and parental unemployment, seldom with direct interest in schools or education. Poverty was not relieved by an effective concept of guaranteed minimal income[77]. The pot of violent protest ad unrest was ready to boil over. The miracle is, not that it happened, but that it does not happen more often as is the case of the Arab Spring.

A socially different phenomenon was that of the Stanley Cup rioting in Vancouver in the spring of 2011. The city population was intensely excited by the possibility that the local professional ice hockey team would win the Stanley Cup North American championship after decades of trying. Months earlier there had been dancing in the central streets, hugging and kissing as the Canadian national team won over the United States in the locally organised Winter Olympics. Surely that spirit would be repeated and the authorities, though careful, were unprepared for what happened.

Hundreds of family members were gathered in the main city centre watching the disastrous game in mammoth open air screens. When the Vancouver team lost the 7th game of the final series and were eliminated the disappointment was profound as is frequently the case with European soccer games.

The crowd, including many young children, slowly packed into the rapid transit system on the way home.

But the city centre itself became the scene of a drunken brawl as both men and women combined to set cars on fire, smash windows and loot stores. Most of the action was recorded on press cameras and smart phones. Deeply ashamed citizens, nearly all youths themselves, cleaned up the mess next day and provided police with images of the rioters. Two years later court cases are still being processed.

Who were the rioters? Not the unemployed or downtrodden. Although liquor was banned in the city centre many had been drinking all afternoon prior to the game. Many were from the outer suburbs, deliberately looking for excitement including a few who were "known to police". Most appeared to be well off with impeccable records and steadily employed. Once the mayhem started, fuelled by liquor, otherwise decent youths created an excited mob. The official enquiry concentrated on the inadequate and unprepare3d police response and the City council stopped all open public gatherings. Some said that the mob had won the day.

What was this about? The enquiry, under pressure to be quick, did not take up the task of seeking causes. In Vancouver there is considerable opportunity to participate in recreation of all kinds, and thus for forms of excitement and risk taking. But many youths are looking for more and when the opportunity comes break out of conformity to engage in behaviour which is otherwise out of bounds – and they know it.. There is a search for danger, for getting away from conformity. To go crazy and let loose. To turn the rules of society upside down, as happened with the cargo cults of Melanesia. And the educational system, though conventionally very good, once again cannot cope, as at presently organised, with concentrating on such issues as non-violence and maturity.

It is dramatic to take notice of such crowd behaviour. The reality of youth life consists largely of suppressing the troublesome tendencies and seeking social acceptance. The youth of Vancouver responded to the rioting by immediately volunteering to clean up the mess and to express their revulsion through social media and posting messages on boarded up shop windows.

To the non youthful observer of a past generation there are some signs of a combination of creative accomplishment and a disquieting malaise in the culture of youth today, world wide. I can only touch on some of the indicators.

Positively, there is an extraordinary quantity and skill of innovative activity. Many of the great internet companies such as Apple. Google and Facebook were conceived when their creators were still at university and they have drawn on similarly youthful colleagues. This also applies to innovation in India and I believe is happening in Africa. Old established mega companies such as those in the oil industry have not yet learned to tap this richness in the young who think outside the box. (Extending the retirement age is in this sense counterproductive.)

In dealing with young volunteers who have recently been helping me in my work I have been enormously impressed by the skill with which some of them combine disparate interests into new forms of activity. For example I think of a young Asian musical student who realised she would not be making a complete living giving chamber music or celebratory concerts so equipped herself to run an enterprise booking events for other young musicians by attending classes in the Faculty of Commerce. Or the young lady who began life as a martial arts instructor and passed through award winning documentary film making to become an outstanding investment broker's assistant. Or the young man who with as partner established a company bringing other's conceptions of electronic invention to engineering and marketing fruition.

It is far from being a rosy panorama however given the enormous scale of un- and under- employment I have mentioned above. Globalisation and world wide migration create remedial possibilities. Much of this has been counter-productive, giving rise to racial animosities and migrant frustration

African and Turkish migration of workers into Europe, where in fact the unemployment is already beyond belief.

Yet a wider conception offers hope. There are parts of the world where there is a major shortage of skilled workers in certain fields such as the construction trades and medical professions and at the same time a need to have a more youthful population to counterbalance the aging demographic. Canada is at the moment one such country and has established a rational immigration policy which takes such factors into account to the benefit of young skilled workers. This is no longer a brain drain but a programme putting to use otherwise unused skills.

It is not without resistance. Canadian coal is essential to China. Special techniques are needed to operate environmentally acceptable mines. Chinese workers are skilled at this: Canadians are not. Yet some parts of the Canadian public objected to the employment of Chinese worker specialists. Canada is doing little to help the youth of Greece and Spain and thus solve Canada's skill shortage.

It is time we thought of the supply and demand for work as a global, not a national, issue.

Perhaps the most publicized areas of youthful expertise are in popular music with its world wide appeal, and professional sports of which soccer and cricket provide international opportunities. For most who are favoured in these domains the fame and income can be short-lived as youth becomes middle aged. Indeed it is in popular music that we begin to notice the destructive challenges facing youths who have a freedom of choice like that of no other time and which some are unable to handle[78].

The time of youthfulness contains within it discomforts, pains of the spirit, not understood and hence troubling challenges and difficult yet life influencing decisions. The cultures of youth have to handle such issues and at the same time are dominated by a quasi-independent series of youth cultures. My treatment is influenced by my age and prejudices. What I see as regrettable dysfunctions can in fact be a prelude to cultural new characteristics which can evolve into behavioural regularities of high value in the rapidly moving global society. I have to leave it to the reader to add modifying perceptions and interpretations.

There is a growing rapidity of sometimes slurred speech which those of other generations find difficult to follow. That demands greater auditory sensitivity with shorter reaction times than heretofore. Yet the world is

213

full of uncontrolled high decibel sound from that of emergency vehicles and large trucks to loud concerts. Some adult workers have ear protection equipment but the raving young do not, with predictable hearing consequences for their later years.

While some forms of group popular dancing do require skill and even acrobatic energy the standard action in nightclubs and accompanying concerts consists of mindless jerks to the beat of percussion with little or no physical contact or communication between partners who are often of the same sex or dancing solo. If this is a symptom of self-immersion it suggests that in the spirits of many youths today there is a dichotomy between popular dance expression and the use of technology (rather than face to face words) to communicate with "friends". Indeed the word "friend" no longer mainly refers to the intimacy and trust of interactions but an association with anyone at all with little discrimination and often with political or manipulatory characteristics. Are youths missing out as the romance of what is now limited to ballroom dancing is no longer a part of their experience? Is society destined to evolve into one of bees or ants, and to what purpose? Survival?

Associated with these phenomena is that of a rise in short attention spans. What might in other circumstances be put down as boredom or laziness in school age youth is nothing of the kind. It can be accompanied with very rapid speech amongst peers, almost a recognition that if a statement takes too long it will not be received. This can be carried over into adult life, though it is tempered by the demands of office and business for clarity in communication.

However it is accepted and reinforced in many institutional ways. Films and TV shows consist more and more of sequences of short clips. Against such a trend is the success of longer documentaries though even here short clips can prevail. Social media such as Twitter and smart phone texting enforce brevity, requiring numerous clarifications and bursts of messaging when the subject does not permit of simple statements to be effective.

It is too early to say but it is just possible that this type of communication is more functional than not. It demands short bursts in the transfer of information which in theory implies that in a given time more information can be transferred – assuming that each burst revives attention. In other words velocity of circulation of ideas increases, also increasing the frequency of innovation as we have seen in Chapter !!.

The Quebec student demonstrations of 2012 were ostensibly a protest against a proposed rise in university tuition fees but soon took on protests against the social and political system of the province. They were evidence that the lesson that crowded protest aided by smart phones is powerful and draws attention to issues like no other political form. It is a modern way of attempting to achieve political change outside the ballot box. As such it lends itself to special interests which may or may not represent the perspectives of the total electorate and cam become an outlet for demagogy. The protests were mainly peaceful although, especially early on, there were clashes with the police.

The reaction in the media revealed divided opinions. On the one hand the students were criticized as being spoiled kids putting their own material issues before the needs of the provincial budget. On the other hand some suggested that student leaders were gaining political and tactical experience and would be at the political leaders of the future, particularly after a failed meeting with the Premier of Quebec. In itself an indicator of the seriousness with which the demonstrations were viewed, the students enlarged their list of objections to elements in the social order with which they disagreed. Thus in April they turned their attention to objecting to the Formula One competition due to take place in Montreal. As the government failed to find a way to stop the protests the sense of empowerment increased.

The Arab Spring achieved much on a grander scale, and with much youth disappointment. The replacement of government does not in itself create wealth or employment.

But attitudes can change as a result, and, given time, advance can be achieved. The 'sixties and 'seventies were the precursor of profound changes in gender relations which had previously been scoffed at as impracticable.

Dare I hope that the young and recently young will take up some of the issues raised in this manifesto, and one way or another inspire the dynamics of change. Thus my motto which eventually will conclude the manifesto.

AdditionalPostscript

- *The Edge* of June 7th 2012 contains a report by Simon Baron-Cohen, who studies development psychopathology, on the work of Sarah-Jayne Blackmore., professor of cognitive neuroscience. Instead of focussing on brain alterations in childhood, the latter has studied what happens in the brains of adolescents, and finds that considerable changes take place. It is not clear whether the changes are promoted by the endocrine system or by the socio-cultural environment. The orientation of this research may have significant implications for the understanding of individual youth behaviour. It may even be possible that the dynamics continue into adulthood

Manifesto for the New Age

VII – The Intersection of Crime, the Law and Health

Changes in attitudes towards crime, the law, and health have been dramatic over the centuries, even over the recent decades. We regard crime and ill-health as unhappy disturbances to well-being, something to be reduced to the minimum. How?

First we must acknowledge that the roots of many issues and problems lie in the subject matter of previous chapters – education and family relationships. If we can achieve changes in those fields we will have done much to improve the conditions we are to discuss in this chapter.

The juxtaposition of the two problems in this chapter has nothing to do with the growing phenomenon which seeks to find biological and genetic causes for crime. While there may be significant advances in that field it will, I am reasonably sure, continue to encompass explanations.[79] for only a relatively small number of individuals. Even where it contains an explanation, social measures are necessary including diagnosis and therapy among the young in the Youth Maturity Institutes. Here I concentrate on the institutions themselves.

At the same time as we are looking again at the problems of crime we are being forced to reconsider our perspectives on ill-health. To be ill is becoming anti-social, a drain on society's resources, and a matter of personal responsibility since we are coming to believe that

219

we can avoid many illnesses if we try. Should we be personally responsible for the consequences of our illnesses? We are also re-thinking, or perhaps redesigning with inadequate thought, the institutions which "deal with" the ill.

Ghosts of Samuel Butler's *Erewhon*?

The analogies must not be overdone. It is evident that what is crime and what is illness is a matter of contemporary cultural definition. Homicide as revenge for rape or an earlier homicide has not always been a crime and is rampant in many cultures where revenge is the norm.[80] In some cultures today the death penalty is considered morally criminal, in others justified. As to sexual harassment....? The discomforts of some women around menstruation or menopause have been classified at different times as involving spiritual danger, normality, and now a treatable form of routine ill-health. Some forms of depression are now seen as illness. Chronic urges to sexual aggression mix the definition of criminal and medical. Homosexuality is no longer a crime in many countries. In the United States to bare a woman's breast on television is getting close to being criminal but is normal in real life elsewhere.

On the whole we still have separate institutions for dealing with crime and health, though they have many similarities, such as restriction of movement to institutional cells in both prisons and hospitals – and submission to authority. I will start with the world knows as that of managing crime.

We would prefer to see a world without crime, for crime is an assault on others or on their interests. The institutions we have to deal with crime do so in countries with a Roman legacy on behalf of the State in the name of the community, which represents the assaulted individual only indirectly. This is an anachronism based on conceptions of Roman centralised power and authority, carried into modernity by first the assertions of feudal power and then that of the centralised State. In other societies the law may be administered on behalf of religion. Police, criminal law, the criminal courts, prisons and rehabilitation agencies are expensive ways of "bringing order" when the State defines that its peace is threatened by behaviour which takes place against itself or its members.

States have a parallel system of civil law which supports lawyers and civil courts without the vast panoply of supporting institutions such as police. The civil law resolves disputes between legal persons according to rules which define equity and acceptable behaviour that does not involve formal criminality which requires State intervention. The expenses of the disputes are borne mostly by the litigants, which rules out access to civil courts by a large number of aggrieved parties.

This chapter deals with crime, since that is perceived as one of the major threats to our values, but what I say about crime-fighting institutions will have major implications for an extension of civil law and the consideration of illness.

Sometimes the relevant institutions are lumped together as "the justice system". Sometimes we hear phrases such as, "There is no justice in this world", or "All I want is justice". When I studied the anthropology of law in the 'fifties I found that both anthropologists and jurists were in agreement. Although "natural justice" is a concept that sometimes, if rarely, has legal expression, there is in fact no such thing in the abstract, standing universally for all people at all times. Justice is an abstract idea which is ambiguous and not universal. The idea of justice, where it exists (and in a vast number of cultures it does not), varies with time and place. It cannot reasonably be referred to as a universal principle against which specific law can be evaluated.

When the words are used they mean in fact that the evaluators believe that at that time and in that context the law does not adequately address specific principles that the evaluators believe to be important. As such the criticisms may be telling and significant. But they are cultural, not natural.

In addition it seems to be the case that when people cry out for justice they are in fact crying out for revenge. They feel hurt and they want that hurt transferred to the perpetrator.

In my view, this is a subject in which we have a great deal to learn from cultures whose law has *not* been derived from Roman or Islamic law. Few will disagree with the observation that the system that deals with criminality is crude and ineffective. A few see the system as a whole in the context of the larger society, as a self-perpetuating growing cancer. I have had the dubious privilege of being embraced by the tentacles of the octopus, wrongly accused of a crime, and living in the world of the incarcerated in France and Switzerland. This was not an anthropologist's "participant observation", but in my unsystematic troubled way my insights were sharpened.

Before that I had seen the way in which some British Columbia Indians, under the influence of drink, social abuse, and severe depression, saw incarceration as a way out, a relief from their desperate world. Some would commit a petty crime, such as breaking a storefront window, to get back in. I had visited prisons as an outsider. The metallic noises were different, but I was impressed by the apparent "normality" of the prisoners. In a vaguely academic way I recognised that prisons constituted cultures in themselves.

As I write, the media, both visual and printed, emphasise the tragedies of the victims of crimes. Persons related to victims find it relatively easy to raise funds for reformist crusades. We see as many relatives with tears running down their faces, their world in chaos, their bitter diatribes, as we do starving African babies. We see women and men expressing their anxieties verging on the paranoid or more aggressively "taking back the dark". The statistics count little. These are individuals, individual cases, made significant by repetition and publicity. Fear stalks the streets, even when we know that it is men more than women who are victims of men, and that, on a population basis, there is in fact less violent crime, and has been, year by year, for at least a decade, in much of industrialised society (including inner cities) where the fears continue to be the greatest.

The reason for the false perception is that the media treat acts of crime as dramatic audience binders, in which the drama is portrayed by people like you and me, with whom we can identify, and in which the story can be followed for several days as in a *Kojak* series, without the payment of actors' and producers' fees..... The criminal series, because it fills the screen regularly and regularly hits the tabloid headlines, is easily but falsely interpreted as the norm.

Underlying nearly all the media-emphasised public reaction there is one theme: revenge. That is, what "justice" has come to mean in nearly all cases, and in some systems overtly. The system is not working unless the victim's right to revenge is recognised. Relatives of victims often demand harsher penalties, the removal of the young from youth court to adult court, in the United States and Canada, or the rigorous application of the death penalty. It doesn't matter that studies show that such measures are ineffective in reducing crime. That is not

224

important, fundamentally. What is important is that the victim, however defined, be revenged, and that this must be done by the State in the name of the State. The victim does not personally see the judicial murder that he or she has been calling for; except in some Muslim countries and where, in the United States, victims may attend an execution, and in communities where reprisal - an eye for an eye and a tooth for a tooth – is sanctioned. The victim is not concerned fundamentally (however much involved in public protest) with the general reduction in crime; rather with the assuagement of anger.[81]

I am more concerned with reducing crime and if possible eliminating it. If revenge stands in the way, revenge must be reduced or eliminated.

Sources of crime are manifold and cannot be lumped together, although I believe one comes through as predominant.

First there is the crime of youth which is an expression of youth. I do not know of a time when this was not a major phenomenon. It seems almost endemic. Some military societies have been able to channel the impulses -- Zulu age regiments are an example. In Nazi times youth was mobilized in uniformed gangs, where certain types of thuggery were mandated. In Imperial times youths were enrolled in military cadet corps which disciplined their aggressive tendencies. In medieval times the fortunate young, even noble teen-agers, commanded armies. Present day creative outlets for energy, aggression, competitiveness, group identity and risk taking are there a-plenty: adventure travel, mountaineering, skiing, boating, sports. They are not available for everyone and are mostly costly. The parental desire to reduce risk comes into conflict and leads some into subterfuge. Physical risk-taking, as an aspect of Youth Maturity Institutes, is an essential part of growing up, of putting one's self to the test.

Independence seeking youth often pulls back from an organisation unless it is self-directed. A gang in such instances can have more meaning than a school volley-ball team. Organisations, even those such as Outward Bound which use risk as a motive, surround their activities with risk-filtering nets. They have to, or they would be put out of business by law suits and parental vengeance. An essential element in competitive risk is to outdo the others. If schools have controlled-risk sports, there will be a clientele for higher-risk events, with clandestine or grand-standing group behaviour. "Look at me." "Look at what I can get away with."

Mixed in with this is sheer opportunism, the temptation to steal, the imagination of working on a break-in, as on television, and of course alienation. Children who are expressing their anger at parents, at perceived *unfairnesses* at school, at the hypocrisy of church-going, at deprivation -- working it out alone, or pulling in accomplices to exercise power. And then the more fundamentally disturbed, who may not see the horrible reality of their acts because the vivid imagination that led to them and the hysterical aggression in the midst of blood and murder has entered their minds as fantasy. One could go on.

As we have seen in the education chapter, a mark of growing from infancy to maturity is the increased respect for others. Some individuals are slow to grow up, a small minority never do. Far from allowing the child within to dominate, we must learn to be adult, even if that means sacrificing some of the desirable features of innocence. When youth breaks into crime it is an indicator that respect for others is deficient. It all starts with the lack of courtesy in using elbows to create space on public transit.....

Hence some of the features of the Youth Maturity Institutes will reduce, but not eliminate, the entry into crime. So will ultimate changes in interpersonal relations, including marriage, some of which I have advocated in earlier chapters. If children too are treated less as property and more as human individuals, without crossing the boundary into lack of parental responsibility, if there is courtesy in the home, the results can only be beneficial. As I write the press is referring to studies which purport to link bullying to "bad" parenting.

It is sometimes pointed out that there is a higher incidence of crime and dysfunctional personalities in "broken homes", by which is meant homes that have been broken by divorce or separation, homes that lack one parent, homes where there is abuse. There are many well balanced survivors of such events, and many interesting children living with single parents. It depends partly on the nature of the child's sensibilities. But even more there is a huge difference between "civilised" splits and argumentative property-driven ones, especially when access to the child is a property right; between comfortable splits and those which result in poverty; between amicable splits and those where the cause has been abuse, violence, alcohol or drugs. Optimistically, this is where the Youth Maturity Institutes and their therapy-oriented professionals can make a difference.

In the meantime, and probably for a long time, the fact will remain that juveniles will be apprehended and sentenced, and that many will come from stable, apparently loving, well-off homes. In their late teens, in some jurisdictions earlier, they will be dealt with as adults. Most civilised juvenile courts endeavour to place the child in the context of his or her life, and seek remedies which have a theoretical healing orientation. I do not have the expertise to know the effectiveness of the approaches in practice. I do know that there is a great deal of criticism to the effect that juvenile courts are "too soft" on young violent criminals, especially those who have committed horrendous violent crimes attended with publicity, and on those whose age and sense of responsibility is at the borderline. The criticisms are once again tinged with the cry for revenge. Whatever changes may be regarded as appropriate at the juvenile level, harsher penalties through adult court are the reverse of what is needed.

Further, what is "adult" in this context? The word is being demeaned. It should mean maturity, the practice of responsibility. It has little to do with age. Those who play stupid fantasy games which result in violence are not adult whatever their age. That is the same sort of demeaning expression as the use of the term "adult movies" for gross pornography; or "adults only" meaning that something is going on in here that is too raunchy or alcoholic for juveniles. Becoming an adult is becoming defined away from what it should mean to "I can now indulge in gross conduct."

We should do away with the term adult altogether, as representing a distinction from childhood, recognising that many young are very mature, and some who are old have never grown up. Since I shall argue that the law should deal entirely with individual cases, not classes of people, save in special cultural circumstances, there need be no distinction between juvenile and adult court.

One would also make more use of the term "citizen", and have formal rites of passage that made manifest the transition from the status of "ward" (child) to that of responsibility ("citizen"). The point of transition would not be defined by age, but by meeting requirements of maturity. I know that such a suggestion will be controversial, especially since I have not yet defined in my mind the sort of tests and ceremonies that would be appropriate.[82] It will be controversial since it raises the spectre that authority may use the distinguishing criteria in such a way that perhaps many potential citizens could be kept out for their idiosyncrasies, including political ones.

Perhaps a citizen should become one without challenge, at a time of his or her choosing, with witnesses to maturity, responsibility, rejection of violence, caring. Will you help work it out? The one thing I know is that some such concept is needed.

How can I say talk of civilised ways of handling crime when the crimes are so violent and horrendous, so dangerous and costly to the public?

The reasons are quite simple.

Being caught and punished does not stop crime. It adds to the risk, which, as we have seen, is a potent motivator for the young.

The process of conviction and punishment does not enter into the minds of many young first offenders. They are being dealt with by an establishment and laws which are remote from their respect and experience and abstract rather than reality-based. Almost by definition, they do not see the consequences as real. They have already discounted them. They are already getting respect from certain peers. They are cynical about adult responsibility and the adult world. They are being noted by older adults as possible tools for further crime.

From the young person's perspective it can be so *unfair* and it creates even more anger. Remember, most of the young people involved are, in their actions, self-centred with minimal regard for others, at least until Youth Maturity Institutes get to grips with the issue. Now, in addition, many, feel boosted by publicity. Then they are isolated, in their view they are alone, ready for introversion and angry brooding. They deal with lawyers who talk technicalities, who may be provided by the State or by legal aid as a duty rather than a commitment, mitigating circumstances are frequently not taken into account, preventative detention is demeaning. These are psychological assaults that confirm the angers and the oppositions. Almost overnight the dangerous prankster or self-centred ego becomes a criminal, out to show he is at war with the system. And if there were any doubt about this, prison will fix it up and make sure of it.

For adults who are first time offenders the dynamics can be similar. My information here is going to be tinged by subjectivity; it cannot be otherwise. It is influenced not only by my personal experience, the full story of which is not appropriate here[83], but also by talking with and observing fellow prisoners, some of whom were acquitted, some already serving sentences. The purpose of my argument is not to set up a temporary set of reforms, but to try to look at the larger scene, raise the long-term issues as we influence our evolution to a mare acceptable world.

In summary I am going to argue that criminality is a sub-system within our society that has its own recruitment, demographics, dynamics, rules, boundaries, culture and life. Tinkering with reforms is unlikely to root it out; it may even help to preserve it. Follow the process of dealing with an offender through its stages. We can do this with some confidence, since despite significant variables in various countries there are broad similarities in their criminal sub-cultures and those of the police and authorities who deal with them.

Not every person charged with a criminal act enters into the dynamics in the same way. Some come out of the experience as responsible reliable citizens. To do this they have to have major informal psychological support, faith in themselves, certainty about what they did or did not do, an ability to overcome the trauma in the short or long term, a restructuring of their values. If any one of these features is absent, it is very unlikely that their future lives will be adequately functional.

Mostly, the central system does not address such features. It concentrates on vocational skills and some half-way house adjustment for those who have had long sentences; and there is help from chaplains and social workers, acting as individuals, and those relatives and friends who remain loyal and caring -- which is often not the case.

It all begins with an event. Police conduct an investigation under various kinds of authority or supervision. In Napoleonic systems they act in the name of an enquiring magistrate, reporting to him. In Anglo-Saxon systems police govern their own investigations, charging on their own initiative or after the agreement of a prosecutor's or public attorney's office. (I am generalising my terminology and descriptions.)

Defence lawyers are continually on guard against police inaccuracy and manipulation, and confirm that sleight-of-hand with regard to truth, while by no means applying to all cases, is widespread. In some instances a conviction or the bringing of a charge would be impossible without police breaking the rules.

I have my own experience, which may be extreme. I was able to observe in detail similar "methods" being used in connection with accused in Switzerland, and have read numerous press reports about the same kinds of actions in Anglo-Saxon countries. During my enforced confinement I talked with prisoners who had been incarcerated in a wide range of countries -- Britain, Netherlands, Switzerland, Germany, Italy, France, African countries, Iran, and so on. Prisoners lie, but they are not necessarily liars. I am confident that there is truth in the regularities.

Once police are confronted with what they believe to be a crime they must do what any other investigator must do, look for evidence, a process which is governed by *theory* and which, ideally, should influence modifications to the emerging theory revision. This is

233

hard to do in any discipline, yes, even in my own of anthropology. For the police the task is much easier if someone with a previous record is somehow connected, or if they can work with some sense of statistical probability. If, for example, there is a murder, they look first for jealousy as a motive, or drugs or money. If there is a person who might be linked through jealousy or drugs, he immediately becomes a target, unless there is *inescapable and immediate* unavoidably strong alternative evidence. The process is not very different from that used in medical practice, for example: use established theory first.

But the police are working in a totally different atmosphere. They are under pressure to solve the crime and bring a charge. To be effective they cannot lose time. The environment is dangerous; often they must react in a split second or their lives could be lost. It is easy to judge in a writing room. Although they did me great harm, I think I understand why they did what they did. Having chosen to become police they do what they believe they have to do to fulfil the mandate *that the **public** places upon them*.

In my own experience threats were issued *sub voce*, but strongly, in circumstances where independent witnesses were not present or could not hear. Witnesses were influenced by the persuasive statement that the police had all the evidence needed to convict and all they needed now were a few confirming details, when in fact they did not have such evidence. Attempts were made to psychologically undermine witnesses (especially women) through false accusations (in one instance, of incest) and domestic harassment (police calling at the front door with sirens in operation and at awkward family times), the presentation of malicious innuendo as truth without independent substantiation, misrepresenting witness statements without securing witness signatures, sequestering the accused in a way that prevented him from tracking down supporting evidence, the use of tape recorders without informing the interviewee, using trickery to gain entrance to a residence when a warrant had been refused. Much of this is suppressed and does not come to light in court but is used to guide and justify the direction of the enquiry and, in Europe, to influence the examining magistrate and even the presiding trial judge.

Other methods may include the planting of evidence, harassing observation, bribing convict witnesses with privilege or reduced sentencing, violence, plea-bargaining.

In many, perhaps most, criminal cases such methods do not come to light. Police are very aware of the risks they run in working in such ways, and are skilled and collegial when it comes to concealing. Most cases involve repetitive crimes, almost routine, in which no one wants to use up resources in an unequal fight. Criminal lawyers are only human. They will challenge police methods, but what is the point when in other respects the case is cut and dried? When there is, perhaps, a confession? Their task is not to get a declared criminal off, but to see that he is treated according to the rules of the court. There are lawyers who will go the whole way, and do, who challenge every police misdemeanour.

But even that is not my essential point. With individuals who have entered a criminal way of life, police malfeasance is accepted as a reality and shrugged off as part of the conditions of work. The main task is not to get caught in the first place. Some "petty" criminals even take police charges as a way of placating their symbiotic colleagues, and expect to serve time, as long as they can get away with other events. When I exchanged talk of my experience with other prisoners they would laugh. The police always do that. When someone new came into the prison on a charge and I heard, step by step what he was facing, I knew that even the words the police interrogators used were exactly the same as they used with me. "We'll respect you if you tell us all about it, then we'll have a beer. Right?" or "If you don't, we'll turn your life upside down, your friends will leave you even if you're not convicted."

What is much more devastating is the effect on first or early offenders. I met literally scores, mostly non-violent, who had no real defences. Young, naive, sometimes innocent, they become more cynical, angry, betrayed. They had little faith in the lawyers who were assigned to them -- usually the accused had no funds -- and were unable to get any other psychological help. There are though lawyers and consular officials who act as friends, take on the role of *pater familias*, and spend far more time than their fees would justify.

I am not setting out the observations in an attempt to excuse young criminals. There are many young people, growing up in similar conditions, who do *not* enter crime. There are those, who, accused and convicted and imprisoned, turn away from crime. It is a question of choice and responsibility, however ill-informed and emotional. Just the same, the majority are vulnerable, weak, poorly supported and allow their experiences to reinforce dormant alienation. The dynamics are deadly and counter-productive.

Prisons for "preventive detention", analogous to "remand", are sometimes in theory independent of police. Again, in theory, such prisons are situated close to relatives. Preventive detention can be used specifically to defeat the accused. The refusal of bail -- very common in Europe -- is a first weapon, consciously or not. In complicated cases it seriously inhibits the collection of defence evidence, which the accused alone can track down. It drags out imprisonment for months or longer, sometimes in nearly solitary conditions, before a court has had a chance to rule. Remember, some of these people are innocent.

The hurts are deep. A high proportion of prisoners awaiting trial are accused of drug or white collar offences. I met West Africans arrested at airports carrying drugs to finance European studies, credit card sharps, purveyors of stolen art, entrepreneurs accused of fraud. The latter were totally at a loss as to how to conduct themselves in prison. The majority had wives, girl friends, expectant mothers.

They were out of their minds with worry. They were not irresponsible within their own worlds. Where they had such affines, their women were working hard to guide defence lawyers, to raise funds. Funds? Yes. For many of the crimes, in France and Switzerland at any rate, involved drug trafficking. The accused negotiated customs duties and concomitant fines, and would not go to a superficial trial until the negotiations were agreed and the funds paid. By which time the accused has in effect served his sentence. Out. We don't want to pay for your cell any more. Now we have our money.

While the accused is in detention, the enquiry proceeds. It has not been completed. In some European countries the accused has a right to the presence of a lawyer during interrogation, an enormous but expensive safeguard, if lawyers take their tasks seriously rather than with a routine shrug of their shoulders. In most industrial countries the police play on anxieties, and try to find weaknesses they can use to more or less bribe the accused. The good cop bad cop routine is real. They try to wear down the accused by taking him to a police cell for interrogation and doing nothing, so that he wonders what is up. They imply that friends are deserting him. Where they have correspondence censorship rights they pick out phrases to use. They attempt to mislead the accused with respect to his juridical position and rights. (Paradoxically in some jurisdictions an accused has the right to lie, to fight back if police use violence, and to escape. In practice, this does not mean much.) When they have no real evidence, they lie that they do.

The reason is simple. It aids the police task inestimably if they can get a confession, whether or not a plea of "not guilty" is entered in court. Indeed, it is quite probable that the majority of court cases, whether successful or not, are brought to court as a result of a confession, direct or implied. This is the object of the psychological warfare between police and accused.

Many accused do not bother to fight back very much. Police pretend to respect this. Police say at least then the accused have the moral strength to pay the price when they are caught. There are typical offers: we have nothing against you as you. We are just doing our job. When you have made our task easier by your admissions we'll be your friend. This is a game the frequent offender knows very well. He understands the hypocrisy involved, although some do in fact, when they are out, have a collegial beer or two.

Police and offenders are in a symbiotic relationship. Without offenders police work would be reduced to that of citizen helpers, directing traffic, giving street directions, reviving the terminology of "sir" and "madam". It is in the police professional interest -- as with other professions -- to dramatise an admittedly often dramatic role, to build up their undoubtedly courageous image, and to exaggerate crime (for this justifies their jobs). Criminals who have been through the system know their "enemy", and, except in the most horrendously violent crimes, play cat and mouse.

Many are so used to the prison system they take it in their stride. One English fellow I knew even published a book about how to survive in prison. For some it is a part of their career, for career it is for many. Many parts of the criminal world have their own professional standards, career decisions and retirement plans. Prison is part of the cost of doing business.

There are others who are so alienated and disturbed that the prison world is their only real world. They cannot survive, emotionally, psychologically, and materially outside of prison. They will commit crimes to get caught and to go back in. For some it is an alternative, however harsh, to sleeping under bridges. For others it is a cocoon, the guards are macho fathers, the rules limit behaviour so that choices do not have to be made any more. They are frightened by choice in the real world.

Periods of prison of a year or more begin to erode the individual's capability of operating in the real world. Vehicular traffic can be anxiety producing, crossing the street a hazard, looking self-satisfied and superior citizens in the eye is a challenge.

Imagine what fifteen or twenty years do. Individuals must face the disapprobation of straight citizens, many of whom are in fact not particularly moral. It is unlikely that a spouse will still be there for them, and if so will be a very different person from the one they once knew. They have forgotten how to act heterosexually (although a few prisons try to keep up the practices by allowing wives or prostitutes to visit). Whatever occupational skills they have acquired are treated with suspicion by employers and are not likely to be up-to-date.[84]

Citizens who clamour for longer sentences don't know what they are doing. They are increasing the likelihood of recidivism. Under these circumstances it is remarkable that repeat offences are not much more frequent. Normally prison does *not* cure. If convicts return to some semblance of non-criminal life, it is by drawing upon their inner strengths, or because they were not leading a criminal way of life in the first place, or because they are just plain frightened, seldom because "prison has reformed them".

Until the nineteenth century, many punishments were public -- the stocks, whipping, hanging. Crime -- partly because of definition[85], partly because of poverty, and partly because of the roughness of life -- was more frequent than it is today, even though now we are more worried by it. Prisons were relatively open; it was often possible for the public to enter, to jeer, or to find friends and relatives behind bars or chained to a wall.

In the late nineteenth century prison reforms changed these ways. The educated middle class did not like seeing the results of conviction. Their fastidiousness led to reduced, more "civilised" sentences for many crimes. It also led to removing prisons and punishments from the public eye.

241

There was a general change in the structure of newer prisons, with cells arranged in linear wings with a control and observation post at the point at which the wings joined. The new design was not only to improve the effectiveness of control but, as part of a reformist theory, to enable guards to give the individual prisoners a sense of their own individual space, a responsibility for themselves that close supervisory approximation destroyed. In addition, the efficacy of observation (when doors had see-through properties) was supposed to make it possible to detect individual psychological problems -- suicidal or manic, for example -- early.

For the philosophy became one of *curing*. The idea, familiar to some modern thought, was that criminal behaviour was an illness. The function of the prison system was to rehabilitate. This was to be achieved by firm but understanding supervision, by in-prison education, and above all by the ethic of work. Trade training became highly significant.

It was an enlightened approach, and there are still many vestiges of it. Minimum security prisons provide opportunities for physical recreation, enlightened educational programmes, creative activities such as theatre and art, discussions and counselling. Sometimes career criminals find their way to such centres. Perhaps they are influenced. The more secure, tougher, prisons also have programmes of this kind, which sometimes speak to individuals.

But in my view there has been a marked deterioration. Neither of the prisons I observed in France and Switzerland had reformist characteristics, even for the long-term convicted. I do know that such prisons do exist in both countries. I also know, from reading, the media, and talking with prisoners, that in France, Britain, Canada and the United States, there are totally dreadful prisons, overcrowded, violent, where the problems of security overshadow most attempts at reform.[86] Prison "work" is frequently minimal wage labour accessed by sharp entrepreneurs, or by charitable organisations who do not recognise what is going on. (In the Swiss prison, prisoners sat in dreadful eye-straining artificial or candle light in their cells, perched on thigh- and back-ruining hunks of wood that served as chairs, hour after hour putting together UNICEF cards on a pitiful piecework arrangement, their hands covered with glue that they often couldn't remove without great difficulty because there was no hot water in the cells, for pitiful "pay" that quickly went on monopoly supplied groceries. What, may I ask, is reformist about this?)

Why the backsliding? Pressure of funding is one force. The unattractiveness of prison management careers another. The size of the prison population a third. The low priority accorded to prisons among competing demands for public support another.

The very inaccessibility of prisons to the general public is a dominant cause. If the public really knew, experienced, the prison culture, opinion would not stand for what goes on. This is not a question of being "soft" on the convicted. It is the degradation of human beings. It is would-be escapees being dragged down iron steps by their heels, heads banging on the iron, step by step. It is screams in the night as adult men have nightmares. It is men going mad spread-eagled against window bars, trying to break their heads and the glass. It is men curled upon an iron cot in a foetal position, unable to respond to food or drink. It is men crying night and day as they think of loved ones. It is being picked out at random, taken to the shower room, stripped naked for the investigation of orifices. It is macho guards who look forward to escape attempts (not illegal in Switzerland) so that they can use their firearms in a hunt. Much more. These I have seen. In the worst prisons, supposedly secure, which I have not seen, drugs, knives, murders, homosexual rapes are frequent. It is a commonplace that within the prison culture there is organisation among the prisoners, especially the long-term ones, with hierarchies and gang rules. This can *only* happen with the connivance of the guards who however are often powerless to do much about it.

These are the toughest prisons, the ones in which security is the dominant priority, everything else coming second. How is it then that drugs and weapons are so frequently encountered? Drugs particularly have to come in from outside. Despite the undoubted ingenuity that convicts evince, which ensure that the prison boundaries will never be 100% secure, I can only come to the conclusion that the drug supply, at least, is condoned, perhaps even unofficially encouraged. The use of medications is frequently abused in prison conditions in order to try to keep individuals tranquillised. The use of drugs may be thought of in a similar way. If so, be open about it. When clandestine it supports corruption among the prison staff and endangers interior security.

So too with interior order. It is not particularly difficult for prisoners to manufacture aggressive weapons. Nor is it difficult -- over years, remember -- to engage in relationships with officials who turn a blind eye.

Did anyone mention reform of the individual? This is a criminal society and culture. It puts together people who *live* their criminality and continue to do so uninterruptedly in prison, reinforced by their peers. Some are one-time offenders. What a university. It has nothing whatsoever to do with the reduction of crime. Well meaning citizens who advocate longer sentences are in effect advocating the perpetuation of criminality -- unless they say, lock them up for good. Then what happens to them is not an issue. Civilised?[87]

It is more than symptomatic that Michael Tonry, possibly the doyen of criminologists in the United States, in his recent publication *Thinking About Crime*, deals almost exclusively with punishment and pours scorn on Dan Kahan's theory of retributive shaming.[88] I support the idea of shame as an essential part of the healing process, though not as part of an idea of punishment. The focus of such writers, and many other criminologists, is on the

245

efficacy or non-efficacy of differing kinds of punishment, measured by the level of recidivism. This is largely folly, for punishment and, especially prison terms, have in themselves very little if any result in reducing crime. The measures I suggest may do so, but ultimately we will have to mark time until the Youth Maturity Institutes can do their part of the job.

Is there an alternative that we can pursue in practical ways? I believe so. For once I do not think it would take expense or decades to bring about. It involves a change of attitudes, a greater weight given to the effectiveness and openness of the processes.

The key I think is this. While we are becoming more and more concerned about the frequency of crime, we also raise ever-more recurrently the plight of victims. Victims are usually quite right, in that the system of criminal "justice", while perhaps listening to their complaints, does nothing for them. Except in "traditional" non-Roman law, there is little or no restitution. The only option is to seek revenge. One cannot criticise victims for this. There seems to be no other way in which to resolve the hurt, trauma and emotional desperation. And in some societies, for example parts of the Balkans and Middle East, the thirst for revenge is such as to threaten the very fabric of inter-ethnic stability and the body politic.[89]

This is no way in which to organise a civilised society when its norms have been breached. Revenge is one of the most destructive forces there is, analogous to jealousy in marital relationships, both to the individual who is expressing deep feelings, and to the social environment. It does nothing to heal the social wounds that a crime has created, in fact leading to generations of inter-family tit for tat strife..

There are other ways. There are older societies from whom we can learn to adapt. They are even, in the midst of this vengeful retributive culture, ways of claiming back some of their older methods.

In a muddled way the United States and Canada are permitting a handful of Indian tribe-nations to exercise juridical processes in the midst of the overwhelming Anglo-Saxon system. In some highly commercialised Indian communities the interests are primarily in administering their own civil law as a method of controlling resources and enterprises, a law which is adapted and borrowed from the mainstream corpus, with little difference.

In other instances mainstream courts allow the representation of tribal authorities when it comes to sentencing. In one example, the court handed over two violent young men to the tribal council. The council and elders banished the young men separately to an island, to live on their own resources for a year, to learn about their inner strengths and contemplate their responsibilities as men, after which they would be placed back in the care of the elders, who would talk with them and ultimately formally reincorporate them back into society.

In another example, with the assistance of tribal police, elders and *healers*, an almost totally demoralised community in Canada, riddled with destitution, dependency, sexual abuse and alcoholism, was given the authority to look after its own problems. They did so through treating the abusers and violent alcoholic offenders as individuals who had lost any vestige of self-esteem, any notion of responsibility for their behaviour toward others. The indigenous psychology of respect for lineal elders, meaning respect for extended family connectivity, shame for exhibiting weakness and the hurt of others, acts of contrition and compensation, the examination of self in isolation, the use of traditional psychological healing arts, worked. Transgressors returned to honour in their community, found their self-esteem, understood the harm they had done to others and themselves, and found satisfying pursuits despite the high rate of unemployment.[90]

In a very few prisons, traditional healing circles are at work.

Such examples are in part helped and made possible by the continuity of tradition which can be recalled, and by the fact that some hitherto demoralised Indian communities have been going through a cultural regeneration. The communities are also, for the most part, small. When they work they are tightly knit, and are still able to reclaim, in crisis, some of their members who have moved into the larger mainstream society, but dysfunctionally. The examples cannot be replicated automatically into the wider culture.

These principles and others are nevertheless worthy of closer study. Here are some of them.

The most useful starting point is that the transgressors are socially ill. Their minds have been filled with thoughts and imaginings which are culturally unhealthy. For a healthy man does not damage other members of his community. To be healthy is his own responsibility, a condition of his being a part of the community's network, to which he contributes, and which supports his functioning. He can be sufficiently mad, mentally unhealthy, to reject the community, in which case he goes off and lives as a "wild man", an uncivilised being, on his own. If the methods of healing that are available do not in themselves bring him back into appropriate relationships, then banishment will be the community's answer. Rejection. But this is a last resort.

Prior to the extreme of banishment, the community may work with the following principle: a transgression is an interruption of the social order. The purpose of a judgement is to put that order back in place[91]. This takes priority over the notion of revenge or punishment, though neither element can be discounted in practice.

The kinship orientation of a number of societies makes the principle workable. If there is violence, even murder, theft, adultery (thought of as criminal), or sexual perversion, the offender is the responsibility of his or her kinsmen, however defined. If the offence is against a member of the offender's own kin group, then that kin group handles it. If it is against a member of another kin group, then, through various mechanisms, including negotiation and ceremonialised warfare, the offended kin group must be satisfied. (Note that, by definitions of exogamy, offences against a spouse may involve *two* kin groups.)

Such systems are also aided by the fact that there are exchanges of wealth at the time of marriage. (In some societies, this is one-sided and can be abused.) If there are problems between spouses, part of a settlement will be restitution or the threat of restitution of at least some of that wealth, depending sometimes on whether divorce is an outcome.

The ultimate settlement will involve such mechanisms as the offending group taking responsibility for controlling the offender, including, perhaps, isolating him or her until he or she returns to sociability. There can be ostracism and, yes, punishment. They will apologise for his offence. They will make recompense by transferring wealth or obligations to the damaged group.

The processes are quite similar to those involved in property disputes, for example disputes over land boundaries or failure to maintain ceremonial obligations. In other words, there is little if any distinction between what we regard as civil and criminal law. And it is true that if negotiations fail there could be violence, and that the process does not work well across cultural boundaries.

I must also make it clear that I am not by any means describing "all traditional societies", among whom there is great variation. And that even for the kind of society I have in mind -- much of North American Indian, many in Africa and Melanesia -- what I have presented is abstract generalisation. The concrete ethnography would show much more complication in detail.

And what can work in small communities will not be suited to mass industrialisation.

Nevertheless there is a great deal here to emulate. For the prime idea is that the social order has been upset, and that the primary task is to restore it. The social order is not considered to be an encompassing state, but a disruption of harmony between individuals which threatens normal interactions between their relatives and friends. To restore the harmony, the victim must be included in the settlement, not left out. Revenge perpetuates the disturbance to the social order. In part, modern state criminal law recognises this, for it does not allow the victim to "take the law into his own hands", that is seek revenge by himself.

The concept that a crime being a threat to the social order is therefore a crime against the state is fraught. The almost universal wish for revenge is a clear indication that the victim is less the state than the individuals who have suffered hurt. This is being admitted in fact in those jurisdictions where the victims are asked to describe the conseluences of the crime as it affects them, information that may be considered in sentencing. But so far it stops short of restitution, of returning the state of affair to what it was before. To rectify this we need a procedure to think less of the state being damaged but more of the victims being damaged.[92]

We should merge civil and criminal law, and treat crime as a tort. And perhaps at the same time we should consider all crime to involve forms of mental disturbance that require varying kinds of treatment; mental disturbance in the sense that there is defective concern for others and for the social consequences, and there is diminished responsibility. (I am *not* implying that such "illness" is appropriately treated by conventional biomedical models: quite different methods may be needed.)

Revenge will not disappear unless we put an alternative effectively in place. My thoughts are of course expressed in great generality; to make progress would require considerable refinement. These are some steps......

The clearest case for what I am proposing is with respect to juveniles. All families, however dysfunctional, should in principle be made directly responsible for the acts of children and youths, sharing accountability and liability with the offender. That said, the family itself may need major therapeutic attention which may require the removal of the offender to another familial, adoptive, or care home environment. While such alternative home environments may, in practicality, have to have an institutional organisation, the less this is done the better, and, except in very extreme circumstances, the offender should not be removed into an institutionalised prison which abstracts him from direct responsibility for his past acts. The objective is to heal by *re*-socialising through restitution and acceptance of responsibility.

Nor will the juvenile offender be removed from Youth Maturity Institutes, where the healing will take place, though he or she may be enrolled in a specialized Institute suited to the youth's needs. As time goes on the observation of youths' psychological and mental states in Youth Maturity Institutes will reduce or even eliminate later anti-social behaviour.

The juvenile offender, to varying degrees, requires special forms of healing. Heshe needs to find hiser inner strength, hiser self-respect, and above all hiser respect for others. The court's task should be to mandate appropriate healing devices.

The primary method is to involve the offender *and the family,* however defined, in acts of restitution toward the victim. I am not talking here about enforced community work that involves an abstraction of public service. I am talking about direct acts in relation to the victim and the victim's relatives. They are not precisely a kind of quid pro quo. They will not mirror the offence. A robbery, yes, will involve restitution of the stolen or damaged material. It can also involve acts like painting a house, garden work, help to an elderly relative or friend of the victim, and so on.

At the same time the offender would undergo direct healing treatment. What it might be would be individualised. It could involve participating in risk-taking adventure groups. (I have been impressed by the principles of a North American organisation called Vision Quest. In lieu of prison, young women with extensive and violent criminal records are sentenced to its care. They heal and find their civilised selves as crew members of a large sailing barque.) It could involve the field study of social issues. It could involve encouragement of creative activity. It could involve therapies of self-awareness, self-testing, aggression control, psychiatry. It could involve, exceptionally, pharmaceutical therapy.

The end of the programme should *not* be determined by a specific time objective. It should be determined by result; when, in the view of qualified assessors, the offender has participated in sufficient restitution to the victim, and when, as a result of this and other activities, he or she is re-socialised.

The end of such a restitutive programme should involve a healing ceremonial in which the victim and the offender, each with their kin, friends or other guarantors, acknowledge that harm has been done, healing has been achieved, and that it was possible now to put the offence away.

At this point it must be acknowledged that in our present Western systems forgiveness and healing of the hurt is extremely difficult. There are indeed hurt parents of a victim who exhibit compassion and concern for the offender. They are notable for being few and far between. Most such parents are themselves victims, not only of the crime, but of a system in which restitution is not institutionalised.[93] Note that acceptance, forgiveness and restitution do not imply what we foolishly describe as "closure", that is the removal of painful memory and its emotions[94].

How much of this can be adapted for adult offenders? In individualised society, the identification of relevant family (and/or friends) to share responsibility will not be possible in many, perhaps most, cases. In societies where this continues to be possible, that responsibility should be maintained. But we must consider the situation in which the individual is just that, alone and personally responsible.

For the most part the same considerations apply, especially for first time offenders. I make this comment because the majority of first time offenders commit petty crimes, for which the possibility of both material and emotional restitution is practicable.

Courts, in non-confrontational consultation with victims, would not establish coded penalties, although this might come with experience. They would establish the offender's restitutive acts and behaviour, including types of therapy and supervision. In an intermediate period until the system were properly installed, offenders would be held in revised prisons, from which they would be removed to undertake both tasks and therapy. As far as possible, the prison society would be broken up, with minimal contact between the convicted (except in those intriguing cases in which the guarantors would include other offenders). The convicted would in fact continue to live in society, although if needed, an institutional home and its officials would be available primarily for supervision, to ensure that tasks were in fact fulfilled, and keeping him or her out of further trouble during non-working non-therapy periods.

Especially for "minor" offences, and offences where there is no victim except the general public (motor offences which do not involve accident or injury), including offences where the law is regulatory in nature, some present remedies are likely to continue -- fines, withdrawal of driving licences, and so forth. Fines should not go into general revenue coffers, or be considered, as they often are now, a source of general revenue, or, perniciously, income for magistrates. They should be allocated to specific relevant remedies (driver training, alcohol control). Where there is a victim, restitutive acts should take precedence over generalised fines. Where possible, remedial requirements should take precedence

256

over fines -- service with an ambulance team, specified hours of controlled driving, for example on major highways at the posted speed.

Certain types of offences would no longer be considered delicts in the present sense. This applies to the remnants of prudish laws (as society permits), such as laws against the baring of breasts or nudity. More importantly, offences where *the adult victim is the adult offender himself*, need to be thoroughly reconsidered. Alcoholism laws have mostly, except when the law includes Moslem-style prohibition, reached this point. It is not an offence to drink, or to engage in private and consensual sexual aberration. Why should it be a *criminal* offence to hurt one's self? Drugs and suicide come under this heading. The removal of the use of drugs from the crime list would probably in itself half-empty prisons and reduce court proceedings. More important, it would remove beginning drug users from the spiralling entanglements of the criminal society. At the same time the removal of these habits from the criminal code does *not* give the addicts *carte blanche* as I am about to argue.

Wait. There are several refinements that derive from our principles. Drug users sometimes *do* harm to others. They sometimes require actions and attention from friends or family, which can be regarded as a form of social stealing. They sometimes engage in criminal activity to earn funds to keep up expensive habits. (So do other addicts). Their personalities change so that they may become aggressive or unable to perform. They require state medical expenditures. The law would be entitled to take such considerations into account for all types of addiction (smoking, alcoholism, gambling). In its *beginning* stages addiction is an anti-social choice.[95]

In short, where there is harm to others, restitutive and therapeutic remedies are in order. Far from solely reducing the field of criminal law, by changing offences to forms of tort one extends the notion of responsibility and remedy to other fields. A smoker would be required to accept his or her responsibility for his or her actions, and undertake some form of recognition, restitution, and mandatory healing. As I shall argue below a person who **becomes** an addict must bear the responsibility of the consequences, including the costs of therapy and of collateral damage to others.

It will immediately be objected to the application of these principles that they will not work for certain kinds of criminal. I agree, especially in the short run though time, experience and the ultimate effect of Youth Maturity Institutes will gradually erode the negative statistics.

In other words the attribution of responsibility should be ascribed to first time addicts, not to those caught up beyond responsibility. The latter should rather be treated as being ill

There are: individuals now so caught up in the present criminal system that they cannot be expected to get out of it on their own, individuals who are so violent or sex-oriented, and of an age, that therapies of whatever kind, as we know them now, are useless, individuals who are so alienated that restitutive acts further internalise alienation, individuals who despite restitution and therapy remain recidivists, individuals whose offences are so large (massive fraud, terrorism) that restitution (but perhaps not other forms of acknowledgement) is impracticable.

Some of these categories, for example the first, are transitional. We do not expect our reforms to be created over night. It would take considerable time and many intermediary moves, to establish the system I have imagined. Yet boldness is needed, for we are caught in a trap. If we do not posit *what we want to achieve* we will never achieve it. I for one **want** the system I have described to be achieved. Join me; and, since you are younger, work for it.

Some of the categories may respond to more imaginative ideas and to new therapies.

Nevertheless, outside the above categories, the punishing prison system would give way to socially and individually effective healing. The kinds of prisons we use now would be substantially reduced and in time eliminated.

For the above transitional categories, the future will tell how long we will continue to need prisons. The inward-looking structures, reinventing a criminal society, help no one. We should give up on no one within the walls no matter how repulsive he or she may seem. While maintaining maximum security until the public agrees to proven new measures, the alteration in other elements of the prison system should help to create adaptive possibilities. Animal-like cages, decrepit buildings which are insecure inside, crowd behaviour with its threat of numerous kinds of assaults and violence, help no one, least of all "society".

Break up the prison society as we know it now. Smaller prisons, more space, more privacy, programmes with more physical and mental challenge, developing prisoner-based responsibilities for internal order, and the use of at least 50% of time and resources on therapies and the encouragement of creativity. That's one way en route to the ideal.

In writing of therapy throughout this discussion, I make no prescriptions, for the data are beyond my command and there are signs that there will be massive advances in knowledge before much of the above is put into effect. Suffice it to say that it includes major reliance on the norms and supports of cultures of which the offenders and victims are members. If these are not taken into account in multi-cultural societies, other methods may be counter-productive. It includes psychological measures, bio-medical measures, alternative therapies, and the use of medicaments in some instances.

I must enter a strong caveat that one must not judge the potentiality of therapies by what is now taking place. There is a major tendency for some therapists who work within the punishment system to adapt their healing techniques and philosophy under the influence of the punitive system which can distort their analyses and also to attempt quick results.

Psychiatrists and psycho-analysts whom I have observed provide one sort of example, as do physicians who deal with problems by the induction of massive tranquillisers. In Switzerland a colleague visited me in prison. She had undertaken considerable controlled examination of the activities of psychiatrists in the context of criminal analysis. What she wrote confirmed my own observations.

Typically, psychiatrists were consulted during the course of the investigation, after an accused had been apprehended. What they did was to look at the police record as the foundation for their thoughts. Not once in numerous consultations that came to my attention did they question that record. They then conducted perhaps half a dozen short interviews with the prisoner. They came to the conclusions of the police, writing their reports in obfuscating jargon or direct language adding little if anything to what was supposedly known. "A man of violent temperament", "A pathological liar".

In short, they were adding material to the police dossier. This had nothing to do with the act of healing,

261

was indeed contrary to it, and a breach of the Hippocratic Oath. No genuine analysis can be based on that kind of information. Analysis alone, let alone therapy, requires lengthy interviews and "thick data" over months, and, in this context, deep discussion with friends and relatives.

When I returned to life after prison my view of all "holding" institutions changed considerably. Hospitals, mental institutions, nursing homes for the elderly, are literally prisons of a kind. In these, you are supervised, confined to certain spaces, fed institutional food, taken, if at all, on supervised trips even to a garden, sought after and brought back if you escape, are restricted in the circumstances in which you are permitted to discharge yourself, treated administratively and medically (sometimes) as if your mind did not exist. Facilities are sometimes no better than in minimum security prisons. In some instances, sadism and cruelty are the order, deliberate or unintentional, as rules are instituted with the best of intentions to regularise procedures, or worst of intentions as understaffed over-pressured aides confine people and push them around.

I know of a case when a 90 year old woman with a stroke was moved from intensive care, where she communicated in smiles with smart professional nurses, to a long term ward in which the nurses disguised themselves in informal clothes, addressed everyone by their first names, jollied the patients along with the utmost of patronising equality. The patient felt confused and insulted, gave up immediately, allowing herself to die as quickly as possible, her integrity threatened, probably believing she was no longer in a professional environment.

I know of homes for the elderly in which drugs are mal-administered, and those who cannot express themselves normally are treated brusquely, with contempt, and sometimes violence. I have heard of them screaming with rage and impotent frustration, not in words, but on the keyboard of a laptop computer, and then having "privileges" withdrawn.

All restrictive institutional settings are potentially subject to abuse.

What is at issue is probably not the doing away with institutions but their revision. In my city the closure of a facility for the mentally ill on the grounds that the patients were better off in society, but without provision for adequate alternative care, resulted in massive homelessness and street begging. In some countries the "problem" is conveniently solved by reducing times spent in hospitals, which is frequently desirable on medical grounds, discharging the non-violent mentally ill, and persuading families and personal homes to care for the elderly.

Mostly, this is escaping collective responsibility, the hidden agenda being presumed financial savings. It is all very well closing psychiatric hospitals, reducing time spent in mammoth city hospitals whose size justifies expenditures on enormous capital and operational equipment, and placing the elderly back in the home. The theory is basically sound *provided* that resources are redistributed to provide alternative support.

The dilemma should be a warning. Our dreams for the future will fail, at least in the short term, if the intermediary stages are not well thought out. For alternatives, now and again we can learn from the developing world, and now and again we must innovate from scratch. Entry into a sanitised hospital with its formal activities can be a frightening experience for many people. In tropical countries, where shelters may be erected with space, greenery and informality, it is often the case that special arrangements are made to permit family, friends, visitors to be present, even to supply food to patients, and perhaps to do simple chores like changing beds. The family circle *enters* the hospital.

Similarly the lack of supply of fully trained doctors, especially in rural areas, means that initial first aid, simple supply of routine medicines (e.g. anti-malarial) and preliminary diagnosis, is administered by often highly competent nurses and intermediary medical practitioners with good, short, limited training. They screen and if necessary send patients off to more sophisticated hospitals. They may have a few beds in their charge. In Canada a beginning has been made to licence nurse practitioners to act as first line family doctors, and to perform duties in emergency wards and drop in clinics..

Organisation and therapy often go hand in hand; nowhere is this more evident than in the poorer world where circumstances force innovative methods. In Madurai, India Dr. Govindappa Venkataswamy runs charity eye hospitals as businesses. He charges for one-third of its operations, and conducts the rest free. (I myself in another country was charged for an intervention on the grounds that his would enable another patient to be treated without charge.) It runs an assembly line style strictly limited to operations for cataracts: nothing else. Through its methods sight is restored to 250 patients a day, or 65,000 a year. It is planning international expansion as an enterprise to enable it to fund extended operations in India.

It may well be that, ancillary to general medical practice, medicine would be more efficient and yield more substantial results if such institutions took care of well defined and open to routine procedures, rather than in general hospitals, and probably through direct patient access as well as referrals.

At the other end of the diagnostic trail, in industrialised countries, in city neighbourhoods as well as in rural districts, local clinics staffed by diagnostic and preliminary aid nurses, male and female, can take much of the burden off the expensive hospitals, and keep patients close to, and possibly in, their homes. Nowadays with computer links to family physicians and specialists, every element of intervention can be recorded and supervised, (a) by a qualified resident doctor in the clinic, and (b) by a patient-chosen family physician. The recording of a patient's treatment and diagnosis by both specialists and other care givers in a shared computer system is being adopted far too slowly. What works in the highly specialised medical environment can be applied to the diagnosis and treatment of those in what is now the prison system.

In Uganda internet connections link rural care givers with the central hospital system so that information and directions can e given and diagnosis refined. And in Britain robots have been developed to undertake tasks including surgeries thus both saving on support staff and, for some tasks, avoiding human error.

Bio-medicine is becoming more and more expensive, less and less cost effective. Enormously complex million dollar machines become necessary not only for treatment, but more and more for diagnosis. They wear down, turn out sometimes to be inaccurate, become outdated, so that their shelf life is relatively short and expensive replacement continuous. The simpler, more direct and hands on intuitive approaches of the poorer world are often more effective.

At the same time the application of technology in aid of the physician's direct contact with the patient is woefully inadequate. What *The Economist* has called the "no computer virus"[96] stalks doctors' surgeries, now in fact offices. Piles and piles of paper records take up the space, each to be hand retrieved. A few savvy doctors have this on immediately searchable computer programmes. A few more have the ability within their own office of pulling up the results of X-rays or eye-scans for immediate careful examination. Most still depend on courier or inadequate fax to move data from one doctor to another. In some geographically challenged places computer connections enable specialists to advise surgeons during operations, but this is rare within urban complexes. The documentary records of retired doctors are in practice unavailable yet can be crucial in diagnosis and in avoiding repetitive testing procedures. Despite notorious hitches, widespread record and data digitalisation and internet connectivity are at last gaining ground.

Mobile technology would make it possible even now for a doctor or diagnostic nurse to get out of the office and into a patient's domestic environment, with immediate access to the full record including images, and to specialist advice where necessary. The expense would be substantially offset by the scale of the production of the equipment, the time saved for both therapist and patient, and efficacy of communication and more detailed observation. Even the monitoring of the health of those who deliberately choose to be homeless would be feasible.

Even more to the point, if the clinical nurses can include house visiting, which should be practicable in neighbourhoods, they can introduce a dimension of diagnosis which is now almost totally lacking in "advanced" countries -- the first hand contact with the client's domestic environment. It is generally agreed that a "holistic" view of the patient is desirable, though not necessarily as defined by "holistic" practitioners, who themselves deal primarily with body and mind as presented in office discussion, and seldom with total life styles based on observation. How conventional doctors can prescribe treatment for many illnesses without first hand contact with living arrangements, observing daily activities, even knowing more about the workplace, beats me. In developing countries such knowledge is almost inescapable.

Almost everywhere family doctors are under pressure as their colleagues become specialists. Well trained diagnostic nurses, available for both office and house visits, alone or in clinics, can take much of the burden from them.

Similarly in so-called sophisticated countries, the seriously handicapped, pseudonymically dubbed "challenged", are being moved out of institutions back into society. For the physically handicapped the adjustments seem to be largely in place -- more awareness in commerce, industry, shopping malls; apartments constructed for their needs; newly formed communities. But for the mentally "challenged" this is not so general. Some, with initial assistance from a social worker, manage quite well. Others are challenged not only by their disability but by sheer poverty (which may be alleviated by the Guaranteed Income advocated in Chapters XV and

XVI. And yet others, in distressing numbers, sleep under bridges, beg, wander the streets confused and in rags, until picked up, with a bit of relief, by the police. That kind of "solution" is sheer cruelty. Thoughtful philanthropists have created villages with stand-in parents for orphaned children. Surely something of the kind can be devised for those who cannot live in our society, through no fault of their own.

The aged who are well off in finance and relatives, can manage through individual choices including well-run homes with maximum independence. But at this time it is unrealistic to expect the indigent and lonely to do the same; they are at the mercy of good and bad operators. And it is, under present circumstances, unrealistic and damaging to expect those families which exist for them to take the aged into their own home, coping with Alzheimer's, seeing mental deterioration day by day, keeping a close watch on wanderers, changing the incontinent. Parents have the responsibility to bring up their own children, and many have to do this while engaged in two or more jobs. Some try very hard, but it can be a recipe for disaster. Institutional arrangements are unavoidable. They require long-term re-thinking, especially for those who are not able to afford to pay themselves. (Paradoxically, the increased creative non-employment that I advocate, coupled with guaranteed income, may make the home environment more adaptable to the care of the infirm, the unstable, and the elderly.)

Personally, if I were to face such institutionalisation for myself I would favour mixed institutions, composed of units each catering to a different set of circumstances. I would not wish to be segregated into a home "for the aged" (though that may be necessary!), defined as such, and patronised as such. I would miss the mix of individuals who constitute society. I would opt for something like a village, yet close to urban facilities (if I were mobile). Parts of the village for fellows like me, parts for the physically disabled, parts for the mentally disturbed, parts for day to day workers, parts for a community clinic, parts for orphans, parts perhaps for the alienated juveniles – all these "parts" mixed up with about fifty per cent, let us say, without any noticeable problems,and the other fifty per cent struggling with their handicaps and illnesses. Speaking for myself, I want to be in contact with youth, for I find that rejuvenating and challenging.

Within such a community I would like to see the segmentation modified through service. There are roles to be performed by each of the categories, there are self-improving and self-reinforcing tasks to be done. Almost every single kind of disability can be turned around and redefined to become useful to others. (In the city where I live there are, for example, two private restaurants, one of which trains individuals with mental limitations to work effectively as cooks and waiters and cashiers; and another which trains ex-convicts. Both have a high success rate in occupational placement.[97]) The elderly can help the young, the mentally disabled escort the physically disabled, both young and old can perform work – often as volunteers - in the clinics, library, other services, and so on. If they have learned to use their creative abilities in Youth Maturity Institutes, then they can have creative recreations (other than Bingo, computer games and the TV) to enjoy.

I would like to touch upon an increasingly significant aspect of therapy, which is the role of alternative therapies. In my sceptical mode I see most of them as unproven, possibly of great value, and sometimes dangerous. One of the confusing realities is their sheer number, the confusing array of differing techniques and claims. More and more, individuals resist the biomedical model, psychiatry, and psycho-analysis for therapy, and search for other modes.

Sometimes the search is based on weak ideological premises, uninformed, desperate and dogmatic. In my view, this applies to the proposition, for example, that "natural remedies, because they are natural, are better than manufactured ones." As a general rule, this cannot be. For example, acetylsalicylic acid (A.S.A.) is a compound found in willow bark, the latter frequently used in folk remedies. Scientists discovered that A.S.A. was one of the active ingredients in the bark, and were able to manufacture pure compounds. In the decades that followed, much was learned about A.S.A., including its side effects as well as its benefits.

The difference between swallowing A.S.A. tablets and absorbing willow bark is that with A.S.A. you know much more about what you are getting, and you know that whatever effects it has can be attributed to A.S.A. With willow bark the ingredients are complex and mixed. There is more than just A.S.A. If something goes wrong you do not know for sure what ingredient is responsible; and because there are many compounds involved the chances of something going wrong are increased. This is true of all natural products, save those which are manufactured into purity. So, inherently, they are less, not more, controllable than manufactured pills.

The components of reputedly beneficial natural and folk medicines are far from being totally studied. What is it about garlic? ginseng? (I happen to consume both). We know something, but not very much. There are thousands of such remedies available, some still to be brought to the attention of science. It would be foolish either to reject these out of hand or to assume as a matter of faith that they do what we expect them to do without other effects.

The role of alternative therapies is even more complex. Men and women must be in charge of their bodies. They cannot simply hand them over to specialists. It is impossible for them to know all they must know to make decisions, so they must turn to specialists for knowledge, and then try to make their own judgements. The vast explosion of data through search engines inevitably contains misinformation or explanatory phrases which require study and evaluation which the ordinary citizen is not equipped to judge. Often the information is contradictory or in its simplification omits essential qualifications. Schools are starting to grapple with this issue as we would hope would Youth Maturity Institutes. I hope readers of the manifesto are both accepting and sceptical.

With exceptions, the more desperate people are, the more they search. The more insoluble their problem is, the more desperate and searching they are likely to be. Handbooks of alternative therapies list hundreds of them. Some, like acupuncture, have been drawn partly into mainstream medicine, though in my opinion sometimes with modifications (shortness of training time and complexity of analysis) that may detract from its original efficacy. Others have no college of supervision, have their basic premises (e.g. those of chiropractic) challenged and competed for by other schools, or require absolutely no training. It seems easy for practitioners of such arts to skirt the law by not claiming to practice "medicine".

The most dramatic examples are those which deal with the mind and the emotions. Alternative magazines must list thirty to forty competing approaches to emotional, spiritual, personal healing, disguised as "counselling", including family, marriage, and personal counselling. The "success rate" is seldom if ever reliably measured by controlled methods. Some unethical clinics create dependencies and use mind control. Individuals in this kind of trouble are extremely vulnerable and open to suggestion. With exceptions that are unfortunately difficult to identify, they can reinforce the very problems they tackle and create others. There is nothing so dangerous to the persona as the half-knowledgeable interference with the mind..

Yet the need is clearly there. If they are working from a massive data base of ignorance, so too, when it comes to the mind, does conventional medical science. It is not surprising that individuals, coached by the media and by the cultural climate of problem reinforcement, are anxious, depressed, hurt, and desperate to find both remedies and *explanations,* turning from one model to another in an endless quest.

Meanwhile, our poor world. It may be that the Youth Maturity Institutes will enable individuals to be more secure in their judgements, and that knowledge will, most probably, improve dramatically. Certainly there now massive increases in our disciplined knowledge of the brain. In the meantime, however, the medical clinics I have proposed above might very well open their doors to selected alternative approaches. This would at least give an opportunity to relate differing approaches one to another, to monitor, and to learn, as well as giving patients more freedom of choice.

We must now be more deliberate in bringing crime and illness together. There are three strands to this exercise.

Both crime and illness are culturally defined. Neither are defined by nature, although we have been accustomed to thinking of illness as a natural pathology. An illness, disease, has to be identified (however unscientifically), named, and culturally recognised as requiring some remedial action, from isolation or banishment of the victim to therapy. Each decade brings the recognition of new constellations of symptoms which were there all the time but which hitherto did not come into this category. Repetitive Movement Disability Syndrome (have I got the name right?) is one of the latest. Some forms of aberrant behaviour are regarded as eccentricities, some as illnesses, some as misdemeanours if not crimes. There is a great deal of variation amongst the populace as to what fits what categories. Sometimes the definition is therapy-driven. For example, new drugs such as Prozac make it possible to define non-extreme depressions as remediable illnesses. If a medicine changes something to do with the body that we don't particularly like, then that something b becomes not a nuisance but an illness.

There has always been a cross-over between crime and illness. The long and the short of it is that some would say that *any* anti-social act is evidence of a disturbance that can be thought of as illness. The issue then becomes, can it, ought it, to be treated, and how, and with what chance of success? Not very different from the way we try to deal with AIDS.

Then there are those illnesses that are brought about by deliberate risk-taking -- smoking, drugs, alcohol in excess -- until they become addictions. Insofar as they start out deliberately as a matter of choice, they can be fingered as having a criminal component. And are not some criminals *addicted* to their crimes, like a drunk or a smoker?

It seems as though the definitions of crime and illness may be in process of merging. If this results in better attention to therapy for offenders, so much the better. Smokers[98], who, knowing the consequences, start smoking, are sick criminals. So are those who *start* taking drugs, robbing, gambling, using violence, and those who are addicted to beating wives or pick pocketing.

Even now, and the more so as the merging proceeds, there are major similarities in the handling of defined crime and defined illness, of which the most notable is institutionalisation. The amelioration of institutional approaches and the treatment of "crime" as a tort, and repetitive "crime" as an illness will bring the two sets of remedies even more closely together.

Crime and illness are destined to coalesce. That, indeed, is the civilised way. Let us hasten the process.

2012Postscript

- The issue of violent crime carries over from education where in the proposed Youth Maturity Institutes the whole child is being trained. In that context the propensity towards violence can be discovered and treated early as a psychological and social illness.

- The excuse that obsession with TV violence of Mixed Martial Arts or the competitive destruction o trucks is cathartic holds no water as it gives both youths and adults the justification that violence is alright.

- Why? Violence makes money from drug dealing to ice hockey.

- Another area of health concern which is amenable to legal control consists of noise pollution. I discuss this in connection with youth behaviour but it extends much further. Some regimes do indeed limit noise levels in the work place, hospital areas or residential districts. Enforcement is up against the practical difficulty in many instances of having an investigator on the spot with appropriate measuring instruments. Hearing damage occurs when there is prolonged noise over 80 decibels. Commonly suffered levels are nevertheless level scan be 115 decibels for leaf blowers, 120 decibels for North American emergency vehicles, 124 decibels or chain saws, 90 decibels in fitness clubs, up to 115 in night clubs and 90 to 125 in rock concerts. Other work place levels are just as high. Workers usually have ear protection equipment, but the problem lies not only for them but for the general public which is exposed to the pollution[99].

- Even death itself has become an entertainment. Witness media reports of death and injury from car crashes or gang shootings with journalists vying for the most "intimate and real" story and scenes of weeping friends and relatives invading their privacy in the name of news.

- There are many instances in which incarceration brings reform. However the evidence is overwhelming that prisons are universities and workshop seminars[100] of crime, and curiously often are helpless to prevent the continuing existence of crime within their own walls. Clever and rich gang leaders are known to continue to conduct their own operations while inside prison.

- Pinker, Steven. *The Better Aspects of our Nature: How violence has declined,* New York Viking 2011. Civilian violence has declined he says but is still rampant..Domestic violence unreported?

- Munchem, Robert. *A History of Violence: From the end of the Middle Ages to the present.* London, Polity, 2011 Suggests that action and crime novels have given young men to indulge in fantasies without committing them

VIII – Diversity Within Community

What we are dealing with here is of critical significance for the innovative dynamics which, in chapter II, we discovered to be crucial if any change, including reformist change, could proceed with efficacy. Diversity, *provided there is communication between the cultures,* increases the size of the cultural capital from which to draw concepts which can be recombined for innovation. This is the context in which our discussion must proceed and it inserts a distinct value judgement, that diversity is to be recognised, promoted and protected.

The significance of communication between individuals in differing cultures is a major variable which must somehow be taken into account without destroying the supportive value of those sets of beliefs and values, subject to the emergence of global ethics.

In contemporary large-scale societies it is common for the individual to feel "lost", little more than a tiny atom in a national or global universe over which he or she has no control. Just as worrying, there is a feeling of helplessness, an inability to influence the course of events. This is a relative matter. Someone in much smaller sixteenth century London, especially if arriving from the countryside, had to find a way, to adjust, and without doubt felt a small spoke whose task it was to attach himself to the large wheel.

It is this feeling which inhibits conscious moves towards our brighter world. We leave it to the politicians. But we have already noted that individuals *do* have power. Time and again in this argument I will be referring to ways to identify that power, and to make it count.

The human psyche has ways of counter-balancing such impersonalisation. In North American culture, and increasingly in other large scale conurbations, therapists lead the way in demanding that we "know ourselves", that we try to understand who we are and how we as individuals got there. As a result of therapy, or because of their own inner strengths (which were in culture before most modern therapy was invented), many individuals do find their way to a personal balance. They use their inner tensions to spur themselves to action, whether that be politics, warfare, entrepreneurship, intellectual activity, loving or isolated meditation. These and similar values enter into the profiles of culture and their individual demand schedules.

The other methods of "finding one's self" and counter-balancing the alienating effects of atomisation existed long before contemporary therapy, which mostly ignores them. In parenthesis it may be observed that traditional societies have been rich in therapies that are oriented to the most powerful of the everlasting methods, namely identification with community. Humans place so much value on identification with others that it may be regarded as biologically induced and culturally defined. Individuals who are so self-reliant or so troubled that they do not want to associate with others we regard as aberrant, eccentric, driven, or emotionally disturbed, states sometimes justified by resultant religious fervour or worldly success.[101]

Two methods I distinguish are the reinforcement of links within a specific culture, and the entry into group-associations. (I use the phrase "group-association" because the groups are not necessarily formally organised. A regular bridge party may serve the purpose as well as a Rotary Club meeting.)

The neglect of much therapy to take this into account is curious and only partly explained by another phenomenon. Throughout known history, but very much increasing in scale nowadays, is the drive to *escape* the group or culture of origin. Individuals express their maturity, adult independence, risk taking, and curiosity by moving *away* from the parental family, more and more into paths that are strange territories to the mother and father. While some children opt for some form of continuity today, many do not. It has been noted that some young people, after nervously experiencing the wider world,, return to the family nest for security. Some regard this as a case of delayed maturity, discussed in earlier chapters.

The majority it seems prefer the adventures of the wider world. This is made evident in the explosion of youth travel and back packing in foreign lands. In 2006 a BBC international poll found that 80% of youths between

15 and 17 inclusive were of the opinion that they should have the *right* to live in any country they chose. Such a finding bears upon our later discussion of the role of the nation State.

The phenomenon is a well known source of strain amongst, for example, Asian families with children growing up in Europe or the Americas, though some Asian families are most adept at redefining and retaining old ties with new practical functions. Asian diasporas are a major source of trading and personal links between countries.

Early students of development suggested that the breakdown of the family and traditional culture (particularly in its religious aspects) was not merely a concomitant but a *necessary* condition for urbanisation, globalisation, industrialisation and economic maturity. They may be forgiven for being wrong. Such breakdowns were at most temporary results of those processes. Where individuals had the psychological and cultural means, they took steps to *re-invent* affinities and groups. From the 'sixties on travellers on airlines between Canada and Europe found themselves in the midst of young people in their teens, who had lost immediate connections with their forbears abroad now returning to their ancestral locations to reinvent family ties and learn their languages of family origin.

Nevertheless perhaps therapy is recognising or suggesting, by concentrating on the individual persona, that individualisation is an evolutionary trend. I cannot be sure that this is wrong. But for my part I suggest two things: if we are to influence the direction of evolution, we do not want that trend to be a total outcome. We do not want such a trend because in its extreme position it is the epitome of selfishness and of the denial of the validity of the other. There is also considerable evidence that the opposite is occurring. As many people become better off, they devote increasing proportions of their income to group identity and to ceremonial such as Carnival or marriage or identification with sport.

Paradoxically we do not want a society in which individuals have to feel uncomfortable in themselves when they decide to be isolated for positive reasons, to be loners. And we do wish to place a monopolistic value on the adaptability of individuals to move from one culture or sub-culture to another for such flexibility is one mark of a dynamic society.

One of my earliest strong impressions of the United States was the flexibility and adaptability of individuals moving from one kind of work to another, and from one part of the country to another, and the way in which society and employers sometimes tried (not always with success) to smooth such transitions. At one time it was also a characteristic of the British Commonwealth, at least for its white citizens, who could move almost seamlessly from one country to another, a characteristic that I personally felt was destroyed with the growth of the trappings of nationalism and the realization that to be a

New Zealander in Canada was no longer a smooth transition.[102] The Commonwealth is an example of the trend to make severe distinctions between residents and citizens[103].

Faced with the influx of "foreigners" who have different ethics, beliefs and behaviours. States are finding ways to homogenise the new populations. Multiculturalism in Canada has its limits: female circumcision is a crime as is acting according the tenets of terrorist jihad. France has gone so far as to outlaw the use of religious emblems in school dress and is fighting the *burka* and head scarf[104]. President Sarkozy made it clear. We wish to maintain our culture intact and anyone coming here must comply with our values. Swiss citizens do *not* have the right to retain their language of origin if they move from one canton to another, but must receive their services and conduct official business of the language of their new canton.

Understandable though they are and legitimate *in extremis* such attitudes fly in the face of history and need to be balanced with the desirability, from a dynamic and innovative viewpoint, of diversity. Centralised France has a long history of mixed populations – Franks, Huns and many others were among the founding fathers and mothers. It is also a country where religious persecution – Huguenots and Cathars for example – did damage to innovative activity. In the case of the Huguenots both Switzerland and Britain benefited from the enforced migrations.

It is not accidental that, faced with the issues of ethnic policy and their tendency to create laws to solve problems, governments are suddenly faced with questions the answers to which they take for granted but cannot define. Who and what are Britons, French, Canadians, Americans or Germans? The fact is that all those peoples and inhabitants of all other countries except some small Pacific islands have had mixed heritages from birth (Even major armies were often composed of soldiers of differing languages and ethnicities in the earliest empires) and contain social groups with quite different values and practices. It could be argued that an English plumber, farmer, pop singer or doctor has more in common with say German or Dutch plumbers, farmers or doctors than between their own compatriots of many other occupations.

The purpose of this chapter, however, is to look more directly at the issues of community and association in themselves.

Humanity is characterised by the fact that its communities, brought together by descent, then reinforced by the needs of material survival and defence, were and are never totally self-bounded. The earliest boundaries, and those of the most isolated tribes, were marked by distrust of strangers, but also, as sophistication increased, by elementary exchange, and the capture of territory, land, humans -- in other words, contact that implied some movement across the boundary. This led early anthropologists to seek for information about the relative force of internal evolutionary innovation on the one hand, and diffusion on the other. The diffusionists tended to win the day

In the present context diffusion is inescapable[105]. Community is still defined by boundaries, but those boundaries are permeable, highly variable one to another and over time. Today, one can even be a citizen member of more than one community, through marriage and migration.

It is worth noting for a moment the nature of the movement across boundaries. First there is marriage. The endogamy inherent in many communities is breaking down, and some communities, such as some Swiss communes, were by preference exogamous (the in-marrying woman retaining her family name and rights to the property of her commune of origin). In other words, there is noticeable movement of people across cultural and political boundaries.

Migration reinforces that dynamic. It does not necessarily mean a break with the community of origin; that is a matter of choice. East Indians often travel "home" to India or Uganda or Fiji, just as early British migrants travelled "home" to England, Wales or Scotland. Young immigrant children re-discover the forgotten language of their parents, and travel to meet unknown relatives; adults keep in contact with their parents and villages. Greeks and Italians are well known for returning to their home lands when they have been financially successful in other countries. Many Chinese migrants have family lineal ties all over the world -- it is not uncommon to have lineal contacts established in Hong Kong or Taiwan, Brasil, Canada, Britain, contacts that can be used for purposes of commerce, education, migrant support. Swiss abroad maintain their required military service, do not lose their communal rights, and have rights of elected representation and social security.

A recent Canadian Broadcasting Corporation documentary exemplified the dynamic adjustment of boundaries. It was about Rankin Inlet, a largely isolated Northern Arctic town. Third World immigrants, finding it difficult in the cities, are sometimes encouraged to use their skills in such places. That was the case with a Filipino woman nurse and a Somali male teacher. From almost opposite ends of the earth they created a nucleus of friendship based on the discovery and daily application of shared values derived from their native cultures and their experiences in the alien, becoming normal, frigid land. A new cultural ethnogenesis[106]?

Across the boundaries flow exchanges, commerce, and above all ideas. The religious innovations in Melanesian communities (both traditional and prophetic) owe much to adapting what is observed elsewhere. We need not spend time on the obvious force of the principle in modern-world communities.

Modern communications, when present, facilitate movement across and within the boundaries[107]. Much commentary has stressed that this moves in the direction of a single global culture (perhaps American dominated). Yes and no; not quite.[108] Ease of communication permits several things. There is a certain core of ideas which becomes global. Slowly but surely all parts of the world arrive at inter-communication. That is, one may communicate from or to a culture without leaving the home culture. As communication becomes faster and less expensive, there is a move towards equalisation; there is no *technical* reason even now why a village in the depths of Burkina-Faso cannot be in touch with the World Wide Web or the Paris stock exchange. Funds for the infrastructure are not sufficiently there now[109], but that is only a matter of time. The technique and *matériel* of communication will be global; so no doubt will be the language. The village in Burkina-Faso will have its culture dramatically changed in more complex ways as its inhabitants make their cultural choices. It will also have the resources, the education, to reinforce and protect those elements in its way of life that it values, and to call on other communities with like-minded priorities. And it can even inform people of other cultures about what its life and ideas are like.

Wealth and communication change culture, there is no doubt of that. But whether it is to the detriment or in reinforcement of culture is a matter of choices. These will not be uniform, in just one direction. It will give individuals more power to make political, commercial and personal choices. Take note.

British Columbia Indian communities, mostly destitute and thoroughly demoralised during the 'twenties to 'fifties, have revived their traditional spirituality and have expanded ceremonial. They are in fact exporting and diffusing elements of their ideas to others, through art and spirituality. There has been an explosion of innovative art based on traditional ideas and modern techniques, far beyond tourist junk, such as major art collectibles with adaptations into high style clothing and jewellery. Political skills have been honed, languages re-learned, education adapted, all with pride in community, expressed as nation-hood[110]. In New Zealand Maori art, politics and language have thrived over the past thirty years to the point at which Maori is taught in schools and the country has an associated name, Ao-tea-roa. Southern Africa is a-bustle with revival in the midst of its poverty.

In Europe, think of the re-invention and restitution of community-reinforcing ceremonials. Medieval football in Florence, the parish-competitive horse races of Siena, carnival in Basle, ethical bull fighting in the South of France, Romany lore, all at one time forbidden or predicted to die. The list can be extended throughout the world, wherever people have resources to expand what they believe in, and the choice to direct their energies. Some activities spread. The dragon boats of Hong Kong, which are community-oriented there, have given rise to associations and international tourneys from Vancouver to Germany, in each case with its own community roots as well as the global spread.

At another level, sociologists have long measured associations and participation in them. Every major centre of population has a myriad. It is a primary sociological task to map the cross-hatching of individual membership, relating it to other cross-hatching themes such as income, religion, cultures, professions, education, and the like. Think of the groups to which you in some way belong or with which you identify; and think of the additional ones you could belong to or identify with. This is an urbanisation, modernisation, phenomenon, applicable in all dynamic parts of the world.

Behind these phenomena are straight-forward principles. People value association with others and gain reinforcement of their own values and self-identity by doing so. The personal linkages created give some status to the otherwise helpless. In the massive-scale world, they provide small-scale fields of activity. The individual plays within a set of rules, dealing with limited possibilities, rather than the hugeness of infinite choice. Those who like to follow can follow, those who like to lead have the chance to do so. One can be influential instead of kow-towing to the boss. Perhaps, even, ideas are welcome. And one, usually, can get out at will[111].

Many do. They change their loyalties. Even communities find this. Loyalty to community is being re-defined. More and more, where it is retained, it is a matter of choice. In the mobile flexible world of the present, even in hitherto untouched areas of the Third World, communities cannot *bind* their young people however much they sometimes try. There was once a dictatorial, authoritarian aspect to communities, a restrictive approach to norms, morality, and activity that is no longer appropriate in this world of choice. The primary exception to this trend comes about when religion and politics are strongly intertwined creating an ideological mystique characteristic of martyrdom. Many, especially in rural areas, are finding that their existence is threatened as their economies are no longer viable in the older way. Communities now must *earn* their loyalties.

But communities are far from dead. They are being redefined. The old parishes and communes of Europe continue, notably in Italy, Germany and Switzerland to say nothing of the Balkans.

In modern cities without centuries of history, neighbourhoods begin to have community meaning. Such a city is Vancouver, only about 150 years in age, where geography creates many niches, separated by microclimates, ravines, coastline, mountains, highways, ethnicity and lifestyle. Developers and planners touch such neighbourhoods at their peril, defensive associations lobby and protest Where neighbourhood and ethnicity coalesce festivals and celebrations turn into newly formed tradition. In older cities such as London or Paris immigrant populations add to the mix of identities, with strong definition. In rural areas, small towns and villages, afraid of dying, turn their creative thoughts to new ways of establishing continued viability. Sometimes they are at least temporarily destroyed by incorporation into suburbia

-- the Netherlands seem like one huge suburb, with commuters criss-crossing like tribes of ants, yet I doubt if what are in effect suburban neighbourhoods entirely lose touch with their historical individuality. The United States and France, both considered to be "melting-pot" nations, are honeycombed with definably different communities and neighbourhoods.

Modern technology does not necessarily interfere with their creation. There are small communities in the United States literally built around the reality of cyberspace. Though small as communities they are the location of firms dealing with computer hardware and software production. The homes, local government, hospitals, emergency services, library and schools are linked by fibre optic cable and e-mail, binding them.

Per Norback, in his contribution to the 2004 World Utopian Competition, describes his initiative in binding together the youth of the small community of Vallentuna in Sweden through e-mail. The focus was to use the tool as a way of discussing local policy issues. E-mail bound together young people who found they had a common interest in their community, an interest that was merely dormant before. In discussing issues they formulated policies and created a "non-political" political party which elected a member to the local council.[112]

The sense of belonging may affect only a small proportion of the community/neighbourhood population in normal times. Indeed another characteristic of many is internal divisiveness, fighting over what the community means, arguments over policy and definition. When it comes to cultural self-expression, thinking about the future, communities of the new kinds have major creative impulses. Cultural events are used as identifiers, or perhaps there is the revitalisation of a declining neighbourhood. They are not necessarily organised into formal local government. There is a spontaneity which brings the notions of community and association together. There is also a perfect opportunity for power trips, the kind of domination and argumentation that the involved individuals could not express in large firms or major government.

Such developments are not necessarily progressive. Many are the communities which resist, for example, the placement of therapeutic institutions in their midst -- half-way houses, homes for the mentally disturbed, "social housing" for the poor, drug rehabilitation centres, abortion clinics. Communities, however, are not all-powerful, and should not be. There needs to be a counter-balance to the potential of communities to insist on total conformity. One of these, of course, is the existence of higher levels of government, about which more later. Another is the increasing ability of individuals to move to and live in the communities of choice, and to leave those they find unpleasant. A third is, to some extent, the growth of varying democratic practices, though these can create rigidities and do not always ensure liberty, and may exclude newcomers from participation. (Witness the urban Swiss commune which insisted that a building, ten centimetres higher than code allowed, be restructured or torn down......)

At present many parts of the world are going through a revival of the bane of ethnic intolerance, even "cleansing". This is not a part of my personal view of the desirable new world. My personal delight in ethnic variation is tempered by my realisation that there are limits to my own tolerance, and reinforced by the functional value of ethnic difference under appropriate conditions. Ethnic difference is the most visible indicator of cultural difference, though not the only one since class, wealth and occupations play their part as well. It is an indicator that is grossly misleading, in that cultural differences that are just as strong exist in modern societies without ethnicity, in its popular sense, being a factor at all. The lumberjack and the doctor, the fisherman and the rock musician, the academic and the money market trader, each have ideas, symbols, values, modes of behaviour -- that is, aspects of culture -- which are unique to their colleagues, which they do not share easily with other citizens. In any given society they constitute at least sub-cultures. In other words, cultural differences permeate society, often without consciousness of what those differences are. Ethnicity in its full sense is only one such cultural binding and differentiating force but it gets the major part of political attention, replacing the Marxist approach to class difference.

Furthermore, nowadays, none of the cultures are bounded within nation States. Patterns of migration and ex-colonial boundaries have resulted in kaleidoscopic patchworks. International travel and communication link members of most sub-cultures together in world-wide webs[113].

Within the patchworks and the global networks, differences continue in modified forms. An anthropologist cannot assume that Sicilians in London, New York and Toronto have the same culture and patterns of behaviour as their forebears in Sicily, or indeed as each other. Each experience brings about a cultural variant. If one were to count cultures one would find that, along these lines, the number of cultures is growing fast, possibly exponentially.

Contrary to popular belief and ideology, political nationalism in the nineteenth century was less a liberation of "national cultures" than a centralising move to control variation. Centralising France, Italy, the Netherlands, England, Prussian Germany, forced in varying ways the adoption of a single language upon culturally and linguistically different communities. In France, Italy, Spain, Canada (even excluding the Québec issue) and Britain, to name just five countries, there are enormous resentments which continue, and sometimes grow, to this day. Only in the early 1990's did Alsace gain the right to teach Alsatian dialect in schools, or expand the teaching of High German, rights which are still fiscally restricted by the centralised organisation of French education. In all countries where nationalism was the rallying cry there are wondrous literatures, often comic and satirical, about the ways in which the dominant elites reinforce their arrogance with blindness.[114]

Indeed, I would go so far as to say that the difference between a State and a tribe is that the latter is culturally uniform, whereas the former gains its character through the ways in which it includes within itself populations of *different* cultures. Anthropologists who look for the processes that created States from tribes identify economo-technical factors, such as the administrative requirements of irrigation or of settled agriculture. My theory is complementary rather than competitive with such explanations. It holds that, for whatever other cause, tribes found themselves in the position of having to handle other kinds of people in sufficient numbers so that an administration was forced upon them. Bantu "kingdoms" are a case in point since they were historically observed in a phase of large land expansion, driven by northern forces to move onto land already settled by others. Their military organisation had to deal with the original settlers as part of their expanding society, and used regimental outposts for control, defence, aggression, keeping rambunctious young men occupied, and asserting cultural inter-dependence. The increasing scale and demands on wealth gave rise to forms of taxation and fiscal organisation.

To the extent that I am right, ethnic cleansing is a return to tribalism, a nasty glitch compromising our move to the world we want. Where it dominates it slows the rate of dynamism and innovation, as I advocated in Chapter II.

The events of the 1990's, continuing into the present century, have shown us the serious dangers that cultural intolerance can produce. Much of this has been reinforced by memories of past struggles which have gained the status of ideological myth and need to be put in context in the educational system[115]. We may have partially overcome the extreme excesses that typified Nazism. But catastrophes in Rwanda, Darfur, ex-Yugoslavia, Chechnya, show that we cannot be complacent; that where ethnic difference is kept in control by central government alone, chaos follows.

In all instances the fierceness that erupted are fuelled by geographical confusion and land claims, and the historically false notion that ethnic difference justifies a new national State. In the countries I have mentioned, such purity is impossible to achieve without repressive and horrendous ethnic cleansing. The ideology the leaders have used is historically and socially false. Nation States gain their identity and strength *from the ways they handle the reality of differing cultures within their borders.* The United States is "American" in large part because of the way it handles large populations of ethnically differentiated immigrants and centuries-old settlers[116]. France is French because of the way it handles language and the Alsatians, Bretons, Languedociens within its borders. Britain is Great Britain, largely because of the Welsh, Irish and Scots, and even more, the Cornish and Yorkshiremen, and now the waves of immigrants. Switzerland is Switzerland because....... Canada is Canadian........ And so on.

In later chapters I will be defining a changed role for the nation state in the context of global government. In this concept the State has more the character of a regional administration. Should that come to pass it should be less of a problem for areas like Alsace or Catalunya to be politically separated from France or Spain.

Extreme ethnic hostility used to be blamed on poverty. It is still a major factor, for example in the Middle East. But it has a great deal to do with land claims and with the mind. Land claims mix with centuries old history, and intersect with family relationships. It is noteworthy that in the most dangerous parts of Europe, the Balkans, social rivalries, competitiveness, and strict views about "honour" were and are expressed, not through the consensual problem-solving I have referred to in Chapter V, but through continued hostility and the institutionalised idea of vengeance. Blood feud, in other words. Land, sex as property, and violence constitute a potent explosive. Ethnicity becomes an excuse, not a cause. It is an excuse in which violence breeds violence, allowing the unscrupulous to attain power, to exercise brutality and repression, through the smokescreen of defending their own people by punishing the others.

The 2005 riots in France seemed initially to be ethnicity driven. But it turned out that the mostly young people involved were frustrated and devastated by their inability to rise in the socio-economic order. They were mostly NOT immigrants. Significantly they were the *children* of immigrants, their parents often successful. But French society did not accept them as such, so there was a mixture of poverty, high expectations, and ethnic discrimination. It is the same kind of frustration and denied expectation that is part of the classic model of the dynamics of messianic cults in other contexts and of Palestinian despair.

It shows that forms of multiculturalism are highly varied and not in themselves enough to be functional. I say again, there must be cross boundary communication and socio-economic-cultural exchanges to make a variant successful and to contribute to the surrounding cultural capital. The patronising stance of French political and cultural elites does not contribute well to this within their own country, although there is more success in welcoming cultural exchanges with persons who may still be counted as representing the "other". Singers, dancers, artists and writers find interaction, especially if they were born elsewhere. The exotic is praised. This is true not only of France, but of England, Italy, Germany, Toronto and Montreal.

For other kinds of people, and especially for the young who wish to be accepted as were their parents, the same societies preach, if they notice at all, "tough luck'. A result is ghetto-isation of the different young, driven almost mad by boredom and frustration and (relative) poverty. It is not accidental that it took a major hurricane to reveal this soft under-belly of poverty and prejudice in surface-happy Louisiana. The Blues are paeans to despair, not to joy, ultimately a way out and up for the creators.

Significantly, this is not new, but seems to be more intense because of legitimately higher expectations. The Blues are matched by the heart-plucking passions of fado, tango and flamenco, rooted in centuries past cultural deprivations. Spain and Portugal provided contrasts, the one with Castilian superiority over Moors and Indians (the latter not invading the metropolis), the other mass converting slaves and patronising democratic sex and miscegenation. In Britain peoples from the Caribbean, South Asia and other Commonwealth countries initially rioted, if at all, as part of the distressed countryside or urban workers. Nearly all European countries, to say nothing of the former Anglo colonies, established ghettos not only for Jews but for skilled immigrants practising trades. By the late twentieth century the descendants of such people had achieved upward mobility and contributed to all ranks of life. The ghetto did not stop external communication in such instances, but it took a long time for that to have a total effect.

It should be noted, too, that many immigrants who were excluded from normal occupations by race bias started tiny enterprises, sometimes growing into large ones. The ever present curry houses of England began with ship jumping sailors from what is now Bangladesh meeting a demand for such food by men and women returning from India in the very early days of the Raj, wanting the spicy food to which they had been introduced.[117]

Two differences between much of the past and much of the present stand out. One is that many of the ghettos used their own resources and skills to create not only expectations but success and respect. Huguenot watch makers, Lebanese traders in Africa and Jewish financiers are well known instances. A clear case has been the long term success of Chinese abroad, with their supportive networks, now, in places like Vancouver, no longer ghetto-ised but mainstream. Much the same can be said for Ismailis escaping Uganda, Armenians, Scots, Welsh and Irish. Can those from the Middle East, Africa and Latin America create a similar fate and use cross-ethnic and inter-ethnic communication to innovate and prosper? It is not generally recognized that the upper echelons of Swiss success, which is historically quite recent, made use of a high number of key immigrants interacting with a Swiss diaspora. Such connections created banking, chocolate making, watch making and cloth manufacture. If Switzerland were more open to an influx from the world, it might regain that dynamic,.

Religion, and the fables of the mind are just as potent. Serbs, Croatians, and Muslims in ex-Yugoslavia, as well as other peoples, are, depending on your criteria, themselves an ethnic hodge-podge of numerous smaller units. They also have unities of culture - the Serbian and Croatian languages differ mostly in the alphabet used and primary religious adherence. Those differences have historical roots. The central European plains were from prehistoric times the routes of invaders, who left behind them patchworks of ethnically different populations. The latest Grand Invasion was that of the Turks[118], who introduced coffee, much of Balkan cooking, a little religion (Muslims in those days were largely tolerant and non-proselytising.) Where the Turks administered, Eastern religions and the Cyrillic alphabet prospered; where they did not there was Roman Catholicism.

Again, religion is a rallying cry. It is a magnificent tool to organise the masses, and sometimes it can be regarded as causative. But in ex-Yugoslavia, a country which in recent years has been characterised by inter-marriage and religious tolerance, I doubt if religion and language would have established the current rule of force had it not been for land and the culture, especially in Bosnia, of blood-feud.

What then of our brand new world? In counteracting the excesses it is necessary to make a choice. If we believe that such excesses are an inherent part of ethnic and cultural difference, we might be well advised to do everything in our power to limit, even destroy, it and create a homogeneous, every-one-the-same global melting pot. This, at least locally, is the rallying cry of many majority ethnic populations who feel that their dominance is threatened by immigration and difference. (It is interesting to note that such populations do not use the word "ethnic" to refer to themselves, but only to minorities. In Canada we have "ethnic" restaurants, which means "of a different style", not recognising that the dominant Canadian cultures are also "ethnic".)

But if we believe that cultural difference is valuable, as I have tried to advocate, we must make clear wherein that value resides.

Cultural diversity is necessarily valuable to the desirable world *in itself.* When cultures turn in upon themselves they become a source of prejudice, false information about the value of others, dogmatism, and static control of individuals, even brain-washing. They can become fanatic and potentially aggressive if the inward turning changes to external action and expansion. We have the example of Hitlerian Germany to inform us forever more.

Once again, the indicators are at the boundary. To what degree and in what ways are there movements of ideas, values, matériel and individuals across the boundaries? If such movements are infinite, we can hardly talk about a discrete culture; it would not exist for the two parts would coincide. A culture implies some limitation of cross-boundary movement in practice, if not in ideology. A culture, or sub-culture, suggests that there is more movement in the networks within the boundary than across it. As I have pointed out, professions and similar value- and network- centred groups have such characteristics, and can be called non-ethnic sub-cultures. From this it follows that individuals can, in this world, belong to several cultures or sub-cultures at once.

That phenomenon establishes different boundaries for individuals for different purposes. What may be restrictive in one context may be opened up to communication in another. A Muslim woman's purdah may be modified by her membership in a medical professional sub-culture. It is next to impossible for a culture to have unmodified boundaries in the modern world.

Such modifications, which still allow a culture to retain its integrity, its sense of unity and of difference with respect to others, are worthwhile. They permit ideas and symbols to flow across the boundaries. They enrich the cultural pool, or capital, that is available to humankind as a whole.

A major primary benefit comes when we consider cultures to be experiments in living. No culture has all the answers to life, and never will. (The last statement follows from my premise in Chapter XIII that knowledge, by its nature, is imperfect.) Varying cultures give us an opportunity to note how others approach problems we ourselves have. We may not like what we see. But even then we are challenged to think about, to reappraise, what we ourselves do, and to evaluate alternatives. There is a sense in which the excitement and stimulus of travel can be replicated in our own cities. The enquiring mind can seek explanations for differences in norms, and perhaps learn from them. My earlier discussion of crime was influenced by the way it is handled in some other cultures.

Another fundamental benefit comes from the fact that, by definition, more cultures mean more ideas, more concepts, a greater variety of activity. To the extent that knowledge of this increased pool circulates, that is crosses cultural boundaries, the greater the rate of innovation. Cultural diversity contributes to the process.

You don't believe me? Here is a hodge-podge of examples. The Swiss chemical industry received its inaugural jump start out of the observations of Swiss in India (dyes); the watch industry from the movement of Huguenots from France; the chocolate industry from a combination of Swiss and American ideas; the metallurgical and heavy engineering from Swiss and Germans; early banking through inputs from Germany and France; aesthetics from the interplay of individuals and resources rooted in the varied Swiss cultures. How could British textiles in the nineteenth century have evolved if Britain had been an island in isolation? Diasporas, in which individuals and families have been forced into contact with other dominant cultures, created commerce that provided inter-cultural links. Asian students, driven by family values and respect for thought, outbid their less-driven North American co-students for places at computer terminals, often in their early twenties establishing new enterprises or moving on to scientific research. There is nothing automatic about such relationships and results. That is not the point. The point is that the *chances* of innovative results are higher when inter-cultural contacts take place. Once again, it is not always ethnic. Interactions and synergies between professional and discipline sub-cultures have similar effects.

Under appropriate circumstance, then, cultural diversity is to be welcomed. It is necessary for our new world. Furthermore, cultural diversity constitutes a kind of data base out of which our thoughts about the desirable future, and about how to get there, will emerge.

It is important to stress and encourage the functional rather than the dysfunctional aspects of such variance. We must not be starry-eyed. If we close our eyes to the strains of some immigration, for example, we will be disappointed and damaged. The right wing French politician Le Pen, building his career on fear and hate, was evidence of damage. Yet we must recognise that behind that fear and hate there are real problems, of which they are the symptoms.

There is a strong obligation for immigrants to understand the source of stereotypes. For this they need help. Tired, exhausted, traumatised refugees cannot be expected to absorb the theory of adjustment. Other immigrants seek the support of being with members of their own culture, a support that is often essential for survival, but thereby losing some adjusting contact with the wider society. It is not simply a matter of understanding the mechanics of shopping and dealing with authority. It is learning what words, gestures, attitudes, points of view will be interpreted as offensive -- a difficult line to convey in adjustment education, since the integrity of viewpoint of the immigrant must also be understood and respected.

By the same token, it is essential for receiving cultures to avoid a static view of what they are. Intolerant anti-immigrants, racist or not, in Britain, France, Germany, Italy, Canada, the United States...... make much of the "threat to our traditional values." To do this they must ignore history. Late twentieth century Britain does not have the same spectrum of values that applied in the nineteenth or even the early twentieth century. The values of Canada and the United States, whatever they are, emerged out of differing experiences of immigrant interplay. Americans often, rightly, puzzle over why Canadians should feel different from them. In North America, to follow the traditionalist anti-immigrant line would logically imply accepting pre-Columbian Indian cultural values and ways of life......

Too often the majority way of acknowledging respect of other cultures in their midst is to encourage "harmless cultural expression" by way of folkloric dances, costumes and foods. This again can be stereotypical. Quaint. It avoids the deeper questions. What do people want in their lives? It is never just money. Money is merely an expression for something else. What do they love? How do families enjoy themselves? What do they think of as being creative? What do they think of as being bad? What are their hopes and their nostalgias? What is it that develops pride in themselves, accomplishment, a sense of failure? How do they perceive the socialisation of children? What is the place of religion, alternative medicine, fear, in their lives? So much more.

In our new world we will make the utmost use of differing values and cultures, seeking not tolerance but *understanding*, preaching not one solution to the structures of multi-cultural society, but many. My major criticism of multiculturalism in Canada is that in some parts of the country we are satisfied with superficial tolerance and stop our thoughts long before understanding has been reached. An indication of a transformation from tolerance to understanding occurs when intermarriage takes place.

Whatever we say, increased communication will induce cross-cultural knowledge. Youth Maturity Institutes will have to encourage understandings, without preaching the adoption of different cultures; and to reveal the nature of stereotypes and the difficult realities that lie behind them. Our world will also be frank about difficulties of adjustments, identifying inner tensions, and the conflicts of values that contain the seeds of danger as well as innovation. Management of danger with minimal interference, is sometimes a tricky balance, especially when it is tempting for politicians and other leaders who dwell on the dangers to opt for simplistic solutions that bring them unthinking support in the polls. Too often they think in terms of regulation or legislation rather than dialogue and discussion.

2012Postscript

- "Nanny" governments are increasingly entering the control and regulation of phenomena which are deemed to be a threat to public health and well-being, creating new civil and criminal offences. The most publicly reported interventions occur when it is an issue of environmental damage. Food safety and labour accidents are other major areas. Yet some major activities deserve more consideration. Perhaps the most obvious would be the control of motor vehicles which cause more deaths in advanced countries than major illnesses. Strict safety rules for the construction of vehicles themselves, speed limitations, and laws intended to ensure that drivers are properly in command of their reactions and senses, are apparently not nearly enough. Citizen values, in this case the love of the car and unwillingness to pay for public transit, stand for now in the way of drastically reducing the use of vehicles.

- It is a disturbing phenomenon that the Israeli government (by no means all the Israel population) whose history has largely emerged from ghetto experiences, has created one of the world's most infamous ghettos in the form of Palestine.

- In May 2012 the Congrès annuel de la Société Quebecoise de science politique organised a workshop on the question Global justice and mobility : is there room for an ethic of emigration ? The organisers presented the following analysis for examination, an analysis which situates cultural diversity in the phenomenon of migratory acceptance and jural rights.

- "There has been a normative tension between emigration and immigration since 1948. Indeed, article 13 of the Universal Declaration of Human Rights states that everyone has a universal right to leave his country, but recognizes only the right to enter only for those who are already citizens of their country.

Thus, citizens have a right to exit and a right to enter. Others hold only a right to exit. What is more, this normative tension has been built up in international law as well. With the rise of mobility regimes in the beginning of the nineties, political thinkers have focused on immigration in order to identify the moral obligations of States that could transform the right to enter into a real universal right. But a number of authors have recently called into question the relative neglect of the right to leave   The purpose of this workshop is to explore the meaning of this turn for political theory. ... Here are some of the questions to be examined: Are the effect of individuals' mobility on those who decide to stay the same in sending countries and in arrivals countries ? Do they vary with what motivates individuals to move or to stay according to gender, to their level of education or to their sector of professional activities ? What are the standards that should be adopted to assess them ? What are the moral obligations of States toward those who decide to stay and those who decide to leave and how best to protect the rights of these individuals? What kind of international institutions does the management of migration flux require?"

  •   Along a similar vein the Department of Anthropology in the University of Sydney organised an international symposium in 2012 on Culture and Rights: Scepticism, Hostility, Mutuality. Focussed on internal multiculturalism the concerns are similar, as expressed by the organisers. "The relationship between the concept of culture and that of human rights has long been complex and contentious."On the one hand, culture and human rights can be seen as locked in a mutually antagonistic embrace. For many human rights activists, culture has been "demonised" as tantamount to "unfreedom" (Sen 1999; England 2004); culture, in this view, is a disguise through which entrenched forms of power and exploitation operate, and a way of naturalizing cultural systems that prevents people from realising their full humanity."Human rights, on the other hand, has been critiqued by anthropologists as a purported universal framing of humanity that conceals metropolitan values, epistemology and interests. Although anthropology and human rights discourse have both been challenged as the metropolitan colonisation of local identity, today the concept of human rights has become a key site of global regimes of accountability as well as a plethora of local struggles over resources, the public voice and the management of the self. As a result, moral and political capital have crystallised around human rights today as both a form of advocacy and a mode of local empowerment.

• Anthropological concepts of cultural difference and universal demands for human rights are not simply antagonistic. The contemporary linkage between global forms of governance and human rights regimes has generated its own anxieties and scepticism within the human rights world, and it is here, Riles suggests, that culture and human rights are mutually oriented towards each other. In the face of this anxiety, culture is not only a set of practices against which rights must be asserted, but culture is increasingly also the ground from which rights take on their meaning."From the point of view of culture, however, rights is the contemporary 'outside' that allows the agents of culture to intervene; to rework their own cultural fabric. In this respect, it is intriguing that rights-based perspectives represent significant competition to the long-standing role played by political economy as the outside of culture."For anthropologists the effects of this symbiotic relationship between culture and human rights can be traced at a number of different levels. The relationship between anthropology and human rights has been a key point of debate in the development of anthropological codes of ethics. Human rights, in its discursive and institutional contexts, has become another thematic aspect of anthropologists' subject matter – rights have been assimilated to culture. The capacity to participate in the dialogue between rights and culture has become integral to the political negotiation of fieldwork in many contemporary contexts, and of its ethical evaluation. It is also the primary discursive frame of a contemporary public anthropology – in the Australian context, the politics of anthropology's engagement in the broader debate about the state 'intervention' in the governance of indigenous communities is particularly revealing. Finally, the increasing interpenetration of rights-based and development-oriented forms of critical inquiry and activism has meant that anthropology's role in the social science division of labour, in both applied and teaching contexts, is mediated by rights discourse. Nevertheless, distinctively historical and political perspectives in anthropological writing have also generated substantial critiques, not only of human rights discourse, but of the ways it has been mobilised in particular social and political contexts."

• One of the pressing issues in cultural diversity is how to open up interaction with the larger society when one culture within it turns in on itself and sets up cultural exchange barriers in order to attempt the preservation of cultural purity. Such situations can arise when a group feels culturally threatened or politically powerless, or wishes to join hands with their relatives across the state's boundary. This is difficult to deal with but such attempts at isolation are doomed to failure especially in this high-tech world when youths are mostly seeking openness. And of course it is incompatible with the goal of innovative stimulus which depends on a high interactive volume of idea transmission. A conference dealing with such issues is organised by the Central European University, Budapest for 2012. Here is how the organisers analyse the issues: "Contemporary European societies have been recently characterized as having entered the age of 'super-diversity'. Migratory flows in particular have contributed to this transformation, due to the heterogeneous ethno-cultural, and religious background of present migrants, as well as their social status, age, and mobility patterns. Among the effects this transformation has brought about is the increased challenge posed to the constitutive principle of the nation-state, i.e., the assumption that identity (nation) and politics (state) can and should be mutually constituent and spatially congruent. Thus, unsurprisingly, many states have started perceiving diversity as a 'problem', potentially threatening national unity, while anti-immigration and xenophobic attitudes have experienced a rapid surge. "Existing scholarship has offered insightful critical analyses of this 'backlash against diversity', documenting therise of repressive state measures designed to limit access of new migrants to the national territory and citizenship. Other scholars have instead moved away from the idea of the nation-state, proposing either post-national solutions, which decouple the cultural (nation) from the political (state), or transnational paradigms, which implicitly discard the focus on the nation-state as not only obsolete but also politically questionable. "Yet, despite important insights from this scholarship, social and political life continues to remain largely structured by discourses, resources and institutions articulated at the national scale. "It is therefore the aim of the proposed conference to explore how 'living together in diversity' is imagined, narrated, organized, justified, and practiced within contemporary national societies. With the stress on 'in' rather than 'with' diversity we want to move away from reifying the dominant 'majority' society perspective, which assumes diversity as something 'carried' solely by immigrants and something that the 'native' society has to cope with. Some of the questions that we are interested in are: What makes multicultural societies circumscribed by state borders cohere together? What are the ways in which the nation becomes re-signified to accommodate the ethno-cultural diversity of its populace?

How do migrants position themselves in national narratives and political structures? What alternative modes and models of belonging are at work within present national societies? In which ways does the national continue to feature as a site of attachment?"The desire to preserve cultural identity within diversity is normally positive in its effects on the larger society, increasing the size of the cultural capital. When though it is aggressive and angry it emerges as a major factor in promoting violence both within and between states[119]. The 2011-12 violence between tribes competing for dominance in Syria and the difficulties in creating a secular government in Libya are to the point.

- Sometimes issues of diversity and especially the recognition or otherwise of nonconventional lifestyles or disabilities opens up the mantra of individual equality. In many contexts this should be clear. No one is justified in claiming that a person who behaves differently but within the law is any less valuable as a human being than his or her conventional peers. That though is a different statement than the assertion that all men and women are equal. They are not: in their beliefs, their skills, their education, their wealth, their status in religion, and many other vectors. We are not yet robots. Those differences are to be cherished and supported as of right. The support of diversity requires the understanding and recognition – though not necessarily approval or agreement.
- The denial of the principle of welcome diversity, despite the growth of multiculturalism in many parts of the world, especially when armed violence is dominating

316

the environment, has, together with environmental disaster, created refugee issues both within countries and internationally of truly massive proportions in this twenty-first century. The calls on international aid, ultimately paid for by citizens of other countries, has probably never been greater[120]. This is partly because of public awareness and media attention: it makes for dramatic and heart wrenching TV, And a major part of the non-material aspects of a solution is to reinforce the value of diversity.

- Cities have a special role to play in ethnic diversity. They attract immigrants who almost always in the modern world move to cities or towns rather than to rural areas for this is where they find people of their original culture and they get security and reinforcement from this. Such a characteristic of cities began in their earliest history. Cities by their nature were places of trade, and thus attracted merchants of numerous kinds. In past centuries foreign merchants were frequently licensed to live in the cities in special enclaves, with strict restrictions on interactions with the native residents. Some were permitted to control their own laws. Such practices lasted well into recent times in many parts of Asia. In Europe there were merchant districts and streets might be set aside for them, and if their practices, religious or otherwise, were considered suspect they could be confined to ghettos. Such separation of course reduces interactions and thus the innovative effects. In modern times legal ghettos are far less frequent but like attracts like and neighbourhoods created distinct ethnic characters. Since these are open to all, in addition to business and employment conditions, inter-ethnic visits and side by side living create a modicum of idea exchange.[121]

- Syria is a classic and nasty case of multiculturalism gone wrong. It has been one of the most diverse cultural and religious societies anywhere. Later we will note the archaic effects of tribalism in Syria. In this context one tribal alliance with a minority religion has succeeded in monopolising power for decades. It has institutionalised the power in the form of the Bath party to which persons of other cultures are admitted only by forswearing other allegiances and toeing the line. Cultural divisions are not linked to mutual respect and equality but to an autocratic exercise of power in which all cultures other than the politically dominant one are treated as inferior and with disdain. Revolt emerges through frustrations but does not necessarily result in democratic unity. It has too many elements of a struggle for power. Later we will be arguing for the relegation of nation states to local administration under a new form of global government. Under such a system cultures which could not get on with their neighbours could become self-administering local powers without upsetting seats on a world government or global political stability. One obvious candidate for such consideration is that of the Kurds, currently spread over Turkey, Syria, Iran and most distinctly Iraq. If it were not for the antics of the anti-Turk PKK armed violence, the patience and hopes of the Kurds should be rewarded.

- Cultural diversity means the existence of differing moralities within the larger community. We have pointed out that the simple application of a law to enforce conformity seldom works since morality implies commitment which often takes precedence over rules from above. If such a difference can be branded as "uncivilized" it behoves the superior power to understand the social and cultural imperatives which underlie the difference and to work with them to achieve change – and to understand and respect the socio-cultural consequences of such a change. This is increasingly relevant, as we have seen, as a global morality, almost a global level of culture emerges through international agreements and global change.[122]

• When we will be discussing issues of business and industrial organisation we will be noting the prevalence of dubious ethics. As it is the responsibility of both governments and the citizenry to respect the human rights inherent in diversity, so it is the responsibility of business in the role of enterprise as citizen.[123]

IX – Humans in Nature and Their Use of Resources

Humans are natural beings. They have been created by and are subject to the same processes and evolutionary patterns as the rest of nature. They are not above nature, they are part of it.

Each species has its own role and characteristic in the natural world.[124]   *Homo sapiens* is different from other species in many respects, but one stands out as relevant to this discussion.

Humanity has more culture, some would say civilization, than other species. It is uniquely equipped to think about consequences including its relations with the other species.

Decades ago Clive Bell[125] defined civilization, or culture, as humanity's control of nature, a point that most anthropologists and ecologists seem to have ignored. Think about it. If we include humanity within nature, as we must, then every bit of our thought and creativity zeroes in on adapting nature, including ourselves, to our wishes. We can't avoid it. That is our nature as part of nature. We use natural air to breathe, we absorb natural products into our bodies for sustenance, we use natural sounds to speak, we use blood cells and electrical impulses in the brain which are dependent on natural nourishment to think and create concepts, we use energy to communicate.

Our ability to *control* major aspects of nature is limited, however much our culture demands that we try. We cannot control earthquakes or volcanic eruptions and, not yet, hurricanes. Nor the weather, except perhaps indirectly through our impact on climate change, but that has not been *deliberate* control. Our attempts to control climate change are in some respects arrogant, the fallout from a technological ideology in which it seems that all things are ultimately possible if only we put our minds to them. We must determine and then accept our limitations and sometimes push beyond them.

The cry "Leave nature alone" is a non-starter. Despite our limitations we do it every moment of our lives.

It behoves us however to be acutely conscious of this symbiosis, and in accord with our goals to be conscious of the consequences and to choose to determine which consequences we want and which we do not want, which we can control and which we can't..

In my first draft I did not include this chapter, largely because if I did I would focus on humanity's environment and on the large debate on climate change, and I felt it was redundant to enter the fray. But in the midst of our concerns it seems necessary to make some points.

Many humans are choosing to protect species, which is their right. They do so because otherwise some species will disappear, and there will be a reduction in the gene pool, which they can argue persuasively is not what we want, especially since elements in the pool may have significant value in adapting or resurrecting human-valued species or their variants. Fair enough.

But wait. Throughout the history of the world species have disappeared, been wiped out. Other species have evolved to take their place. The desire to save species from extinction is a human value not shared by nature as a whole. Intervention in the processes of nature, even when the threatened disappearance is attributable to human actions is debatable. It is a *cultural* phenomenon and thus a part of humanity's behaviour in attempting to control nature, just as is humanity's action leading to the specie disappearance. And by no means all the disappearances are the result of human action *per se*.

An interesting and challenging thesis appears in the course of a novel by Martin Cruz Smith.[126] Drawing upon rapid species changes in the area of the Chernobyl disaster it speculates that one way of "saving nature" from humanity would be to cover the globe with high radiation atom bombs, leading to massive species adaptation. For that is what is happening in Chernobyl. Some species have adapted for purposes of survival and thus added to the census numbers of world species..

This is more than a fictional notion since revivals and adaptations have been observed and recorded. The history of the earth has been one of impacts from extra-terrestrial objects which have had profound effects on species forms and distribution.

A more disciplined argument for the disappearance and re-adaptation of species may be found in the work of S.R. Reice[127], who writes "catastrophes can ultimately have positive effects on natural communities. The core idea is that disturbances foster increases in biodiversity....and these in turn provide...nutrient cycling, decomposition and the increase in production of plants and animals....." Perhaps the most common example is the regeneration of plant life after fire, and I myself have seen tropical plants and trees, pulverised by volcanic explosion, return to life with a differing balance.

The upshot is that general ideological positions will not be accurate enough to help us properly. We cannot escape the fact that humans because of their intelligence bear an ultimate responsibility for what happens in the natural world, even if that control is both limited in its power and often muddled. To the extent that it is possible, each decision affecting the environment and even nature outside the immediate human environment, requires careful study and analysis. Consequences are specific to the case in hand, not derived from a generalised global axiom.

These matters involve value judgements, about which we will need to make up our minds as we seek the better world.

Half a century ago the great worry was that humanity would unleash a devastating nuclear war. That concern has now lessened but it is still there as a consequence of nuclear competition, lack of security in the handling of dangerous stock piles, and terrorist possibilities as well as the absence of a legitimate world government.. One solution will emerge through the joint creation of Youth Maturity Institutes and an effective Global Government.

What has replaced that particular worry is fear of the consequences of climate change, which are seen as a challenge to humanity's ability to control the rest of nature. That is a proper worry, confused by emotion though it may be, which should concern us not only in this generation but as I shall show in every generation which follows.

The first point to make is that the global climate has always changed dramatically as a result of forces beyond humanity's control. We know of past ice ages and global warmings. What are now tropical animals used to roam Europe. At the time of the initial overseas expansions of Dutch, British and French maritime empires, the fleets, both commercial and navy, were manned in part by refugees from the farm lands of Northern Europe, ruined by a descending mini-ice-age. Greenhouse gases and other human interventions had nothing to do with such phenomena. They will re-occur.

It appears that in the next century or so we can expect to have a non-human initiated warming globe as a predecessor to a bounce back to at least a mini ice period, *whatever humanity decides to do about it.*

I was taken aback in a web discussion group when a colleague asserted: "The earth is always in the same position with respect to the sun. It never changes". That is simply not so. Quite apart from the effect of the varying strength of sun spots with short term effects on the earth, there are much greater long term variations in what is known as the Minkovich cycles.

These describe an elliptical variation in the earth's orbit, a variable tilting in the earth's axis and a wobble as the earth spins. It has been common knowledge certainly since I was a boy that the magnetic North pole shifts over time, sometimes quite suddenly. The cycles I have mentioned take 100.000 years,, 41,000 years and 23,000 years respectively. (I wonder what would happen if the peaks of the cycles, however defined, coincided!) In between there are numerous other variations which have been the causes of both historical and pre-historical global warming and ice ages of known record.

That of course does not let humanity off the hook. We are bound by our cultures to seek to control, and we do have a responsibility. What I have written above does not in the slightest remove our own notable effects on the cycles. We know that human engendered changes overlay the natural timing. We know that changes in our behaviour will lessen the impact, though even if we stopped such effects immediately, it could take a decade or two for results to be seriously noticeable.

What we are experiencing now is quite drastic even though it is picayune by comparison which what will hit us as a result of astronomical (no pun intended) phenomena sometime in the future,

Currently the main focus is upon greenhouse gases in the form of CO2 creating holes in the "skin" of the stratosphere around the earth which then permits higher warming penetrations of the sun's rays. Humankind produces much of these emissions in the form of transport, industrial and agricultural activity. The action is pervasive – even the droppings of farm animals are major contributors. To fully control this would require many more alterations in our behaviour from getting around (the main focus now) to what we eat and how much we produce. (on the latter point the chapter on commerce and industry will be relevant.)

That cause, though major, is not the only element in the dynamics of warming. When warming begins it does other things which create a further impetus. Water begins to evaporate and the increased humidity itself has an additional warming effect. One study asserts that the increase in water vapour has had a more potent effect on warming in Europe than CO2 emissions[128].

Although many current effects are noticeable and studied there is considerable debate, unresolved, about the general global conditions and the politics of causation. From this point of view the Copenhagen world summit on climate change in 2009 and the similar one in Rio de Janeiro in 2012 were disasters, but they were also symptomatic of the state of the world's politics. Their failure must b e kept in mind when we arrive at our discussion of the role of nation states and the reform of global government. At the same time it is probable that even the most coordinated practical approaches to remedies would be far too late for this round of climate change which in some form we will have to live with.

Climate warming is fully on the way and we had better take note and get used to it. Mankind is supposed to be the most adaptable of fauna and must needs start on the road to adaptation right away.

Let me remind us all of what we know now. *It is beside the point* as to whether our culture has been causative or whether there are other additional or even more important causes which we don't yet understand. I repeat, climate warming is already here and marching forward by deliberate steps. We can do a little to mitigate it but we will not stop it. The dynamic has already set in. If there was any hope of stopping it the global political system has put paid to that idea. The question now is, are nation states ready and is the United Nations ready, to guide our adaptation?

Here are a few things we already know.

1) The Arctic is warming fast[129] and glaciers and ice packs are melting. The Northwest Passage has opened up to shipping as has the route north of Russia. This opens the possibility of exploitation of material undersea resources and

international disputes over rights and sovereignty.

2) In northern Mali fertile lands have become arid because of the retreat of the river and lake waters. Techniques are available and were being used to restore irrigation for crops but funds are lacking to make these effective. And the Tuareg occupation has stopped the efforts,

3) Australia, one of the worst polluters because of its coal industry, is now being ravaged by fires year after year. The wine industry, agriculture and city water supplies are threatened by the loss of water in rivers. There are massive heat waves.

4) Soils are becoming warmer no matter what it is being used for. In the U.K. this is causing soils to exhale more carbon dioxides[130].

5) Warmer plant growth itself creates an increase in Co2 emissions.[131]

6) African agriculture and pastoralism is being hurt by rainfall changes, affecting national gross domestic production figures.[132]

7) Countries such as China in the Sudan and South Korea in Madagascar[133], searching for more agricultural land, are reducing the availability of irrigated water to the local people in times of increasing shortage. In Madagascar this had political repercussions and a change of government.

8) California's water supply is threatening cities and agriculture becoming the major political issue in the State.

9) As countries strive to obtain control of decreasing resources for food production, hostile disputes are likely to erupt. Control of the Laos plan to dm the upper Mekong against the interests of Thailand, Cambodia and Viet-Nam is a case in point.

10) Pollution of the oceans and changes in water temperatures are causing havoc in fisheries at this moment from the coast of Africa to the Mediterranean and the Pacific. Vast stocks are threatened and the list o endangered species, many of food importance, is growing rapidly[134].

11) Some parts of the world may on balance benefit, for example as semi-tropical crops move into temperate climes (provided water and soil resources remain adequate.) It is predicted that increased rain will benefit the areas of India which have perennial water shortages. (see below for a note on the accuracy of predictions.)

12) There is increased desertification.

13) Ocean water levels are rising, largely as a result of the melting of Arctic ice (though the flow of water from rivers must be decreasing.) This threatens river deltas and the populations living there. The most dramatic example is that of Bangladesh where the residence and

livelihoods of millions are directly at stake. But other deltas will be threatened, from North America (Fraser River) and other parts of Asia to Africa and Latin America.
14) Nepal is already suffering from increased heat and water shortages which are reducing crop harvests[135]
15) One study observes that the earth is warmer than it has been for 400 years. We should note that 400 years takes us back only to the seventeenth century. This is just a mini-second wobble in the earth's long history[136].

Now we must note some major qualifications. I have listed above results of observations which can mostly be made not only by scientists but by populations. *Both* sources are subject o error. The scientific method, as we shall note in a later chapter is based upon testing existing knowledge against contradictory or alternative hypotheses and data. Each one of the observations above can be invalidated. Indeed in the years from 2008 the literature has been full of *mea culpas* from scientists admitting or being challenged for errors[137]. Yet it is unlikely that *all* of them will be amended, and so the general conclusion that the earth is going through a warming period and that some of this at least is due to human behaviour, stands for now.

Despite these results the prediction of future conditions is mightily uncertain. Although there is global information and predictions based upon those such as the rise in sea levels, many of the data link to local conditions and perils. There are still a number of scientific sceptics.[138] It is also generally agreed that predictions about the future are "notoriously unreliable".[139] This, however, is not to dispute the known trends, but only to question their accuracy in detail, scale and impact and the rate of change, which can in fact be faster, not slower, than estimated. Those who hold this opinion use it to call for more *exact* studies. As I argue when I write about the acquisition of knowledge, policies cannot wait for the certitude of complete accuracy, but must deal with what is currently known. Even the trite observation that *all* policies will have unforeseen consequences to some degree, we have to work with what we have. The excuse of uncertainty is not an excuse.

So what can we do?

First it must be accepted that *any* effective or even partially effective remedial action will be mightily expensive. All policy makers from the global government to municipal authorities must balance those costs – many of them guess work – against other demands such as the provision of Youth Maturity Institutes and reformed health services. In some instances human settlements may need to be abandoned or seriously changed in size and occupation. We must take that on the chin and not pretend, as did King Canute, that we can order the rising tides to depart.

We must draw the conclusion once again, the pessimistic one, that (a) global policies are unlikely to be achieved given the world's current political structure, and (b) even if they were, and were put into effect, it is far too late to prevent the current dynamism toward increased global warming – which is already here.

The realisation of this is slowly bringing about an overdue change of emphasis - from expensive and unrealistic prevention to local efforts to deal with climate change *effects*. In the long run humankind will have but very limited influence on terrestrial climate change, both hot and cold, and must therefore make use of its characteristic as one of the most adaptable of animals. Let's get on with the task of adapting. So what should we be attending to? As I surf the literature I find no credible *global* answers. The remedies are specific and addressed to individual locations and conditions. (This of course does not preclude example and learning across continents where conditions are similar.) Thus we have an ad hoc list which exemplify problems and possibilities and some of these mix the issue of modifying climate effects as well as addressing problems caused by climate change.

So here we go.

The most talked about is reducing dependence on fossil fuels. This is so much talked about that I hardly need to mention it. Alternatives are being explored actively, but each has its own problems apart from costs.

And new sources are discovered, as in the Arctic and Nebraska which tend to put off the most dire predictions.

Biofuels do damage to the environment including deforestation and to other desirable crop production to feed a hungry world[140]. Jean Ziegler, UN special reporter on the Right to Food, condemns biofuels as destroying food crop availability and sending prices to record levels.[141] The report from the charity Grain amplifies recent warnings from the Food and Agriculture Organization (FAO) that some biofuels produce hardly any carbon savings at all. [142] Grain says: "The numbers involved are mind-boggling. The Indian government is talking of planting 14 million hectares of land with jatropha."

Harnessing the power of tides has not yet proved cost effective, but if did so it would have fewer harmful side effects than many other solutions except perhaps on already threatened sea life. Wind power uses up land, is unsightly, but, more expensively, can be operated on the seas. Solar panels are being planned for vast desert areas – for example Sahara installations on a massive scale to enhance Europe's power supply (and we would hope Africa's although that has not to my knowledge been mentioned.)

Bands of mirrors in outer space reflecting the sun's rays back to the sun could theoretically also be a source of power as well as being used to modify the earth's climate. Their cost would be horrendous if in space in numbers to make a difference, the technology seems light years away, and any such solution would need (a) to take care of local variations in conditions and (b) possible effects on the extra-terrestrial environment.

Carbon trade schemes appear to my untutored mind to reward the polluters (The World Wildlife Fund asserts European scheme are set to fail.[143]). Carbon tax schemes seem to have a more direct impact. They should not be ignored but as I have pointed out are like shutting the door when the horses have escaped.

More directly and in ore limited ways we can take immediate measures to finance and design remedial and protective measures.

Work is proceeding to modify food crops to enable them to withstand the effects of increased temperatures and lower humidity and water supply[144]. Much of this involves genetic engineering which, despite ideological criticisms, may prove yet to be an essential element in reducing hunger, especially in the poorer parts of the world.

A by-product of climate change is in some parts of the world such as South Asia is increased rainfall and river flooding. This often involves rivers which flow through more than one country (e.g. India and Bangladesh) so that remedial actions to control the floods involve bilateral or even multilateral agreements and administration. This has proved possible but often less than efficient when it has involved hydroelectric dams upstream. Can the flood protection schemes be implemented in time, especially when such flooding meets the effects of rising sea levels in the respective deltas? The revised national and global structures advocated in later chapters are likely to be far too late to resolve the inefficiencies which are currently apparent.

Massive improvement in dykes and similar protective measures can be achieved without such complications, especially to avert rising sea levels. In the one case I have noted myself, that of the Fraser river Delta in British Columbia local, provincial and national governments have shown no sign of action while population growth is exacerbating the eventual problem. (In this case the issue is even more serious since the area is close to high tectonic activity with the probability of an eventual tsunami.) Rising sea levels and other effects of climate change could threaten the Vancouver International Airport which is located on low level land surrounded by water. There is a major residential and commercial area, the city of Richmond, which lies on drained land. A combination of rising sea level, high ride and even tsunami will eventually push back the waters of the river from the sea to its inland reaches. My reckoning suggests that only massive, expensive, and debatable raising and creation of dykes could protect the residential and farming areas from massive inundation. An effective but unlikely solution would be too move the residences at least from the low lying area. The issue of rising Fraser river waters is known and debated but the commitment of funds and policies for a solution is almost completely lacking.

If this is the case in a sophisticated and wealthy location, how much more will it be a problem in the deltas of the poorer countries such as Bangladesh or the oil rich swamp waters of Nigeria?

The year 2005 was something of a record for natural disasters – the South Asian tsunami, the devastating hurricane season in the Caribbean, Mexico and the United States. The human response has been to deal with the effects through massive national and international relief aid. It is most unlikely that we can do much if anything to stop such events, but improvements in forecasting are under way, and there is talk of creating a permanent revolving disaster fund under UN auspices that would provide the money, if not the people on the ground, for immediate instead of delayed responses. The relief efforts are bedevilled by national interests and rivalries (which affect our analysis of dysfunctional government and ideas for Global Government), and also by an unwillingness to give the UN the powers and authority to fully coordinate both governmental and private efforts.

But the problem and its mitigation run deeper. Disaster and human settlement authorities have long pointed out that, for example, housing construction in many of the threatened areas are dangerous in earthquakes – it is seldom the tremors that kill, but rather sub-standard buildings. This is not so dangerous in tropical areas where homes are made of thatch, but is lethal in areas where heavier materials are normal. There exist in the United

Nations system specifications for non-lethal construction, which countries such as Pakistan and India ignore. Meanwhile older codes and their avoidance in countries like Italy and Turkey are death trap recipes.

And what about a further moral dilemma. To what extent should populations be encouraged, even allowed, to remain in seriously threatened areas, in inaccessible mountain areas or tsunami threatened coastlines? The disaster of New Orleans in 2005 could have been mostly averted by heeding warnings of floods waiting to happen as a result of poor engineering, and even better by relocating the city away from the water tap.

Relocation however runs against a deep rooted and almost universal rule. Populations return to areas of disaster like lemmings. The psychology of this phenomenon has not been adequately studied – the natural drive of poor populations to avoid the unknown, in direct opposition to the migratory tendencies of others. Both "solutions" involve the assessment of risk, about which it is the role of governments to advise, perhaps not to enforce. And probability falsely advises "It has happened now. It will be generations before it happens again."

We must take note of the effects of ever increasing urban sprawl and invasions of productive land for tourism, industry and other purposes. Multimillion cities with their square kilometres of heat inducing macadam and housing that replace vegetation create centres of natural destruction. Humans in their civilisation are supposed to be able to control nature for the globe's benefit........

In cities like Kinshasa smart city workers emerge from simple huts, but those huts are located on small plots of land, with fruit trees, shrubs and vegetables. That is one kind of suburbia, common to Europe and North America except that the plots are seldom devoted to food crops as much as they could be and animals such as poultry or milch goats are seldom encouraged. It is at the expense of intensive agriculture or forestation, and in the largest cities does not survive population pressure. In an attempt to soften the effects of expanding residential land use, cities like Vancouver opt to use air space instead, thrusting apartments into the sky, with major effects on urban living and working. This has also created a change from dull deserted streets to vibrant interactive living. But it has not gone the next desirable step of *requiring* that all roofs be constructed to support and develop green gardens on the top of all buildings. This would do much to restore land areas to vegetation.

Whether suburban or towering urban, insufficient attention has been given to greening criteria. There are movements afoot to persuade city planners to insist that roof tops be green and even food productive, though so far with insufficient effect. Tailored parks do not do the job since buildings have replaced green lands to a much larger extent. And to convert the dysfunctional capital of buildings into structures that are not only eco-friendly in themselves, but contribute to the vegetation stock of the world, is a mammoth task. But we should surely require it to be undertaken. We cannot sit back in the lethargy of denial.

What should we say about population control as an aspect of human's nature? It may be that the globe as at present constituted cannot support very much more by way of increased population. This has been said since the nineteenth century and almost nothing has been done about it. Direct population control measures (China and India) have mostly failed. Improvement in wealth and education reduce the propensity of women to have children. This can be carried further as women experience a reduced need for male sexual partners as we have mentioned earlier. That however is speculation. But Innovation will improve the carrying capacity of the world in as yet unknown ways.

Paradoxically social evolution may be moving in this direction. Increased awareness of the rights and role of women does not necessarily reduce the birth rate, unless accompanied by birth control facilities and access to abortion. Despite my remarks about homosexuality in Chapter IV, perhaps this could be nature's way of controlling the birth rate. And so could the increased empowerment of women, who, as I pointed out in that chapter, no longer need men for biological purposes in the traditional ways. We need to devote attention to removing any brakes which exist on the spread of women's empowerment throughout global cultures.

Humanity's involvement with nature (including itself of course) involves many other priority issues, such as, for example, the application of genetic engineering. Some of these I will refer to in the next chapter on Knowledge. For there is no doubt that we need to know more, and urgently, if we are to be able to control our future. And that may require more and more reliance on an effective Global Government which we still need to design.

2012Postscript

- The world's fisheries are being decimated[145] by a combination of massive over-fishing, even off the coasts of Africa, and pollution from plastic and other materials sent down rivers to the sea, some of which is found in the stomachs of dying fish. The pollution dynamics suggest that the problem is increasing. Will we be left with only fish farms of limited species?

- There are no indications that evolution has somehow stopped. The self-modification of flu viruses and the reaction of bacteria to the over use of anti-bacterial medications are cases in point. We can also assert that to greater and greater degrees humankind has been affecting the very principles of evolution. Plant and animal breeding have been used for centuries. The methods are becoming more refined and genetic modification has speeded the process. Ethical worries emerge especially as scientists attempt to manipulate human change.

• The increasing use of the earth's atmosphere and outer space raises unresolved jural and ethical dilemmas. Does the nineteenth century principle of sovereignty acquisition apply? So far it has not. There would be an unstoppable objection of the United States were to assert its unique sovereignty over the moon and its possible riches on the grounds that its citizens were the first to land there and raise the United States flag. Surely this should become of major concern to a world government which should perhaps assert global sovereignty. An analogues issue has arisen over the control of Arctic waters and what lies beneath them as the ice retreats. Fortunately the neighbouring countries have, at least for now, come to an agreement over jurisdictional boundaries. Would it not have been better for the United Nations to have taken control? However the United Nations does not qualify as a world government and is dominated by national vested interest as we shall see in our penultimate chapter.

• A major problem in the use of the earth's atmosphere and outer space originates in the periodic flares of the sun's energy. These can knock out satellites as well as global communications. They require research into the protection of such potential institutions as orbiting solar capturing energy devices. And who will control such devices – governments, companies which build them, or world government?

• Similar issues arise over the already serious problem of atmospheric debris. Will a new world government enforce clean up and impose sanctions on offending parties?

- Our wastage of water is leading to movements to flush toilets, purify the water and recycle. In most of the developing world such measures are... a pipe dream.

- "An estimated 10 million people are affected by the Horn of Africa's worst drought in years. Somalia, wracked by 20 years of conflict, is hardest hit. Dr Hussein Sheikh Qassim, who works in the Médecins Sans Frontières hospital in Marere, southern Somalia, described what he saw on Friday: "The situation is extremely dire... The malnutrition ward is beyond full – of young children, most of them too weak even to eat... Some of these children had to walk for many kilometres to get here because their parents couldn't afford transport and were too weak to carry them on their backs..."[146]

- In many parts of the world possible aquifers are not being tapped and what there is is contaminated. Increased population strains domestic supplies and growing industry – even nuclear reactors – is thirstier than ever. Where water supplies touch on state boundaries the competition becomes political and requires international mediation[147].

- Diminished water supplies also affect animal husbandry – and wild stocks –straining other parts of the human food chain[148] and competing with other uses of lands and forests in a seemingly never-ending cycle. (Dramatic TV accounts of desertification, with carcases of herded cattle strewn over arid plains are evidence of a mere fraction of the immensity of damaging anti-developments.) Does the artificial creation of animal-like proteins in the laboratory (itself demanding raw materials) offer any possibility of matching the scale of such threats?

- On July 28th 2010 the *Globe and Mail* summarizes a report involving 300 scientists from various countries led by Derek Arndt of University of East Anglia titled *State of the Climate* by the U.S. National Oceanic and Atmospheric Administration. According to this report 2009 was the warmest since records began. Note however that *long before* records began the globe suffered *both* protracted ice ages and hot ages with Europe occupied by tropical mammals.

- Many forms of energy substitution raise negative issues which can be almost the equivalent of climate change damage. Thus both Brasil and the United States have found that ethanol production on a major scale requires the conversion of land devoted to other garniture and herding and the diminution of forest lands, the latter creating its own negative effect on the atmosphere.. Wind turbines eat up land and devastate birds, although placing them on rooftops or in the oceans may just possibly have lesser effects. Tide controlled turbines have at least localised impacts on tidal creatures. Solar panels require manufacturing with some climate effects and the gigantic proposal to install them in the Sahara to supply Europe requires transmission facilities and would stop any animal nomadism in the region. It is much less disturbing if the panels are installed on buildings and vehicle roofs. As I have pointed out civilisation, culture, human activity always involves the manipulation of the natural world. This is just another example though policy makers nowadays must take the costs of environmental interference into account and compare them with the benefits.

• Nuclear fusion was once thought to be contrary to the laws of physics. Yet an experimental nuclear fusion plant is under construction in France and is intended to go on line in 2017.[149] Whether it will be as controversial as current nuclear plants is unclear. Japan, after suffering meltdown during the tsunami of 2012 is in June bringing a damaged but rebuilt plant back online since the country cannot meet energy demands.

• Climate change is irreversible even with zero emissions. Researchers at the Universities of Calgary, Edmonton and Victoria point to the rising sea level increased flooding, more desertification in North Africa in *Nature Geoscience* journal 2010.

• Mirrors in space could send heat back into the universe. Also tapping the sun's energy from space could provide solar energy without using up land. How would we control the effects on weather without using transmission lines, and what impact would they have through the manufacturing and transport processes? And would the owners submit to World Government control?

• The present United Nations, based as it is on rivalrous nation states, is not equipped to deal with the tensions, group violence, civil wars and war between governments and their rivals. As I write climate effects and control issues combined with tribal loyalties are undermining the stability of Syria, Mali, the two Sudans and even Libya. The implications are examined in later chapters.

• The UN meeting on Climate Change in Durban December 2011 a fiasco. So was the 2012 meeting in Rio de Janeiro. Very few of the earlier promises have been met by the states which made them. Only an effective world government will change this, and by then the environmental situation will have different implications from what is now known.

• Peter Fedow in Vancouver, one of many, is making fuel for his diesel vehicle from cooking oil recycled from a local pub[150].

• Huge Antarctic ice shelves are melting under the influence of warmer water beneath them. This will result in major rises in sea levels which could be over a metre[151].

• Climate change with cold snaps is influenced by the solar cycle[152]. Sun spot cycles last about 11 years of waxing and waning. Occasionally sun spots disappear, coinciding with cold earth temperatures. In 2011 Frank Hill and others at the American National Solar Observatory argued that a "new extended solar minimum" is about to occur involving a cooling of the earth's climate.

• "Solar power companies are struggling. Bur the survivor will have a bright future.'[153]

• A 2008 conference under the auspices of the American Philosophical Society noted the likelihood of major volcanic eruptions, a comet collision with the earth, the return of an ice age and increased aridity as among the major environmental disasters for which we should be prepared.[154]

•　New technologies make more oil salvageable. Much more gas is available. Given the rapid expansion of demand especially in Asia and Africa, carbon dioxide goals of 450 parts per million is "not remotely likely".[155] (Unless alternative energy sources such as solar energy for vehicles proceed at a far more rapid and economical pace.)

•　Scientific results linking humans to other aspects of nature, as affecting practice, are far too often accepted in isolation from related variables (see also next chapter) a natural simplification in journalistic reporting but too often influenced by ideology or wishful thinking. Currently it is fashionable, for example, to preach the mantra that local food supply is better for the climate than sourcing food from a distance. In a specific case this can be true but the truth depends on other variables. It is often the case that local food which can be sourced elsewhere have a higher price than their competition. When this is so it indicates that nearby producers are less efficient than those at a further distance. In other words the carbon credit through less transport can be outweighed by higher carbon production on local farms. The devil is in the details, not in an a priori manta. Of course the proposition does not take into account the wider benefits of international trade or the economic advantages of specialisation .

•　Architects in Thailand have created a model of a floating city which would relocate a population threatened by rising floods or sea levels.[156]

The present model does not allow for motor vehicles but no doubt the pathways could be fitted with moving sidewalks. (Working class settlements on the Western side of the Prao Chaya river across from are on stilts above swamps with wooden paths raised above the water. Presumably such a city would be solar powered.

X The Hopes and Traps of Science and Knowledge[157]

It goes without saying that if we are to design the best possible world we need the best possible knowledge of the way the world works. We also need to know what knowledge is available in relation to particular issues since this will give us a partial guide to choosing which issues are most likely to be resolved. If we know that there is knowledge about an issue it will suggest that this is one we can profitably tackle. If there is no knowledge about an issue we will spend much more by way of time and money and experiment to get a result, and that may discourage us.

On the other hand we should not let this principle be the only one which affects our priorities. We need to remove violence from our lives even if we do not know everything about its causes and cures. That priority and many others stay regardless of the state of our knowledge.

Furthermore all knowledge is subject to change. What is approved of today is quite likely to be out of date tomorrow. This is especially true of consequences. The creation of policies are seldom holistic: policies are made to address specific questions. Side effects are seldom examined and if examined are subject to inaccuracy and may be more serious than anticipated in a cost benefit analysis. That is in the nature of policy making. We have to be in a hurry and cannot wait for an unquestionable truth to emerge. So far our ability to map a truly holistic future, despite great advances in massive computer calculations and models, is beyond us even in important "natural" events such as weather forecasting, let alone societal predictions.

This is still true despite the exponential advance of knowledge and its increasing availability through the revolutionary, and still not completely designed, operations of the internet.

For it is not only the existence of knowledge which counts but its availability, its circulation. We have already noted this variable when it comes to innovation. We can expect the explosion of the internet and its availability to result in a massive explosion of innovation in all fields of life.

During the past two decades the internet has put knowledge within reach of every person who has access, and that means most of the world. The costs of access have dropped significantly in the poorer world, where some countries are beginning to leap frog over the restrictions imposed by inadequate land lines.

Even more startling has been the dramatic and seemingly permanent arrival in the past half decade of what are misleadingly called "social networks". These indeed began as social networks with the function of extending contacts between individuals and building interactive friendships. They are now much more than that, permitting scientists to regularly exchange information beyond their usual contacts, providing inexpensive avenues of informational advertising that would have been beyond the pockets of entrepreneurs using standard media, and opening up information channels literally to multi-millions of people. A great deal of this is trivial from the perspective of advancing the circulation of significant ideas but the likely innovative effects are as yet only just beginning.

The most widely reported effects of these conversations and information sharing has been political, enabling individuals in such places as Iran, Georgia and even China to inform the international world of events suppressed in the official media. However this dramatic phenomenon but scratches the surface. Behind it lies a host of knowledge sharing which supplements printed sources from business news to scientific thought.

Such interactive networks include several which are focussed in their applications; for example ResearchGATE provides interactive space for scientists of all stripes. This is invaluable not only for specialists who wish to expand their contacts but for discovering accidental cross-disciplinary information.

The scale and impact of such networks is represented by the largest of them, Facebook and Twitter.

From humble beginnings with restricted objectives Facebook services have expanded technique by technique with new tools. In October 2009 it had 430.2 million unique visitors. The *Economist* pointed out that its population of users is surpassed only by the populations of China and India as far as countries go.[158] Furthermore 70% "of its audience live outside the United States so that it is a strong influence toward an ultimate equalising of knowledge internationally, although that is yet to be maximised. From the point of view of the circulation of ideas and a potential effect on innovation it is noteworthy that it experienced 35 million updates as day comprising 2,5 *billion* pieces of content every week. Those figures will by now have multiplied several fold. Enough said.

The internet and open networking do contain major inefficiencies. Numerous recombinations of ideas will be premature or otherwise have no effect on our behaviour and lives. That happens in physical experimentation too and is an essential cost of advance.

The internet is an equalising and internationalising tool, however imperfect. It is there for curious individuals to find things out before they make decisions, from private behaviour such as finding an appropriate off the counter medication to understanding of policy jargon such as "emergence from economic depression".

Just because anyone can make their views available on the internet the system is also known for misinformation. What some people see as misinformation may in fact be an as yet untried alternative solution. The internet is a massive tool for debate, even if the debates fail to reach a fully accepted conclusion.

At its present state of evolution the internet, except in totalitarian countries, is a chaotic free for all. Once again it is a major task for Youth Maturity Institutes to educate youth in the perils of accepting simple affirmation as truth and how to use skills of logic and data analysis to improve the value of their web searching enquiries, skills which are even more significant than they were in the days when the acquisition of knowledge was limited to the use of libraries and media propaganda.

To this end we need to pay attention to the presentation of purported knowledge in traditional media not only for its own sake but as illustrations about traps which lurk in the internet itself.

To illustrate, there is a problem, which I find particularly in the presentation and methodology of medical research but which constitutes a warning about interpreting any form of research for the public through the mediation of journalism and individual reporting of all forms. Time and again we learn of a causative relationship discovered on the basis of a statistical enquiry, sometimes minimal, sometimes massive. Later, we find another study which, with similar methodology but a different set of variables, provides alternative or contradictory causation. Tucked away in a footnote, or completely omitted in the popularisation, you often find that the researchers are puzzled as to *how* the relationship comes about.

What is missing is the fact that statistics deal with *probability* not final proof. A statistical statement is almost useless *in itself*. It has meaning *only* as providing a serious hypothesis, unless and until it is embedded in the context of a wider theory of explanation, linked to *other* relationships by abstract general statements, which could, in principle, be disproven. If the researchers admit they don't know *why* the relationship exists statistically, their data must be treated with the utmost caution, as the subject for further research, *not* the presentation of a conclusion which has enormous implications for human life. The recent history of nutrition surely shows this. At one time margarine not butter, now butter not margarine. What is the cholesterol implication of consuming eggs? Milk, dairy products, the effects of digesting fish. Generalisations about these and so many more technical nutritional and medical matters have, literally, been upset or modified within the past few *weeks* of my writing this.

To my relief – for I am never certain about what I say – an entry in *The Economist* for September 3rd, 2005 refers to a significant study by Dr .John Ioannidis of the University of Ioannina published in *PLOS Medicine*[159]. He examined studies in the *Journal of the American Medical Association* and found that a *third* of them were later refuted. The problems were rooted into a misunderstanding of the meaning of "statistical significance" and to unprofessional use of the statistical methods.

Again, especially in medicine, while the statistical norm certainly matters, it is the individual organism which is at issue. The variations from the norm are as significant as the norm itself. Probability is just that, probability. It is *not* certainty about each and every one of the instances which have been aggregated. In many areas of study, the fact is that even one single instance which does not conform to the norm implies that the theoretical basis for the norm has been disproven as a generalised statement. There is something else at work. The human organism -- and so many other objects of investigation -- contains so many variables that the essential tool of statistics has to be treated with great caution, the only certainty being that it cannot remove doubt. Indeed, the single seemingly aberrant instance, if closely examined, may yield more theoretical innovation and understanding than the instances that are statistically normal.

In every section thus far we have touched upon imperfect knowledge. I opened with the assertion that knowledge, not even in the most ideal of worlds can be a certain thing. We must live with fuzzy logic and uncertainty, take pleasure in them for they represent excitement and human challenge, not be afraid of them.

If a little knowledge is a dangerous thing, the danger is necessary. Since uncertainty surrounds us, we cannot wait for certainty in order to act. We must get on with the job.

A merit of democracy is that it implicitly recognises that technocrats and scientists are limited in what they know, especially outside their own disciplines; that the little knowledge of each individual adds up to great principles -- freedom, understanding -- that since no one individual has superior knowledge about all of life's affairs, the ignorance of one is more than counterbalanced by the sum total of the wisdom of many. Provided, of course, that the many are not swayed out of their strongly felt reason by the more than strongly felt hype and hysteria of inflamed rhetoric or crowd drive. That, once again, is where the central importance of logic and rhetoric in Youth Maturity Institutes' comes in.

There are degrees of littleness. While we cannot wait for knowledge to be perfect, while commissions of enquiry and statements of uncertainty are often used to inhibit action, it is nevertheless appropriate that we should improve the pool of knowledge, support investigations of strategic questions, and distribute that knowledge as widely as practicable.

But what is knowledge? Are there such things as truths and lies? Is knowledge simply that which someone believes to be true?

I see three primary kinds of knowledge, and two apparent dichotomies. As I mentioned before, there is knowledge based upon faith, which we can call religious. I believe, therefore it is. There is knowledge based upon and communicated by art in its manifold forms. I express and you receive that which your own spirit tells you to receive, amending the message as you do so. And there is knowledge based upon sceptical questioning, with answers provided by attempts at control, and the tests of logic and falsity, and an ability to replicate or a failure to do so, namely science.

All three deal with concepts of more or less, even when the assertions are couched as absolutes or aesthetic values. More sin or less sin. Total renunciation or none. Great beauty, less beauty, or great ugliness. The harmony of form or its disharmony. High probability or low. Warm or cold. For each, differences of degree are possible whether or not they are explicitly stated. Differences of degree can, theoretically, be translated into at least ordinal quantification, though the specific method of acquiring knowledge may, at least for now, abjure that.

"Subjectivity" and "objectivity" are always mixed. Once the assumptions of a faith are disclosed, logic may be applied to the consequences and implications of those assumptions. Theology, political philosophy, exposition of values follow. Initial faith may be challenged by logical attack, but if the faith is deep, it is impervious. That does not mean it is a lie. Even if "disproven" by some investigation, it is true to believers, and must be counted within the pool of knowledge with which people use for action. Knowledge can be mistaken objectively. Intuition is arriving at conclusions without evidence or reasoning, conclusions which may in fact be supported by other methods. Those of us, like myself, who believe in scepticism have a form of faith -- commitment to scepticism; so have the rationalists. Ultimately we have no means of proving beyond doubt that rationality and scepticism are the ways the natural universe intends us to think. We can, however, argue about it.

There is a sense in which art differs from science mainly in the fact that art addresses individual phenomena, teasing out implications, instead of grouping phenomena together and testing the significance of variables. It is just as empirical as science. Even when the art is embodied in words, in poetry or literature, its message cannot fully be agreed upon by verbal criticism, which in itself is a subjective art. The message is between the artist and the viewer, the hearer, the reader. Again, the difference between art and science is not the sensory base of the communication, for all communication is sensory. Scientific and mathematical judgement is full of terms such as "elegance", "simplicity". Attempts to objectify the terms do not remove the fundamental subjectivity on which they rest. And the choice of the scientific enquiry, however much bolstered by argument and rational justification, is totally subjective. I *choose* to be a mathematical biologist or an astronomer and try to answer such and such a specific question.

We must therefore not separate specific forms of knowledge too certainly in a hierarchy of method and truth, though there are major differences in the central types of communication. Faith asserts, art seduces, science is expository. But here again faith can result in exposition and can use seductive methods; some art is programmatic; and scientists love to seduce through simplistic but dramatic exhibits.

Knowledge is communicated for it depends on innovation. It is often the case that the root of a piece of knowledge is indeed not directly communicated, other than to those who share that knowledge. Those who have the faith share it with others of the same mind. We seem to be going through a temporary phase in which some artists club together with other artists and feel purposeful in so doing. Scientists often look down on those who try to communicate beyond the sacred walls (newly challenged, as we have seen, by the internet). Knowledge leads, then, to monastic orders; but at least within those there is communication. Knowledge, as I asserted in Chapter II, grows from that communication, and could not do so without it. The isolated person who has in his sensibility some truth or invention is not dealing with knowledge but an interior emotion.

Knowledge, then, is communicated insight.

That insight deals with generalised relationships. "It is a beautiful sunset" has little to do with nature. It compares the phenomenon to other sunsets. It tests the insight against ideas of beauty. Those ideas relate, for example, to the shape, intensity and spectrum of colour, all of which are in a particular relationship, comparable to and differentiated from the relationships set out in other sunsets -- and indeed other phenomena, such as dawn, reflections on water or a painting. They may relate the sunset to emotional experience, to love, to romantic opportunity. That the judgement is made in a split second does not remove that characteristic. That is why abstract thinking and rationality, which attempt to reveal relationships, have a special influence in the way we think about knowledge.

I suggested above that the great methods of acquiring knowledge are mixed together and not to be put into some sort of absolute hierarchy. In my usual contrary way, however, I now assert that not all bearers of knowledge are equal, and that they never will be. Indeed, as we have noted, an amazing defect in some theory and practice of childhood and university education (now fortunately mostly abandoned) was the assertion in the classroom that anybody's idea, however arrived at, is as valid as the next person's especially in matters of the "humanities". Democratically, that may be so. It may even be that someone is nursing an idea that, when he or she comes to maturity, turns out to be revolutionary in its implications. But ideas are not at all equal. Those ideas which influence other ideas have greater significance than those which stay isolated or fall on deaf ears or whose methodology or background is suspect.

Standards of enquiry are inevitable and necessary. Genius may be hidden, but most of us, though capable of more than we let on, are not Genius. Genius takes a swathe of contemporary knowledge, combines it with some other swathe of knowledge, and turns everything topsy turvy. But to do that Genius has first to find the swathes of knowledge that pre-exist. It has to choose what elements to master, but mastered they must be, so that they may be changed and developed.

By mastery I do not mean that the school or university has a monopoly of the swathes of knowledge that Genius or lesser mortals will eventually play with. Much will come from outside.

The school and university do have the responsibility to show how knowledge is gained, and what devices we have for testing knowledge in its various forms, how it is communicated within and without the monastic halls, and how people go about making their judgements about what is valid and what is not. A child has to learn to put his thoughts to tests, yet ultimately not to be constrained by those tests; to accept disagreement, yet be strong enough not to be disheartened by it -- nor even necessarily to agree with the disagreement.

In the population at large we are going through a time in which democratisation of knowledge, that is the widespread sharing of it, is being exponentially expanded by communication methods. The time and space constraints of the media, to say nothing of their commercialisation, insist on reducing complexity and uncertainty to simplicity and certainty. The time frame of television documentaries requires enormous skill to convey complex questions, a skill and an aim which is most frequently not there. The space and structure of newspaper "stories", though able to complement these with longer, more analytical treatments, stress a dominant theme at the expense of other themes which are just as significant for interpretation. At the same time sources and counter-sources are usually not adequately revealed. There are millions of examples every day. I shall take two to illustrate.

A doctor conducts a major study of the use of temoxisen, a drug that is effective in the prevention of the spread of breast cancer under certain conditions. The object is to try to quantify the risks of numerous side effects which previous studies had reported. In medical research there are large numbers of statistical studies which are not definitive because numbers are too small for the control of variables, or the statistical tools are simplistic. These are widely reported in the media as if they were truth, or definitive break-throughs, whereas they should be interpreted only as presenting possibilities or hypotheses for further enquiry.

This study was, however, thorough. It traced large numbers of side effects, among which was an increased risk of cervical cancer. The press seized on the last point, trumpeting the danger, and creating considerable anxiety in patients, with which no amount of reasoned discussion could compete. The facts revealed (as probabilities only) that without temoxisen there was a 2% likelihood of a breast cancer patient acquiring cervical cancer. With temoxisen there was a 6% likelihood. Further studies will most likely show why, and perhaps which women are most likely to be at risk.

The figures show that in the meantime caution is required and that women should be informed of the risk. If they opt to take temoxisen they and their medical advisers should watch for the first signs of cervical cancer, which, I am informed, is, relative to breast cancer, a low risk and a treatable disease. The discovery, which was not new but was properly evaluated in the study, did not justify the kind of fear promoted by some of the U.S. national press. (In fairness, I have to say that I heard the "balanced" approach during a discussion by a woman doctor on television. But for that I would not have had my information modified.) In other words the media, in reporting the study, exaggerated one of its elements for dramatic impact, corrupting the implications of its results.

The Canadian Broadcasting Corporation has built up a reputation for being stolid. Perhaps to make up for this it sometimes goes overboard in trying to be at the forefront of scandal mongering. In 1995 it decided to follow through on allegations that Care Canada, a non-governmental aid agency, had wasted monies raised from the public to provide relief to Somalia. They alleged that "not a penny" of what had been raised had gone to Somalian food or medical relief; that instead money had been spent on security guards in Kenya and a public relations officer in Mogadishu; that air tickets were at full economy rates instead of bargain basement rates; that officials had stayed at a $225 a night hotel in Sydney, Australia during a conference. Before the telecast Care Canada officials had declined responding to what had been put to them as a general problem of allocating money, since they believed the untruth would be apparent and the programme would not air, at least in that way.

It did, causing an immediate stir amongst all Canadian aid agencies, since there was a strong likelihood that the public, believing the stories, would become disenchanted with giving to anyone.

There are indeed private fund raisers, even some who harp on religion, who are open to suspicion, and who are more concerned with maintaining their competitive advantage than with delivering help. But Care Canada is one of those with a fifty year record, and one which is regularly audited in various ways, including by government agencies who provide some of the funds.

A reliable account would have approached the matter differently. It would have placed the complaints in the context of the dynamics of aid delivery. That would have shown, for example, that in Mogadishu at the time journalists from all over the world were harassing aid workers and preventing them from getting on with the job. A public relations officer was a defence to enable the agencies to meet the emergency.

It would have shown that to allocate money in advance too rigidly would prevent aid agencies from adapting to unforeseen and rapidly changing emergencies. Thousands of Somalis needing help were in Kenya; Care Canada, in coordination and consultation with other agencies, was mandated to focus on them. The complaint that private donors thought the money was going to Somalia (which, incidentally, no donor had then been able to do) was splitting hairs in a damaging way -- it was going to Somalis. The charge that the money was in part being used for security guards instead of for food shows extraordinary naiveté. Massive looting, unrest, violence, interference with convoys, if not checked, would have prevented *any* food reaching the sufferers. As I know to my cost, full economy air tickets are necessary if travellers are to be able to change their plans to meet emergencies at a moment's notice -- and in this case, travel agents gave rebates. As for hotel charges, the "investigators" quoted the published full tariff rate at the hotel, not the amount actually paid. That amount was at a reduced conference rate. It *might* have been possible to get a room at even less, though that would have to be demonstrated under the conditions of the case. But staying at the conference appointed hotel is part of the cost of doing business; not staying there indeed raises ethical questions, since if those who attend do not stay there, if the guaranteed rooms are not occupied, then the conference is liable to pay for conference meeting rooms that it otherwise gets free or at a nominal charge. The hotel booking is in fact a subsidy to the conference, without which it could not take place.

If a television producer and writer did not have the knowledge of the principles underlying these statements they would not be qualified to undertake such a documentary, and would be doing so simply out of muckraking hubris. But, ethics apart, it shows how dangerous a little misleading information can be.

The CBC presentation was, in my opinion, anti-knowledge. As I have said, no knowledge is perfect. But there are degrees of imperfection. Misleading statements are all the more serious when they come from media outlets that the public is trying to trust.

In this context, the point of both examples is that it is not just the media who are responsible for interpretation. The public is responsible too. Until the internet came of age it has been almost *only* through the media that the public has obtained its knowledge. In our best world the public will not tolerate deliberate or careless mis-information. It will demand accuracy. It will demand that scientific journalists do not depend solely on the press handouts of scientists, but go to the original sources, and to the scientific debates. It will demand that muckraking is not enough, that information revealed be put in context, for only then does it become possible for individuals to make their own interpretations. Knowledge is not just something hidden in universities or research labs -- it is something every one of us amasses every day.

Fortunately the conventional media are being supplemented and challenged by the internet.

So far I have treated the media as purveyors and creators of knowledge. Behind them is the panoply of research institutions, artists, private investigators, universities, technical schools, inventors, corporate research facilities and specialised journals.

Amongst these I shall focus on universities[160].

I would define a university as an adult institution with the central objectives of: generating enquiry and creativity through teaching and research, expanding cultural resources, including knowledge in the sciences and the humanities and arts, developing powers of scientific, aesthetic and moral judgement, *using the technique of rational enquiry.*

A university is by no means the *only* location in which such activitiestake place. Indeed, artistic endeavour, for example, is best located outside a university, since the constraints of rational scholarship and of other demands inhibit artistic freedom. The reason for this is that a university distinguishes itself, ideally, from other institutions by its use of rationality to advance knowledge. It criticises and explains rather than writes novels. It explores the historical genesis of art movements, rather than paints.

Immediately I must make the point that once again that terminology is likely to be thoroughly misleading. First, not all institutions which name themselves universities concentrate on these functions. Some, in many parts of the world, are more concerned with learning outcomes defined as packages of facts, rote instruction, and the control and use of knowledge as a service to industry, rather than because it is in itself creative.

Other institutions might well be considered of a university kind, especially some of the great Institutes of Technology, Schools of Art, Colleges and so forth. Elements of universities are in many places. And even universities which meet the definition are seldom "pure": They balance budgets through military and industrial contracts; they have to teach the elements of languages by drill and exercise; some of the non-creative things that universities do are but a means to a creative end. They cannot afford to lose a good mind because it cannot put words on paper properly, hence they may dip into coaching techniques to reach the constructive goal. If they do this too much they may find themselves, as do most North American universities, including a component that is little more than that of a high school, and not even a good one at that.

The last statement points to a tricky balance. To create, there must be a basis for creation. As I have pointed out, the basis consists of at least some of what has gone before. So the university, in order to do its job, must take part in the preservation of what has gone before, retaining and communicating the pool of culture. It does not have to communicate solely to formal students and scholars. Communicating to *anyone* who wants to listen is surely part of its mandate.

It is beyond my task here to go into the terrible dysfunctions and anti-creativity processes that go on in most named universities, except to plead that we can if we choose make them go away, or transfer them to other places where they are not damaging. One such dysfunction is the North American obsession with course-work, comprehensive examinations and the like in Ph.D. programmes, course-work which is either not needed or more properly insisted upon at the M.A. stage, comprehensive examinations which, if needed at all, should be part of the student entry and selection process; both dulling, sometimes forever, the enthusiastic creative mind. It is sometimes a miracle that creative minds survive such attacks upon them.

Knowledge is not to be neatly packaged. Though organisation of knowledge is essential to the rational mind -- and, remember, universities are involved with rationality -- those who are searching, both students and those who have passed the degree test, must be free to wander. The tricky balance is to draw the attention of students to the rigours of argument and areas of subject matter that the student is not aware of, on the one hand, and to encourage his or her freedom to search for associations, synergies, anywhere. And to demand that assertions reveal their locus in scholarship, their relevance for enquiry and for further thought.

Furthermore *anything* is open to challenge. Professional schools, by definition, have at least tiny places where challenge is seldom open -- I refer to the statement of conduct that defines the ethics of the profession. Such Faculties have to watch that this central orthodoxy does not permeate, and, if they call themselves universities, to be open to challenge even here.

Since anything is open to challenge, there is no room for blind faith, except in rationality, though that may rationally be challenged. (I am NOT saying that rationality is the only, or even the best, way to knowledge. I AM saying that it is the special tool of universities, and that there is as yet nothing of equal merit for the effective and relatively precise communication of ideas. Faith and ambiguity flourish primarily elsewhere. Universities do not have a monopoly in the modes of searching.)

This means that those who cannot stand up to such challenges, who are disturbed rather than stimulated by them, who are liable to suffer psychologically if their faith or aesthetic intuitions are hurt, should avoid universities. The point means that students, to understand their position, to act appropriately, must be capable of reasonably mature judgement and know rather specifically what universities are about. Secondary school counsellors too frequently limit their talk to careers and job hunts. Although universities indubitably affect, even create, careers, that is a by-product of their primary concerns. It is not the contemporary university's fundamental job to train skilled doctors; that can be done in independently accredited medical schools. It *is* the university's job to assist enquiring minds, whether they belong to doctors or philosophers, to think about medical matters, to be a locus for medical research and debate, and to educate those would-be doctors who wish to think creatively about their profession, its human context, its science. Too often so-called universities allow parts of themselves to be training schools, rather than horizon-wideners.

The social role of the university is not to provide *technology* for tomorrow. Since it is dedicated to discovery, that will happen as a by-product. The many forms of rational creativity to which the university is devoted are valued now and will be even more so in future for additional reasons. Youth Maturity Institutes as we have seen will be concerned with the non-vocational aspects of living. Universities do not do this directly. But the emphasis on rational creativity, on discovery, on searching, on finding out, will be of immense benefit to those millions who, in the future, will be released from day-to-day other-directed work.[161] Universities will attract the increasing numbers of non-gainfully employed whom we envisage in our chapter on work, free to follow their creative impulses. To handle this, universities must reverse the unthinking surrender that is taking place, surrender to pressures to make them directly vocational, directly subservient to industrial and commercial needs. Let there be other types of programmed research or technical institutes to do that.

It might be thought that I am advocating ivory towers divorced from their communities. Not at all. There is a pent-up demand for thought, intellectual exploration, knowledge in communities -- the movement of the elderly into the realm of educational tours, short courses of higher education, even degrees, is noticeable. Unfortunately, a great deal of this is "talking down". Universities will have an increasing role to play in opening doors to those who are interested in learning, not just for its own sake", but as a means to a creative adult life; and designing methods, uninhibited by the swaddling of degree rules and regulations, to respond to the intellectual potentialities of the population.

Furthermore I have advocated, and still advocate, community involvement where it matters -- not so much in the university board rooms, not in academic decision-making as such, but in talking with staff about the intellectual and community issues of concern to them. In other words, faculties and colleges might well have liaison and consultative committees drawn from the community to discuss such matters as the possibility of stimulating courses addressing new questions of interest or the techniques of discussion and dissemination. University staff naturally tend to address issues, especially in the sciences, which are determined by their peers. As a result a large number of matters of concern to the public are not on the priority list for investigation (see later). Remember, I am suggesting *consultation*, not problem-oriented control. There are many factors involved in making decisions about priorities for enquiry -

- funding, aptitudes and capacities of personnel, the unfettered passion to solve a problem however unpopular it might seem among others. The consultative groups must learn to understand these, to stimulate, not to demand; to be useful through stimulation.

And I am not abjuring applied research. Indeed I feel that in the social sciences, for example, applied research is not accorded the intellectual status that should be accorded to it -- largely the responsibility of the practitioners. In these subjects it is through applied research that we may address matters of great significance -- for example the testing of hypotheses, the investigation of ethno-social science (the hypotheses about cause and effect with which every manager and politician, counsellor and lover, operates), the elucidation of the values and goals into which technology should be fitted, and the discovery of new questions. In making the point I am readily aware that this is a part of knowledge that is in its infancy.

I cannot foresee the structure of research in the next century. Ideas I may have about the organisation of enquiry on the whole, changes in the communication of data and knowledge, the relevance of such buzz-words as "interdisciplinarity", about funding -- these are matters of technical detail which are changing rapidly and profoundly. There is no one right way. May many flowers bloom. Let them be wild as well as cultivated. Let them invade the desert spaces that men and women have been cruelly fashioning for themselves, desert spaces called the emptying of the spirit.

I do not want to leave this topic without indicating the vastness of our ignorance, the infinite terrain that is there to be explored. We are accustomed to the idea that knowledge is increasing at an exponential rate, that the number of enquirers living now is more than equal to the sum total of all those who lived before. That the output of data is getting beyond control, creating difficulties of management, access, quality control, and absorption.

If this is so now, what may it be like soon, let alone in our new world? Democratisation is an inevitable and welcome feature. With democratisation will come even greater magnitudes. Even greater difficulty is finding the diamonds in the sand, the need for even huger data-managing machines. But also there may come a breaking away from the constraints, not of mental discipline, but of artificial discipline boundaries. Academics will potentially be in much greater contact with non-academic creators. Academics will be challenged as never before. The amateur, as in the first days of science, may well find his or her niche. The hidden minds of the third world will come to the forefront. If only we learn to turn the electronic age toward its rightful purposes....

Many years ago I suggested to fellow-anthropologists that we should stop the print publication of heavily subsidised primary journals -- those concerned with data reporting and initial interpretation -- leaving the print field only to those which were concerned with synthesising and theorising. I suggested also that we should try to develop electronic intercommunication through the nascent Internet in such a way that workers in the field could transmit their data and papers openly, and access library resources on line as needed. This, I argued, could be of immense benefit to third world anthropologists, whose ideas are rejected by referees because they are not embedded in the literature for the simple reason the literature has not been available to them, even in libraries in their country. I saw this as potentially being a heaven-sent equaliser.[162]

It was of course quite impracticable in those years ago as an immediate goal. Portable field computers did not have the power. Telephone lines were missing, and telephone systems unreliable and expensive.

This is just about not so any more. Technological change in just two years has seen the passionate expansion of smart phones from Nigeria and India to China and the Middle East – in fact everywhere – with reading tablets on the way with access to global literature. Countries like Rwanda are ambitiously laying optic cables to link all schools to the internet, as private companies stretch connecting cables from Africa to India and thus to the world..

This does not mean the loss of books, smaller demand for paper, or the disappearance of printed journals. Although it is far more effective to write to a modern computer screen than on paper it is still more appropriate to use hard copy printouts for most reading and many reference purposes, despite the arrival of e-book digital readers[163]. Most scholarly journals -- as many already are -- should become "on demand" journals, available to everyone who can electronically skim tables of contents and summaries, and then read selected material and order printouts or store on disc. Journals and books will be in a limited number of central libraries and data centres. The most valuable will be those which synthesise out of the chaos, the imaginative rather than the descriptive.

For the Internet, as it is now, will be swamped with junk. I do not believe this will go on in the present form. It is now possible to determine in advance which home pages and chats are serious, though there are a tremendous number of home pages which are little more than publicity brochures and most of the chatting is hardly intellectual. Users can learn ways of escaping from cyber babble. The Google service for scholars which restricts searches to primary papers and documents is in fact a major initiative, as is Google's programme to digitalize and make available the contents of five of the world's great libraries – and now ambitiously all books in print as well. I fail to see the objection of some authors to having their work made available in this way. Since Google has made arrangements to pay author royalties – and arrangement which no doubt could be improved, but extends the income base of authors[164].

But note. The origins of the World Wide Web as we know it (as distinct from the first scholarly internet) go back less than three decades; its democratisation perhaps five years; its sudden popularity and the beginnings of its vast expansion and growing commercialisation only since about 1994. As a communicator of knowledge it is in its infancy. As a generator of knowledge, it has hardly yet begun.

An essential condition for the proper operation of universities, and of the knowledgeable world outside of universities, is freedom of ideas and communication. I abhor the entry of politicized racism into scholarship, but I defend the right of such miscreants to express their thoughts. The only university remedy is confrontation with reasoned argument rather than emotional demos. To me it is a shocking that there have been incidents of *de facto* censorship, including the cancellation of scholarly visits, at such venerable institutions as Harvard and Oxford, let alone dozens of minor players.

Much of this has to do with the power of "political correctness", a phenomenon which has no place in true universities.

In the Muslim world, in particular, different forms of political correctness prevail.

The International Union of Anthropological and Ethnological Sciences, of which I was then president, accepted an invitation from Egyptian colleagues to hold an international meeting in Alexandria close to Christmas. Egypt then had diplomatic ties with Israel. In accordance with policy the IUAES had received assurances that no person would be excluded on the grounds of citizenship or religion. A few days before the meeting we received word that the local organisers had cancelled the arrangements – because students at the American University in Cairo were threatening mayhem if Israelis were permitted.[165] This act was contrary to open procedures of international scholarly bodies.

In 2005 an international academic historians conference was to be held in Istanbul, examining the issue of the slaughter of Armenians in the wake of World War I, a slaughter which outside critics dub "genocide", an appellation the Turkish government refuses to acknowledge, describing the victims as traitors. The Turkish government heavy handedly proscribed the meeting. This from a country that is seeking to join the European Union. The issue continues to trouble the country and the principle that untrammelled scholarship, as objectively conducted as possible, should be open and encouraged meets undesirable political resistance which those of us who are committed to the broad idea of a best possible world must work to reject.

There must be many instances of meetings in Muslim universities which do not involve such censorship. There are also Christian "universities" which demand that ideology be the foundation of understanding. And there are many Muslim calls for the opening of freer internal discussions. Until such issues are addressed frankly and firmly the Muslim intellectual world will be unable to maintain the full respect that is its historical due. and will be unable to make its creative voice heard the way it should be heard[166].

Let me turn now to set out a number of subjects which I believe are under-investigated by contemporary science and scholarship. This is not intended as an exhaustive trip into the unknown, but rather as a demonstration that the unknown is very much still out there, despite the fact that we now have the tools, if not the will, to create a socio-political desirable world. In some respects, scientific knowledge now is to knowledge by the end of the twenty-first century as scientific knowledge in Ancient Greece is to scientific knowledge now. The ability of the human mind to keep up with such a vast leap forward will be sorely tested, as will the capacity of scientists to create intelligible interpretations of what they explore. I anticipate that demands on the mind will prompt its evolution in ways that draw upon as yet unused mental powers. Science, all knowledge, is, when it all boils down, a matter of imagining and transforming rules of the universe into terms that the human mind recognises. Perhaps the universe has no rules; those little dangling bits of probability that are unaccounted for may, one way or another, remain dangling forever. But as long as we can use the mind's predispositions, and yet be prepared to accept uncertainty, we seem to be able to find enough by way of regularity to function.

Everything we have by way of perception, knowledge and feeling is organised and made conscious within what we call the mind. We believe that the mind is the activity of the brain made conscious. (There are of course a host of other meanings, from soul to memory.) It would seem that if we are to understand knowledge, we must understand the mind. Until recently our knowledge about the mind has come from internal reflection, observing what happens when we are conscious of thinking and meditating, and from uncontrolled inferences that come from asserted probing into the subconscious, to which we add the body of psychology and the analysis of culture and of behaviour. It is a huge amount, but, curiously, gives us very little data (though it has increased substantially during the past years) about how the physiological body interacts with what seems to be known from these approaches, (even though psychology began with attempts to understand the senses and to relate these to perceptions and thought through philosophy).

As the major working hypothesis we locate the physiological processes of the mind in the brain. It is notoriously difficult to study living brains.[167] Yet to understand them, to be able to account for what happens within them, is the major missing factor in the comprehension of the mind, and hence of the generation and filtered retention of knowledge. The more we understand those processes, the more we will understand how it is we know and believe what we do, the more that understanding progresses, the more we will understand how the rules of knowledge link with the rules of nature, or depart from them.

Thus I place enquiry into the brain and the mind at the top of my priorities in research. The challenge is indeed being taken seriously within the constraints of contemporary science. As a layman, it seems to me that neurological and physiological studies are proceeding at a rate far exceeding that of the past -- but that the data are still not ready to lead us beyond speculative models. The development of mood changing drugs such as Prozac, with some understanding of why chemical intervention affects the brain's processes, and the location of areas of the brain linked to behaviour and emotions, indicate increasing interest and success. Some of the studies provide a physiological basis for understanding ways in which the *total* bodily system, including the senses and organic malfunctions, affect the brain and its consciousness. But by comparison with what we don't know, this is as yet picayune[168].

Consideration of the brain opens up the can of worms that the current methods of science are probably not enough, indeed may well be epistemologically insufficient, to understand. Innovation, remember, is linked to what is already known. Epistemologically, this means reliance on modifying, or tinkering, with what is already tried and apparently true. We advance with analogies and depart from them at our risk. When they are departed from, it requires others to recognise that the departure has use. The history of science is populated by those who reversed a known principle (Galileo), linked hitherto unlinked observations (some new) together (Newton, Darwin, Freud), and so on. Recall the resistances, not based on criticism of what was proposed but on ideology and on the conservatism that results from the inevitable dependency on what has gone on before. The paradox is that what has gone on before cannot be allowed to inhibit changing our perception of it, *building* upon it, and even destroying parts of it.

It may be that we are awaiting more such revolutions in the investigation of the brain. Those who suggest that there are phenomena connected to the functioning of the brain that the epistemology of contemporary science is not equipped to reveal are frequently dubbed as cranks. In some sense many are at least confusing science and faith. But behind the confusion lie some real questions.

The term paranormal is indicative. Science on the whole deals with the normal world, a world of tested methods and the predictability of their usefulness. In that body of concepts there are primary notions of energy. Never mind that these notions are being revised almost continuously as atomic physicists and astrophysicists and brain researchers learn more. There is a set of concepts that are organised in such a way that the kind of energy represented in nature is consistent and coherent. We sort of know what we mean by magnetism, light, sound, radio waves, electrical charges, gravity, and the ways in which particles play with each other, inventing the concept of anti-matter to make sense of it. We know that scientists observe and measure these things. As they do so problems keep cropping up requiring more refined measurements and observations and new loci of energy.[169] We also know that three hundred years ago some of the types of energy that are talked of today were not known as such.

Let us start with the kinds of energy we know about. If you place a suitable designed receiver at any spot in the world that is not shielded from radio waves you will be able to receive and translate radio signals from thousands of transmitters. Any amateur can do this, as I did as a boy. The basic premise has to be that all the thousands of signals are *simultaneously* passing through the one place where the receiver sorts them out.

If the brain is not shielded, the signals must be passing through the brains of each of us. Each of us is a potential radio and television receiver. Sci-fi apart, that is not my point. The point is that we are not conscious that this is happening to us. The waves exist in nature, so that to some extent the brain during its evolution had to deal with such invasions. What do we know about this? I understand that there is a considerable literature on, for example, microwaves. Most issues that are argued about in the press deal with potential associations with physiological disrupture such as anaemia or cancer. And I apologise (as I must throughout the discussion here) if there is a major body of knowledge of which I am unaware. I would expect that the passage of such waves through the body would have some effects. This does not mean that they cause anaemia or cancer. The relationship between energy waves and bodily functioning seems to me to be likely to be subtle and undramatic, but nevertheless there, just as the effects of food intake are there. It may even be that the body has defence mechanisms to inhibit such invasions from having effects, from, for example, disturbing its internal electrical impulses. Existing scientific methods should be able to tell us something.

On the other hand, are there other energy systems, or other energy sources which are consistent with the current paradigm, that a study of the brain may reveal? I most certainly do not believe everything I hear about the paranormal. But I regard the fantasies as the expectable outcome when humans are trying to deal with, and manipulate, that which is *not* understood. Is this not a portrait of alchemy dealing with the unknowns of chemistry? And, as with alchemy, there are those who, in limited ways, try to investigate paranormal phenomena. They find fraud, trickery and hypnotism. But they also find indications that "there is something unexplained".

I do not have to provide a comprehensive list. Human auras captured on photograph. Close-to-death experiences. The transmission of feeling between persons in physical proximity. A part of what in anthropology is called "mana", exuding power and charisma. The capturing of thought across space. Faith healing. *Déja vu.* The consciousness of events, such as the death of a loved one, which occur far beyond immediate perception.

My scepticism extends to the dismissal of such reports as nonsense. Many are not. It may turn out that there are as yet unknown psychological processes of an ordinary kind which explain them. It does not seem likely that such explanations will be valid for all instances. My scepticism suggests that dismissal is based upon the unquestioning belief in present scientific paradigms, at least to the extent that they cannot be revolutionised.

It may well be that existing energy concepts will be capable of handling such questions; but not if they remain relatively uninvestigated. If they are so investigated, much that we do not know about the brain will be revealed; including, in the extreme, ways in which the brain constructs fantasies and communicates them to others. But in my view the investigations are unlikely to be fully revelatory unless the investigators are prepared to use as hypothesis that there may be kinds of energy linked to the human body that we do *not* know about, and which may not be measurable with the kinds of instruments at our disposal. *The energies of contemporary physics may not be the only kinds.* Perhaps we need a concept of the transmission of force, or power, that uses quite different metaphors.

We cannot talk of the mind without raising problems in psychoanalysis. It has been shown on many occasions that Freudian and Jungian procedures, for example, are based on faith, that curative claims for the procedures are defective, and that there have been very few attempts at controlled studies of outcomes, a process that is foreign to the movements. I am not concerned with those charges, which are common to almost the whole body of alternative therapies, partly because the practitioners have been driven, at various times, into self-defence cults through opposition (itself failing to set up controlled studies). I am instead concerned with the basic underlying concepts as subjects for investigation.

These concepts are those of the subconscious, the collective unconscious, and, by extension, archetypes and the place of dreams in what I am calling the mind. I find the concepts so chillingly lacking in accuracy, yet adhered to in their psychoanalytic form by so many respected intelligences, that I wonder what I must be missing. That in itself doesn't matter: the reader will be able to correct. But the *issue* matters because I have asserted that a precise knowledge of the mind-as-brain is essential to us in so many ways.

There can be no doubt at all that there is a subconscious although this may be a portmanteau word for several phenomena. If that were not so, the brain, in order to function as a memory bank would be flooding us with millions of images, in a totally chaotic way. They have to be stored away, ready to come forward on call.

We also know that most of our memories are not literally true, or are true only to some degree. We only have to think back and check against realities, such as diaries of the time. I have done this and am surprised at what my memory of my youth is and at the discrepancy with diaries. Psychoanalysts would argue that this is because we are suppressing though some of the memories are inaccuracies rather than full suppressions. That suppression takes place is also agreed. The connotations of suppression and forgetfulness are different. Is an Alzheimer's sufferer suppressing? I think not. Suppression implies a deliberate act, sometimes of the conscious mind, and unconsciously through biases, some would say distortions, of the psyche, especially when troubled. Forgetfulness and inaccuracy of memory are different.

Two points immediately arise. If it is in our nature as humans to suppress in the more deliberate sense, or even to forget, the questions are how and why? A functional and evolutionary approach would suggest that there is good reason, that we are *meant* to do these things for the good functioning of the socio-biological unit. If so, to pull these out of the subconscious could be a dangerous game, and may account for therapy failure. Forgetfulness may of course result from the need to clear the brain's storage capacity of space, rather like clearing a document from a hard drive. The address to the location is wiped, but it remains around somewhere and may be retrieved by appropriate searches that do not depend on the address unless it has been over-written. A troubling feature of a psychoanalytical approach is that it is directed not only at those who declare themselves to be sick and who seek help, but also at those who in normal society are considered healthy. Freudian-based psychoanalysis demands that a qualified analyst be analysed to know himself or herself. The process -- apart from its secret society overtones -- implies that what the organism spontaneously does is not organically sound. Psychoanalysis is somehow God's gift to make up for the mistakes of nature, and can only be understood through immediate subjective experience of it.

The other point is that retrieved memory is not necessarily accurate -- in fact it won't be, for memory never is. There will be errors, trivial or significant. To base remedial action on memory, spontaneous or retrieved, has to be the case. Memory, it has been pointed out, is a *living thing*, a part of a living, ever-changing, ever-renewing body. To assume that what is retrieved through analysis is any more accurate, without independent verification, than spontaneous memory is too big a jump.

Thus we need vastly more research on how this all happens within the brain. In parenthesis we may remark that discrimination in memory has positive effects (in addition to avoiding the unpleasant), since as a result we put our knowledge together in various new shapes and forms. In other words we are predisposed to create. It might well be that if we had complete and accurate memories of our past we could not function.

The search for the collective unconscious, and of archetypes, is a different matter, for the issue here becomes one of nature versus nurture. It is distressing that both Freud and Jung necessarily drew upon an anthropology that was in its infancy for their stimulation and claims of universality. It would nowadays be argued, for example, that the interpretations that Jung made on the basis of short-term African experience must by their nature be flawed. No one, it would be argued, could reasonably interpret myth, religious and spiritual concepts, psychological orientations, dreams, or any sensitive materials in which ideas require contextual interpretation, without extensive participatory enquiry into the depths of culture, which in turn requires the mastery of language. Which does not necessarily mean that Jung was wrong; rather that he could not know if he was correct or not.

Another field of enquiry which I would emphasize, perhaps more urgently, is in the field of pedagogy.

Our plans for Youth Maturity Institutes can so easily be watered down, trivialized and made ineffective by weak pedagogical instruments. Colleges of Education have been derided in the past, especially in North America, for insignificant, frivolous and inept research activities. This is unfair to those individuals who have maintained high standards on serious issues and I am sure that the research ambience has changed foe the better.

In part weaknesses have been caused by time spent on looking into marginal or logistical questions rather than fundamental ones. What we desperately need to know are answers to such problems as: How, and with what approaches, can Youth Maturity Institutes, with their anticipated resources, most effectively counteract violent tendencies or alienation in youth? Classroom exhortation is clearly not enough. How can prejudice and charity be turned into understanding? What classroom methods can be devised to ensure the effectiveness of the Youth Maturity Institute goals? How do these intersect with non-classroom activities? What indicators can be made available, or developed, to enable observers to detect the emergence of individual stresses and psychological issues in the children? How can hidden sources of creativity be discovered most effectively?

Another subject of major concern for enquiry is the potential capability of humankind to live elsewhere than on this planet. Humankind discounts the future in terrible ways. We turn our backs on doing anything about volcanic eruptions or earthquakes or even global warming because it seems to be not here today but maybe decades later. Astronomers are good at noticing alien bodies about to impact the earth. The sighting and tracking of a significantly damaging body can start when it is many years away. Research is taking place[170] to attempt to destroy many of the lesser bodies before they hit ground. A truly cataclysmic body capable of destroying the earth's surface would surely, by its very destruction if that were possible, have other devastating effects which would threaten life on earth as we know it. We cannot wait to know how to evacuate the earth until just the moment the danger is sighted, long though our warning might be. For the answer to where do we go has not even begun and is hugely complex. So, rather than waste money on huge earthly missile defence systems (when the answer to that danger lies in Global Government) we must start knowing about a future homeland and how to get there. This is for the 21st century to start, not the fiftieth.

We have no knowledge as yet of how to organise a mass evacuation of earth. Nor do we know where such an evacuation should end up. While we are continuously looking for signs of life elsewhere comparable to humanity, there is very little we know on that subject with reasonable degrees of certainty, given the vastness of the universe. And we definitely don't know how much time we have got. Because cataclysm is unlikely to hit the living generation in any but critically manageable form, we assign relatively low priority to such studies. Enquiry of long-term, very long-term, significance should be more than equal to the resolution of the immediate.

Quite possibly linked to our future fates is the controversial domain of hyperspace, the theoretical and applied study of multi-dimensions -- I am told up to ten dimensional space as it exists now. Such words raise science fiction thoughts of parallel universes, of the possibility that living beings can arrive on earth in dimensions we cannot or can only partially, detect. I say "raise thoughts" because the understanding of ten or so dimensions is totally beyond me, and in truth I have no idea whether the concepts have any relationship at all to what science fiction writers imagine.

The point is, however, worth making because of the innovative dynamics outlined in Chapter II. However unimaginable are the imagined worlds of science fiction, they consist of weaving together conceptual strands that are already in our web of culture, so that the whole cloth, consisting of newly imagined relationships between existing culture-facts, is like a magic carpet transported from another, yes, dimension, to float within our minds. Quite often, elements in science fiction are not far ahead of what scientists are already addressing. Sometimes the imagined cultures consist of the present, satirised to be sure, with existing phenomena exaggerated and extended toward the impossible, which later turns out to be real. It is false to think of such imaginings as minor. Electronic tracking devices for humans, communication from any human body to any other located anywhere on the globe (or even in space), video surveillance, robotic domestic and medical services, semi-intelligence devices working with fuzzy logic, instant data banks on everyone, electronic identity cards containing one's personal history, surveillance cameras tracking every movement -- these, the stuff of science fiction's paraphernalia that underlie imagined social and political systems, these are already here, awaiting refinement which is coming at a pace not seriously believed to be likely forty years ago.

Imagination is the stuff of knowledge, and, in whatever form it is presented to us, sparks disciplined thought, which, I believe, will increase in intensity the more human beings are released from drudgery so that they may, each in their own way, live creatively.

Remember, our hoped for world is a creative society and in the chapter on Work, we shall see that it is possible.

Thinking about ecosystems has become indeed a major preoccupation for those who enquire conventionally, those who manage commercially and politically, for those who show their concerns by joining with others and attempting to influence outcomes, by schoolchildren. The remaining issues of ecology are still, not only serious, but on a scale that requires much more disciplined attention.

The natural world on earth is so enormously complex, with so many trillions of interacting elements, that I am confident that what we believe to be sound knowledge today (sound knowledge that is seldom agreed to by all) will look quite different in the future.

The study of minimal eco-systems can embrace for simple manpower reasons only a tiny proportion of what could be known. Another set of studies, interacting with the former, deals with wider eco-systems. The task of integrating all these, and other forces, into global models is, literally, in its adolescence. Data on effects of global warming are capable of several interpretations. When one seems to be prepotent, other sets of data, themselves necessarily imperfect, call for a re-arrangement of the factors, another set of explanations. This is necessary, will go on possibly *ad infinitum*, but surely clearer knowledge will emerge. [171]

Two interferences with nature in the name of science are worthy of note. One is the frequent call for the preservation of a species on the verge of distinction, often, though by no means always as a result of human action or the changing climate. Here humankind, as an integral part of nature, is denying the natural dynamics of its own role and, on the other hand, adapting its role as a part of nature to intelligently interfere with evolution. There is a tendency to discount the point that evolution continues its march, and that drastic cataclysm, can sometimes result, as at Chernobyl, in a new adaptation of a species rather than its total destruction. The other theme is to artificially preserve species in a bank of nature, in case in the future we need to study or even regenerate a species. Zoos and the cloning of animal life are part of this value laden research task. Vaults of seeds, plant materials and DNA banks are now operative.[172] Both sets of efforts are bedevilled by the continuous discovery of new species

Many of the consequences of global warming, and of the large cycles of natural warming and freezing, are inadequately studied. These include protection issues – defences against rising waters, conditions in which population shifts may be necessary, and, as I pointed out in the previous chapter, the adjustment of food supplies through modifications in the food chain to fit new climatic conditions. In previous tropical or ice ages mankind did not have the tools to undertake such studies or modifications. Now, once again, we do, but do we have the determination and the will to do so?

Which question leads immediately in to the issue of genetic modification......

Genetic modification has become a buzz phrase carrying ideological premises as if every form of genetic modification equated every other. There are dangers in slap dash, careless, not considering the consequences, references to genetic modification because of their variety. All such activities carry implications for the future, not all of which may be known. This is true of other man induced controls of nature as well. There are other acts of genetic modification which are as well controlled as is humanly possible, and the controls continue to be improved. In other words it is false to tar each act of genetic modification with the same brush. Each action must be judged on its individual merit, weighing the costs and benefits..

Furthermore, genetic modification has been with us since the invention of breeding animals and cross fertilizing crops, and very often the results have been the reverse of what was wanted. But the crosses which persist have been invaluable – new strains of wheat and rice increased yields in the Third World, relieving some poverty. Even a new animal, the mule, came into being, to say nothing of specialist wool bearing or flesh enhanced sheep, and quite different strains of horses and cattle. It is my contention that the difference between this and laboratory genetic manipulation is that there are more controls with the latter, and that there is no reason in principle to ban it, or to ban the use of the results. There is every reason to insist on maximum investigation of consequences before any product is released to the public.

Indeed this is a field which demands major priorities in research, for the simple reason that it holds one of the answers to the effects of phenomena such as global warming. Humanity needs, in very short order, to adjust its crops and animal husbandry to the swings of climate change – of global warming in the now future, and of at least a mini ice age further down the centuries. Genetic modification is probably the fastest way of doing this – and given the huge diversity of domesticated species, no time should be lost. Where once humankind left it more or less to nature to produce the results, that caused long term suffering. The contemporary spread of dense population restricts the possibilities of consequent migration. Ironically, a form of genetic modification is already normal in human therapeutics – the identification of genes responsible for certain illnesses, leading to the use of this knowledge to create gene-suppressing medication.

So much work is going on in the world of medical science, with exponential growth in research and its costs, and in its results that it may seem redundant to stress it. However the balance seems awry. The profit motive, which I do not deride, has the consequence of making drugs out of reach even for governments. New and more technical machines arrive and after all their absence are suddenly deemed to be essential at the cost of millions, and perhaps of advances in other medical fields. In small part this is counterbalanced by the increased use of robots in the United Kingdom and Japan for both housekeeping and surgical procedures, reducing the demand for labour.

One of the despairing features of medical and pharmaceutical research is the way its priorities are governed by national immediacies and the attendant commercial priorities. Scholarly associations in various countries do try to draw attention to imbalances, but governments are chary of listening. Despite the sometimes successful efforts of the World Health Organisation, global issues get little attention unless, like influenza, there is a probability of direct impact of a country's population. All too rarely, it takes the initiative of a major private donor to break through the confines.

Thus it has taken the private initiative of Bill and Marilyn Gates to start to address one of the major imbalances. Profit-oriented research focuses to a major degree on the ills of financially advanced countries. Would the scourge of AIDS in the poor world have received attention if it had not also devastated the West? I think not. But malaria, disease of the poor, kills as many in the countries where it is present. Europe and North America got rid of it only a couple of centuries ago, but they did. Bill Gates, noting the few resources available for the study of anti-malarial vaccines, drugs and therapies, established a well endowed Foundation to concentrate on the issues. He has also created a specific fund to endow researchers in areas of medical study that are inadequately supported by conventional funding sources.

I will also be advocating in a later chapter the use of higher education and institutional research as a method of alleviating poverty in destitute countries. This would also have as a by-product the likelihood that new research priorities would emerge in otherwise under studied areas.

There are few benefactors with the wealth or sensitivity to do the same for the other scourges – ebola, the tsetse fly, locusts (for a different branch of science), sleeping sickness, cholera, hepatitis, schistosomiasis, and many others.

Once again governments, until the problem jumps over borders, sit on their figurative hands. They tend to put it off until it really does start to become or to threaten a pandemic. Dangerous short-sightedness and selfishness.

The only governmental organisation capable of taking a world view is the World Health Organisation (or its successor forecast in the chapter on Global Government). It needs a massive injection of research funds by the Global Government – Bill Gates multiplied by ten. Note my later call for the concentration of military power in the hands of Global Government to relieve the budgets of states.

A word about anthropology. Like economics used to be, anthropology is not a discipline but consists of points of view that make use of varying disciplines. I do not hold a brief for anthropology in its present state. But if we are to examine the potential paths toward our anticipated world, to trace them, and if that world is to be recognisant of and based upon sound knowledge of the ways in which societies and cultures work, then what anthropology, somewhat unknowingly, stands for, is essential, even if by some other name. In its underlying but imperfectly applied philosophy anthropology is in fact the nub from which a holistic, synthesising interpretation of the world can emerge.

The statement rests upon the fact that anthropology draws into itself theories, methods, perspectives and sometimes data from all other disciplines which bear upon the nature of human behaviour. The most effective anthropologist, from this point of view, is one who has been trained to the graduate level in another subject (once a mandatory requirement, in effect, at the London School of Economics). Obviously, no scholar can encompass the whole of what has been achieved in other subjects. But his or her knowledge of at least one of history, biology, psychology, economics, some sociology, music, art, mathematics, political science, will inevitably enter into his or her methodology, question-formulation and theoretical constructions.

This is necessary to anthropology, a central part of its system, currently undermined by a too early specialisation. To construct explanations, it must try to put the phenomena it examines *in context*. It is clearly, at this point, extremely difficult if not impossible to achieve totality in accounting for a context. But that is the aim, whether the problem be connected with incest, the money market, or the ways in which illnesses are recognised.

After the contextualisation comes the simplification, the reduction of the data to abstract principles. To do this we need data bases, some of which are known as "thick ethnography", of great detail, of many dimensions, and at a relatively low level of abstraction. Unfortunately, the creation of thick ethnography is often thought of as a goal in itself. It cannot be, if the powers of anthropology are to be released. Anthropology needs many more abstracting minds at work, if its answers are to be applicable to humankind.

There is literally no subject area of human existence, at any time or place, which is beyond anthropological study, in which questions of anthropological relevance are not embedded. This is a point that most non-anthropological social scientists do not at present realise.

In part, they do not realise it because anthropology lacks the enormous man and woman power to obtain not only its data base but to emphasise its links with colleagues in other subjects. This is reflected in the conservative organisation of scholarship. Ph.D's do the work, often alone. In my view they need to be supplemented by hosts of simply trained data gatherers, whom we may call para-anthropologists -- recruited from professionals like teachers, nurses, agricultural officers in the field. And also, why not, some of the army of the non-employed who will emerge from the reformed employment conditions and guaranteed income proposals to be outlined later.

It is also a reflection of the fact that the weight of anthropological enquiry moves with fashion, and that very few specialties within anthropology have enough critical mass to meet their goals, let alone make them known outside the profession. To make its rightful impact, for example, economic anthropology would need to have almost as many practitioners as the whole of anthropology now. How else can it cover the territory? All times, places and questions? And that is the same for several score of anthropology's other interacting parts.

I have tried to give examples of long term, very long term issues that come to mind, and I do so as a corrective to the current intense preoccupation with immediate and even payable results. Readers will identify other domains of knowledge which in their view are equally, perhaps more, significant, to our future. Good.

For what it all adds up to is that our desirable world is knowledge-based, and that to get there we need expanding understandings. Other chapters have brought forward the notion that humankind, the individuals who make it up, seldom have the challenge or opportunity to use their creative minds to the fullest. There are vast mental energies which are underused. This, rather than in wage-earning, is the true unemployment we face.

It is here that the venture lies. This will be the location of human contentment, growing out of grappling with challenges. It will be through these kinds of activities, or never at all, that we reach our desired world.

2012   Postscript

- Measurement and counting have played an enorm99us role in science and we need more of it, properly focussed, in the social sciences The practice has also played a central role in public affairs, particularly in commercial judgement, but needs handling with care. Cf. Allen, Douglas W. *The Institutional Revolution. Measurement and the economic emergence of the modern world.* Chicago, University of Chicago Press, 2012.
- The existence of the Cloud which links computers together to expand the capacity of software, data volumes and the ability to daw logical inferences raises issues about the human brain. To some extent the brain makes use of electrical connections and dynamics. We are far from understanding the ways these work. When we do it might well be possible to link brains together to resolve issues on the analogy of the Cloud. This could put together in one dynamic whole a host of memories, knowledge conceptions and ideas, and imaginations far

beyond the storage of any single individual – or even seminars or scholarly conferences.

• It appears that an indicator of possible life, in rudimentary forms at least, is the presence of water which is essential for life as we know it. But there's the rub. This imaginative example worthy of science fiction suggests though that we should open our minds to the possibilities of life *without water*. We certainly do not at present know under *what* other conditions, but science should at least be open to the shock such an observation would afford. After all water itself requires other ingredients before life emerges in it or in connection with it.

• Among the themes in the social operation of science are (a) nothing in the body of scientific knowledge is immune from challenge and (b) somewhat contradictorily, science deals in certainties (expressed through such devices as measurement and mathematical argument.) Science does not like ambiguities or observations which cannot be "explained" in terms of associated processes. Much of research involves addressing such dislikes. There is little room for the acceptance that ambiguity and chance can be essential to accurate and essential explanation.[173]

• The relationship between political authority and science is tendentious. Political authority answers to the values of its citizens or its power elite. Science answers to the objectivity of controlled observation and logical argument. Recommendations of scientific bodies , especially those created by the political authority are frequently filed for further examination or emasculated by putting side recommendations which are unpopular with elements of the population, considered to be of less importance in the competition for resources, or simply misunderstood. We are all aware of the difficulty in following scientific knowledge when it comes to environmental, forestry, or fisheries policy, to say nothing of crime and education. It is not uncommon for scientists to be ordered not to publish openly or speak to the press or even speak at meetings of colleagues. and unpopular scientific views can result in the dismissal of scientists who are government employees. It is often the case that governments appoint commissions of enquiry on subjects dealt with by science with a judge in charge. While this usually ensures objectivity, the operation involves as many lawyers as scientists, lawyers to defend a non-scientific perspective. For example one such enquiry into aspects of polygamy in British Columbia in 2011 used as data only one such institution (fraught with contentions problems) totally ignoring the methodological principle of examining a large number of such institutions, often analysed in anthropological studies with observations of general application.

- The genetic selection of babies is now available for gender choice. Parental decisions can thus have a major new effect on population structures. For example the effect of preference for male children in many cultures is likely to be exacerbated. There are even more worrying possibilities if genetic control of babies expands, for example influencing eugenics decisions, skin colour, eye colour, hair, muscle tone, and perhaps eventually personality and obedience. One wonders if the brilliant scientists involved in this breakthrough considered the effects and ethics of what they were up to.

• It is likely that the creation of an HIV vaccine will influence the cultures of sexual activity, although this is not known and may occur anyway.

• Initially the democratisation of the digital age was begun by the requirement of scholars to communicate faster and more readily. In the early days this meant that ideas and papers could be moved around researchers in the richer world with greater effects on innovation. Today the capabilities are being shared by thinkers in Latin America, Asia and Africa. This is now more of a two way circulation. Indian innovations in the supply of health care are to the point.

• As the experience of Nazi Germany taught us only too well, science and technology in the wrong hands creates enormous political and policy dilemmas. The initial research does not even have to be in the wrong hands. Chemical researchers are unable to interfere with the work of other chemical researchers who use the former's results in the cause of chemical warfare. Biologists who study flies discover that colleagues are perfecting ways of using the insects to disseminate toxins to enemies in times of warfare[174] and computer technologists are active not only in hacking crime but in attacks on foreign computer systems, amounting in fact to clandestine aggression.

• There is much expressed fear that we humans are in danger of becoming tools at the service of technological instruments, even including robots and the physical and mental demands of gadgets. Supporting open, even uncontrolled, creativity in education (advocated in earlier chapters and through the guaranteed income policy (to be advocated in a later chapter) would do something to counterbalance this.

- The exponential growth in accessible data creates enormous problems in management, sorting and economically accessing what is useful. This is particularly true in business information as data is stored in the digital cloud. It can also obscure what is useful to science or stored for scientific purposes. Digital programmes help but do not cure.

- The social sciences are also caught up in these dilemmas. Of particular concern is the state of economic analysis, as I have complained above, since economists have a disproportionate role in policy decisions. Nobel Laureate Paul Krugman has written "The economics profession went astray because economists, as a group, mistook beauty, clad in impressive looking mathematics, for truth..... The central cause of the profession's failure was the desire for an all-encompassing, intellectually elegant approach that gave economists a chance to show off their mathematical prowess." Economics of choice rather than modelling might be more realistic.[175]

- A major source of misunderstandings in both the social sciences and journalism's reporting of science results (particularly medicine) is the misunderstanding of the significance of statistical correlations. In its raw state a statistical relationship merely creates a hypothesis which is yet to be ratified either by logic or further experiment. Far too often such a relationship is presented as a new final truth, which it not.[176] The social sciences are also caught up in these dilemmas. Of particular concern is the state of economic analysis, as I have complained above, since economists have a disproportionate role in policy decisions. Nobel Laureate Paul Krugman has written "The economics profession went astray because economists, as a group, mistook beauty, clad in impressive looking mathematics, for truth..... The central cause of the profession's failure was the desire for an all-encompassing, intellectually elegant approach that gave economists a chance to show off their mathematical prowess." Economics of choice rather than modelling might be more realistic.[177]

• It has been estimated that the volume of digital data is growing at five trillion bits per second[178]

• Note: Sprnberger, Joe *Dreams and Due Diligence: Till and McCulloch's stem cell discovery and legacy.* Toronto, University of Toronto Press. Daar, Abdallah and Peter Singer, *The Grandest Challenge: Taking life-saving science from lab to village* New York Doubleday.

• The growing sophistication of robots raises issues about the ethics of replacing humans in the work force and as with computers, in the intellectual work force. However the past experience of industrial revolutions suggests that the most likely outcome may be *increased* demand for such skills as they adapt after a period of disruption.

• If we are to achieve the goals addressed in this *Manifesto* we will need all the help we can get from the social sciences, since the design of effective action lies in the purview of sociology, economics, anthropology, political science and their adjuncts. Of these only economics has the regular ear of policy makers. I noted when I attended a meeting of UNESC's General Assembly's discussion of the humanities and social science, very few of the country delegates were qualified in the social sciences.[179]

• Nineteenth century economics was in effect the study of mankind's choices, even when it considered institutions, as with the economics of industry. However as the twentieth century advanced economics moved further in emphasising its roles studying those events which could be related to "the measuring rod of money" and the sometime became hypnotised by mathematical models. Some of this was invaluable to policy makers who themselves seemed hypnotised by this established science and economists became their agents of prediction. Some of this was quite wrong but that was hardly noticed until the banking and sovereign debt crises of 2011-12. The reason for this appears to be not only the abandonment of the study of choice itself[180]. It seemed to me also that economists ignored the other social sciences with disdain and seldom accrete their methods or findings until they, the economists belatedly discovered them indecently thus giving them the requisite caché.

• A research institute in Bangkok has created a solar powered lunch which is constructed as a floating water purifier. It is intended to supply purified water from polluted sources to communities whose supply has been rendered inoperable by floods.[181]

XI – Of Terrorism and Freedom

The shock of 9-11 in the United States sent the world into a tizzy and, in the U.S., into paranoia. 9-11 was not the first, the largest, the most brutal, or the last of terrorist massacres, for the definition of terrorism, although nowadays usually implying individual acts, has to be also applied to armed conflict with harasses that terrorises and kills civilians even as "peripheral" consequences and quite often deliberately. 9-11 was pitifully small by comparison with the official wars of the last century, and does not compare with what has been going on in Darfur[182] or the Congo, or until recently in Rwanda. Che Guevara got away with murder and became a hero in the process.

Terrorism has been with humanity in one form or another for centuries – remember the Assassins?[183] They were a branch of Ismaili Shi'as, a group who once ruled Egypt, had castles on the offensive and defensive in Sunni and Mongol Mesopotamia, and whose swirling dervish rituals and food practices[184] had a significant though peaceful hold in Turkey. Certainly present day followers of the Aga Khan cannot be accused of bloodthirsty intentions, which give hope ultimately for peaceful segmentation and evolution.

Criminal murder is often a form of terrorism. Suicide often has similarities in creating guilts and anxieties in others. Violent death takes place in order to dramatise a grievance and cause fear in relatives. Contemporary terrorism is distinguishable in that it targets the innocent. The Assassins and the anarchists of the nineteenth and early twentieth centuries targeted those they believed to be guilty, thus taking the law into their own bloody hands, although other terrorists and, yes, official armies, have been guilty of indiscriminate massacres over the centuries. The most famous successful act was the murder in the street of Archduke Ferdinand which provided an excuse for the outbreak of the First World War. The consequences of terrorism are not to be underestimated.

Why have terrorists won this stage? The Western world, largely following the United States, put the defeat of individual terrorism, but not of more damaging wars, at the top of its policy agendas, making almost all other policies subservient to it. That perhaps natural reaction is just what current terrorists want – it is their best public relations. *Fear* of terrorism is rampant and has led to hideously expensive and intrusive and largely inefficient so-called protective measures.

President Bush characterized the defence against terror as a "war", with huge consequences for the deployment of arms, the demonization of opponents, and the disposition of treasure. By doing so he used the identical public relations strategy as the terrorists – *Jihad*

410

and war both become justifications. This has diverted funds from the handling of social ills in his own country and undermined the United States' ability to act as the wise leader of the free world and a champion of freedom.

That is only a small part of the current terrorist victory. In embracing war, the United States leads the way in its attack on freedoms, freedoms which most of the world believed it cherished as a founding principle. The Patriot Act, the unilateral limiting of the Geneva Convention, the extreme controls over the movement of visitors to the country, the detention of suspects without trial or access to legal support or time limit, the intrusion of racial profiling, represent a major step backwards from the strange and imperfect liberty that the French statue in New York harbour upholds as a beacon to the oppressed of the world. Terrorists have successfully destroyed the moral leadership of the United States as the defender of freedom.

The assault on due process is mirrored in other countries, even Britain, that supposed bastion of freedom, and France, the land of liberty, equality and fraternity. It is like a nasty virus which has escaped the control of the WHO.

Justified by war? In this case the word is a mere slip of the tongue insofar as terrorists are concerned. If war, then where is the Geneva Convention? A declaration of war is a declaration that the warrior hopes to attain a victory. No victory is in sight and even in Afghanistan in

2010 the NATO forces were having trouble in defining the nature of a victory and were backtracking from defeating the Taliban to suggesting negotiations with them, a sure sign of frustration.

Justified by 9-11? Only by paranoids, however understandable is the reaction to the horror and tragedy. The trouble is that the paranoia has persisted, dragged out by the continued freedom of the presumed Al Qaeda leader, of which more below, and the limitations of policy in Iraq and Afghanistan[185]. Thus the attack on liberty not only prevails but has become routine in the practices of governments, which some suspect to be politically motivated in order to control public opinion.

Over the centuries men and women fought for the acquisition of liberty and the rule of balanced law. It is symptomatic of the state of affairs that I feel the need to remind fellow citizens of this, of the huge sacrifices made, often in vain, of the way the Second World War was fought for freedom, of the wave of populist determination to turn autocracy and nepotism into freedom in Georgia, Ukraine, and now Libya and Egypt and hopefully in Afghanistan and Iraq.

There has been no acquisition of liberty without pain and sacrifice. The deaths at 9-11 were not an excuse for war and more violence. The correct memorial is that the country becomes more than ever determined to stand up for its liberties, not giving an inch of them away. Reaffirming and celebrating them. But we are a long way from this. Vengeance, the vengeance of the terrorist, has gripped the United States, giving the terrorists the tactical victory. An eye for an eye and a tooth for a tooth has bedevilled domestic life and politics in the Balkans and the Middle East. Has it now arrived in the West? In such a climate the introduction of Youth Maturity Institutes is both fraught and more than ever necessary.

Military abuses in Guantanamo Bay, Afghanistan, and Abu Ghaira should surprise no one. Canadians in Somalia. British in Iraq, have been caught in the same way. They go unnoticed in full scale war. If we want to stop them the first thing to do is to stop war. They also reveal a gun toting macho mentality which has deep roots, and a culture of abuse and shame in U.S. prisons which is part of U.S. culture and spreads amongst its young unarmed men, as do the sloppy trigger happy lethal reactions of a small minority of frightened soldiers.

Pitifully President Obama, elected on promises to reduce such abuses including the closing of Guantanamo Bay, has done nothing to restore freedoms in the policies of his own country. As a result of a failed terrorist incident in December 2009 he in fact strengthened intrusive measures to screen airline passengers, measures which fed into and increased civilian paranoia and which are most unlikely to stop a skilled terrorist as distinct from an amateur one.

In his handling of Guantanamo he has totally missed the point. Some prisoners are to be tried in U.S.

civilian courts. Fair enough and overdue. For the others the notion of closing the prison simply means the transfer of prisoners to other prisons, some in the United States, and others in foreign lands. This does not tackle the fundamental issue. Prisoners have been held for year after year, in some cases growing from adolescence into manhood, without trial *for lack of evidence.* Without the evidence officials continue to refer to these prisoners as bad and dangerous men. President Obama and his allies are not defending or applying the principle that only evidence supports the procedure of holding a person in prison, awaiting a speedy fair trial. Perhaps some of these men are dangerous. The fact is that this is guesswork, that the experience of Guantanamo is likely to *make* them dangerous, and that the authorities would surely be keeping a watchful eye on the activities of any released prisoners.

In such a context the boast of U.S. Presidents that they will support liberty and defend it in every part of the world is hollow, naïvely hypocritical and thoroughly mistrusted. In countries where it counts, as perhaps in Lebanon, it is shallow and even counter-productive, giving strength to the nationalist opponents of liberty and U.S. interference. The demand for liberty comes from within. Outsiders can help but not impose it. "U S Presidents," too often is the cry, "put your own house in order", a cry the Chinese use with effect, and undermines genuine moves towards democracy in other countries. President Obama's welcome "soft" approach to international relations rings very tinny indeed when his own country is so rife with abuse. To make it worse, the freedom loving United States too often supports autocratic regimes and is suspicious of the Arab springs because the *sine qua non* of their support requires that the country or movement concerned openly joins the fight against Al Qaida. In fact dubious regimes such as Russia and its satellites use the threat of Al Qaida as a stick to beat down some oppositions.

It is the thesis of this work that violence in *any* form, whether domestic. criminal, in war or in terrorism, is to be rigorously done away with. (In a later chapter I do give a revised global government the sole right to international policing which can involve meeting violence with violence. I will regard the use of violence by *any* nation state as illegitimate.

The nasty responses to terrorism are legion. Imprisonment without trial, torture, airline security are perhaps the most dramatic. The 2010 Winter Olympics in Vancouver and the 20112 Summer ones in London called forth a vast assembly of armed forces, naval and air patrols, and thousands of extra police. Yet no one can guarantee that this expenditure, which could be used to remedy the issues of homelessness, can truly prevent the actions of a skilled and determined terrorist, especially one who is dubbed a martyr. Most optimistically they could catch such a person in the act, or after he or she has done the worst. In Britain there are upwards of 4.2 million CCTV cameras in operation, leading the country to be dubbed "a surveillance society". Other countries have followed suit. In Canada I discovered that the system has intruded into private companies when I was told that my every move I made in a supermarket as I made my purchases and drank a glass of wine had been taped by security cameras. Intrusions of this kind become pervasive as the citizenry allow them to proceed unchecked.

The language of terror defence has spread into the justification of other acts. The damage caused by unmanned drones and other devices on civilians in Afghanistan and Pakistan is defended as an "unfortunate" by-product of the war on terror. The suppression of civil rights, the imprisonment and mistreatment, even murder, of activists, the totalitarian occupation of Chechnya are all justified by the need to suppress what is called terrorism in public relations handouts. One may have differing views of the legitimacy of the Tamil uprising in Sri Lanka. It is too easy and simple, as has been done for example in Canadian policy, to dismiss the Tamil Tigers as a terrorist organisation. The distinction between that and a freedom fighter is shady and mute. And in Sri Lanka military victory has been followed by the attempted suppression of non-Tamil opposition.

Terrorism at the present time[186] is mostly Islamist, though others join the fray for psychological, pillaging or additional motives.

In the Non-Muslim world popular opinion makes some fundamental mistaken interpretations. The west, both in colonial times and the present, has an unspoken reverence for leadership. When meeting an unknown ethnic community, naval, military and colonial authorities had a habit of seeking out someone who, they surmised was the leader of the community. This sometimes led to hilarious mistakes, but more seriously when such leaders were found they became the intermediaries in what became known as "indirect rule".

The approach to terrorism and Islamist movements had much of the same characteristic. Osama bin Laden was we are assured the mind behind 9-11! We know that, as with all messianic leaders, he had a bevy of skilled aides, who no doubt were responsible for many of the effective procedures.

The concentration on killing bin Laden contained major misinterpretations however valuable it may have been as political propaganda, Al Qaeda is not a unified military or political organisation. In spreading globally the name is in many respects a public relations exercise, enabling perpetrators to claim some sort of authority and use the name to scare the public. It is easy for any violent group to claim such an association.

. Nor is the Taliban[187] a single cohesive group: it is made up of many factions (which lies behind NATO's idea of bribing adherents to leave the movement.) From time to time we hear that an Al Qaeda leader has been killed. Celebration. Surprise, surprise, a new leader emerges and the organisation continues without a tremor

(and sometimes civilians have been killed in the process, leading to more anger.)

The occasional targeting of Muslims as terrorist activists or sympathisers is of course far too easy and dangerous a profiling. Islam is possibly the world's most democratic and loosely bound of religions. There is indeed a hierarchy of religious leadership, up to the Grand Mufti of Egypt, but it by no means centrally organised. Not only are there major differences as between, for example, Shi'a and Sunni and Ismaili and others as there are in Christian sects but local imams are only influenced, not controlled, by more famous clerics. Most stress the peaceful, non-violent elements of their religion. Some of this majority of imams are indeed trying to remedy the costs of such decentralisation by bringing together like minded leaders to pronounce on freedom and liberty and non-violence.[188]

It is easy for us to throw u our hands and say that the only defence is to increase security and give up freedoms. I aver that this is the worst possible of possibilities. Warfare is just another form of violence with insupportable costs and civilian casualties.

There are other strategies to consider.

One is on the battlefield. The great surge has taken place and already there have been unacceptable civilian casualties. The strategy is one of acquiring territorial control of areas of Taliban strength supplementing

Pakistani military efforts across the border. Firstly this is likely to result in the Taliban and if applicable Al Qaeda slipping away into the mountains and reappearing as guerrillas and terrorists in "freed" cities and rural areas.

On this level the alternative is much more subtle. To some extent it is being started with the offer for unhappy Taliban to desert. That stills leaves the hard core who are quite capable of deadly infiltration.

The answer is to use Taliban style tactics against them. Instead of massive armour and high tech equipment, which limits armies to territorial strategy, the alternative is to use guerrilla type infiltration, booby trap Taliban lines of action and supply, and pop up behind Taliban locations. It is probable that the Afghan forces would be most effective in this, provided NATO is not training them *out* of their skills. Afghans are quite used to this kind of warfare.

This then is where the Taliban in self-defence sneak back in to mix with civilians.

So the second type of action attacks them where it hurts most, but is slower to b ear results. This is to mount a major ideological offensive. One trump card would be to be able to demonstrate massive material progress in Afghanistan. As is Iraq the Allies were far too slow to embark on material reconstruction and improvement, although valiant efforts have been made.

That in itself does not defeat ideological fanaticism, but it does influence civilians to distrust the Taliban's message and provides temptation from their waverers.

It would take time and patience. It would depend on the Afghan government itself. It requires the joint effort of Muslim preachers of all variations to come together and infiltrate Taliban ranks with men who suggest alternative interpretations of the Q'ran. Start worrying debates one way or another – including radio – to create doubt and dissent.

The final and only sure fire answer requires even more patience, determination, and long term strategy. Terrorism is but one form of violence. It can be bred in the young. A joint attack on frustration in the Muslim world and anti-violence education is called for. Terrorism will not disappear – it will only take newer forms – unless this is done. We cannot afford to be in denial and put off such tasks because they are extremely difficult to put into practice. We owe it t o ourselves and the future of the world to tackle these issues directly, beginning NOW.

As in Darfur[189] violence and terrorism can be openly organised, even State supported but this is not the global form. It therefore behoves the Islamic world to support the basic premise – the removal of the cult of violence amongst the minority of its adherents. Islamic Youth Maturity Institutes. Only when the ideological power of Islam focuses on well-being, and takes responsibility for the disaffected young, will this specific kind of terrorism, perhaps to be replaced by some other until Youth Maturity Institutes take hold. This will not happen overnight.

First, the Muslim world needs time to embrace the Youth Maturity Institute concept, then it requires practical organising, and then it will be years before the first full graduates reach adult citizenship influence and leadership. If religious schools in, say, Pakistan, were to take up the idea, immense progress would have been started. In the meantime Muslim, Christian and Jewish schools must be prevented from preaching, approving, let alone sanctifying, violence.

Acts of terrorism are justified as part of a war against evil, defined by the terrorist's peers.[190] This perspective argues that evil is best countered by persuasion and example, and that violence is never justified.

There are a few good signs in such a direction. Influential mullahs in Saudi Arabia on both sides of the action met together for public theological debates. May their influence spread. Following the London bombings, for the first time imams globally issued *fatwa's* condemning terrorist violence as un-Islamic and inexcusable. And Pakistan has been taking draconian measures in an attempt to root out terrorist indoctrination from religious schools. It is minds and hearts which count.

That works the other way too. The increasing persecution of both Arabs and Jews in Europe not only contributes to terrorism but is ugly in its own character.

Terrorisms root causes? There are many, not just one.

Poverty is often cited. Based on the history of peasant and messianic movements, this is too simplistic. People who are in the depths of poverty do not usually engage in terrorist martyrdom. Instead, there must be a relationship between the level of poverty and expectations. Usually this occurs when the level of poverty is decreasing or has decreased, but all around there is wealth, and the poverty population asks why not us?

To poverty must be added claustrophobia. This is particularly relevant in Palestine, but there is also a kind of psychological claustrophobia in Afghanistan and Iraq and much of the Arab world.[191] Not only is there poverty and unemployment, but there seems to be no way out in the minds of many. It takes little imagination to empathise with Palestinian teenagers, growing up already in an atmosphere of repressive hostility, of rock throwing and aggression, with communication by graffiti, with the presence of troops ready to kill, to impose curfews (however justified) and in the midst of competitive violent factions. As in the Syrian conflict live in a society in which for hours on end you are confined in your homes, with no power or water and no news and inadequate food and medical help, totally against your will. That is what terrorism has invited and the occupying power falls into the trap with more repression. It is extraordinary that official Israel, as distinct from many of its people, fails to recognise this, and to admit that is policies are creating the very terror and hostility the policy is intended to repress. It must be one of the most self-defeating policies of a government in the world.

We have seen in earlier chapters the major importance of risk-taking in the lives of growing energetic youths. In such conditions, and in the lesser ones of Afghanistan and elsewhere, risk-taking means breaking curfews, jeering at occupying soldiers, establishing enemies whom you can taunt, risking your life by painting a graffiti. This adolescent extremism, an equivalent of Western road racing, obtains justification and extension as adult "responsibility" grows and finds the religious justification of terrorism congruent and appealing. The adolescent adopts the beard of the converted religious activist and finds that risk taking has its serious rewards.

What we have is a mismatch between the level of living on the one hand and aspirations, whether material or ideological, or religious on the other. We also have an ideological leadership supported by an executive of ability.

A driving supportive force, from which the ideology takes its message is in the Christian/Islamic extension of Judaism with its beliefs in the Messiah, prophets, and martyrdom. It is no accident that a considerable degree of education and religious knowledge is required to justify and act upon the terrorist message. Osama bin Laden was neither a fool nor dumb and those around him have considerable education. Che Guevara and the Bader-Meinhoff gang represented varieties of terrorism with more secular ideologies, unless we count Marxism as being in the Judeo-Christian-Islamic tradition.

On the basis of this theory in 1976 I published a prediction that the Palestinian diaspora and particularly the refugee camps were ripe for a fully blown messianic movement.[192] I was wrong. But on reflection not as wrong as all that. By focusing on the Palestinian diaspora I completely neglected, or was ignorant of, the widespread disaffection of millions in the Arab Islamic world outside Palestine.

The Islamist phenomenon differs from the conventional messianic and millennial templates in several respects, yet may be considered to be an extension of such phenomena into the modern Islamic world. The first is the very size of the populations that are open to the relevant dynamics. From Palestine and Iraq to Iran and Afghanistan to say nothing of the North African littoral the forces are at work. This is a huge population which dwarfs those of the medieval peasant revolts and even more so the localized millennial movements of Asia Africa and the South Seas in the nineteenth and twentieth centuries.

Allied to this is the efficacy of modern communications which are open in principle to everyone. Television and the internet are powerful unifying forces which supplement the effectiveness of localized graffiti which carry *sub rosa* details.

The leaders of millennial movements seldom proclaim that they are messiahs, but in effect they carry a holy message. In Palestine the messages of the crippled imam Abdullah Azzam are, in the words of one observer, treated "almost as if they were holy writ".[193] Sometimes, though not in Islam, there is indeed a messianic claim, as with the Lord's Liberation Army in Uganda, which also used abducted children to reinforce its vague message..

Another factor with Islam is the absence of a religious hierarchy in the normal meaning of the term. There are leaders who, because of their positions, hold important doctrinal sway. But in addition to the natural sectarian divisions, imams essentially are responsible to their individual mosques, though of course they are open to pressure from other religious leaders. On the one hand they are localized, but on the other their message and influence penetrates far more widely because of the velocity of circulation of ideas that the modern world brings with it.

Al Qaeda is the most notorious and clear example. I do not know that Osama bin Laden has ever claimed to be a messiah, and he mixed the political with the religious in his messages to carry them to a different even more potent level. As with many such movements, his failures to achieve his results (apart of frightening the West) did not undermine faith in his calls to arms.

We do not have to posit some kind of spider web global organisation. Clever organisers he had, but the culture of revenge and violence is at the fingertips of any would be follower, not necessarily with clear organisational links beyond inspiration and encouragement. By no means all of the events in Iraq are attributed to al-Qaeda, but enough are, and they provide a model for other acts of terrorism with sometimes quite different motives[194].

The underlying characteristic of conventional millennial movements is also missing, though one could argue that it is present in a different but analogous form. Millennial movements are typically social-community based – a village or a region or an occupation. In this case the unifying ideology is that of a set of religious ideas which impact on the life story of individuals from widely differing communities. The martyrs are individuals, not communities. They are not bringing the millennium to their fellows here on earth. All the evidence is that they truly believe in the reality of Paradise with its carnal and other-worldly pleasures, a joyous relief from the horrors of the earth, and a powerful and real reward for martyrdom, which asserts that the secular life is unworthy by comparison.

It is difficult for secular minded politicians, or those like George W Bush from different religions, to imagine the appeal of such martyrdom, even though Bush used a great deal of religious hyperbole in his discourses, hyperbole which falls on completely deaf ears because in a contest with committed martyrdom there is no contest. For the individual involved, a suicidal attack has an almost automatic scenario, a state that approaches that of an active trance. Nothing matters accept the planned action. The mind and body during the act are impervious to outside influence, to the environment except as it is a part of the scenario, and certainly to reason. In the successful events there has been a long build-up, not only of ideology and religious reference, but in something approaching ecstasy.

I may be well off base in my analysis of how individuals are open to such influences in Islamic society because my imperfect knowledge of the Middle East[195]. But I suspect much lies in family life and resultant psychosis, exacerbated by Palestinian like claustrophobia. It is common, though variable, in Arabic Muslim societies for children to be brought up by the women of the family, with fathers initially more remote figures. Then all of a sudden around the age of puberty the fathers take charge of the boys and introduce them to a male society from which women are excluded and strictly separated, unless they be women deemed to have low virtue and thus open to sexual exploitation. Or in the diaspora and many refugee camps the boys are let loose, with little fatherly guidance. I can imagine little that would be more dysfunctional, confusing than the sexual stresses of puberty in such a context[196].

Thus in the mix we have young people dealing with deep sexual frustration and malfunction, a domain of sub-conscious psychological trouble to add to all their other disappointments, angers and frustrations. We do not have to go far to find sources of fanaticism.

That this perpetuates men's view of women there can be little doubt. However by no means all men become terrorists as a result. Far from it. The human child is highly malleable and survives the worst of horrors, amongst which this can hardly be counted. But an impressionable and sensitive and intelligent boy, and now girl, with a predisposition to psychosis would find the need for extreme outlets, into which the ideology of violence and terror fits like a glove. And what better than Paradise?

Durre S. Ahmed analyses what I believe to be the result, by distinguishing the psychology of elite well educated fundamentalist males on the one hand and the masses on the other. The former, it is argued, are cold in their application of fundamental beliefs, repressive even brutal in their relations with women, and praising of violence in the service of their faith. The uneducated masses find emotional pleasure in following the lead. Both repress "eros" in favour of the power of "logos" - the word.[197]

Once again I remark that the authoritarian response is to use force, and to go for the leader, the figurehead, who is deemed to be responsible. If only Bin Laden had not appeared the world would be alright. Let's get him. What rubbish. The West is confronting a non-hierarchical anarchist style movement not at all dependent on organisational leaders.

No. It will take a long time to resolve the issues, but it can be done within this century. It is a battle of ideas, not guns. And the debates must, will, be undertaken within the Arab and Muslim communities themselves. The ideas of non-violence, courtesy, understanding and empathy are needed on both sides of the struggle. These are Muslim, Christian and secular values to which by far the majority of the population adhere.

Let them be stressed in Youth Maturity Institutes in the Middle East as everywhere else, and let those Institutes be equipped to understand and help with emergent psychoses and extreme social grievances.

At the beginning of this chapter I proclaimed that the terrorists have won. They have undermined liberty and created a climate of distrust and nervousness. The defence against terrorism has avoided the primary causes and concentrated on violence and counter-violence with more violence.

A main theme running through our wished for society is that of responsible liberty in its most creative forms. Events following 9-11 have set that principle back perhaps for a decade or more. Armies and anti-missile defence systems have diverted thought, energy and money from the real issues. Current policies sacrifice liberty, and are not even good *realpolitik.*

As I write this, individuals suspected of the July 2005 bomb attacks in London are arrested in what seems to me to be brilliant police work. But, as with the Iraq invasion, what of the aftermath? It appears to me that there will be trials, in accordance with current judicial thinking. I imagine that, if found guilty, the result will be long prison sentences. With what result? Unless the guilty are in solitary confinement for the rest of their lives – cruel and unusual punishment – they will mix with other prisoners in the world's most effective school for crime.

Terrorism is a form of crime, murder and kidnapping and blackmail. The mere imprisonment of terrorists creates breeding schools in prison. If some innocent people die during terrorist acts, they die in the name of freedom. Do not destroy freedom in their name. however tragically, they are paying its price. Let the courts, as described earlier, decide, and work on restitutive justice.

2012Postscript

- Terrorism in the form of massacres, bombardments, arrests, torture and persecution is a persistent form of intimidation used by states and their oppositions. The International Criminal Court is the main instrument to bring charges against perpetrators since international governments are reluctant to intervene in another state's "affairs", despite the growth of international moral principles. Tribal and religious divisions (sometimes co-existent) and extreme positions are difficult to eradicate Thus we must strive for an armed police force of an effective World Government.

• Of course governments find it easier to abuse powers when the population involved is far from the daily media attention. Indonesia's abuses in Timor went unnoticed for decades until international action was mobilised, and similar abusive policies continue in Irian Jaya, which few foreigners visit[198]. Terror from suicide bombings, abduction of children, the burning of religious gathering places, rape and sheer massacre are among the distorted instruments curiously designed to win populations over to minority ideological and political positions.

• In many respects terrorism and other forms of violence are fed by the media. A major motive for the perpetrator is to obtain widespread publicity for their cause and their martyrdom or the circumstances which led to the violence. Social media make this dimension even more relevant. The general public is of course interested from the point of view of implications for their own safety, which gives an emotional titillation. Individuals wonder if they themselves could become violent. The good guy bad guy struggle always fascinates.[199]

- Almost all major religious faiths officially proscribe violence except in the admonition of criminals. Yet all contain elements which justify violence in defence of or in the interests of the faith. As a formal justification for terrorism, religion is the predominant excuse whatever the political objective.[200]

- As reported in the main text, the events of 9-11 sparked a worldwide introduction of protective and restrictive measures which infringed on previous liberties..[201] Repressive regimes try to counter criticism by describing the victims as terrorists, often without evidence using the name Al Qaeda

The extreme measures created to counter terrorism and protect populations in most countries are based on a false idea of the terrorists' strategy. It is NOT the killing and the destructive mayhem of the act itself. That is merely the tactical instrument to establish the ultimate objective. That objective is to *create* fear and in doing so disrupt the normal way of life of the targets. The publicity given to both fear and the counter-measures is precisely what is wanted. It involves anxieties which would normally not be there, suspicion amongst citizens, disruption of normal operations such as air traffic, and a great deal of diversion of resources both in funds and personnel.

Manifesto for the New Age

XII - Work Poverty Inequality and Creative Leisure

Contradictions and paradoxes abound. I do not seek them out; it would be easier if they were not there. They present themselves. Just as with crime and health, there is a symbiotic relationship between work and leisure. We need to untangle this if we are to create a wiser world.[202]

Perhaps the most tricky issue is that of striking a balance between work for payment or material income and spending time without payment or material income. Even our vocabulary fails us. The differences are usually expressed as between employment and unemployment, work and leisure, work and play -- or free time, recreation, spare time. Reflect upon each, and you will notice immediately that none correspond even approximately to the realities denoted by the phrases work for payment and spending time without payment, for the latter has numerous manifestations.

The distinction between work and enjoyment-implying phrases does not apply. While, for many, paid work is drudgery, for many others, and at many times, work is enjoyment. Writing this book is work. It is not employment, but, I hope, it will result in payment. When I finish writing in the late morning I feel a sense of accomplishment. Whether what I write turns out to be drivel or otherwise, it feels good. I don't have to do it: I choose to do so and I am beholden to no one else.

Retirees often regret the pleasure that going to work gave them – despite its annoyances and hassles it kept them on their toes, alive.

The explosive entry of women into the "work force" is mostly determined first by their *desire* to work, because working brings them into contact with a world that being a housewife does not; it provides them with a stimulating challenge, the ability to do things that once were men's preserves. It enables them to earn their own income, to be more equal. Then they find perhaps that they are trapped, just as men are, by the need to balance income and expenditure. Before they know it, two incomes become a necessity for a family. Nevertheless, for both men and women the workplace is an *escape* from domesticity. If they are lucky they enjoy parts of their paid work and would not want to give those parts up. The pains are a price to pay for other benefits.

Agricultural advisers in developing countries sometimes endeavour to introduce what, to them, are more efficient instruments, for example a spade instead of a digging stick, and are surprised at its rejection. What appears to them as an innate conservatism that rejects the new is not conservatism as such but a judgement about the wider context of efficiency. The digging stick may or may not have some technical advantages, but more importantly it requires the use of quite different muscles, and often a different kind of rapport with fellow workers. The discomfort of using different muscles is a cost; so is the loss of enjoyable rhythms and banter.

Work is not to be equated with employment. In my city Italian, Hungarian and Chinese suburban residents grow luscious vegetables in back gardens. They tend to specialise in one or two crops, growing much more than they need. They then exchange "over the garden fence" tomatoes for corn or peppers, apples for pears.

Probably to the detriment of the monetary system, there is an upsurge of unpaid voluntary work, in charities, ecological movements, struggling little printed papers, neighbourhood television -- wherever you look it is there. It is not employment in the financial sense; it is carried out because the workers feel it to be right, that is, they gain a sense of value from it. Many are driven to it for the same reason that others are driven to seek employment -- the *need to do* something, to contribute, to gain self-worth, and enjoy human contact. Work around the house -- carpentry, sewing -- is driven as much by enjoyment as by duty. In any cost benefit analysis, this must be recognised.

I wrote that such work may be to the detriment of the monetary system. That system depends for the generation of wealth on the velocity of circulation of money. If money is not moving around fast, the opportunities for profit taking and the re-investment of profits is missed. This was as true of socialist countries as of capitalist ones. The exchanges in kind can be regarded as a sort of circulation, but the speed and efficiency is much less than with the intermediation of money. If a large portion of the gross domestic product is outside the monetary system, with volunteers, it is contributing only to direct production, with few spin-offs that come from multiplying effects beyond the immediate actions..

The point relates to one of the weaknesses of community development in non-industrialised countries. The movement relies largely on do-it-yourself techniques. These can be extremely valuable in getting things done when money is not available, but by the same token they inhibit the growth of specialist enterprises -- house construction, well boring, brick making -- and the division of labour, without which the circulation of money is restricted. If community development moves from a valuable innovation to a dogma or entrenched habit, it will have provided merely one step along the path of change, not a dynamic. It must transcend itself and create specialized work to evolve into a dynamic force.

Yet it is possible that the return to voluntarism and self-help in the last 21st century was indicative of an evolution. If my notions are correct, the benefits of the monetary system need somehow to be extended beyond employment in much more significant ways than they are now. Those who are not working for gain will nevertheless need to be compensated. The old communist adage "from whom according to his ability, to whom according to his need" describes in fact where we are headed. But it needs to be seriously redefined, and it needs to be blended with the mechanics of capitalism.

To some extent this has already been done, for wealthy countries have created expensive social safety nets. Capitalism almost "with a heart" made this possible, without, it seemed at first, restricting the economy. Now we know that in almost every country the form in which social security became established required growing indebtedness that the fiscal systems could not easily handle. And there is a backlash against high taxation which restricts freedom of expenditure and creates a situation in which individual discretionary real expenditures are often falling. Since my argument will imply more, not less, by way of public expenditure on what may be built in to social security, we will have to deal with this issue head on the chapter on fiscal responsibility.

At present there is an extraordinary resistance in the public mind to facing up to some obvious realities. Governments, both conservative and social democratic, are gaining public approbation for facing up to the reality of reducing debt, demanding more efficiency from social services, and embracing slogans such as "Get people into employment, make them get off welfare." We have proposals to force single mothers whose babies reach six months of age into the full time work force. There is talk of moving the age of retirement upwards, from, say, 65 to 67, or 60 to 63 -- for fiscal reasons. (All that does is to increase negative pressure on the entry of the young into the work force.)

Stop a moment or two. What is this? What is the objective of living? Where do we want to go? Will it next be child labour? Is that the answer to youthful alienation? Do we not *care*?

Ironically, every major economic ideology in theory looks forward to a time when there will need to be *less* work, imagined as *less* employment, *less* drudgery, and *more* leisure. Capitalism is justified by the steady increase in capital, which is competitive to labour. For decades, governments heeded. They attacked child labour, slavery, and destructive work weeks.

Now puritanism has returned. Paid labour seems to have regained its position as a moral force. If you are not in employment, or self-employed for gain, there is something wrong with you. Paradoxically, and in my view correctly, there have been moves to reduce the work week in some countries (and to demand more energy in work habits in others).[203]

Levels of unemployment, so defined, became at the highest since the Great Depression, and remained steadily for a good decade. The 2008 containing bank and credit crisis dramatically interrupted this trend. As I shall analyse in a later chapter for two years governmental remedial actions concentrated on banks and less effectively on credit and only in 2010 did the pain of the unemployed become a higher priority although austerity measure have introduced an almost never ending dimension to the issue.. Our present system simply has no tools to handle what we have designed as the pain of no paid employment.

Minuscule reductions are greeted as political triumphs. "Downsizing" is the buzz word, and downsizing means reducing the work force in particular enterprises -- including governments, which are trying to reduce the civil service at rates not seen before. That creates unemployment as a matter of policy, by governments who are sworn to reduce it.

The policies of governments and of private enterprises are not likely to change quickly or drastically, since the major restructurings are responses to realities, financial truth, and technical change. It may well be that technical change often creates new employment, just as computers increase rather than decrease the use of paper. Thus policy makers can argue that the unemployment which is being created is temporary, a blip, a friction, in the process of adjustment. To some extent they are right, and I cannot claim for sure that they are wrong: I remain sceptical. Should we be considering the possibility that reductions in paid labour for industrial economies is here to stay? And that we should try to find ways to embrace it?

We are in fact living in the midst of a change, the knowledge revolution, which is as great as that of the industrial revolution. Knowledge has always been an (unrecognised) prime commodity, but now it dominates. It translates into rapidity of communication, management of vast data, exponential growth of innovation, and electronic marvels. Many marvels reduce the need for large work forces, whether of management or on the production line, and make it desirable for companies to spread activities more evenly across the globe. New countries sometimes have an advantage not only in labour costs but in not having to write off or destroy or rebuild old capital investments to make way for the temporarily modern.

The distinction between workplace and home is becoming blurred. Perhaps we should say rediscovered, since the home as workplace is still typical of agriculture and activities in developing countries, and was normal for artisans and many others during past centuries -- the separation seems to have been a recent phenomenon. From the point of view of efficient synergy there are pros and cons to working at home rather than in a main office or workplace. Just the same it is often feasible. Electronic communication strongly affects and loosens up the location of the knowledge industries. Pleasant working environments and synergetic communities and data bases are becoming more significant than locating in an industrial park, though the population and idea concentration of urban centres still have their efficiency effects..

Unemployment, coupled with the necessity to earn income, has sparked more innovation. Individuals turn to entrepreneurship, self-employment. Many have done so with innovative fervour, adding to the supply of services, small industries, and employment which still does not provide work for all. I have also noticed that there has been a semi-explosion of artistic activity. If you can't get employment, do something you like and feel are good at, and get some cash for it in the process. Pottery, crafts, bands, specialist foods, art, even busking. There are creative impulses on which to build. Alas, many do not cover the bills.

There are several ways in which national policies could solve the paradox. The one that seems to be uppermost is to create jobs at any price. Governments force unemployed into re-training programmes. That is all very fine and might be worthwhile, but training implies a decision as to what for and it takes time. Most training programmes create competition with individuals who are trained by other means. When training is finished, there is no guarantee of employment. The requirements of commerce and industry may also have changed overnight. Effects on employment are minimal, though they could be extended if training were to be on-site for specific jobs in specific enterprises. Pushing newly trained people into hunts for non-existent or over-subscribed jobs is alienating, and damaging to the spirit.

Another is to enter into a command economy or to heavily subsidise unprofitable enterprises, that is pay people to pay others. Both are destructive of production. I do not have to demonstrate the point at this moment in the history of Eastern Europe. Because effective production is limited, they create more and more demand for more and more unproductive jobs, viciously spiralling downwards.

The unbridled single-minded search for greater employment could have disastrous side-effects. In "under-developed" countries the danger is already expressed. Ecologically sound policies cannot be afforded; employment has to come first. This could be the case in industrialised countries. Although environmentally protective industries themselves create employment, there are many voices to be heard resisting eco-friendly measures if they affect an industry that is already an employer.

We could also encourage the production of any and all "widgets" (to borrow *The Economist's* evocative word) irrespective of their social value. More dangerous toys. More drugs. More useless souvenirs. Subsidise the production and distribution of pornography. More and more armaments. A jolly good world war. In effect, we do much of this now. Certainly we could achieve full employment and much bankruptcy . Do as India does and former communists did -- enrol the unemployed in the civil service, whether they have anything to do or not.

We shouldn't want to. That is not our preferred world. Stop pretending.

As a matter of fact, I do guess that the richer industrialised countries could possibly achieve near full employment for themselves by globally free commercial policies, although it would only be temporary *and full employment should not be our goal.* The creation of the ponderous World Trade Organisation as the child of GATT, dedicated by international agreement to global free trade, helps. It is a truism that increasing the volume of trade increases wealth in general. That translates into global purchasing power. Specifically, poor countries that can produce if there is a market will have a greater chance to improve their wealth if markets are opened up to them. That increases their purchasing power, which can be used to provide a market for the things the industrialised countries can do best. Despite this elementary piece of economics, national governments still react to myopic pressure groups by placing barriers on trade with under-developed countries, *in the name of protecting national employment.* By doing so they limit their own wealth growth, create dangerous tensions between North and South, and do nothing for the figures of employment because poor countries are inhibited from earning income which creates the purchasing power necessary for the purchase of goods and services which richer countries are poised to sell............,,,,,,,,,, And so the silly circle keeps expanding.

Thus the need for greater equality of opportunity. What I have written above applies to the foreseeable future. But the long run which interests us we may conceive of an equilibrium in which access to education and knowledge are evenly spread throughout the world. Comparative advantage, opportunity costs and the location of enterprise will be based less on those two factors, or indeed any of the factors of production that are used in analysis today except supply of capital.

They will be based on *cultural* factors. Decisions as to what to do by way of production, including services, will be taken with financial criteria in mind. We will not have created a state of perfect competition in which economists will at last be at home, though we will be much closer to it than we are now. Individuals will become entrepreneurs not out of individual necessity but because it fits their personal dreams, because they enjoy doing what they are doing.

I have argued and continue to argue that cultural difference should be nurtured, that it has its own momentums, that indeed it is a mainspring of innovation, of stimulus. It will be the root of the re-emergence of opportunity variables. Cultures will continue to differ in some of their consumption demands, thus requiring variations in supply. Perhaps more significantly, they will differ in their values, in the emphasis they place on elements in their way of life. While there will be a sub-stratum (or super-stratum?) of unity, of human commonality, differing cultures will place variable weight on such matters as demand for leisure, recreational pursuits, abstract thought, spirituality, hierarchy, children, risk-taking.

As I do not argue that, for example, "national character" dictates that culture A likes risk more than culture B. Or that culture A likes to accumulate wealth more than culture B. There is considerable evidence that such comparisons are not correct and that any such data will change over time, despite the popularity of national character constructs at one time. What differs is the opportunity to express latent values. The difference between A and B, if opportunities are equal, consists (a) in the actual way the values are expressed, conceived, and felt; and (b) the distribution of individual expressions of the values through real actions in specific historical contexts.

Cut through the mumbo-jumbo. In our desired world, differing cultures will always want to do different things. These differences will maintain divisions of labour, that is differences in production and services in each country, and in styles of living. Good.

I now move to maintain that so-called *unemployment or under-employment is in fact **desirable*** and achievable, supporting a reasonably good life.

Of course right now it is *not* desirable or achievable, except for some lucky individuals, many of whom do not know what to do with it. Under-employment is touted as a curse in poor countries, because it means limitations on earning power, and consumption. But this is a function of income and education. Under-employment even there sometimes has side benefits -- closeness to nature, child-rearing, even creative pursuits. On balance, though, it can produce destitution, famine, inter-cultural violence, disease.

At present unemployed individuals are socially stigmatised. We created social safety nets to help. Now we blame the unemployed for using them. Despite the percentage of unemployed, we still urge them to get out and find jobs, preaching from our own positions of comfort. Food banks and soup kitchens are reminiscent of the line-ups of the Great Depression, and the shame of being on the dole. Public revulsion against the dole led to the safety networks being created from the idealism that followed the war. Now hopeless faces scan the notice boards. There is resistance to helping single parents, who are restricted in their work and job searches without that help. We are not far from saying the unemployed should be punished.

This is totally wrong, both morally and functionally. It is demeaning and destructive of the individual. The more we do this the more we create alienation, violence, addiction and damaged children. In some parts of the world there is a direct link to terrorism especially as intellectuals think about the wrongs of it. Why should people who are expected to do the impossible, who have no hope, not seek solace in addiction? Why should they not feel and express anger (it is amazing they do not do so more often – they do not have the energy)?

Once again, we cannot change this, the disgrace of industrial, rich, "civilisation" overnight. The employed feel threatened themselves. They see what they may become if they are fired.. Some turn their fears into genuine charity. An increasing number project their fears into demands to use forceful draconian measures on the unfortunate and destitute. Get them out of sight. Create work camps (maybe in the form of stimulus packages). Withdraw support.

No. The opposite is what we should be striving for.

First we need a major change in public attitudes. Unemployment is *not* a disgrace. It is a social fact of life. Indeed it could be argued that it is a necessary concomitant to the rewarding jobs that others have.

Further, *there is nothing morally wrong with unemployment as a way of life.* Look at it this way. If you like your job, want it, and are afraid of losing it, the person unemployed *by choice* is not going to take it away from you.

Again, non-employment may and can be creative living. For gain or not for gain, creative and worthwhile endeavours may be there. This indeed is what we look forward to, *what we want*, as characteristic.

The unemployed themselves are not prepared for such a change in attitude. I may not be making a judgement about a beggar on the street. But if that person is there against his will, as distinct from being a professional beggar, he will imagine I am, and he will make that judgement for me. It is very hard for a skilled, well-earning person, to enter the job line-ups and face the overly sympathetic looks of neighbours and friends.

Politicians and civic leaders can help to change such attitudes in the shortish term. In the longer, more fundamental, course of events we are thrust back onto the role of education.

The young must know when they leave Youth Maturity Institutes, that during the course of employment, as a matter of choice, and in retirement, there will be long periods, even perhaps a lifetime, in which they will not be directed by an employer. This they must see as an opportunity, a challenge, a chance to do things they would not otherwise have time for.[204]

They must learn the arts of time-budgeting as well as money-budgeting. They must know how to be self-reliant and how to regard sociability creatively. They must judge whether to work full-time or part-time, in terms of their own personae. They must know about their creative impulses and potentialities, how to nurture them. They must discover how to use time to be of service to themselves and others.

The impact of Youth Maturity Institutes taking on this task will be multiplying. Their change in policy will not come about without parental and political support. If that can happen, the philosophy will by definition be percolating through social attitudes and the uses of time.

There are some useful indications. Many young people are not waiting for employment but turning what they want to do into earning power -- the most visible sign being the plethora of bands, but remarkable elsewhere in the economy. There are many, both young and older, who are opting for part-time work; and others who seek contracts or flexible hours to alter the balance between time spent on doing what someone else wants you to do and doing what you yourself want to do. Some unemployed are being successfully guided into conceiving and running their own independent businesses as entrepreneurs.

Indeed one partial solution to the problem is through the shortening, not extension, of working hours, through longer vacations, earlier retirement, and the limiting of overtime, thus sharing the available work more widely. The solution meets resistance from those already in the work force, since it also spreads income more evenly and means either higher costs for employers or lower hourly income for the now-employed.

None of the above reactions, however, will deal with the present volume of available free time, or the widespread desire for more of it.

There is no escaping the only adequate remedy -- the social safety net. The non-employed must be retained as viable human beings who are of benefit to society, whose self-directed time is culturally worthwhile, who make their own individual contributions to total well-being, to thought, to ideas, to behaviour. They must in fact be nurtured.

What we are coming to is a substantial, an adequate, guaranteed minimum income. If that were where my tax contributions were going, I would be glad, instead of being resentful at some programmes such as expenditure on military force as at present.

Naysayers say, and will say, that it is subsidising people for being idle. Absolutely. *I want to do that.* For my conception is that very few would be idle if their abilities and interests had been maximised because pure idleness is dreadfully boring after a time. Do you know how boring it is to be idle? They would be free, a very different proposition. Free, not of social responsibility, but to do, individually, what the human spirit dictates. There is no better freedom. Individuals will carve out innovative niches with their own dynamic, rather than being under the control of socially distant executives.

Most people will still want to elect for paid work. There is no danger of industry breaking down. Most will be driven by the insatiable demand for consumption goods. Many will simply want to get out of the house. Others will find that employment releases their creativity

451

in ways they could not achieve outside of the workplace. Others will find that their creative pursuits lead them into entrepreneurial, organising, activity. Others will do it because their friends do and they need the sociability of the workplace. Living at the guaranteed minimum income, however generous as it should be, will not be for all, by any means.

It will, however be substantial, and a major item in any national budget and the subject of our chapter on fiscal responsibility. Moreover, it is likely to grow over the decades, maybe the centuries. Because, fundamentally, most men and women want a better balance between other-direction and self-direction.

2011Postscript

• Men, and women, are not born equal, as other manifestos would have it, unless guaranteed in the decisions of the law, in the control of the ballot box, or in the ethics of opportunity. We differ in bodily forms and health, in personality characteristics, in gender, in the use of our minds, in our formation, in our friends and partners, and much else indeed. Those whose level of living give them feelings of legitimate aspirations to rise at least another notch in the pecking order of wealth, give voice to their demands with the hyperbole of equality which, alas, is only hyperbole. It is notable that in the American dream it is individuals, not groups or classes of people who rise from poverty to riches[205]. And in the United States there is now surely an aristocracy of the wealthy not very different from the somewhat faded aristocracies of Britain and Europe. The success of publicised individuals who have risen from illiteracy in slums to major roles in enterprise and politics cannot obscure the fact that such changes are not for the majority unless accompanied by major reforms in the operation of society, politics and the economy.[206]

• The idea of the guaranteed income for all, to be examined further in connection with fiscal balance, is slowly gaining momentum as it is seen to considerably remove hardship, remove wasteful social payments, and contribute to economic growth. Further it is morally justified in an ethical society where humanity opens areas of creative wellbeing instead of closing doors through ruthless assertions of superiority.[207] [208]

• We cannot afford the costs of poverty.[209]

• Social and medical costs of poverty, not only in the poorer countries but in the richer ones which have numerous endemic poverty sectors, are grave. They include, for example cholera, rickets, malnutrition, osteoporosis, goitre, diarrhoea, blindness, birth defects, scurvy – all of which can be reduced by an improved level of income.[210]

• Cholera spreads when populations cannot afford proper toilets.

• One in five New York residents depend on food stamps.[211]

• Poverty is often discussed in terms of socio-economic inequality. While we may abhor some forms of inequality for other reasons, reduction of poverty should not be dependent on that issue alone.[212]

•   The horrendous rise in unemployment in 2011-12 has undermined the morale of youths as we have seen in a previous chapter, but the employment crisis is affecting the morale of adults in all walks of life in industrialised countries. The consequent reduction in demand establishes a vicious circle of deprivation. Sackings of civil servants to save public indebtedness – and the banks – and dismissal of high ranking money administrators are but the most newsworthy of the widespread employment turndown. This is bound to affect not only material but health well being.[213]

Manifesto for the New Age

X - Fiscal Balance – Paying for Reforms

Aaron Pereira and his colleagues at Action Canada have called for a taxation change from income to consumption. I am going to go further.

Any reasonable critic, whether or not in agreement with the objectives I have tried to work out so far will by now throwing hands to the sky and saying "All very well. But how on earth can we pay for it............?"

Such a reaction would be in conformity with the contemporary mood. My task here will be to show that modification in spending priorities will do much to move state budgets into a mode that is more healthy for society and the globe itself; and then to show that there is a great need to re-examine the nature of state finances so that *both* revenue and expenditure move away from what in effect are taxes on initiative.

Between now and the arrival of a desired globe, world product and levels of living will no doubt have risen enormously[214]. That in itself does not resolve the difficulty, since costly steps are needed en route and population will also have risen sharply.

Before reaching the fundamentals it is necessary to write somewhat of the short term reactions to the 2008+

banking crisis which threatened and complicated national finances and is still going on into 2013..

It is symptomatic of distorted values and their damaging application that governments almost unanimously rushed to vastly increase national indebtedness to bail out the major banks in an attempt to revive the global economy. In doing so they turned common sense on its head. Many banks had got themselves in trouble through supporting unwise mortgage policies which failed because consumers did not have the income to support the payments. Instead of re-contracting the mortgages to allow payments to continue at reduced but stable rates lenders foreclosed. In doing so they lost a stream of (reduced) revenue to place on their books the value of properties which no longer had value. Self-defeating.

Meanwhile (a) small businesses were not helped at all: only size it seemed mattered, and (b) banks became afraid and reduced lending to both businesses and consumers, making such profits as they had on other aspects of their business.

Governments then enjoined banks to resume consumer lending in a big way. The banks have done some of that reluctantly. The point however is that the whole mess is based on the notion that it is credit that drives the economy. Having been bitten by unwise credit, governments and financial managers are enjoining businesses and consumer to embrace credit once more.

Belatedly, in 2010, the emphasis moved to what should have been obvious from the start: unemployment. Bank bailouts did not produce jobs. Lower incomes reduced the ability of individuals to exercise demand, slowing the re-growth of suppliers.

If the *generous* guaranteed minimum income described in the last chapter had been in place *none* of this need have happened. Mortgages would have been adjusted to such an income and money used to bailout the banks would have been available if needed to apply directly to consumer incomer and employer security. Banks would not have got into the same trouble.

Another similar solution could have been the long standing Canadian approach to consumer banking. This is the policy whereby deposits in banks up to a certain amount are insured by government against bank failure. That would have made it possible for governments instead of rewarding banks for their lack of due diligence, could have let the miscreants fail and at the same time maintained consumer confidence in the economy protecting at least some purchasing power. The non-consumer customers of the banks would temporarily have themselves been in crisis until their business was transferred to the more reliable surviving or new institutions or even a government support fund.

The main flaw in this argument is that such solutions run counter to the ideologies present in the United States (the first country to experience the financial crisis) since it would be branded as socialist. Which raises an important point for the globe's well-being – should the global society be held hostage to the ideological backwardness of the United States?

This situation will make it much more difficult for governments to put in place a desirable fiscal reform, although far-reaching reform is ever more urgently needed. Rather than undermining the proposals I shall make the crisis increases the need for some new thinking and some far-reaching changes, whether or not you agree with my specific thoughts.

Here at the expenditure end are some of the charges I have in mind[215]:

- increased fundamental education of youth,
- massive support for higher education in poorer countries,
- guaranteed income for all,
- universal health care and reduction of crime costs,
- support of aesthetic and scientific creativity,
- support of older age cohorts, with earlier retirement and guaranteed income,
- suppression of the arms trade, including possible losses to the gross global product (to be argued later),
- measures taken by richer countries to reduce global inequalities and manage migration.
- taking care of the global eco-system,

- financing the Global Government, including effective legislature, courts, and military-police units (to be argued later),
- greater weight given to the search for and dissemination of fundamental knowledge.

Before you throw up your hands at the bill, reserve your judgement until I have outlined the ways in which some massive current costs should be eliminated, making room for the above priorities.

This is a tall order but is the minimum for a civilised global society.

Fortunately, many, perhaps the most important, requirements for meeting our objectives do not call for direct expenditures since they are based on changes in attitudes and perspectives. It is not enough, however, to rely on these to bring about all the needed changes. More mature and civilised attitudes to sex, interpersonal relationships, crime and punishment will help create a climate of opinion and a view of a warm, desirable, world which will make institutional change, and the inevitable fiscal reforms, acceptable.

Further, some significant costs -- and their resulting benefits -- will be met in the course of doing business, especially if fiscal reform requires that it be so. It is now apparent that measures to protect the eco-system create profitable industries.

As I write I cannot tell how much of what are now regarded as public services are appropriate for private enterprise. *A priori* it seems eminently suitable for public works and transportation to be politically designated but privately financed, constructed, operated, and charged for. The more finances can be removed from the public charge the better. Should not schools, hospitals, office blocks, be privately constructed, and rented to the public users? Would this not permit them to be turned to other uses when their original need was no longer required, for demographic or technical reasons? (For example, when schools or hospitals are no longer in demographically needed areas?) Would this likelihood not encourage the design of more flexible-use buildings? Once the public interest had been defined, the market, with greater or less state intervention, would determine time-priorities and viability.

Such approaches, which are gaining some favour, obviously do not resolve the major fiscal issues, though they create a little more flexibility. Schools and hospitals are just part of the costs of education and health service. The costs of individuals using them must still be met, and require public inputs to make them accessible, whether arrived at by subsidy, reimbursement of fees, or placing the operations within the public budget.

So many stages will have to be passed through, and so many alternatives judged, that it would be misleading, indeed impossible, to do a significant calculation of the costs of the reformed world. It is my judgement, however, that the social service elements, and especially the provision of a respectable guaranteed income, substantially above the poverty level, would represent an enormous additional charge at present not represented nearly adequately in state budgets. To this must be added the other elements I have bulleted above, and no doubt others that I have not foreseen. The reductions achieved by turning some operations over to private enterprise would not be nearly enough to balance accounts.

What to do?

It seems clear that nothing short of a complete rearrangement of the structure of public finances will suffice.

On the way there are two major savings that will be achieved bit by bit. One is the reduction in prison expenses, partly offset by the greater complexity in arriving at court decisions, and in supervising court judgements, and the loss of some fines to the public purse. The other will be the enormous saving achieved by the reduction of military forces, a major thrust in the arguments of later chapters which envisage a ban on national armed forces in favour of global government.. Once this is completed, even the most powerful Global Government force would cost but a fraction of what must be the most obscene use of taxation that one can imagine, other than repression in a totalitarian state, namely the maintenance of armed forces excessive even for self

462

defence, as we shall see, rendered illegal except for minimal police roles.

It is possible that those two measures would finance the proposed improvement in social services without affecting taxation levels; but it is quite unlikely that they alone would finance guaranteed income.

An underlying thrust of my argument is that world reforms will be wanted because they fulfil individual desires for civilisation, a civilisation based upon warm human interactions, human differences and the originalities of the human spirit. In other words, it is based upon trust, respect, and responsibility. It allows for the probability that some members of humankind will *not* be civilised in such a sense; but that the overwhelming majority of the population will be.

The structure of government proposes to emphasise such characteristics, to build upon them. So too should the fiscal structure.

Speaking very broadly, the main sources of government revenue are customs and excise, wealth or income taxes and expenditure or consumption taxes. Customs and excise should disappear with the growth of free trade, and, insofar as they remain, be subsumed under consumption taxes outlined below.

Wealth taxes, including income taxes, have been clumsy attempts to redistribute income. The greater their level, more especially with income tax, the greater the interference with individual choice. Income tax is the most direct form of indicating to the public that the state knows best how to use your money, and that the vote is less powerful than the internal revenue office.

To finance the changed priorities through income tax would essentially mean little individual income. This is obviously a contradiction in terms, since spending is one of the few ways in which individuals exercise their choices. To have no income is not to spend, not to exercise choice, and to destroy the economy..

If corporate taxes can in some fundamental sense be equalised so that there is a level playing field, it might not matter if they were raised to the roof. We would simply be in a world in which the prices were denominated at a higher percentage overall. But I do not see it as a level playing field. For example, a good may pass through, say, ten companies or twenty as it moves from a raw state to the consumer. Corporate taxes reflected in the ultimate price run a risk of being very much higher in the second case than in the first, however they are levied.

Corporate taxes are a tax on initiative. The more successful the company, the more, at present, it pays in tax. The more workers it employs the more it pays in payroll taxes. This is no way to stimulate an economy.

The exception is to require corporations to pay for goods and services they now get freely, and to pay the full costs to society of their doing business. If they pollute, they pay for it, is the prime example. If they use roads, they pay for the use. If they employ educated people, they contribute to education. If they cause illness, they pay for the cures. If they move people from one location to another, they pay the full costs of such an operation. If they destroy forests, they pay. If they fish, they pay for the maintenance of the fishery. They are not subsidised from the public purse.. They pay their way, and charge accordingly. The public then knows the true costs of the things it is choosing to buy and can make its choices accordingly.

If present corporate taxes are removed and replaced by payments for social services and social costs, one can assume that corporations are paying directly for those things they choose to use. While this would cover a substantial amount of social services and public costs (which have become a primary item in state expenditure) there would still be a major proportion of public expenditures not yet covered. I imagine -- and it is not a calculation -- that perhaps fifty per cent of public expenditure would be met by this revenue item, reflected in costs to consumers, replacing taxation on initiative.

Income tax is also a tax on initiative. The more you earn the more you pay (even in flat tax systems) and in most countries the rate of tax can increase.[216] Customs duties are a small proportion of revenues in most countries. Again they increase the costs of production when the goods are destined for industry, can be protective in defiance of free trade, and are costly to collect. It is time to remove both income tax and customs duties entirely, and examine the roots of taxation with a clean slate.

So I turn to the direct consumption taxes mostly in the form of Sales tax or Value Added Tax.

There are two contradictory principles at work. On the one hand, much consumption is apparently wasteful of resources. I object to creating employment for employment's sake, since this can, among other objections, lead to the production of useless widgets, using up scarce resources, and made available to consumers by artificial means. My position is somewhat snobbish. The tourists who line up from buses to buy junk are exercising their choices. Who am I to say them nay? If corporate taxation is amended as suggested above the social costs will be reflected in price.

The other principle extends the recognition of freedom of choice. This does not mean no taxation on consumption. It means *equal* taxation on different forms of consumption (it again being assumed that social costs have been reflected in the course of production itself). Alcohol might be taxed at the production level to cover costs of alcoholism, a tax reflected in wholesale price; at the consumption level it is taxed at the same level as bread. The consumer then chooses.

If this is so, the effects on the individual consumer will be at the margins of his expenditures. The pattern of expenditure will be modified, but freedom of choice will remain. The individual will still control what happens with his income. This is not the case with income tax, in which choice is removed. If consumption tax moves from 5% to 100% the choice between expenditures still remains. I would far prefer to pay even 100% on consumption than 40 or 60% on income, *provided the consumption tax was universal* and the revenue went into social services and guaranteed income rather than the military. On that assumption, a consumption tax feels less like state robbery and control, *and it enables me to determine how much tax I shall pay.* By consuming less I pay less. By consuming more I pay more. To a much larger degree it is in my control. The public's choices totally control consumption tax revenue. I can also factor in the ethics of consuming particular products.

Unlike a flat income tax, the consumption tax is progressive, even though it is the same for all categories of consumption. Taking the extreme of a 100% rate, the millionaire may buy a Ferrari now priced at $200,000 for the new price of $400,000, of which $200,000 goes to the state. The starving (but he will disappear with guaranteed income) student or artist buys a jalopy now priced at $100 for $200 of which only $100 goes to the state.

Further, the relief from corporate and employment taxation, though partially balanced by charges for environmental and social costs, enables firms to pay higher wages and salaries.

Admittedly, an extreme 100% consumption tax (a figure that would be unlikely) would overnight create a onetime halving of the value of money to the consumer. However, it is again unlikely that such a tax would be introduced overnight (though it could be with a return of income taxes paid). Fiscal authorities would have a major task to perform in adjusting the supply of money, and ensuring its spread to the population. Draconian measures of this sort have indeed been applied from time to time in the history of governments, some successful, some not. The adjustment is not beyond the bounds of our ingenious. And once achieved, particularly on a global scale, the major crisis of adjustment would be over.

In other words I consider that society as a whole will reflect individual values better with equalised consumption taxes than with income taxes, whatever the rate of the consumption taxes. The individual also knows that there will be no fiscal penalty attached to earning more, only on spending more. This will keep motivated individuals in the work place as needed, rather than holding on to the guaranteed income floor because work is no longer taxed away. Once again, the combination of guaranteed income and no income tax allows individuals to make reasonable choices.

Furthermore, consumption taxes, in making the consumer think more about specific expenditures, could have important effects on the quality of life, reducing spending on widgets and giving an opportunity for consumers to think about such matters as the ecological or fair trade implications of their choices. *And, once again, the individual is in control over how much tax he or she pays.* If I purchase that Ferrari, think of the tax I would be paying to a government I don't like. But if I *do* like government expenditure policies, buying the Ferrari would not only satisfy me, but be a political statement.

The ideal, especially with free trade, is that such taxes be at the same level throughout the world, perhaps even set by Global Government instead of state government, collected by state governments to be placed in Global accounts, and shared. However at the point at which this becomes practicable, regional disparities and differences will continue, for ethnological and geographical reasons. We are not talking about uniformity of life. It is for this reason that attempts to put low or no tax rates on some goods and high ones on others (necessities as against luxuries, for example) would be next to impossible to administer globally, so different are the cultural definitions. While one would thus argue for global uniformity in tax rates, state governments, in agreement with the Global Government, would have the right to influence the level of income at which the consumption tax kicks in or is rebated for special considerations.

For example, state government could rebate the consumption tax on necessities of life for those on the guaranteed minimum income, as defined by the culture applicable in the country.

Customs would not disappear. Officials would now be trained not only to prevent the entry of contraband, but to make sure that taxes on imported consumption goods are included in the price, this to make cross border shopping equitable. And it would be necessary to have a tax refund system for non-residents returning to their homes, as is the case with sales taxes and VAT now.

So here we have it. No corporate, individual or customs taxes. All revenues based on consumption or on eco-social costs.

On the expenditure side, there will be no or minimal military spending. No subventions to individual corporations. Removal of all current social service payments, which at present vary according to the power base of segments of the disadvantaged. Introduce guaranteed income for all at a liveable rate which does away with special funds for segments of the poor – the unemployed, the halt and the lame. Guaranteed income for all removes the competitive disparities in handouts to the disadvantaged – the unemployed, the sick, the destitute, returned service men and women, first time job seekers, artists.

I wonder which country will be the first to translate this argument into reality? Many changes in social service payments were adopted after the second world war, though many, such as the dole, existed previously. Graduated income taxes have not existed for all time. It took innovation to establish them and one country was the first to do so, leading the way. We need to make a start – and in this as in so many other facets of reform, half measures are troublemaking. A recent change in consumer takes in Canada resulted in public anger. Why? Because it was an *increase* in taxation *not* accompanied by a *decrease* in income tax. Again, half measures are likely to result in public misunderstanding. Only the *total* package makes sense.

XIII – Rethinking Organisational Design and the Economy

Do the remarks of the last chapter imply some such revolution as the end of capitalism? Not at all. Fiscal change removes a major burden on corporations as well as individuals. But corporations would be channelled into thinking about their place in life, about the effects of their actions in the wider culture and society. For too many centuries most have ignored such responsibilities because they did not enter into their balance sheets. With fiscal change they would have to watch their steps much more carefully, for a mis-step could mean ruin.

The population may be conceived as having three parts: (a) those who are part of organisations which use money for accounting purposes but whose purpose is not to make a profit -- universities, schools, voluntary and charitable groups, public service, military, hospitals; (b) those who are part of organisations whose intent and legal status require that profits be made; and (c) those who are not part of either (retired, unemployed, youth). There are overlaps: individuals who are in (b) may also participate in (a). Some whose time is mostly spent in (c) may nevertheless participate in (a). For individuals, the distinctions are not watertight in their daily living; there are matters of degree of commitment here. Some university professors (a) operate entrepreneurial enterprises (b).

472

Even though there are overlaps, nevertheless the distinctions are real. The three categories represent, broadly, three differing cultures, each with their sub-cultures, which carry over from the centres of operation into family life and social interactions and discourses. Between the cultures there are many fundamental misunderstandings and lacks of knowledge. Most entrepreneurs and workers, white collar or blue collar, in category (b) have little understanding of, and indeed often an antipathy to, workers in category (a), especially, for example, teachers, university professors, doctors and nurses. The reverse is true also. Most university professors and civil servants, many adherents of single cause organisations such as those dealing with the ecosystem, have little or no knowledge of the decisions, the risks and the manipulation of factors of production that managers have to deal with every day. Yet it is what managers decide, with all the insecurities involved, that governs the material world in which we live, from the food on the table to television programmes. How much of the artistic world -- plays, for instance -- apart from some popular literature, is rooted in management themes that have such a major influence on who we are? Why is the culture of management such a tiny (perhaps growing) part of contemporary social anthropology?

Meanwhile, let us note that ideological preoccupations with the simplicity of social class categories, from left and right, have diverted our attention from these other, more dividing and troublesome, cleavages. Class as a descriptive category indicating a number of people who are positioned close together on a scale measuring a given criterion (wealth, education), helps scholars analyse relationships between criteria. Other than that it has no reality: it is an arbitrary academic construct. Class in the Marxist sense goes further, arguing that broad categories (workers, peasants, bourgeois) had so many conditions, objectives and interests in common that they constituted organic entities with historical roles. That, as I have argued elsewhere, is simply not true[217], save for brief periods in history when members of one group brought themselves together for action. Peasant revolts might be an instance. It is intriguing to me that, particularly amongst those trying to challenge authority, leadership more often than not came from outside the group concerned, and that such groups did not embrace the totality of the assigned class, among whom considerable difference of opinion, even opposition, existed. Significant numbers of the British "working class" have consistently voted Conservative. As we struggle toward our goals class concepts, in this second sense, are of no use.

What may be of more use is to think of various kinds of organisations, not only in terms of their conventional effectiveness, but in terms of their interactions and overall norms within society as a whole. As a short-hand I shall use the categories I proposed at the beginning, and the divisions within them. However, just as I point out the limitations of assigning an individual to a class according to his or her position on a given scale, because on other criteria his position changes, so too I caution against using my broad categories to define the characteristics of an organisation *a priori.*

It is now customary to have individuals who are familiar with profit and the bottom line in board, management or consultancy positions in category (a) organisations, and to try to borrow management techniques from (b) to (a). I am not opposing this, but consider it to be inadequate as a tool in itself, and possibly damaging if other tools are not developed.

What *are* the objectives of a university or a hospital or a military unit? What are they there to do? Financial efficiency and not getting into bankruptcy; the greatest economy of material or personnel resources, as measured in profit-making institutions, may simply not be relevant. If not profit, what is the output that should be selected against which to make the measurements? Are the true costs monetary? What about the destruction of an individual assigned to work in ways he or she can't handle, because he or she can't be let go? What about children who are mistaught social studies because a teacher, counted as doing the job, has no knowledge of history, sociology, political science, or anthropology? What about hospitals which refuse to allow nurses to handle procedures of which they are capable because they are not doctors? How do you measure the efficiency of a military unit which is up to strength, has all its assigned equipment, is well field-trained, but is racist or is personally loyal to a dissident commander? Is a policeman's efficiency to be measured by his salary divided by the number of arrests?

Such conundrums put enormous complications into judgements about how well organisations in category (a) are doing their job. Just because the judgements are complicated, such organisations must not be left off the hook. The judgements have important uses -- by funding donors, by taxpayers, by patrons buying tickets at a certain price. I do not have nice easy answers, but there are alternatives awaiting development.

Once upon a time economists (do they still?) pointed out that their subject was the study of the ways in which scarce means were administered in order to fulfil competing ends in the most satisfying manner. For obvious reasons, of which analytical manageability was the main one, this became mixed up with the use of money as a *scientific* measuring rod, instead of a means and an end mixed together in real life, competing with other means and ends such as religious belief or love, the joy of physical activity or teaching a child manners. If money doesn't come into it, the main schools of thought in practice believed, we can't handle the dynamics or the judgements. And if *we* can't nobody can. Not many challenged this canard.

The original propositions of economics posited the balancing of different ends to achieve the optimum result, the latter determined not by the observer but by the subject. No use buying a Macerate if that meant going without a combination of food and opera and dressing the children properly. But if resources change one might do all those things. Or, once confronted with the fact, one might effectively decide it would be more satisfying to redo the kitchen, pay for John's university, and have annual holidays in East Africa. The potential ideas floating in one's head do not necessarily become prepotent when the chips are down. There are many models in the various disciplines that play with these kinds of issues, and their complements, the varying choices which individuals make in the task of combining different kinds of resources to produce the result.

With some limitations, for individuals read organisations. Organisations in category (a) need goal plans, a statement of objectives. But those goals, are not simply things like graduating so many students in so many fields, undertaking so many heart transplants a year, or making sure that we can raise so many millions to redistribute to yet other organisations. The *quality* of what is done is at least as significant.

Statements of objectives in such organisations require *qualitative* assessments. In category (b) organisations it may be assumed, though probably inaccurately, that the qualitative issues are reflected in competitive advantage, and hence the bottom line, at least insofar as customers and clients value them. This is not so in category (a) organisations. One needs to adjust the easily quantifiable factors for the less precise but nevertheless paramount qualitative ones. One needs comparative data on the quality of learning and initiative in graduating students, on long-term health of discharged hospital patients, on the quality of life of aged clients in long-term care facilities, on the re-insertion into society of prisoners, on the accuracy of analysis and capacity to provide effective services by charities, and so on.

Of course such examinations and analyses do take place. But I consider we have a long way to go before they meet the standards of desirable analysis. In part, we are bemused by cardinal measurement. Ordinal measurement usually implies comparison, for example, very much happier, quite a lot happier, happier, about the same, less happy, a bit miserable, very miserable, desperate, by comparison with some standard. We already know that vested interests hate such measurements and comparisons, even if less subjective than the extreme example I have chosen. School teachers jump onto the attack if the quality of schools are compared. Doctors and lawyers resist any public comparison of their activities. Very few studies are done comparing charitable or lobbying organisations, exceptin terms of fiscal accountability. Academics hate it when objective criteria of scholarly or teaching value are applied to their proposals for new courses of study. School teachers sometimes go on strike to stop its implementation. Yet when applied to things rather than activities we do it all the time. This is a beautiful sunrise. I'd rather go to this cafe because the coffee is better.

We must be in a position to make judgements about organisational objectives and efficacy, just as we try to do when such organisations apply for grants. The more we can refine our tools for doing so the better. For the most part, this involves being clearer about the *whole mix* of organisational goals -- the schedule of ends, material and other, or of the wants they are there to satisfy.

In fact similar principles apply, with differing tools, to organisations in category (b). I am not arguing against profitability or the use of money in exchange. Far from it. Whether it is easily apparent or not, all societies have standards of exchange value. Inefficient standards exist in barter, and in some so-called "non-monetary" societies which have different measures of value for different purposes. There is no escaping the reality and efficacy of the principle that the more rapid the circulation of money the more opportunities there are for profits to be taken; that those profits can be summed as a large quantity of profit in society as a whole; which means a greater opportunity for capital accumulation and its investment. Utopia must be monetary, for even in Utopia I do not see the day, nor desire it, when all wants can be satisfied without exchange, or when there is no possibility for the improvement of anything (which implies investment). How utterly boring. A pox on communitarian non-monetarists.

However that is a *very* different thing from saying high-riding capitalism, as we know it today, is the most

479

effective and desirable way of satisfying human goals. It is not.

The reason it is not is straightforward. In present capitalism money-based profit-taking enterprises usually define their goals as narrowly as they can, and make manipulative use of public services that are provided to them, some free of cost except through damaging taxation.

If I want to make widgets or provide internet services I will do my best to economise on costs. In doing so I do not pay for the air I breathe, and it is very unlikely that I pay my share of my polluting effects or the development costs that have been incurred in placing technologies in the public domain. If I lay off workers so that I can down-size or move to a less costly country, I may, or may not as the case may be, pay the costs incurred by the dismissed people.

In other words, the goals are defined in such a simple way that the true costs are hidden. Neither the individual enterprises, nor the consumers in buying the products, count or pay the full cost. In one sense, the consumers do, through current modes of taxation, which in effect subsidise industry and commerce.

Such a reality is not particularly difficult to grasp. But what do Utopians *do* about it?

Legislation can sometimes ensure that companies take a spectrum of goals into account, translated into their financial bottom line. Thus certain payments to laid-off workers can be legislated, and protection of an eco-system can be mandated. (Why do executives get generous termination packages, but not workers???)

But there are two problems that modify and corrupt such legislation, and put the brakes on it.

If strict ecological rules are enforced for the hewers of wood, but not legislated for formers of concrete or developers of housing estates, the market is improperly distorted. Developers will cut down the trees and there will be a move toward concrete instead of wooden houses. This might be desirable, but it can only be assessed if *all* enterprises have to meet the same social objectives, writ broadly, but interpreted in detail for each industry.

Similarly, if one country adopts stringent objectives and rules, there is a financial temptation for industry to move elsewhere. It is argued that this imbalance will correct itself in the long run, and that developing countries will never catch up if they are charged costs that the rich countries did not have to bear when they were creating their strengths. In the middle term, there is no point and much danger in being too harsh and rigorously inflexible.

But in the long run, we must require near universality, modified by cultural differences, in its approach to identifying and charging for social costs. Only universality will establish the beloved "level playing field". We are rapidly reaching the point at which "national" governments cannot do the job required of them; only a global approach will ultimately do. There will still be major differences because of cultural variations which will affect the location of enterprise; I am not saying that the level playing field does away with, or ought to do away with, comparative advantage. But the principle of the obligation to meet social costs should not be a matter of difference between countries.

The universality of the imposition of social costs and the inclusion of social goals in enterprises will indeed mean a rise in prices. This is another argument for across the board standards: we do not want to reward industries which are excused or which avoid paying their social costs. There will still be differences. Those enterprises which legitimately incur fewer social costs will have a cost-price advantage over those which have more. This is as it should be. If you want things that have high social costs, jolly well pay for them directly, not indirectly through assessments. Then you may understand the meaning of what you are doing.

Such changes will of course mean considerable changes in management, including the criteria for successful management. Social costs will be a factor of production, to be analysed as such.

There are other elements of present capitalist structure which derive from history and have become entrenched, but should be questioned.[218]

For example, there is the relationship between owners, management, lenders, and workers.

Financial capital is a factor of production which in large part underwrites other factors of production -- labour, capital equipment, knowledge, etc. -- insofar as costs are not immediately met out of current revenue but incur often massive indebtedness. There are three main ways of raising financial capital: by government grant, by interest paying loans, and by the selling of shares. By now so many techniques of raising capital have been invented that there are all sorts of permutations in the implications of particular arrangements. For example, shares may or may not involve rights of ownership which influence management; they may be issued with varying degrees of priority when it comes to rights to income or assets. Thus it is necessary for me to simplify down to the typical prime essentials.

Each of these may imply a legal seat on the management board, which acts as executive supervisor for the owners. Who gets to be on the board varies according to the laws of countries, and, within those laws, the practices and statutes of specific firms. One major variant typical of Germany is that worker representatives sit on the board. This is, however, rare. Usually the board consists of representatives of, that is persons elected by, those shareholders who are accorded such rights, that is providers of financial capital plus others who buy-in later or are appointed. (In Switzerland, for example, foreign shareholders may be excluded from such rights.) In Europe and some other countries it is common for banks which have provided finance to acquire ownership and/or management rights as a result. Occasionally, depending on circumstances and political philosophy, governments insist on board representation as partial security for their financial involvement, especially during these bailout times. In the remnants of communist countries, such control can be still dominant and politically motivated, but they have been giving way to the other forms. Private firms, usually led by families or close partnerships, do their best to avoid giving up control when they raise capital.

Whatever the variants, one thing is clear. Capital is the primary factor of production which carries with it ownership privileges, and the power to control the destiny of firms. In this sense, certainly, we are in the midst of the capitalist age[219].

It appears that major industrial and commercial undertakings have established the norm that operations and forward planning are properly underpinned by massive debt. This is not necessary for the *concept* of capitalism. A firm which operates out of revenue and avoids debt except in emergency is still capitalistic, though it is now extremely rare.[220] The process is reinforced by the teachings and ideologies of business schools which are responsible for the points of view and operations of most business executives.[221] And, as I shall argue below, pushes entrepreneurs into the gambling maelstrom of financial markets

Is this what is needed and desirable? I don't believe so, not quite. Capitalism is needed, but capitalist practices need modification.

The reason capital, with private entrepreneurship, has been the main factor of production to be recognised in this way is that it has been, historically, the most difficult thing to put together. It is mistakenly held that price is the determinant of the supply of capital. This is only partially true. Interest rates are mainly governed by the ratio of supply and demand for money, true. But in this new century the entry of funds into both the stock markets and the international exchange markets is largely influenced by speculative considerations, including guesses as to the future policies of central banks, as much as by the need for enterprise capital[222]. In other words, motivations which create the flow of money into such markets are based upon *guesses* about the future rise or fall in relevant prices. I do not know of any well supported and publicised anthropological studies of the culture of stock and money trading. Even the acquisition or sale of firms is governed largely by financial considerations -- the desire to raise cash, re-organise debt, or acquire a money-making opportunity, the last being a speculative judgement about the future.

The fact of the matter is that when it comes to a firm raising capital, especially to get started, subjective matters come to the fore; interest rates will even be adjusted to take these factors into account. The lender *judges* the track record of the borrower. It has become somewhat scandalous that money is often not available *at any price* to women, to those such as Indians living on common reserves who have no individual security, to new would-be entrepreneurs who are innovative but have no track record. It is just as common that if you are in a social relationship with those who control the flow of finance, you will find it easier to raise millions[223]. The downfall of many a great entrepreneurial holding company has come about when, in time of sudden difficulty, the lenders realised that their connection was too optimistic; it was time to look behind the man to the reality -- and then, often, as in the case of the initial Canary Wharf original fiasco or the Conrad Black empire, not look enough forward to see the conception ultimately come into reality. Risk is serious. The judgement of risk, despite all the charts, is ultimately subjective. The market deals with it only partially by a manipulation of interest rates. It can say absolutely no to $1,000 at desperately punitive interest rates, and absolutely yes to $1 billion at preferred interest rates, based on little more than friendly or unfriendly eye-contact, golf games, or earlier business deals. The formal papers are not irrelevant for most routine transactions. But they are little more than background for negotiation in many significant instances.

The relevance of such considerations is increased by the custom of appointing or electing to board members who have "connections" but without professional knowledge of the technology or marketing of the enterprise. The appointment of representatives of external lenders onto boards is seldom a matter of tighter supervision -- such companies are usually very well run in any event -- but a pipeline to further capital should it be needed, and a possible exclusion of other lenders.

Why should financial capital be the primary, if not the only, factor of production (apart from initial entrepreneurship), to be represented in ownership and the government of firms? Historical power has to be the answer.

The only other influences on factors of production which conceivably could have had such power, historically, have been labour and government. (Government policy has not usually been listed among factors of production. But in some form it is a variable which is highly influential on the conduct of business, whose managers manipulate its powers as a possible resource.) Government has indeed used its power to influence and dominate enterprise, often with disastrous and distorting results, of which both fascism and communism represent examples I do not need to examine.

Labour is a more puzzling story. I suggest that labour's failure to enter into ownership derives from its organised origins in the nineteenth century, in which labour unions literally had to fight for almost every decency in the workplace that we now take for granted in the major countries. Save for a few enlightened employers, the typical response to requests for decency was to deny them, to use ownership by the entrepreneurs and stockholders, and the socio-political relationships with the lawmakers, to fight them down every inch of the way.

No wonder Marx talked of socio-political classes. More to the point, no wonder that unions, fighting for their very existence, learned the hard way that the only road forward was for confrontation, not only with the management but with the politicians. They had to search for, fight for, power, and after many decades, with many ups and downs, they eventually got much of it.

In Switzerland, in the 1930s, the conflict reached such a point of violence, and the threats from outside were so intense, that in an abrupt *volte face,* all those involved knew that the confrontations were about to destroy the country, literally. The idea of Switzerland as a genetically peaceful country is totally false. To the extent it is peaceful, it is a matter of deliberate decision translated into policy, because the alternatives don't work. Certainly confrontation continues in many aspects of Swiss life. But in labour-management issues confrontation changed dramatically into consultation and consensus even in such matters as company overall strategy. To achieve this, both sides had to change their methods and their modes of thinking enormously, to work on the premise that the health of the firms required frank openness and the joint working out of the firms' objectives and methods. Since such solutions, and those of Germany in which workers' representatives sit on boards, depend on the state of trust, openness, and the external socio-economic-political climate, they cannot be regarded as permanent or fixed, especially in a world where, for the most part, confrontation between unions and management is still the convention.

What do we want and need in this arena? Why should the capital providers have priority in ownership over the workers? Is there any logic to this at all? History perhaps, but logic? Efficacy? The logic might say that workers, by reason of their background, point of view, and education, are not fit to make management policy decisions, whereas moneylenders are. Perhaps moneylenders are indeed, at least insofar as financial manipulation is concerned. But perhaps one might argue that enterprises are driven far too much by financial wheeling and dealing[224]. That issues like spinning off companies or parts of an enterprise, or merging and acquisition, while sometimes driven by supposed "synergy" or the lack of it, by desires to broaden a holding company's portfolio and to spread risk -- or to do the opposite by retrenching so that a company can concentrate on its core business, are far too often driven by management's personal pocketbook or effects on share prices rather than productivity.

I see no compelling reason, other than that they are risk-takers, why shareholders should have the sole say in choosing and "controlling" management. (And surely workers are the prime risk takers since their very livelihood is dominantly at stake when managers make decisions.) Except for the larger shareholders, whose interests may not coincide with those of the smaller ones, the majority of shareholders take very little interest in the specifics of management. They may express disapproval by selling shares, but give away their proxies for annual meetings. Further, workers, suppliers, dependent customers, anyone who enters into a contract with the firm, are exposed to the firm's risk. For the workers the risk is the greatest of all, for if the firm goes belly-up they are without their livelihood. In principle the workers have more interest in the firm/s success than any other stakeholders. Period,

For most of the industrial world except perhaps Switzerland and Germany, the risk to workers, and their selfish interest in the success of the company, have been obscured by the union convention of confrontation and the employers' elitist denial. The nineteenth century ethos that the boss is the enemy is built into the activity and ideology of the most powerful unions, whose leadership, that is their own management, lives on aggressive stances. Certainly, under these circumstances, the boss *is* the enemy, for he feels he has to fight back to save his company. There is still an attitude of union-bashing, if the boss can find ways to do it.

Unions were necessary, at least until World War II, and in the short run may become necessary again. They are necessary in many parts of the world where conditions of employment are dreadful. In most of the industrialised world, in most occupations, unions are the workers' worst enemies, or at least as much so as are the bosses.

Some unions are so large and powerful, and so monopolistic in their areas of activity, that they are in fact entrepreneurial businesses, sellers of labour. In these, no one can get a job without holding a union card and being nominated in union controlled labour exchanges. In others strict rules of seniority rather than ability apply. Inter-union agreements, forced into labour contracts, govern, sometimes in minute and anti-efficiency detail, the division of labour.

Thus my experience the other day when a trolley-bus came off its wires with trivial damage such that the bus could not proceed. On board was an off-duty driver who had the skills necessary to effect the repair on the spot. "Don't touch it," said the duty driver, "or the union will get you." Instead of proceeding on its way, the bus stood still awaiting the arrival of a union-certified electrician from the other side of town. Rules of this kind create feather-bedding, inflexibility in the allocation of work, idleness in some workers while they wait for a call, and gross inefficiency and extra costs.

Unions are run as businesses in themselves. The capital raised through membership fees, the need to invest strike emergency funds and pension plans, makes some of them among the largest corporate investors in the market. A few can make or break industries through their investment decisions.

The management-shareholder-union scenario, (coupled with large business bureaucracy, which is another story) must be one of the most inefficient and socially damaging patterns of organisation one could imagine for a sophisticated economy. Despite itself, it has great achievements to its credit. I do not dispute that -- how could I, looking around at my world? The mind in fact boggles at the way management and workers, together, have used knowledge and innovation and organisational skills to bring food to the table, clothing and shelter, and a range of technological marvels requiring ever-more complex lines of supply from nature to the user. This is not to be sneered at in some high and mighty way, or despised because of some ideological *a priori* principle.

But I am not writing about that; I am writing about the best of all possible worlds. And, for that there is still room for improvement. For *debate* I shall set out a model.

I have already argued that firms should bear the social and ecological costs of their activities.

To be interpreted in similar context is the curious distinction between salaried and non-salaried employees. Once again, this is an archaic socially disruptive historical distinction, deriving from the days in which it was expected and accepted that humans be treated as disposable factors of production like any other. They are not.

Perhaps once their low level of education provided some callous justification. Today in many countries they are now well educated, often highly skilled, unwilling to be in banal lobs. Youth Maturity Inspirers will increase their personal aptitudes.

When firms get into a bad patch, the easiest target for retrenchment to pay for management's errors consists of the non-salaried employees. It is true that of recent years salaried employees are being dismissed during cut-backs, but this is done usually through such devices as early retirement, severance packages, and the like. By contrast, non-salaried employees are sometimes treated as completely disposable although there are now numerous techniques to soften the blow of redundancy. This is most dramatically evident in large-scale industries where demand changes have immediate effects on supply -- forestry, automobile manufacture, construction and so on.

It cannot be argued that retrenchment cannot occur. Of course it must. But, in equity and for social values, the distinction between blue collar and white collar, between salaried and non-salaried, is an anachronism and improper. Put the blue collars on salary..............

Management can then certainly find other ways of smoothing out the ups and downs of demand than making the workforce pay through a cycle of hiring and layoff; and where dismissals have to take place blue collar workers have similar needs to those of white collar ones. Indeed technology is rapidly reducing the distinction for more and more blue collar workers must have skills and technical education.

A modification to this argument, for both white and blue collars will occur when the argument of the last chapter is adopted – namely that there be a minimum but liveable guaranteed income for al. It is though not a matter of either or, but of both solutions.

I now argue that it is no longer necessary or desirable for the suppliers of finance to hold ownership and management rights. True, it will be necessary to post the assets of a company as security for finance. Given that, there are, except for small start-up enterprises, sufficient methods of supplying funds through ordinary borrowing techniques. (I have already argued that government lending and subsidy is normally a distortion of the market.)

Close down the stock exchanges which fundamentally reward gambling. Some form of risk taking, without perfect knowledge, in inevitable. The stock exchanges though, turn the supply of finance into a global sweepstake, run by the largest casinos in the world. As we have seen during the bailouts of banks, whose investment arms are the sacred pedestals of gambling run wild, where executives who do the gambling are rewarded far beyond the leaders of other industries, mistakes in risk taking procedures have far too dire an influence on the global economy to be tolerated any further.

Figure out the implications. Number one is the minimalisation or removal of financial gambling, the speculative drives which, rather than rationality (for the future is unpredictable and what knowledge there is, is unevenly distributed) determine the fate of companies and the state of currencies.

The start-up entrepreneur and his partners will usually place their own funds in the company to get it going, supplemented by borrowing. Ownership resides in those who register the company as owners, and who operate it as partners, not in relatives or institutions from whom they may borrow. Applying to the stock exchange for an IPO usually comes much later.

Since we are no longer talking of companies financed through the stock exchange, the structure of management is open. There is no longer a need for a board to act as a tame watchdog for shareholders. We are talking management, pure and simple. Remember, also, that we have created more effective education, and that guaranteed incomes ensure that workers can live reasonably outside the workforce. Under these conditions, employees from sales staff to production line have the intelligence, imagination and self-interest to identify with the future of the enterprise as partners in it; otherwise they are unlikely to be there at all. Wise and efficient firms will make the utmost use of this, placing workers on management boards and consultative committees, and inducting them into ownership, depending on the size and structure of the firm and the nature of its work.

The firm is part and parcel of culture and society. It is not neutral. Its present arrangements do not have to be taken as holy. The firm has served society in its present forms very well indeed. But society in its present forms is defective. So is the firm. As society adjusts, so too must the firm, or instead of being the valuable provider it will be the liability working *against* the lives we want to lead.

To sum up, society will raise capital through loans, not the stock market. Firms will take social costs into account as factors of production. They will not be supported by government funds. Workers will be partners, salaried. And, drawing from other chapters, firms will be relieved of corporate taxes, excise and customs duties[225].

2012Postscript

- Except for countries or organizations with the uppermost and lowermost GDP distinctions in its measurement – or the measurement of *any* productivity criteria – are unreliable.[226] And for *all* officially accepted measurements the criteria for performance or results lack consideration of non-monetary and non-material objectives. This applies most obviously in the measurement of costs, where slowly environmental, social and cultural costs are being thought about. One of the first serious attempts to break through this barrier was made by the United Nations Research Institute for Social Development in Geneva in the 1960's to no policy effect since the "intangibles" were not quantified. In 2012 there has been a better accepted way of assessing "wealth" through the UN University's "Inclusive Wealth Report 2012" [227] I remain sceptical about the degree to which it will be incorporated into policies.

- The speed with which investment decisions have to be mad on stock market does not augur well for rationality or solid information.

- Emanuel Wallenstein, in an interview on YouTube speculates that contemporary capitalism is on the verge of self-destruction. Certainly major changes are taking place, largely as a result of the crises of 2011-? But it is likely that capitalism ado[t major changes, some of which I will mention below, rather than morphing into a totally new system, or into chaos.[228]

- The investment scandals of 2011--? made public what those in the business world knew only too well – that in the pursuit of limitless money business executives too frequently let their ethics go by the board and excuse to themselves cheating, disloyal and underhand tactics, corruption, bribery, treachery, clandestine manipulations of other people's money, falsification of documents and records, ponzi schemes, embezzlement, dishonest stock market moves, and more. Success is measured in monetary gain and devil take the hindmost. For this the executives in charge have been reaping and still reap enormous bonuses to which the world is beginning to object. I do not know of much needed studies of the upbringing and background of executives of large scale companies, or of their transformation into ruthless sharks. We also need anthropological studies of financiers' culture – of more value it seems to me than judicial enquiries of limited events. Laws and regulations alone will not remove these practices –the temptations are too great - and the deliberate changing of executive culture is fraught with difficulty. Introducing ethically trained and responsible men and women into boardrooms and executive ranks usually isolates them as a minority under pressure to conform to previously established behaviour. Must we wait for Youth Maturity Institutes? Now, having set out the indictment the defence must rightly argue that it is wrong to chastise individuals for being members of a category – a kind of cultural racism. By far the majority of persons in that category are innocent of such charges. Unfortunately the guilty are in positions of untoward influence and power;

• Dependence on committees in the name of democracy reduces the exercise of responsibility and takes an enormous amount of time in corporations and other organisations. They are of course of great value, as is one to one consultation, when there is need for a variety of expert advice in pursuit of a given result. Organisations, though, might be well advised to periodically review standing committees and remove those which lack functionality or are techniques for a decision maker to avoid personal responsibility.

- Attempts to deal with the financial crises of 2010 - ? at first identified mortgage failures and then investment company mismanagement and then the extraordinary overextension of sovereign debt. The immediate response was to take measures which reformed and rescued governments and through them banks and other financial institutions. In doing so authorities ignored the banks' failed responsibility to exercise due diligence in their lending practices[229] to both home buyers and governments. Bankers used premature foreclosure creating unsalable housing instead of settling for more realistic repayment plans. Also in doing so the authorities all but ignored the principle that it is demand which runs the economy and took measures which weakened demand and prompted more recession. In Canada bank deposits are state insured up to a certain limit thus reducing individual exposure to the crisis and helping to maintain demand. The election of French President François Hollande together with riots in Greece and demonstrations in Spain jolted the financial powers to give more attention to economic growth as the engine of recovery and the peoples' democratic desire. Canada's Minister of Finance declared that demand was the variable which was the key to recovery. But to make matters worse many banks operated both retail and investment segments so that restrictive credit policies now invaded the public retail sector making credit more difficult for small and medium enterprise just when that was needed[230].

- Large corporations are sitting on considerable amounts of cash. In August 2012 the Governor of the Bank of Canada urged them to give most of the estimated over 900 billion in Canada alone, after holding some back for emergencies, back to their shareholders as a way of stimulating economic growth.[231] This would surely apply to Europe as well, thus easing the burden on government funds.

XII – The Future of the Poorer World

The reference to countries which have not shared in the industrialisation and commercialisation of the Western and advancing Asian worlds has changed over the decades from under-developed to developing to emerging, to Third World (the Second being communist and the Fourth the inner city poverty) and so on, each reflecting the analytic presuppositions of the writers. For the present, I prefer to use the descriptive term "the Poorer World" which I think makes no assumptions about developing dynamics or other processes. It is there, there are many causes, many movements, and a tumultuous range of conditions. And it is embedded in parts of the richer countries also.

The very term "poverty" disguisesmany significant variations and is open to multiple interpretations. The displaced agricultural workers of Europe and their surviving villagers of the eighteenth century and those affected by the disastrous famine of the potato (an introduced staple) crop in Ireland later, had much in common with those living in the disaster areas of Africa today. I do not recall any of the great explorers of the South Pacific using the term poverty in describing the level of living of the South Sea Islanders (though they often despised the cultures). Had they done so they would have been treated with ridicule because of a potential comparison with the conditions of their seamen, or with the country folk of their homes, where destitution was forcing men to go to sea and flock to unemployment in the cities.

Today we have measures. A great deal of intelligence has gone into the construction of international definitions of poverty, such is our passion for quantification, and the attempt to capture misery in figures. We don't really need to do this, except as a justification for bureaucratic and charitable intervention. Images on television, selective though they be, do the job for us. And further the very scale of the figures is disheartening, whereas the one image can make us angry. Half a billion? A billion? True, figures sometimes tell us whether it is getting worse or better. But even here there are so many assumptions and inaccuracies in the compilations – just as there are in assessing the death rate in Darfur. If poverty were at one tenth of the scale posited, it is still unacceptable.

There are cross cultural implications in the idea of poverty. Many populations are in fact dying out as the result of poverty induced disease, malnutrition, and migration. These are not always in Africa or Asia. There are Italian, French, German, and Swiss mountain villages, to say nothing of those in the new EU countries of Eastern Europe, and inner city slums and destitution which fit the bill. But in those places there are state initiatives of partial help which are not available in many other parts of the world. However the gross rise in unemployment and retrenchments in social safety nets typical of Europe in 2012 show that the disease has spread astronomically, a factor which will continue until major changes are effected in the political will.

Quite often we read reports that such and such an area is living on less than, say, ten dollars or less a month. To Westerners this is shocking, and in many conditions so it should be. But such figures and their implications occasionally need a dash of scepticism, more particularly in communities where some agricultural supply is not mediated through money. To the extent that lack of momentary income is true of urban poverty and depressed labour, it is indicative of severe human suffering. It can also ignore the subsidisation of urban life by family goods trickling in freely from the countryside from family to family by-passing the market. It can often ignore the miracle of self-help. Intimate studies of shanty towns in Latin America (admittedly sometimes higher on the income scale than many other communities) reveal initiatives, a *joie de vivre*, and creative energy that has material results in improved physical conditions, noticeable if you visit them from decade to decade[232]. This can be in the midst of drugs and violence.

The qualifications are even more of a problem when assessments are made of the level of rural living. Is the help of kin or community in the building of a home, however simple, or in parts of agricultural or forestry labour counted as income? Are stories, music and laughter quantified? Is the Western observer distressed at the "wastage" of marriage ceremonies, failing to take into account the reciprocal activities between kinsfolk over time, the cancellation of debts and the creation of new obligations, and the social benefit of marital stability – in short, the notional income derived from the social organisation of which it is the evidence?[233]

Such international measures ignore cross-cultural definitions of poverty. They imply Western standards of health, education, above all material income, and similar factors. The measures, being international, are imposed from outside with little reference to the specific goals and wishes of the people in question. Increased material wealth may go into ceremonial or non-material events, from Carnaval to bride price, from mosques to moving into urban slums which, despite much misery, can be exciting in comparison to an isolated village and are indeed magnets for population movements. The slums of Mumbai and their homeless on the pavements are populated by many people who have migrated from what they believe to have been worse and to which they do not return. This is not just a poorer country issue. It happens in Europe and the Americas.

Indeed it is false to talk of poverty and wealth in simplistic terms. Economists by and large fail to take into account the non-material values that always compete with the material. Indeed a better term, though still containing ambiguities, is "societal progress". By this we mean a state of affairs that moves from one set of conditions to another *in accordance with the total values of the people in question.* This is not easy to do with precision, the only ultimate indicator at present being *what people actually choose to achieve given changing costs and benefits,* material and non-material alike. Unless academics and policy makers investigate actual and potential changes in such demand schedules, their policies are as likely to be off as much as on target.[234]   I will however continue to use "poverty" as an easier-to-read shorthand.

Oh my, you are going to think, the man is justifying poverty.

Not at all.   There are parts of the poorer world where these observations do not apply, where children are dying and parents starving or too stricken by disease to function. No, this is *not* a suggestion that we turn a blind eye. It is a recommendation that we take non-material as well as material values into the analysis. In pushing for material goals we can sometimes in fact *reduce* the overall satisfactions of life.

I am saying that in the very depths of the poorest world there is hope.   Given a chance, the people everywhere are showing that they have resilience and are determined to improve their lot by increasing their energies devoted to traditional culture or by seeking new lives. Given a chance, free of guns, free of disease, managing climatic traumas.

The societies of which the poor are a part are organic networks which even have extremely rich and often corrupt individuals. There are millionaires in Gaza. They are also organically part of the global community. Changes in politics, power rivalries, entrepreneurial conditions, the approach to tradition, access to markets, between men and women, taxation, education, health services, power supply, and so often overlooked, physical infrastructure, have profound consequences. Not all of them are welcomed. A change in one can have deep effects which ripple throughout the society, polity and economy. The opening of a road to a hitherto unserviced community can have major multiplying effects on every single one of the factors I have listed. Whether it does or not will depend on the points of view of everyone involved, from State departments to village elders and individuals who decide whether they intend to take advantage or not. The poor are not just passive recipients of hand outs, and we must avoid that dogma. They *choose* what to accept, ignore, try and discard.

Poverty is a function of societal conditions. Development economists have pointed out two sets of these. First, there is the situation in which the lack of one or more elements in a functional economy vitiates the ability of the system to work. The list is well known – inappropriate education, ill health, malnutrition, corruption, inadequate distribution system, frictions in access to markets, poor transport, social mores weakening the role of women,[235] lack of capital. The work of the wider world is to stimulate the removal of such dysfunctions, *as approved by the affected population.*

Sometimes the imbalance in the social conditions will stimulate further growth and innovation. An educational stride ahead may stimulate demand for better health services, for more employment, for better adult knowledge. The entry of internet centres into villages may increase the velocity of circulation of information (including current agricultural prices in the nearby market) in circumstances where post and telephone are lacking. It may put cities in poor countries in active touch with the global sources of capital. The eradication of malaria may revolutionise agricultural practice, and vice versa, through the replacement of wet by dry framing.

What is our role in bringing the poorer world closer to achieving its potential cultural-political-economic demand schedule? Aid? Technical assistance? Charity and crisis relief? Military intervention? Sanctions for improper government conduct? Free trade? Improving national government?

None of these are simple.

The most dramatic of these is international charitable aid in times of crisis – tsunami, violence, drought, earthquakes. The popularity of giving direct aid under such circumstances is unquestionable and represents the best of values. However, despite the skills of many of the charitable NGOs, it is not often enough directed towards the dynamic substitution of wealth increase for poverty, that is of dynamic social progress replacing stasis. Nor is it often enough directed toward the movement of populations away from locations of potential or repeated natural disaster. We cannot as yet control all such disasters, though we can alleviate them.[236]

Manmade disaster, and particularly the use of violence and of autocratic corruption, is a different matter. We expect Youth Maturity Institutes to play a major role in the correction of such causes; this will take perhaps two generations after creation which itself is far away.. Global Government, with the monopolisation of weapons and the use of rapid intervention will be needed. Criteria for controlling or replacing governments under Global Trusteeship can be arrived at quite rapidly, though the mechanisms for enforcing this will be inefficient until Global Government is reformed. What is without doubt is that the situation in such countries as the Congo, Myanmar, Darfur and formerly Rwanda cannot be allowed to continue in a modern world. The growth of international morality puts limits on the destructive parts of the independence of states.

Non-crisis technical assistance and international aid are the quiet undramatic and effective methods of transferring the knowledge and practices that transform static communities and economies into dynamic ones, capable of slowly changing the poverty spectrum. Despite its good intentions, however, such aid is often limited in its objectivity. The limitations are legion. In thinking about this we should distinguish, as we go along, financial aid given to government entities, and direct aid attributed to workers in the field, in assisting communities and direct production units, including those which support the arts and ceremony.

Direct financial aid is fraught with misunderstandings, misuse and criticism. I myself do not have the data to make reasonable comments overall. In some instances the good intentions are thwarted by the practice of some donor governments to insist that funds be spent on their own industries, which is why recipient countries prefer such assistance to come from UN or other international agencies. And of course there is corruption, diversion of funds to non authorised uses, and other malpractices.

Direct technical assistance avoids these problems though it deals with more subtle concerns and requires a great deal of sensitivity with inter-personal and inter-cultural understanding. It must be admitted that aid agencies, both private and official, vary hugely in such matters.

The early attempts to design aid often had naïve expectations of indigenous societies in the poorer world. Two of the most important movements were to stimulate the formation of cooperatives and a movement known as Community Development. There have been some excellent results which however, globally speaking, have been patchy. And there have been movements, such as the micro bank systems in Bangladesh, where tiny amounts of individual deposits amount to sums that provide loans for capital purposes, and have been imitated elsewhere with success. (There have even been copies in the richer countries, such as the community development movement in Saskatchewan, which came from experiences in India, and micro loans for the urban poor in major cities). I myself urged the formation of cooperatives, seeing these as consistent with indigenous values and social structure, when an administrative officer in the Solomon Islands in the 1940's.

But a review of United Nations supported community development[237] and also field work in Fiji[238] convinced me that, given the high percentage of failures in some countries, this was no panacea. The naïve view of indigenous culture is that the natural thing to do is for everyone to work together – and indeed there is a great deal of truth in that.

This approach hides dysfunctional tendencies and the variation of individual interests. It works best when the material conditions of life are limited, and collegial help is essential, for example, to build a traditional house. The moment it goes beyond that to the point where, theoretically, wants become expanding and unlimited (as happens when money takes hold and a people can witness the ways in which riches can help both material and non-material ambitions) internal rivalries and competition start to take hold. Defections occur, quarrels ensue, rival camps emerge, and individualistic entrepreneurs seize their chance. This is not to deny that, sufficiently motivated, groups will combine for specific purposes – reforestation, irrigation, public health installations, or, as with many North American Indians, the use of collective resources for commercial enterprises supported by politically organized revenues, including taxes.

Nor is it wiser to come to the conclusion that society must break up into a mass of individual entrepreneurs for societal progress to take place. Especially in their start up stage, but even if they become wealthy, entrepreneurs in most poorer countries still must observe the socio-cultural norms of generosity, social responsibility and familial distribution. (Ironically, the Sicilian mafia "families" provide a case study of this kind of motivation.) Western observers often consider this phenomenon to be a brake on growth, diverting liquid and capital resources into non-material objectives. But for many an entrepreneur this is part of his/her motivation. To destroy such motivations is in fact to destroy enterprise.

Indeed, in my critique of Community Development mentioned above I argued that it could often hold back growth. The reason is based on a simple economics principle. Accumulation depends upon "taking in other people's washing". Community Development is most frequently based on everybody doing the same thing for everybody else without exchange. We all get together to build everyone a better house. We combine to build latrines. In theory it is the obverse of the division of labour, based on the fact that there is little or no money to do otherwise. That's all very well, and is sometimes the only way forward. But as a principle of dynamics it is flawed.

"Taking in each other's washing" is a better principle. It means that numerous transactions take place, and that each transaction creates a profit, however miniscule. Those miniscule amounts add up, and while much may go in consumption or ceremonial support, bits accumulate for capital improvement. The sum of those bits create monetary wealth. Just ask the women traders of West Africa. Let there be a specialist washer-woman in the village, and see what happens – if there are other specialists such as a village carpenter, water purveyor, thatcher, goat herder. After all, when it comes to ceremonial affairs there are likely to be numerous specialists such as priests or lineage leaders in various stages of the proceedings, so the concept is by no means completely unknown.

In the 'nineties aid donors, tired of the weaknesses of governmental practices, moved almost in concert to transfer much of their support to local non-governmental organisations, hoping to avoid corruption and to tap into the very sense of community that characterized the theory of Community Development. The decade was characterized by a jump in progress and enthusiasm, followed by disillusion and despair as so many of the hopeful organisations yielded to corruption, mismanagement, bureaucratic interference,[239] argument, personal rivalry, power broking, and segmentation.[240] [241]

Richer Governments which give direct aid are more than likely to be motivated by political strategy, choosing countries in accordance with the donor's global interests. This was particularly the case during the Cold War, but is still practised. Sometimes legitimise (e.g. accounting) strictures and conditions in the use of aid by one country are negated by the offer of aid without such strictures by another donor. Donor countries frequently insist that their money be spent on their own products or technical experts, even though cheaper or more effective sources are available (which is why channelling aid through the United Nations is preferable and more effective). The effectiveness of Canadian aid, for example, is limited by the requirement that wherever possible the aid be furnished by Canadian suppliers, whether these are or are not the most economical and effective. Sweden has a deserved reputation for being more liberal in such matters (and is in the forefront of those countries using the social sciences to help design aid effectively.) In the case of some more sophisticated recipients government departments can be rewarded in their national budgets if they succeed in attracting aid, at the expense of departments that do not do so: and the "experts" find that their task is simply to evaluate and perhaps rubber stamp proposals which equally competent national civil servants have already formulated.

As well, country donors frequently assess aid requirements in terms of meeting a static goal. Increase rice production by x%. Provide the funds for more school buildings. Dig how many water wells. Treat a thousand

AIDS victims. Useful and not to be ignored. But not *development* aid unless the process not only continues when the donors have left, but establishes multiplying effects throughout the society. with static rather than dynamic effects.[242] Static aid is more like charity than development.

For the dangers of charity must be avoided. Poor people are not objects to be patronised. They are men and women with brains and feelings and potential skills. They can be creative, and indeed are. Not many citizens of the rich world could survive under their conditions, but survive they do. They must not be turned into mendicants, but given the chance to better achieve their own goals.

Thus in the meantime aid must become more objective, more dynamic, perhaps less romantic. This is by no means to decry the self-sacrificing efforts of the most effective donors and especially the United Nations and the those NGOs who know these lessons and these facts and take care of them. International aid must move from bilateral to multilateral, including the use of the effective NGOs.[243]

Ultimately we speak of the best of all worlds. Can we remove the extremes of poverty? Yes. Absolutely. Let's get on with it.

Economists – and I – have long preached the mantra of DEVELOPMENT. This buzz-word can mean so many different things in practice. Jeffrey Sachs, one of the most vigorous and influential proponents implies the conversion of economic systems into the Western free market model.[244]   I am a free marketer myself, in that I abhor the dead hand of bureaucratic intervention and distortions. But we must recognize that nowhere in the world has the free market, or even state management of the economic system, has resulted in the abolition of poverty. They both create the rich and the poor, the advantaged and the disadvantaged.

There must be some form of redistribution, and there should be recognition that for some communities, development does NOT equate with social progress – in fact occasionally the reverse. Believe it or not, some people are becoming disenchanted with the consumer society of infinite growth, which is the philosophical foundation of the uninhibited free market. Insofar as redistribution is concerned, as I pointed out in earlier chapters ways must be invented to create systems of guaranteed minimum income which can   take into account, where necessary, the realities of subsistence farming and similar institutions.

But development in one form or another is still an operative concept and we must keep returning to it.

The record of the international community with respect to the creation of appropriate tools is patchy to say the least. Bilateral aid is driven too much by country interests – tempted to pressure the people to, for example, build a specific number of latrines, the marketing of commerce, political influence. Multinational aid sometimes runs up against rivalries between aid donors, inexpert experts, crisis resolution. Both have high costs, and are limited in the way they learn from experience.

Again, the last phrase I use advisedly. Aid projects have frequently achieved excellent results, even where side effects have not been known. The improvement of rice strains, the monitoring of locust explosions, fish harvesting techniques, some eradication of disease, some educational advance, are only a few in a long list.

Yet very seldom are projects conscientiously submitted to what I would call *developmental* evaluation. While there is now more attention given to hitherto unsuspected side effects – on the ecosystem even more than on the basic socio-cultural system – objectives are almost always given in static terms rather than in the dynamic ones that genuine movement embraces. We need to *judge projects on their multiplier effects*, not on the way they reach a single target. It is as though we are content if we know that A moves to B, even if the world stops at B. We do not often ask what happens after B, whether C and D will follow *ad infinitum*.

It is not as if we have not been told that the objective, both to be valid and to be successful, should be defined in ways that meet the people's own concepts of their desired aspirations. We have. Many grass roots "developers" do just that – the more "grass roots" they are, the more likely the developmental success.

Government ministries, many regional officials, most official aid experts, avoid such disturbing problems by retreating into the position that "they know best". Only now are pastoral officers in East Africa beginning to understand that there are values to the cattle complexes and the indigenous uses of camels amongst the populations that they, the experts, were not cognizant of.[245]

What do people want improvement for? What price in values are they prepared to pay to get there? What happens when the aid project comes to an end? Does it just die on the vine because it ignored the reality of the people? Or perhaps it is renewed as permanent subsidised aid *ad infinitum*? These are among the most often overlooked beginning questions.[246]

There are many more such conceptual difficulties involved in the aid process. When is aid designed to stimulate a dynamic, and when is it merely self-satisfying charity or power-based intellectualism? There are answers already in the literature and in experience, but they are too often disregarded.[247]

The correction of inequities will be necessary every step of the way toward the world we want. It is not to be done in ways that remove decision-making from the populace. In fact one of the most important principles that community development tried to grapple with (mostly unsuccessfully, as the movement became bureaucratised) was to give people the right to say "No, no, and no again."

These remarks are not intended to advocate the reduction of resources allocated for aid; far from it. The world is considerably below agreed targets, as minimal as 1% of G.D.P. At the 1985 G8 summit not all members agreed to raise their contributions to 0.7 % by 2012. At the 2005 G8 summit they did exactly the same, and it was touted as a revolutionary breakthrough! In some countries such as Canada international aid is regarded as a luxury to be chopped, as in 2010, during a budgetary recession, with lower priority than support for the military.

As the poorer countries begin to solve their problems, to create increased levels of living and better qualities of life, so too will their expectations grow. New dangers then develop; dangers of aggression because the pace of improvement is too slow; and more determined and experienced demands for a better life. The objects are legitimate and part of the dream for everyone even when leading to competitive tensions. A new threat emerges when poorer countries are threatened by climate change – a threat that this can lead to military tension and even action.

Similar remarks apply to migration, the movement of populations. The pitifully tragic mass migration that is the response to violence and natural disaster cannot adequately be handled by international refugee organisations, however hard and selflessly they try. The scale in the 1990s was and is now in the 21st century enormous. According to the World Watch Institute, about 125 million people live elsewhere than where they were born (most legally and by choice). In the 'seventies there were about 2.5 million new refugees a year. In the 'nineties the figure rose to four million. There are 27 million internal refugees, whose plight is more serious than most of those who flee their country, and an estimated 10 million illegal migrants. Ten million people are removed from their homes by public works projects, such as dams or roads, usually with insufficient attempts to soften the blow of a change of living.[248]

Too often men and women in the field have to stand by, confronting massacres, unreasoning panic, mass death by disease, the distortion of humanity by starvation, psychological trauma. In the twenty-first century? In the age of the Internet and ever increasing technological advance?

The unremitting tragedies have given rise to commerce similar to that of slavery in the last century. The illegal trade in population movement has the status of a massive industry, comparable to that of trade in some drugs. Thousands of dollars change hands in individual cases. Unlucky victims often find themselves literally in conditions of slavery, from Germany to California.

Global Government has to be able to respond quickly and to interfere if states refuse to admit help or to give help. It has to be able to declare such situations to be disasters as great as those of natural cataclysms, to be totally unacceptable to civilisation. It has to be able to act effectively.

Even more troubling are certain situations where, it seems, no amount of intervention, no amount of development-directed change, will help. I refer to regions of endemic disaster and poverty of resources. Here we must be careful once again to respect the values of the population that lives in such conditions. We must not assume that because life, to our eyes, is unbelievably hard, that it is therefore non-valued; that the population would be happier tucked in bed with television. *It is up to the people to decide.* If they don't want change, if they can manage, leave them alone.

But if they do want change, as a result of suffering, persecution, or wider horizons, they are right to seek it, and we are right, have a duty even, to help them on the way.

In some instances it can be argued that cases which are otherwise hopeless can, with education and communication, carve out niches in the world economy. Hong Kong and Singapore, investment havens, resorts. It is unrealistic, however, to expect every difficult situation to be resolved like that, or that all such cases can support the subsequent population level. There are surely diminishing returns on resort creation.

Richer countries are still having trouble learning that is it is not usually effective to revive dying industries. Populations cannot always be kept in place when industries die or are replaced. Adjustment includes population movement. If richer countries try to create

520

artificial population stability within their own borders they subsidise ineffectively.

If this is true nationally, it is also true internationally. The population level in a few countries will simply not be viable, not because of high birth rates but because of lack or destruction of productive possibilities coupled with the inability to finance education that will make the reduction of paid employment acceptable.

The world as we know it today is the result of continuous migrations. Mankind has never been without them. Many were the result of military force, a process that we have partially overcome. Others were the result of poverty, nomadism, the search for better pastures, and the restlessness of the human spirit which we can never do without. Diasporas are universally present, even in Japan. Even though many have been politically and culturally persecuted, that has been because of their very effectiveness, creating jealousy and envy. Their world linkages have promoted enterprise and trade. There is no reason to believe that their positive effects will not continue. Not only do they contribute to the dynamics of the host country, but they frequently re-invest in their countries of origin.

Thus a major tool for the reduction of inequities is steady migration, even if host countries initially pay a price that may not be returned until the next generation. To have optimal effects, migration should be spared the ups and downs of welcoming and hostility, and should be within the capacity of host countries to manage, provided the concept of management is long-term rather than in response to short-term costs and prejudices.

Much has been made, correctly, of the stranglehold of debt that kills off positive movement in many of the poorer countries.[249] To reduce or even eradicate past indebtedness from the poorest countries was indeed one of the new promises of the 2005 G8 summit. It sounds very good, but is it much more than public relations? Will it happen? And why just the poorest countries? Is this not discriminating against those poor countries that have in fact pulled themselves out of the quagmire – in effect saying "Do well according to *our* standards, and we will then arbitrarily refuse to countenance debt relief."?

This is topsy-turvy aid, especially when much of the indebtedness has been wasted on corruption, military expenditures and gross inefficiency. And may it not simply start the cycle of indebtedness once again?

Of course international finance is needed, and of course special considerations by way of repayment schedules and interest rates are necessary. But discipline is needed. Cut off the tap if the funds are going into private pockets (though see my later analysis of corruption) or into excessive military or similar hardware. In fact, as I hint in the discussion of nation states and global government, refuse aid to countries which spend on militarism. Under Global Government supervision freeze and sequester overseas bank accounts of leaders and officials which do not correspond to their legal incomes.

In the long term we hope that much of this will be beside the point. More fundamentally, poorer countries need to be able to *earn their own living* on a level playing field. Open international trade is not a complete answer, but it the major plank. There are poorer countries which resist this, because they wish to protect inefficient industries. That is like post-war Britain, which blindly tried to prop up dying industries, even towns, delaying recovery by perhaps a decade. There are industries in the poorer world which must be allowed to die, with appropriate help and adjustment.

At the same time some dying industries might even sometimes survive if poorer countries, particularly in Africa, eliminated tariffs between themselves. Way back in the 'forties, as a graduate student, I had two articles accepted by a "Special Correspondent" for *The Economist*. One of these suggested that too much attention was being given to trade between African countries and their colonial metro poles. More attention should be given to within-continent trade, and for this to happen massive investment in infrastructure connecting the countries through trade channels – roads and railways particularly – ways one of the ways forward. Sixty years later, although there have been some notable investments and grand plans, *the need is still there.*

That does not let the richer world off the hook. Once again the 2005 G8 summit made good noises, about reducing, even eliminating the protective barriers that they have set up to protect their agriculture, particularly, from poorer world competition. At least, at this meeting President Bush announced that protection of cotton would be phased out. That is but a tiny conceptual beginning in words if not in deeds. Indeed in 2010 Brasil found it necessary to impose restrictions on United States imports because the promised reduction of subsidies had not been honoured. And where are you Europe with your one sided and wasteful agricultural support policies?

Quite often this is not a matter of bold strategic sweeps, but of little, almost unnoticed adjustments. Canada permits raw Thai silk without duty, but Thai silk clothing gets punished. Obviously this is on the theory that to import the raw material creates Canadian manufacturing jobs – yet Canadian manufacturing hardly uses the stuff. To remove the tariff would create more jobs in Thailand. Isn't that what we should be aiming for, to the benefit of both countries? We will not create wealthier workers in the poorer countries, with income to spare to spend on richer country goods, if we deny them some competitive advantage.

Now it will become apparent that this kind of trade is dependent on the existence of appropriate resources in the relevant countries, resources that are not at this moment being used to everyone's advantage. And some countries just don't have those kinds of resources.

Or so it is thought.

Yet they do have people. It may of course be the case that those populations do not want to bear the inevitable costs of development. Fine, let them alone. But for the others there is an answer, and India has shown part of the way. The people are the resource, but un-nurtured, their capacities unfulfilled.

So here we go. Massive investment in education as the number one priority, regardless. Within a decade, good high schools, if necessary to begin with imported teachers. Instruction in English, French or Spanish as a second but fully functioning language. Universities and technical institutes.[250] Education in commerce, engineering, architecture, agriculture, applied science, social sciences, computer science, the arts. Make it possible for the people to become *creative* on the world stage.[251]

Although India is a very different country, starting with the advantage of good education in English up to the highest level for at least a corpus of innovative people, much can be learned from its experience. What has been noteworthy in less than the past decade, is the application of skills and knowledge to jump over slow evolution into the revolution of internet technology. (This is but one field - engineering, pharmaceuticals, textiles are others, but it is the most relevant for this discussion.) Most of us know of Bangalore, the Silicon Valley of the country because of its success in capturing a proportion of the world's internet service work. The people who are responsible are not village communitarians but advanced entrepreneurs, often in partnership with the world's largest firms. And Bangalore is now significant not just for services but as a location for creative software and hardware development of a world standard.

The important point is that it is not limited to Bangalore. There is a significant trickle down effect as the process of innovation is leading to the creation of new systems of both hardware and services to the poor. On such is an enterprise called Hole in the Wall. This is the brain child of the NIIT organisation started as long ago as 1981 to bring computers and people together – at a time when computers were a long, long way from their commonplace now. In 2001 it began a project called Minimal Invasive Education which now has operations in scores of slum locations, and conceived as an alternative to the expensive and elitist provision of computers in formal classrooms.

The operation is simplicity itself, but to be successful required innovative skills in bringing known elements into focus as solutions for unexpected problems. Computer screens are typically located in series along a slum street where children are at play. Behind the wall is simple equipment and technology to gather information about the use of the monitors. To each monitor is attached the equivalent of a mouse – but that had to be completely redesigned to withstand the roughness of the children's enthusiastic hands and fingers. It was also discovered that the children opened too many screens for the computers to handle so that they crashed. Hence devices had to be invented to limit the number of screens open at one time. And so on.

The children are left alone to get on with it. They quickly learn searching skills and move from games to information as they wish in self-directed education.

Another type of computer extension into the countryside is offered by an organisation which puts computers into villages for anybody to use. The computers are in a sense old fashioned, going back to software basics, but in another sense are highly advanced since they must be protected against rough handling, pollution and dust and must shut down automatically when the temperature is too high. These are not high street models. They must also face interruptions of power supply, so that they come equipped with a backup battery charged with solar panels. To supplant poor telephone connections, plans are being formed to find ways to make use of large area wireless technology. Indeed the demands of this kind of countryside may make advances in that technology more economical and practical than its attempted applications in the richer world.

Once the system is working it has numerous applications. Farmers can check market prices in various nearby locations before they decide which one they should take their produce to. They seek immediate advice on cropping problems. The computer may be linked to an electronic bulletin board with community information. In short the rural village changes its character and enterprise is supported. Knowledge is power over one's destiny, and the computer is its messenger.

Perhaps too much attention is being focussed on free trade for *existing* products. But what about new ones? Much of this is dependent on richer world policies too. Here is but one example.

Sugar has bedevilled the economies of many countries (rather like dependence on oil). Like bananas, it has often emerged as the major product earning overseas revenues (apart from tourism) in tropical countries. There is a global over-supply to present markets. Former colonial powers protect the supply from former colonies.

At the same time the richer countries are gas guzzlers and at the same time over-consumption of sugar is known to have negative effects on weight and diet. An alternative fuel (used with success in Brasil) is ethanol. Poorer countries could in theory contribute to both these issues by manufacturing at home – ethanol and sucralose, a sugar alcohol suitable for diabetics and other dieters. Inexpensive and readily available ethanol would remove the excuses which lead to the manufacture of petrol powered vehicles and to human induced global warming.[252]

A major deterrent for the production of ethanol in temperate countries is that it diverts production from foodstuffs leading to price inflation. That is less of an issue with sugar.

Postscript2012

• The *Economist* queries whether Rwanda will be the next Singapore. 25 February 2012 p. 80
• China's entry into African agricultural and resource development. Africans restive.
• Peerlman, Janice. *Favela; Four decades of living on the edge in Rio de Janeiro.* London and New York, Oxford University Press 2010 Rio favelas, in anticipation of the soccer World Cup and the Olympics, have been cleared of drugs and obvious gangs, and are being developed as high price real estate.
• Refugees place heavy burdens on developing countries. Note Somalis in Kenya.
• Innovation in hospital design – open structures rather than cement high rises.
• For issues of aid and technical assistance. Cf. Nutt, Samantha *Damned Nations: Greed, Guns, Armies and Aid* Oxford, Signal, 2011
• Latin American poverty rate is declining substantially. From nearly 50% in 1990 to 30^% in 2011 - ECLAC report quoted in the *Economist* 3 Dec 2011
• Overseas investment by China and India, and Arab states such as Qatar[253]
• Note: Smillie, Ian *Blood on the Stone: Greed. Corruption and war in the global diamond trade.* Anthenm Press, 2010. The destruction of society in the Eastern Congo is a case in point.

- Why do poor people eat so badly? FAO asks. In richer countries they nosh on junk food because much of it is cheaper. In other countries many of the poor are in lands subject to drought and warfare or as in Bangladesh over population. In many parts of the world rural people are moving to cities where they do not find jobs and foods are increasingly expensive. In some instances their morale is very low and they compensate with such things as sugared drinks or even drugs rather than food. The presence of diseases such as tuberculosis can negate hunger. Migrant workers can leave families struggling to make ends meet.

- While many favela, shanty towns and urban slums are devoid of basic services upon which improvement may be based, where there is income they evolve into permanent suburbs. In India and China forcible clearing sometimes without warning increases strain and destitution. In Kenya alternative planning and housing nibbles at the edges of shanty towns and in South Africa some have turned into major suburbs.

- In 2012 worldwide refugee movements place great strains on receiving countries and emergency charity services. Rich countries pledge vast sums in relief but sometimes cannot deliver because of their own budgetary woes and taxpayer questioning.. In Bangladesh the authorities resist a minority Muslim population trying to escape persecution in Myanmar. The Arab spring displaces millions fleeing violence ad in Libya foreign African workers fled to Italy. Kenya not only establishes camps for fleeing Somalis but invades their country to try to remove the Islamic revolutionary forces which are dividing that county. In Columbia some communities caught between the military and he FARC rebels are declaring "a pox on both of vies" and achieving some success in pushing armed groups out of their territory.

- In some countries innovation in housing techniques can help improving living. The New Mexican use of adobe clay blocks and designs of cheap modular construction and even the use of cargo containers can make a substantial difference in Africa. In Fiji however I noted that congenitally designed units of commercial materials had layouts which made certain kinds of domestic, hospitality and ceremonial arrangements no longer feasible so that only those who were ready to adapt their culture thought of making use of them.

- International aid for development[254] is not only distorted by corruption programmes or emergency relief is sometimes becoming literally a matter of life or death. So-called safety aid corridors in locations of warfare are notoriously difficult to arrange and are highly dangerous to operate. It has become a source of income and publicity for resistance movements to kidnap aid workers.

- Far too many countries which have major exploitations by foreign countries of one or two resources fail miserably to translate those riches into public services including infrastructure or the wealth of workers leading to civil discontent and sometimes slave like and/or highly dangerous working conditions. Oil, cocoa and diamond[255] industries are major offenders.

When Nestle was accused of obtaining cocoa from child labour the firm investigated and reported that there was a major difficulty in that they could often not trace the supply to its source because of the intermediation of middlemen. Critics did not accept this excuse and Nestle vowed to do better.

- Improved income does not guarantee that there will be no unseen concomitant costs. As wealth increases so does the incidence of chronic disease such as heart problems, diabetes cancer.[256] This is NOT an argument for continuing poverty but rather linking such matters holistically to governmental values, structure, financial priorities and organisation.

XV - The Importance of Traditional Social Organisation in States Today

Most policy makers appear to consider that many forms of traditional social organisation belong to the past. Their only relevance is that of finding ways to convert them to urban or peasant models. This, however, is a false analysis. We are now in the twenty-first century, but although often threatened by socio-economic and political factors, traditional social organisation is still real and of high relevance and has sometimes has great adaptability in the face of pressures.

Let us then examine a few examples and consider their place in the ideal world.

Much of Western Europe knows communes as the fundamental political organisation. In France the commune is a unit of local government. However the commune is a geographical unit rather than a grouping of kin so that it now has more in common with urban government than heretofore.

In Switzerland the basic unit of constitutional politics is the canton (In Germany lande). For example constitutional amendments and plebiscites must be approved by a majority vote of the population at large plus the majority agreement of the total cantons.

The cantons, however, are made up of communes. These are localized descent groups, *owning* tracts of land. To become a Swiss citizen, it is obligatory for the applicant *first* to be formally accepted into a commune. The land of the commune earns income. *Both* men and women have participatory rights. Thus it is quite common for a woman to have a joint hyphenated name, that of her husband preceded by her own family name. Wherever she may live, somewhere else in Switzerland or abroad, she has rights of income sharing in her home commune. Commune members may be entitled to social assistance in case of need, again wherever in fact they live, at home or abroad. (They must also fulfil obligations to the Swiss citizen army.)

The centuries old social organisation continues to play a vital role in Swiss life and politics. It can have a bearing on the requirements of modern life.

One example. The Alpine city station of Montana-Crans was created early by the British who there invented Kandahar skiing and invested in hotels and sanatoria on a small plateau looking down on vineyards and the Rhone valley. It became a focus for high end boutiques, restaurants and other services. It needed banks. When the first branch opened in Montana its manager was a member of the Montana commune. The Crans part of the town had to have a bank too. Its manager was from the Crans commune.

A more widespread organisation of major significance today is that of nomadic tribes, often overlooked by Westerners more impressed by the more familiar peasant land holdings, inherited from feudalism, and by the significance of large cities.

Yet today this phenomenon persists since the earliest times and has major implications not only for social life but for the functioning of the related state systems. Throughout Northern Africa and much of Asia, especially Central Asia. nomadic tribes persist and often dominate. They are particularly noticeable in high mountain and desert areas where geographical conditions favour a nomadic way of life. (European transhumance – the movement of herds from high pastures to low ones according to the season is a much modified form of nomadism.) The steppes of Russia and neighbouring areas were another location until transformed forcibly into settled peasantry in Soviet times.

First a small warning. The term "tribe" has been used anthropologically and politically in many senses, primarily denoting a cohesive kin group descended from a common ancestor. Thus, for example, India officialdom and academics refer to certain groups within the country who do not follow a peasant way of life as "tribals". Most African tribes practice settled agriculture or pastoralism though the type of social organisation I am describing here applies to groups in the Sudan and similar areas.

In the situation to which I am referring here, a tribe bears the name of its founding ancestor. They can consist of a several hundred, even thousands, or as little as tens of families. They place a considerable emphasis on tribal cohesion and honour, and often practice honour killing, so important to them are women as breeders of the tribal future.

It is typical for tribes to engage in aggression. Even today war parties, numbering a dozen or so men or hundreds, will set out to avenge a wrong perpetrated by another tribe. The idea of state policing is foreign. Members of the tribe must stand together and defend themselves. This is of the essence, what Salzman has called "balanced opposition".[257]

Nomadic tribes are by no means antiquated curiosities We may think so to our detriment because most Western education ignores the history and operation of what has been the largest Empire in world history – that of the Mongols, begum by Ghengis Khan and brought to fruition by his son Obudai and their descendents..In its heyday the empire stretched from Korea to Hungary, including what is now Russia, Poland, Iran, Turkey to the gates of Budapest and touching on Egypt and India. But for the death of Obudai it would have easily reached the Atlantic. Much of the dynamics and organisation of the

Mongols applies in less dramatic form to nomadic tribes today. We can look there for the essential model.

The empire was headed by the Great Khan. Groupings of tribes of lesser stature were headed by khans. Ghengis Khan used military force from his own tribe to gain the respect and adherence of others. Their military alliance made it possible to attract other tribes who swore allegiance. This led to the successful invasion of China.

He placed brothers, sons, nephews and close friends to head the armies thus ensnaring loyalty and obedience. The armies embarked on a major expedition which eventually ended with the victory at Buda-Pesht when the armies were recalled to Karakoram on Obudai's death. They developed a tactic of feigned retreat which enabled them to surround and decimate pursuing armies. They were aiming for the Atlantic and would undoubtedly have reached it had they persisted.

Despite the withdrawal from Hungary the empire comprised vast territories. Once again the Great Khan ensured that his relatives and trusted advisers ruled great populations, such as those of Russia and Persia.

At first the Mongols used the terror of massacre as a weapon against towns (including Moscow). The armies lived by plunder. Yet after victory they learned to nurse the wealth of cities, justified by trade of the rural produce. And always the Great Khan had to be a descendant of

537

Ghengis.[258]   Communication and control was effected through couriers who made use of an extraordinary (for the time) chains of postal stations placed and defended at regular intervals, providing fresh ponies for the onward travel of messages and mail.,

This system eventually spelled the end of the empire. The substantial subsidiary khanates (Persia and the Golden Horde in Russia, for example) became independent minded, at first judging for themselves whether they would follow the instructions and advice from the centre, and eventually finding excuses to resist control and break away.

The Mongol rulers were highly tolerant of religions other than their own, employing Christians, Muslims, Nestorians, Buddhists and others in the highest bureaucratic positions. There was thus no difficulty when Islam swept much of the region or when Christianity dominated Russia.

History irrelevant for the modern world? Not at all. In fact knowledge of the tribes' political structure is an essential element in the interpretation of current dynamics in the troubled regions of North Africa and the idle East.

Bedouins and Arabs fell heir to much the same underlying systemic structure. Many modern state systems are based on similar underlying principles, however centralised the formal government may seem. As we have noted, success in defending and expanding individual tribes leads to prestige and its lack leads to despising. Psychologically and for self-respect, this is all important.

It is no accident then that throughout the Middle East and North Africa, and perhaps even in Central Asia, the individuals who gain control of the state apparatus, whether they be monarchs or presidents, have arrived at that position through the dominance of their own tribe, sometimes indeed through ruthless aggressions, and that many of the significant power positions are held by relatives or acolytes. Salzman gives a telling list (with my own additional thoughts).[259]

In **Iraq** parliament has numerous representatives of tribes, often practising one of the main competitive Islamic sects.

In **Syria** the Alamites[260] rule, after major violent aggressions against restless subordinate tribes which today are specially targeted for bombing.. A major competitor is centred in the town of Hamas, which was raised with brutality by Assad's father early in the regime, thus ensuring its political dominance and is in 2011 a centre of revolt and vicious suppression.

In **Jordan** the kingdom is controlled by the Hashemite and the army is mostly composed of members of Bedouin tribes.

In **Saudi Arabia** the Wahabi support is reinforced by the use of Bedouin tribes.

Libya was a classic example (my interpretation) of balanced competition in practice. Qadaffi's tribe obtained ascendancy in the West, based on Tripoli as his prestige and leadership were reinforced by his successful coup supported by his tribal allies. The 2011 revolt was led from Benghazi, the centre for the tribal leaders of the former Cirenaica.

Algeria has an ongoing civil war in which the tribal affiliation of the government clash with opposition tribes (my interpretation).

In **Morocco** the dynasty is based on a "sacred lineage".

In **Iran** where tribes still operate in northern districts, the religious revolt replaced the Pahlavis.

Afghanistan's political scheme of things is dominated by tribal warlords, a situation to which I shall refer below.

You can see that Salzman's balanced opposition leads to agreed or enforced domination. The competition is in fact endemic and in the earlier tribal systems which did not have quite the same institutions of enforcement, or the current global genuflection toward the state, competition leading to major prestige was a prime mover.

Tribes which agreed to the power of a leader could always, once upon a time, defect with relative ease, and even associate themselves with an alternative leader. In the modern world this is supposed to be possible through the ballot box, but that is in fact very seldom the case and we have the phenomenon of violence writ large. This is what the Arab Spring is largely about where there are desert tribes as distinct from peasantries.[261]

To me it is quite amazing that military leaders and civilian Western policy makers, despite the immense amount of anthropological work in such countries, have seemingly quite failed to take it into account. If some of them have in fact done so they have not made it publicly known. Admittedly there is a political problem in that many anthropologists , especially in the United States, do not wish to work with authority, in my view a serious mistake to the detriment of improving the world and in some instances avoiding tragedy, suffering and bloodshed. Such purity has consequences.

In any event, let us speculate about policy in Afghanistan. Here a U.S. NATO commander committed one of the most ignorant and unhelpful error of judgement when he invited anthropologists to help. What did he expect them to do? Believe it or not, to sort out the language map of Afghanistan............

In the meantime official policy of NATO and its allies seems to be a mirage.

The term *Jurga* is applied to assemblies of the people's representatives and is used to denote the National Assembly introduced by Western pressure for reform of the state. But it also applies to another assembly which President Karzai called after he was being severely criticized, in order to legitimate his leadership with the people. Elections were one thing, but the *jurga* another.

It was in fact an assembly of tribal leaders. For that is what the so-called "War Lords" are. They have achieved their power through aggressive manipulation, which can include success in feuds, business deals including narcotise trading, and wheeling and dealing. By no means all such leaders are engaged in nefarious practices, but we do have here an example of competition between tribes in the provinces. And Karzai admitted that this gathering., whether in fact assembled or not, was at the time the location of legitimacy. With this in mind Karzai supported legislation that, to Western eyes, weakened the position of women. Western protests secured some modifications, but legislation from the elected National Assembly has little meaning in practice in village society though perhaps in some cities.

The Western powers, intent on defeating the Taliban thus made their first and enduring mistake, in a neo-colonial manner attempting to enforce a western style legislature on the country with the model and expectations of a European style state in mind. In Kabul and perhaps other cities an urban population somewhat agreed, but that was an exception in other areas.[262]

The second ethnocentric error was in the conduct of the warfare with the Taliban. Here of course I must confess that my position is that of an armchair critic, not trained or experienced in the realities of modern warfare. Nevertheless my argument requires acceptance, modification, or rebuttal.

Afghans are a warlike people who have had much experience and success over the centuries, including the twentieth. They are experts in tribal raids and in resisting the invasions of foreign armies. Their trademark consists of rapid aggression, pillage and rapine, and making the utmost use of the terrain, especially in the mountains, to ambush. This is also the hallmark of Taliban tactics with the addition of infiltration with bombs.

By contrast the foreign armies work with massive high-tech equipment, heavy and less manoeuvrable except for the imprecise use of air power. Air power itself often alienates the Afghan population with endless collateral damage, and is ineffective when the enemy merges with civilians or is invisible in forests or melts into the landscape. Additionally NATO armies seem to operate exclusively with the strategy of controlling swathes of territory, a policy which does not prevent daring raids by the Taliban within that territory, even when characterized as "secure".

It appears to me that an alternative or supplementary strategy would be to make the utmost use of commando raiders hitting the Taliban with doses of their own medicine, coupled with an essential propaganda effort making the use of Muslim clerics operating dangerously perhaps within Taliban encampments. And of course doing whatever it takes to cut off Taliban delivery of armaments and other supplies, an activity which also indicates the significance of commando raids.

The NATO strategy also employs the supreme irony of "training" Afghan forces, presumably in their apparently erroneous procedures. Admittedly they are working with formerly civilian recruits who have had no other experience of warfare. The questions remain. Have they studied Afghan military operations of the recent past? Have they attempted to select or seek the advice of Afghans who have experience of traditional methods? On the surface it does not seem that they have done so, at any rate effectively. Have they learned from Afghans themselves? Are they willing to do so? It is possible that if they had done so from the beginning the war would have been closer to a successful outcome.

Let us now turn to Libya. Some of the same sorts of arguments apply. In this case Western intervention was limited by the relevant United Nations resolution, and appropriate modifications of strategy might not have been.

Colonel Qadafi had not promoted himself to be general. That would not be appropriate under Libyan tribal mores[263]. He is rather *primus inter pares*, the leader of the most prestigious tribe in what was once Tripolitania, a position enhanced through respect for his victory in his military coup. In true tribal manner he has appointed relatives and close collaborators to the power positions in the armed forces.

The state of Libya is composed of two former Italian colonies, Tripolitania and Cyrenaica. Each of these parts has its own set of tribes, in the east partially crossing into neighbouring Egypt. At the beginning the eastern tribes accepted this pre-eminence. But Qadafi made the unpardonable mistake of persecuting some of the more restless members, resident in cities, tactics which included public hangings, a total mark of disrespect.

Led by their urbanised and disaffected youth, eastern tribes took matters into their own hand and challenged Qadafi directly. To experience such a challenge and to fail in suppressing it, is a sever kind of blow to a tribal leader's prestige. Members of western tribes, again centred in cities, began to overtly question the leader's power and prestige and some moved into open revolt. I do not know for sure, but I suspect that the military leaders and civilian authorities who deserted Qadafi where not members of his tribe. In addition the armed forces who remained loyal contained a very large proportion of mercenaries.

Did this have implications for a strategy aimed at removing Qadafi? I think it could have. Such a strategy might have aimed deliberately and with precision to continue to undermine the leader's reputation and prestige, ultimately within his own tribe. One key is to establish an anti-Qadafi opinion *in the desert*. There were some signs that the rebel forces, severely lacking in military hardware and, even more importantly, experience, did learn to strike not merely along the coastal roads, but from units attacking from the desert.

Bound by their legal instructions NATO forces, with surprising limitations on the use of navies, concentrated on the Qadafi army units and, with obvious danger of collateral damage, cities. They were unable to pay more attention to the power of the desert. The famous desert tribe of the Touareg who allied with the Qadafids in support of the dictator and are now semi-exiles competing for the control of Northern Mali with extreme Islamists.

As I have pointed out earlier in the discussion of circumcision and similar practices, changes in deep rooted values and practices seldom come about through legislative fiats – they require time and the education of new generations of both men and women.

2012Postscript

• I should acknowledge an apparent contradiction in my earlier yet. In it I pointed out the extraordinarily rapid changes in morals and practices in the Western world exhibiting for example the acceptance of homosexuality and partnerships without marriage. Yet in this chapter we have examples of social organisations which have persisted through the centuries and are resistant to change. .

• The usual Western interpretation of the Syrian uprising points to a desire for democracy and/or the recognition of the majority Muslim religion as distinct from that of Assad's minority but politically dominant variant which is regarded as sac religious in other parts of the Muslim world. There is much truth in this analysis but it nevertheless hides some realities to which policy makers and interpreters should give attention. Syria is a conservative tribal society which also has a significant presence of Kurds in the northeast who did reasonably well under Assad but are now tempted by the possibility of independence. It is highly unlikely that references to democracy are much more than a papering over of the aims of the opposition, though there is surely at least a minority of believers. Initially the opposition had the greatest difficulty in bringing together its various elements which are the expression of distinct tribal interests. It is the case that well organised tribes, which have existed since before Mongolian times and were reinforced by Mongol rule adopt their religious beliefs as a unity under the authority of a ruling sheik. That also provides an ideology for unit political action. But the material interests of the tribe come first. Tribes often come together politically under the most successful of their leaders. This has not yet happened amongst the anti-Assad opposition. One tribe may not in fact secure the allegiance of all the others, but if one does it could well be one of those involved in the potential capture of Aleppo since this would be clear evidence of military prowess and the attainment of material superiority.

- Journalists very seldom do what anthropologists would do as a first priority upon arriving in a culture – get a grasp on family and social structure. Thus they have seldom taken into account the political organisations to which I have referred above and tend to rest content with the buzz words which come from those they interview, who wish to impress with what they in their turn believe westerners want to hear – words like democracy, freedom, equality, terrorism. But the media could not escape this issue when the al-Meqdad tribe (clan) in Lebanon embarked on a programme of kidnappings which they swore would continue until one of their members had been freed in Damascus.[264]

XVI – The Archaic State and Bureaucratic Culture[265] [266]

The state co-ordinates the affairs of a country. This gives it geographical boundaries, which are there for purposes of effective internal organisation, defence of a population and control of trade and migration. The boundaries enable scholars, arbitrarily, to simplify the world by denoting the activities within them as societies, by abstracting the values and symbols within them and calling them cultures, by counting the transactions that take place within them, and summing them as economies. The boundaries are indeed real, but the only sociological reality that coincides with them is the polity with its clearly defined and hierarchical authority; and even there the independence and power of such a polity is severely modified through external forces including treaties and internal pressures. The ways in which states collect data, especially as national statistics, and apply their laws, reinforces the concept of a national county and the mores and actions of the dominant culture within the state reinforce its presentation of q unique entity.

As for matters deemed sociological, cultural, or economic, the political boundaries constitute frictions in the mobility of people, goods and ideas but do not eliminate such mobility. Cross boundary movements imply that the only full society, culture and economy are those of the globe itself, and that analyses limited to what occurs within polities are by their nature artefacts of scholars and politicians which do not fully reflect reality. These considerations will affect the notion of Global Government. and the issues discussed in the chapter on that topic.

Although there are states based, for example, on religion, and although in the Soviet era some emphasised the organisation of production and distribution in an effort to prop up the system, it still remains that nationalism is the ideological principle, carried further into the notion of self-determination of peoples, that states use to justify their existence. Seldom has there been a more cynical, yet effective, rallying cry. It is a slogan, like so many others, that is manipulated to legitimate the most blatant and naked assumptions of power.

The nineteenth century politicised the principle, as radical heroes across Europe, and especially from Britain -- already an amalgam of Scots, Welsh, Irish, Cornish, and others, certainly not Britons -- carried the flag for assumed ethnic uprisings against tyrants -- Italians (who were they?) against Hapsburgs, Greeks (despite the absorption of almost a total cuisine from their Turkish masters and centuries of miscegenation) against their cousins the Turks, who themselves had been affected deeply by Greek influences), and Germans of considerable variety whose populations were inextricably mixed with those of other ethnicities (such as Swedish).

Once the movements achieved centralised government, *internal* variants of nationalism were put to bed, became traitorous. England ensured the dominance of English language, and received Irish resistance and lesser centrifugal movements for its self-righteousness. France seemed to do better, but merely, with arrogance, swept nationalisms under the rug. Anger, often satirical, and long historical memories, sometimes of religious massacre, affected many of the attitudes in Brittany, the Langue d'Oc, Provence and Alsace. Italians seem to accept Italian as a *lingua franca*, as Germans do High German, but some citizens of those countries have difficulty speaking beyond dialect, and ethnicity and regionalisation grow rather than disappear.

In Canada, and possibly elsewhere, part of the *dialogue des sourdes* which characterises argument between centre and region, is reinforced by geography and by linguistic misunderstanding -- in the sense of using key political words in differing senses. For French Canadians, nation retains the meanings of its Latin roots -- tribe, if you will. Tribe is defined as a group having a distinct way of life, a culture, and paramountly a language. The English cannot be tribes in the plural because they speak the same language. When it suits French Canadians they can lump English Canadians in with Americans and immigrants who have differing original languages, although most do admit there is some sort of distinction. Their debate becomes English nation in partnership on equal terms with French-Quebec nation.

The English nation sees it differently. First, "nation" means the Nation State, whatever its origins. Canada, including Quebec, is the nation. However, if you must insist on tribal-cultural criteria of difference, English Canada is not one. Apart from some dialect, the commonality of English is misleading and irrelevant. Toronto, the Maritimes and prairies, to say nothing of the North and the First Nations and Vancouver are not the same in spirit, ethos, culture.

As a matter of fact I cannot think of any Nation states -- except perhaps Andorra and Niue -- which are ethnically "pure". Ideologically speaking, the idea of the Nation state is a double-edged sword. Quebec separatists are already discovering that First Nation Indians and Inuit within Quebec want their own separatism; and that some immigrants are less than enchanted with the idea of being compelled into a uniform French-Canadian culture; that Anglophones can be a dangerous bloc. Not Turkey, not Iran, not the international community which speaks of the "inviolability of borders" will recognise that the ideology of the Nation state demands that millions of Kurds look forward to their own polity. The idea of the Nation state, of nationalism, is there to be used and manipulated, like all sacred texts, when it suits those in power or wishing to be in power.

In the nineteenth and first half of the twentieth century, aided by the appeal of self-determination (which Hitler soon made use of for his own purposes), nationalism justified boundaries. Certainly, maps were not drawn with ethnic precision. In the former colonial world, colonial boundaries (established to divide continents between powers) were mostly maintained, cutting through the middle of ethnically homogeneous peoples. Amazingly and curiously, national identity in Africa began to be identified with the artificial creations; peasants showed allegiance to central governments. In Europe, Sicilians think of themselves secondarily as Italians, in Britain Scots and Welsh feel themselves secondarily, surely not as Englishmen, but part of Britain. Languedociens. Alsaciens, Bretons, Provençals are French but also members of their specific communities, Corsicans less so. But all have complaints about the centralisation of French cultural power, affecting as it does education, literature, and feelings of identity. The issues are clearer in Spain with the overt dynamics, politicised, of Catalan and Basque insistence on autonomy.

Press another button, and the spin-off forces win. The principle seems to have a relationship to authoritarianism. Yugoslavia, to the outsider, seemed to be working. My visits to Croatia revealed the strong nationalist rivalries between Zagreb and Belgrade, even in scholarly matters. But within Croatia personal relationships, inter-marriage, burial in the same cemetery, laughter, regional restaurants, seemed to indicate that religious difference, blood feud and hatred were not realities, and were overcome by an over-layer of respect and friendship. That over-layer was definitely there, and not only in Croatia: in Sarajevo for example. But its fragility, surprising to the West, was open to manipulation by the power hungry, macho spirits with vicious guns. Using nationalism as the myth of cohesion carries dangerous messages. With the breakup of Yugoslavia incipient rivalries and centuries old hatreds came to the fore. The patchwork nap of cultures, religions and languages increased the rivalrous intensity and there was enough bitterness for leaders to turn into vicious violence and even massacre. Since no set of state boundaries encloses uniform ethnicity, the myth enables minorities to claim the right to separation -- strongly exercised after the break-up of the Soviet Union. Conversely the argument that the state is a nation justifies the forced incorporation of unwilling minorities.

The problem with authoritarian regimes is that one does not know how much volatility is there because the stopper is in the bottle. How many genies remain to sneak out. In the 21st century we have begun to find out.

The whole matter is tied in with boundaries and the land within. Let us examine them once again. The boundaries of polities are supposed to be neat and tidy, binding together a coherent population of individuals inter-acting with each other much more than they do with others outside the boundary.

Boundaries define the geographical territory within which the state exerts its control and power over individuals and their activities. State boundaries are the location at which the authority is exerted over individuals, goods, services, even bacteria and viruses, animals, plants and fish who would enter or leave. Within the boundaries it is normal but not universal that individuals may move freely. Authoritarian states frequently control such movements with internal passports, residence permits, and the like. Even democratic states like Switzerland require commune permission for permanent residence. The provinces of Canada restrict the flow between them of, for example, liquor, and supplies directed to the public service.

The myth that states have full control over their destiny and what goes on within their boundaries continues to flourish. But as a description of fact it is wrong, and as the fundamental normative principle that applies to the global system it is, to put it mildly, debatable as a desired situation.

As to fact. Without any recourse to world government states are subject to the international environment in which they live. What they do is limited, as even Hitler discovered, by the reactions of other states. They are also a part of a global eco-system, so that pollution, water flows, air flows, the spontaneous and man-induced migrations of natural life, all impinge upon their internal affairs. While even democratic states try to do so through cultural policies, in the long run ideas, which are the dominant factor in innovation, cannot successfully be forbidden at the boundary.

States have also entered freely into alliances and treaties which place obligations on them and guide their behaviour in restricted fields. More and more, bilateral agreements are being replaced by multilateral ones. International agreements governing fishing are a mix of global and bilateral conventions, with the weight moving toward global understandings. In particular fields, global organisations stand above regional and bilateral moves, working out treaties and conventions to which all or nearly all states subscribe, at least in words. The United Nations "family of organisations" is the obvious example.

The state has in fact given up many of its powers, a fact which is reinforced by the many regional arrangements and organisations, from river basin management to military matters. States have inputs and influence, through delegations and representatives. They initiate policy ideas and undertake lobbying and back-room deals. They administer their responsibilities under the policy meticulously or with obfuscation. But they must persuade the other members of the organisation if policies are to change. They can opt out, though usually, as with the World Trade Organisation, the results could be very damaging both to them and to others. Paradoxically, self-interest binds them to others.

States can only inhibit the movement of ideas, not stop it. Even national patent and copyright laws have limited effect internationally but holders of such certificates must consider what happens outside the political boundaries. The time comes when they run out and the outside world invades more seriously. The advances in technology are such that similar results can be achieved by other methods, by-passing the patents. Prozac was followed by half a dozen related drugs within a few years. Microsoft created Windows to produce similar easy-to-use software hitherto dominated by Apple Computer. Authors know how next to impossible it is to gain their rightful income from reprography or to have their interests respected in, say, China.[267] Reproduction of materials on computer disks is now so easy that there are major industries doing just that in India, China and elsewhere, without compensation, and it is often difficult to tell whether you are buying an authorised version or a pirated one. The full policing of micro-satellite dishes and availability of unauthorised decoders for television is next to impossible.

In many fields prohibition or regulation may inhibit consumption but at the same time create added-value, increased interest, even addiction and smuggling. This is obvious with drugs. Remember samizdat underground papers in the Soviet Union? Putting a quota on foreign (usually U.S.) films suggests they have greater value to the consumer than local films, increases demand for what is available, encourages local film producers to copycat, and magnifies the demand for authorised or unauthorised videos. Television reception moves to international satellite. Culture, despite its national and ethnic value, is quintessentially made up of individual decisions and preferences. It is not easy, and not desirable, for official policy to do more than make sure the options are open, from which people may choose. Restriction has the danger of turning individuals to the very options the State wishes to discourage. The emphasis should be positive, on encouragement not negative on discouragement.

The state is the "internal administrator" of countries in this modern world. For it to do so, our new Global Government will be democratic for the setting of world policy and standards of behaviour. Alas, the word "democratic" has so many meanings as to be useless in itself. One-party states call themselves democratic, even if so-called elections are rigged. British style representative democracy is in effect autocratic rule by the majority party, or its coalition, until the next election, or until the coalition breaks apart. In British style democracies, the prime minister, during this period, wields immense personal power through various devices such as the party whip and the threat to call an election if his cabinet does not stay in line. In most parliamentary democracies the mode of discussion is oppositional. Loyal oppositions consider it their duty to oppose everything that can be opposed, even though, if returned to power, they find it expedient to put into effect the very policies they derided.

Constitutions are usually conceived from the top down instead of from the bottom up. The primary exception is Switzerland, which is a *con*federation of sovereign States, in which all power *not* allocated by agreement to the central government is exercised by the cantons. In the United States, constitutional amendment requires both popular and internal-state support. However, the usual approach to constitutions, except in Switzerland, is one in which the central government is defined, and other levels of government are adapted to it.

It is this characteristic of government that makes a mess of ethnic and regional diversity and aspirations. Centralisation usually means that, in democracies, all individuals are equal -- that is, they each have a vote and the law applies equally and in the same way to each person. Policy, with a few exceptions such as in illness or disability, and now equal opportunity mechanisms, assumes that all persons are the same as each other. The constitutional structure, then, should be the same for Cornishmen as for Yorkshiremen, for Parisians as for Bretons, for Newfoundlanders as for Quebeckers, for Los Angelinos as for Bostonians. And differences, which must be consistent with the overall constitution, will be expressed by the content of policies created by "lower" levels of government. Rednecks in Canada object to the modernisation and rectification of Indian treaty provisions, or Sikhs wearing turbans in ex-servicemen clubs, or Muslim girls wearing head scarves in some Toronto schools, on the grounds that equality means that everyone should subscribe to Anglo-Canadian practices. France in 2010 is making explicit the policy that newcomers must respect and subscribe to a centralised idea of French habits and culture.

Despite the Quebec arguments that the policy has not gone far enough, Canada has been forced to accord constitutional and quasi-constitutional variation not only to Quebec, but to Indian First Nations. The ability to do this in a limited way is now part of the Canadian political structure. But it is still the top approving the design, which must not upset the overall constitution.

The nationalist myth helped create another; that significance accrues only to what happens inside political-geographical borders. This latter myth has never corresponded with reality, yet is so well entrenched that we speak of the British, or French, or Russian economy in those terms, to say nothing of their respective polities, cultures and societies. Scholars and journalists do of course pay attention to cross boundary phenomena, and governments secure rights of extra-territoriality to administer issues concerning their citizens abroad. And in unpublished study I have asserted that the stimulus for industrial and commercial growth in, say, Britain, the Netherlands, or Switzerland, was caused in part by (a) the diaspora of their citizens who paid their country back by importing and adapting techniques and ideas from abroad, and (b) the acceptance of foreigners into the functional life of the country, foreigners who brought new ideas finance and methods, and adapted themto local conditions.

Thus the model should be that British society should include all those within the geographical bounds plus all contacts and interactions across those boundaries. The concept of the permeable boundary with variable phenomena is all important to the notion, and is ignored to our peril.[268]   The United States is probably the most aggressive in its conscious assertion of extra-territorial jurisdiction yet has itself incurred a huge indebtedness to the ideas and actions of immigrants.

So far so good. But herein lies the danger. When circumstances warrant, state policies obvert the proposition and assert not only protectionism but a truly unholy competitive jostling for supremacy in matters from the cultural to the commercial.

Thus in such events as World Trade Forums and the like, and in the journalism of economics, we find worried attention being given to changes in the distribution of production. There are significant signs that China, India and Brasil are competing effectively in certain industries with the European Union and the United States, and may even become leaders in GDP. Horrors! So we have the introduction of trade quotas to "protect" local industries and their workers, and the spectacle of millions of dollars worth of inexpensive Chinese, Indian or Malaysian clothing held up in warehouses because they are above quota, and then the Ministers scurrying to find a way to withdraw the finger from the dyke. Because China is a major market for Western goods, including armaments its population must be able to earn money to finance the imports.

What is missing in this analysis is the Globe, *tout court*. Governments of course have a right to look after displaced workers, and should be shifting the country's production to work where there is a comparative advantage, and by the use of guaranteed income.

Please then Economists and business tycoons and politicians, when you meet in World Trade Forums or influence the policies of the World Trade Organisation, take the welfare of the *Globe* as your unit. Do not be blind-sided by selfish and mistaken state protective competitiveness. This though is precisely what states, by their competitive structure *are reluctant and incompetent to do*. In their present form states are a *danger* to world prosperity and peace.

State policy is executed, and sometimes created, by the bureaucracy. At this point I must clarify that bureaucracies are by no means limited to political organisations such as the state. Bureaucracies are present in any large organisations, including corporations and universities. Hence this part of my analysis will cross-refer between these institutions.

There is an enormous tension between the conservative and innovatory sides of a bureaucracy, an extreme example being the difficulties with former apparatchiks in Russia. The British system of an a-political bureaucracy, advanced on merit, has been, with little doubt, together with the constitutional role of royalty, a force limiting the temptation of politicians, not only in Britain but in similar parts of the Commonwealth, to use their powers dishonestly or autocratically. On the other hand, a bureaucracy can become entrenched in its ways, too independent-minded, so that the politicians find it resistant to their mandate, and sometimes even paradoxically suspect wise advice to be opposition motivated.

Two results then occur. One, endemic in the United States, increasingly used in Canada, France, Britain and present elsewhere, is to by-pass the bureaucracy with political appointments and outside consultants, selected to give the "right" answers. The next government sacks them all and appoints a fresh contingent. Long term civil servants are then less "ideas" men and women but guardians of the archives, designers of forms, helpers to fill out forms, collectors of statistics and fees.

Another is corruption. Bureaucrats are then controlled by payments. They have power, not to influence policy so much, but to manipulate. They are not in the seats of so-called political power, but exercise power, instead, in their day to day relationship with individuals. They corruptly do what individual ministers tell them or bribe them to do, sharing in the profits. They charge fees, often exorbitant, for services rendered. It is said that in India one of the most difficult elements in bureaucracy is the power of bureaucrats to hold up or subvert applications by complex delaying tactics. When they are in uniform, armed with a high powered gun, they put tolls on the roads, as once in Nigeria, and demand recompense for allowing you to go home at night. This kind of bureaucracy is usually to be found in ex-colonies and in totalitarian regimes where the authority of the centre is invested in the lowliest of bureaucrats.

One of the least admired features of bureaucracies is to be found in corporations as well as in government. Whether the organisation consults with its membership (employees) or not during the formulation of policy, it is necessary that the execution be co-ordinated between the different sub-divisions and that employees, in exercising any initiative they may have, do so in conformity with the overall objectives and methods as expressed in regulations. I am here less concerned with the internal smooth running of the enterprise or the government department, than with the manner in which it articulates with the outside world -- customers, clients, John Q. Public, suppliers, other organisations.

Sophisticated government bureaucracies used to be castigated for their insensitivities and defects, and denigrated by comparison with private companies. While I can understand annoyance at those insensitivities and defects, I cannot understand why the comparison should be made in this way. I do not know of controlled comparative studies. My own experience, coupled with anecdotal evidence from friends and people in private companies suggests to me that the latter have as many problems in their public interface, even when their profits suffer as a result, as do governmental bureaucracies. Some companies do much better, as do some government departments.

But here is a list of the kinds of things that occur.

Passing the buck. This is not my responsibility, it belongs elsewhere in the system. Or it belongs in another department or firm. Go there. The new contact sends you to another, or even back to the first one. Mail or a delivery is missing. The post office or shipper sends you to a central complaints office. They give you a form that requires impossible to remember detail. Back to the post office to check on some of the information. You understand of course that it is not the mailman at fault, it's the contracted courier. It couldn't have happened here, it must have happened at the point of mailing. But I had all my summer clothes in the parcel. Sorry, you didn't insure, we can take no responsibility. But **You You You** lost **My Summer CLOTHES.....** Not our fault, we accept no claim unless insured. But I paid for it to be delivered, it was in your hands, you lost my property..........

Remote registration of the problem. You want your computer repaired. Instead of dealing directly with a technician, you are made to phone long distance to a central sorting office which takes your complaint (often without the necessary technical knowledge), sends authorisation to the out sourced technician, who then contacts you when you are out.

Middlemen and warehouses. In smaller countries such as Switzerland, this is less of a problem in the private sector, since distribution is so good that, for example, auto parts can reach any location in the country in a few hours. It does become a problem when auto parts are not stocked in Switzerland, but in France, Germany or Italy. In a vast country such as Canada, parts, CDs, books are likely to be warehoused as far from the retailer as the original manufacturer or publisher. Warehouses run out of supplies, or distribute with priority to the nearby retailers, letting the distant ones wait. I have searched for parts for national and international brands in vain, phoned the national office, been put on hold until they find someone who knows the wholesaler list, approached the wholesalers to hear they can only sell to "resellers", gone back to a retailer on the wholesaler's list, find he doesn't stock the part, but will make a special order, with an additional charge, then finding the wholesaler has to back-order the part from the manufacturer....... Even big box supermarkets and department stores often deal only with certain wholesalers and will not order goods stocked by another, or from the manufacturer. In the public sector, this sort of thing is less relevant, but it still crops up. Postage rates change, but the stamps aren't in the post offices. At income tax deadline specialised forms are not available. Explanation? It's not my fault, it's someone up the ladder.

Failure to address complaints or explain observations. You are passed over to a public relations or consumer relations office, whose expertise is to draft replies that show they have not read your letter, since they address other issues; or they send out a form letter which simply summarises and affirms the policy that is giving you trouble. You point this out. You get the same document back again. When you do get to someone in real authority, a lawyer drafts the letter and again talks past you, not with you.

Refusing to make a precise appointment, or not honouring it. Result, queues in doctor's offices where the patient's time is worth less than the doctor's. Waiting for a plumber all day when you have other work to do and then he doesn't arrive. Agreeing to phone an income tax auditor at a specified time, only to find he's gone off on a course, no-one knows when he will be back, and, no, nobody else can deal with your file. Thank you very much for calling us..

There's no point in going on and on. My meaning is clear. I include the private sector in my diatribe, since by doing so I indicate that the problems are inherent in insensitive organisation of any kind (including charitable organisations and universities). Remedies start with the acceptance that public relations is not simply an exercise undertaken by specialists who make a profession out of common sense. *It is elementary courtesy.* True democracy is based on courtesy. Our world must be based on courtesy. Enter Youth Maturity Institutes.

But real courtesy, not the pro forma kind. Not civil *servants* whose imagination stops at making sure that you, the citizen, fill out the forms correctly and obey the rules minutely. Who do not have the will or the power to guide you to the place at which the rule might be reconsidered, changed, or deemed not applicable.[269]

Once the civil service letters I wrote (when I was one sixty years ago!) and received ended with something like, "I have the honour to be, sir, your most obedient and loyal servant." Let that archaic formula return -- but let it have *meaning* which it did not have when it was but a formula. Let employees who deal with the public be trained so that they know they are like body cells on the skin, an essential component which draws substance and information into the organism, returns information to the environment, at the same time protecting the organism, not by rejection, but by exchanges that allow the organism to adapt. They are not there simply to do the routine tasks, but to send signals to wherever the brain might be when there is a problem. The brain can then react to deal with it, rather than ignore it at its peril.

Ironically, in the much maligned colonial service, I was counselled that my job was not to push aside people with problems, *but to find solutions*, not to work by the rules (though God help me if my accounts showed a half-penny that shouldn't be there.) but to find acceptable ways around them; not to deny that a problem existed, but to deal with it constructively.

Rules provide small men and women with power. Rather than saying "I am using my judgement, and I find it appropriate that you do such and such, or that you don't do it" the rule-administrator points to a section in regulations. If he is in private enterprise, he says "it is not our policy". The only recourse then is to go to the top and try to get the policy changed, even on the most trivial of issues. To be able to point to rules impersonalises the judgement, (admittedly minimising personal bias or emotion or lack of intelligence) puts the appellant in a class along with all other people with the same problem, abstracts the issue. The rule-administrator can present himself as an unwilling pawn; he does not to have to confront the act of thinking or of standing up to another's argument.

Frequently rules exist because the rule maker of then works with a different set of assumptions from those used by those to whom the rules apply. Sometimes the challenge to those assumptions, coupled with some sort of outcry, makes it possible to change or ignore the rules. In Vancouver -- and I know this has happened in other cities -- public health inspectors have tried to apply rules defining the safe and acceptable temperatures at which barbecued ducks would be cooked, displayed and stored -- the high-tech methods the inspectors require dry out the meat unacceptably. They have told sausage makers to use preservatives if they insist on hanging their dried meats in the air. Perfectly safe tandoori ovens were attacked by fire inspectors because they did not conform to an unnecessary technicality, even though the inspectors could not prove that they were a fire hazard. In none of the above cases there had never been a customer complaint about the "objectionable" procedure or a health or fire crisis, and the safety history of age-old cooking methods was simply not addressed. Public outcry forced Ottawa to reverse a decision to ban the importation of unpasteurised cheese: similarly it forced the Vancouver health inspector to reverse his ban on Chinese poultry cooked slowly in restaurant windows, as had been the custom for decades (and still is).

The main trouble with rules, however, is that they become everlasting. It is harder to get a rule off the books than it is to put it on. When the public objects to rules or they become out of date, the public, when it does not have to negotiate an outcome such as a successful application, ignores the rule, making a mockery of that part of the law, until it is no longer applied. In Vancouver there are rules about dress on city beaches, which are enforced. But nudists adopted a relatively secluded area where they disrobed. After a time the police, who regularly patrol, gave their attention to drugs and theft rather than to absent clothing and a vibrant self-governing community, even with gardens and food suppliers, evolved.

Such a reaction to rule by pettiness is not always feasible. At my university a group of colleagues joined to try to empower a Senate committee to review all rules and regulations to determine which could be discarded. They failed.

Bureaucracies almost always think inside the box. Otherwise they disturb their political masters. It takes a cataclysm such as World War II to enable thinkers such as Lord Beveridge to touch the political nerve of a nation with his plan for universal social security, a plan modified in other countries as it in turn became bureaucratised in Britain. When thinking outside the box, which usually means thinking outside bureaucracy, happens, miracles can follow.

Once again think of the failureofstate bureaucracies to address health epidemics in the poorer world, where private corporations are notoriously unwilling to invest. Private individuals, Bill and Melinda Gates, thinking outside the box, established away of beating patents and developing drugs to target devastating illnesses. Victoria Hale has created the Institute for One World Health, which searches for promising medications protected by patent but never developed. With the help of the World Health Organisation, and financial support (once again) from the capitalist rooted Bill and Melinda Gates Foundation the Institute is testing and arranging for the development and applications of drugs for major diseases which have so far resisted treatment – and therapeutic support (because no one else has been sufficiently interested). This is the kind of initiative that will create immense benefits for poorer countries that archaic states fail to address.

Does that not strike your conscience? If it does not make you angry, it should. States, however necessary, are letting their peoples and the world down. They are not living up to global ideals. One day issues of this kind will bring feeling and thinking people out onto the streets, just like Orange and Gene Revolutions.

In the colonial service I was told that all rules existed to be broken. I believe almost that. With enough ingenuity you can find circumstances in which the strict application of a rule results in dysfunction or is an assault on common sense or public interest. Rules replace human judgement, which, while imperfect, is the better for its exercise. *If we wish to be civilised, we will replace rules by judgement whenever we can.*

Because these things are cultural, they can change, just as sexual mores have partially changed. The public interface roles can be redefined to allow more creative participation of front-line workers in the organisation. If other aspects of our new world are in place, we can expect more courtesy to be natural. We can also expect that those who are working will know in a sense that they are in an environment in which paid work cannot be taken for granted, that, in fact, they are dependent on their clients who deserve respect and answers. More importantly -- and perhaps this is the most difficult part of all -- we must find ways to ensure that managers are not artificially shielded from what is going on at the boundaries, on the skin, of their organisation.

After all this, what is the justification for the state? A common answer is that it protects and defends the individuals living within its boundaries. But it regulates them in minute detail, even in democracies, in ways that only in the most indirect sense have to do with protection. It can be said that taxes are needed to provide a social security network and a military force and police but we have already seen how irrational current systems are. Ponderous regulations govern income tax, corporate tax, sales tax, customs and excise. Ignorance of such laws is not a defence, yet they often puzzle specialists. But not all taxes go to such concerns. There are immense bail-outs of failing private and semi-public enterprises. How do state-run airlines meet the criteria? Could not infrastructure projects be financed and operated outside the public sector, with public supervision? Military defence, in the defence of boundary, or defence of interests, is becoming less relevant and indeed must go with the creation of Global Government.

More and more it seems, states endeavour openly or under-handedly to divert tax payer's money to propping up failing industry. This is most noticeably dramatic in the aircraft industry – Canadian Bombardier v. Brasil's Embraer; U.S. Boeing v. Europe's Airbus, supported by massive taxpayer funds, and spending enormous sums in vicious battles before the World Trade Organisation - but it affects and distorts all industries and agriculture. To my knowledge, only Switzerland has this under control – and yet it subsidises its alpine farmers. There the control is effected by writing into the constitution the principles and programmes that govern the use of taxpayers' money, *a feature which should be inserted into all state constitutions.* It is extremely difficult to get a constitutional amendment passed that would permit expenditures on the above handouts. Perhaps also Global Government could strengthen world trade legislation on such matters with binding force.

The United States government calls itself an administration. It is a very political one, with politics running deep into every petty function, so that the word seems a misnomer. Yet if we look at the situation in global terms, the state apparatus of decision making and policy execution in all countries is indeed mostly administrative. The more global concerns increase in weight, the more states will appear to be just one more level of administration between the community and the whole world. The more we can look forward to an effective world government, the more states will be concerned with variations, mostly cultural, within the world order. They will be concerned with maintaining and supporting differences in ethos and style rather than determining pollution standards or trade procedures, which will be global. States will be less sovereign competitive entities with military tools to warn off others than country administrators living peacefully under a Global Government.

Except in the smallest countries, and to some extent in Switzerland, central state government seems remote to its citizens. To show that the centre is in fact concerned with communities, politicians are driven to establish projects, particularly in identifiable buildings and transport links, which enable them to say "we are looking after you". There is an inherently corrupt and patronising attitude that creeps in. The visibility of the central government becomes a matter of major importance, influencing otherwise technical judgements.

Relationships are topsy-turvy. The reality of life, for individuals, is highly selective and relatively localised. Culturally speaking, there is a cross-hatch of international connections and local residential roots. While the international, horizontal and vertical, connections are rapidly increasing, it is a geographical fact that, simultaneously, the individual is in a primarily limited space at any one time. There are connective sequences -- home to work to play to home; London to Los Angeles to Cannes -- but in each of the locations there is a set of perceptions, communications, interests which help to define political and policy interests. In each place there is a combination of very local everyday housekeeping and style concerns, and broader country-wide and international ones. They influence one another, but when it comes to public action representing those concerns they must, for practical reasons, be applied at different contextual-geographical levels.

What this means is that political structures should influence the individual from the world down, and be responsive to the individual from the home and community up. Present political structures do neither very effectively. We must do better. How?

Some years ago I undertook a study comparing the Swiss and Canadian political structures,[270] with passing glances elsewhere. I have personally been hurt and damaged by some Swiss practices, so have no incentive to idealise the Swiss or their institutions. I do believe however, that both are improperly caricatured outside the

575

country, and that they have mastered extremely difficult issues, not because of misleading tradition (William Tell and all that), but through sheer determination to do so, as a result of relatively recent crises, which at various times threatened the very survival of the country.[271]

The Canadian federation, I opined, is built and conceived from the top down; the Swiss from the bottom up. Canadian linguistic and multi-cultural policy, which helps to define the "nation", is almost the reverse of the Swiss. What elements of each, and of others, are best suited to the evolving world?

In making my choice I acknowledge that the mode of linking individual and community to the state will vary in accord with the rich diversity of cultures. Relatively homogeneous Japan may stay that way. If it is by choice, and if it does not attempt to influence other countries that homogeneity is best, World Government will simply record that state, individual, and community are in harmony[272]. My guess is that one century hence, however, the Ainu will have asserted their own sense of community, and that regional-occupational differences (as now between rice growers and urban dwellers) will emphasise community differences within the state. As for the United States, China, and Russia, the powerful forces of national identity will, I believe, have to come to terms more seriously with growing regional-community difference sometime in the future[273].

However that may be, let me propose for debate that the community is worth emphasis in the global political picture. I do not believe my proposal is that of the communitarian movement, as I understand it. I call for recognition of community as *one* basic building block, but not the only one, and not dominant. This is neither a romantic return to the past, nor a revival of the autocracy of community. The reinforcing and humanistic values of community provide many forms of security, which need to be countered by outlandish creativity, freedom to move to other forms of community, and shaking off the burdens of conformity.

In the past, and in most regions today, community, land, production, religion and language go together. These are mostly the poorest and most conservative parts of the world, though poverty and community are by no means correlated. The poorer ones will either disappear, as with some mountain communities of Europe, or grow richer and more vibrant with changes in technology, with the loss of some population and the gaining of newcomers. In some rich cities with a lively cultural tradition, parishes, communes, neighbourhoods are finding new roles, even though they may not be recognised in the political process, and even though residence may not be tied to property ownership or occupations.

One of the weaknesses of Swiss communes is that their conservative political tendencies often predominate, so that newcomers are not fully incorporated in the political process save in special circumstances. There are two sorts of excuses for this. One is land and property, some of which belongs to the commune, whose members are also traditional land-owners in their own individual right. To accord rights to newcomers means the danger of diluting the concentrations of land, and modifying lineage and other kin structures. Linked to this is religion and language. Contrary to much popular belief, Switzerland does not accord equal rights to the four main languages under all circumstances. It is expected that immigrants will adapt to the language of their new residence, whether or not they are accorded membership in the commune. Italian speakers do not expect Italian language schools in francophone Switzerland and in the federal capita;. German speaking Berne, until a decade or so ago there was no public school in French even to accommodate French speaking civil servants.. .

I would like to see something like the Swiss arrangement, but with modifications to make it less restrictive and autocratic. The commune should have the power to be the major influence in its cultural and political identity.

In most parts of the rural world, this would not be difficult to design because the communities are already there. In cities it would require more thought and ingenuity, and the powers accorded to the communes (or neighbourhoods) would be more directly modified in the interests of providing large-scale services, and even large-scale character.

The powers of communes to control residence and to be the first step in the citizenship process require modification. It is inconsistent to build a global polity with respect for societal dynamics, minimal rules, and individual freedom if nationals are stopped from residing where they wish. The communes are not intended to be monuments to stasis. They are intended to be places which represent differing life styles within the larger mass, to be one of the loci of identity and sharing with others, and to change as society changes.

In this world, in-migration would change the nature of the commune. Even the language, conceived as the local language, would change. Cities would have locations where different languages would be regarded as local. In much of Canada's prairies German, Ukrainian or Russian rather than English or French, would be the recognised local language; Punjabi, Cantonese, Portuguese, Vietnamese, Spanish, Italian, to say nothing of First Nations languages elsewhere.[274]

Levels of government between commune and central authority -- metropolitan, regional, state, province, canton -- they too will need to be structured to reflect the concerns of the communes which make them up.

The Swiss example has more to say about the structure of the higher authorities and their modes of decision making.

The constitution is such that it defines the principles of government as well as the powers of authorities. If a law includes a new or a changed principle, it must be confirmed by constitutional amendment. This involves approval in parliament, and a referendum. The referendum is preceded by major consultations with cantons representing communes, and with the major identity-locating organisations -- trade unions, employers' associations, churches, co-operative groups, and the like. To pass, the referendum must be approved by a vote in which the majority of all citizens in the country is tallied, together with another tally in which they are counted by canton to determine whether the majority of cantons also agrees. Thus there is further force given to regional concerns.

In the central parliament, the upper chamber consists of cantonal representatives, much like the Senate in the United States. The lower chamber is by electorate. Several parties are represented. *Groups of individuals* may propose laws and constitutional amendments, which, if sufficiently supported, must go through the same process of discussion and decision.

Although the cabinet is by no means powerless, and in fact initiates the bulk of policy, its method of operation is strikingly different from that of other democracies. Because of the power of the constitution, and the difference between principle and application, the day-to-day work of the government is administration. On principle, the cabinet may propose, the electorate disposes. And the cabinet is constructed to make administration happen. The cabinet may not change the principles of government without referendum; it applies those principles in detail.

The cabinet is restricted to five members, one of whom acts as President-chairperson, a position that rotates once a year among the members. He is by no means a Prime Minister or a French or U.S. President. He is usually hardly known to the public. The cabinet itself is consensual. In practice (I do not think by law) it consists of members belonging to political parties, distributed as far as possible according to the representation of those parties in the legislature, and including at least one German, French and Italian speaker (not necessarily Romansch). That means in effect that opposition parties are members of the cabinet. This is not rule by majority; it is not rule by gaining a majority through intra-party negotiation. Each member of the cabinet is elected by the legislature, which respects these principles.

It is said that Switzerland operates through consensus because of its long democratic tradition and the hand-raising of the Canton of Appenzell. Maybe. I doubt it very much. Switzerland was the only country to reject Napoleonic reforms, fighting an internal war against his occupation because the reforms were *too democratic* for an oligarchic society. It is said that women were politically suppressed. No more, but it was true until very recently.

No. Political debates, especially in referendums, are as strong and as viciously vigorous as anywhere. It is only a few decades since bombs were used to gain the "rights" of Jura as a canton. There are extreme radical movements, both left and right.

The system as we know it today evolved as a result of a crisis in the desperate Great Depression days of the 'thirties. Horrified Swiss citizens saw worker demonstrations dispersed with brutality, horsepower and fire power. On the other side of their borders Hitler, Mussolini and French étatism were a visible threat. The pragmatists of Switzerland decided, consciously and deliberately, that if they fought like this amongst themselves, Switzerland would no longer exist. They needed each other to resist the outsiders. They opted *consciously and deliberately* for consensus, as recently as the 1930s.

Since that was a deliberate decision by men and women with opposing interests, languages and philosophies, I have good hopes that our way to new state forms will be marked by similar deliberate decisions. At the same time I fear that it may take disaster and crises to knock our silly heads together. We have to decide to start on the way. Isn't the fear of terrorism, nuclear proliferation, international crime, eco-devastation, poverty, enough? If only these ideas were in the forefront of 2012 Greek and Spanish reformers.....

For state reforms I prefer the Swiss cabinet. I prefer referendums. I prefer the linkage of community to state. I dislike the histrionics of oppositional parties, and the almost unbridled powers of a majority. I do not like powerful executive Presidents, although executive decisiveness is essential. It is a matter of judging values as well as mechanisms.

And to that I add elements of cabinet-ministry operations which have been introduced in Sweden -- the use of electronic technology to make ministers able to carry out duties with less of a disturbance to their private lives -- thus humanising the operation and drawing on a wider group of candidates for the job. A minister in most democracies may live out of the capital for most of the time, visiting only where the ministerial presence is physically necessary. For the rest, the minister may talk to bureaucrats on screen, deal with documents and data electronically, from a home office. This is the kind of contact that minimises family disruption, appealing to child carers, and to those for whom nature, perhaps quiet, is more stimulating for good work than the hurly burly of a lobby-filled capital.

The closeness of the legislator to his constituency should be safeguarded but not complete. He is elected as a person who stands for certain things, a person whose *judgement* the electorate can trust. He is not a cipher, going back time and again to the local opinion polls to tell him what to do. If that were the case, get rid of legislatures and set up computerised polling booths. Polls do not allow for full information, full reflection, and the balancing of a local issue against wider, even global, ones. There should be no recall on the basis that the representative voted contrary to popular opinion. He is there to lead, as well as represent; if that balancing act is tampered with, there will be no political change except through the demagoguery of those outside parliament who catch the public ear.

Let us return for a moment to an aspect of democratic state constitutions. I am writing from the Kingdom of Canada which follows British parliamentary principles. Next to Canada is the United States, a world leading Republic.

The following are among the *constitutional* monarchies: United Kingdom, Canada, Australia, New Zealand, Japan, Netherlands, Sweden, Spain, Denmark, Thailand. I leave out of consideration absolute monarchies, and monarchies of the past, even into the twentieth century, in which modern constitutional principles were not at work. I also leave out non-constitutional monarchies, such as Nepal.

The prime characteristic of constitutional monarchies (even in Britain, paradoxically without a written constitution) is that, although the monarchs sign law into effect and justice is administered in the name of the Crown, the monarch has no legal authority over such matters. That authority is in the hands of parliaments and Ministers.

Except. Except the signature is necessary, *and in dire circumstances could be withheld.* Usually, the monarch dismisses parliament and authorises elections on the advice of the Prime Minister (who has been defeated in Parliament).

But wait. A constitutional monarch can, in very dire circumstances, dismiss parliament and call for new elections without the Prime Minister's say so. This power has been used very infrequently indeed, on evidence of serious corruption or autocratic instead of parliamentary behaviour. But it is there, and a useful reminder to democrats gown awry.

A more immediate power is that the monarch appoints the Prime Minister. Usually this is symbolic, for the obvious candidate is he or she who commands the Parliament.

But if the Prime Minister loses that confidence in a motion of Parliament, or if he does not command an automatic party majority. The monarch may, for example, invite another parliamentarian to try to form a government, or indeed call a fresh election. This power for instance has been of major importance during the Martin Liberal 2005 minority government of Canada. That government was defeated by a motion on a minor matter which included the word "confidence". The Governor-General, the Queen's representative, after much studying of constitutional precedents, did not rule, leaving the government in power, because the matter was too trivial and the public was not in the mood for an election. However a few days later a full confidence motion took place on a budget bill in which the government just scraped by. If it had lost, the Queen's representative could either have called on another party leader to attempt to form a cabinet with confidence or have called an election.

In 2011 the Prime Minister of Canada, for political reasons decided to prorogue (suspend) parliament. To do this he had to obtain the consent of the Governor-General, the Queen's representative. She could have called an election and many expected her to do so. The meeting between the Prime Minister and the Governor-General lasted a full four hours in which both the substance and the constitutional legality of the move was thrashed out. In the end the prorogation was accepted.

The monarch does not run the government and does not interfere in the country's affairs. But the monarch is an important independent unelected automatically-acting safety valve which no republican system can emulate.[275]

Republics vary in structure. In some, like Germany, the President is Head of State with powers vary similar to those of a constitutional monarch. In others, such as the United States and France, he is both Head of State and Chief Executive. In others, which we need not examine, he is dictator.

The problem with such Heads of State is often that they are in fact the political masters of the country. Balance of powers theoretically intended to keep them in line look good on paper but in practice they are extremely unwieldy and depend upon other politicians, with their own agendas, to operate. In the United States elections are for fixed terms, so that, apart from individual recall provisions, there is no mechanism for a fall of or dismissal of government.

It is true that most other republican systems, such as Germany and Italy, operate with parliaments where the government can be defeated leading to an election and the President has similar options to those of a monarch. But the President is a politician and cannot be above the fray, immune to political rather than constitutional pressures. Note the re-appointment of Prime Minister Berlusconi in 2005 after his parliamentary defeat.

If indeed we compare constitutional monarchies with republics, it is evident that constitutional monarchies are stable[276] and less open to political corruption (though not entirely without it).

This is not to say that republics cannot achieve similar standards, as Ireland and perhaps the Baltic States, bear witness. But they are few.

Under the revised political system we envisage, Global Government and its auxiliaries (treaties, conventions and the like) will stimulate what are now state governments to evolve their roles. No longer competitive military powers, they will be able to innovate and concentrate on and be responsible for the cultural, economic and social implications of the new world, within their countries. They will humanize their relations with their citizens, listening as it were with ground placed antennas, ensuring that localized requirements will be met, rethinking their fiscal operations, creating Youth Maturity Institutes.

They will not at first change willingly. For this to happen we much mobilize public pressures.[277] [278]

<u>2012 Postscript</u>

• The following contains an analysis of institutions which control life outside that of a competitive government: Clarkson, Sephen and Matto Mildenberger *Dependent America? How Canada and Mexico construct U.S, Power.* Toronto, University of Toronto Press. Analysis from the Center for the Study of Democracy, University of California, Irvine

---

- Providing political integration in multi-ethnic societies is one of the pressing issues of democratic governance in the 21st century.
- Over a half-century ago, a distinguished American political scientist, E.E. Schattschneider said that to speak of democracy and political representation is "to speak of political parties". In the proposed conferences, we plan on combining the themes of civic inclusion and the study of the ethnic basis of political party organization within the widen rubric of ethnic conflict resolution.
- When ethnic divides serve as focal points for political division, we may see ethnically based political parties and/or parties that seek to bridge ethnic divisions in the society (Horowitz, 1985, Birnir, 2007, Chandra, 2004, Chandra, 2005, Van Cott, 2005, Norris, 2004: 209-229) . However, multi-ethnic parties remain rare in divided societies, while they are much more common in plural societies, where ethnicity plays a weaker role in setting the course of political competition (Nordlinger, 1972, Horowitz, 1985, Grofman and Stockwell, 2003).Savoie, Donald J. *Power: Where is it?* Montreal, McGill Queens University Press, 2010. Diffused through society.
- The Arab Spring, riots in Britain and France, The Occupy Wall street movement and the need for populism and its focus.
- Failed States. Ghani, Ashraf and Clare Lockhart, *Fixing Failed States: A Framework for Building a Fractured World.* New York Oxford University Press, 2008 Does not consider idea of UN Trusteeship.
- Seguin, Denis. *What Makes a Country?* In *Toronto, The Globe and Mail* July 30, 2011 pp F4-. Suggests: Permanent population, defined territory, Government and relations
- Hont, Istvan *Jealousy of Trade: International Competition and the Nation-State in Historical Perspective* Cambridge,Harvard University Press,2005. Demonstrates the many ways in which nation states distort trade.

XVII - The Conditions of Peace and the Scandal of Armed Violence

The most distressing characteristic of humankind in the 21st century is its propensity for establishing violent groups armed with death dealing weapons. We may perhaps excuse those groups which have democratic credentials and resort to violence in order to defend their existence. Perhaps too we may excuse those groups which seek an international mandate with a high moral stance and who orient their aggression to put down violators of human rights or globe threatening activities. Such excuses however are the expression of a world in which national states take it upon themselves to act as policemen with or without the sanction of the United Nations which is not authorised to act as a true and independent global government, the subject of the next chapter

Many factors contribute to this situation but one clearly stands out – the ever increasing sophistication and availability of industrial arms. Even a respected journal such as the *Economist* carries stories which analyze the latest tools of modern warfare as if they were simply another expression of an industry contributing to GDP. Anti environmental industries receive critical appraisal, but the industry or arms production does not. Otherwise peaceable citizens continue to invest in them. How can we expect a country such as the United States to take a lead in global disarmament when it is unwilling to control the possession of weapons among its own citizenry? And when arms production is such an important part of its industrial output? It is sickening to see the way in which industrial countries compete to supply arms to both sides in the Syrian conflict.

It is sometimes argued that in the absence of industrial arms aggressors would simply resort to machetes and swords with similar devastating effects upon the unarmed. The violence of Rwandan genocide and other outbursts of mob action give credence to this view as does the widespread use of homemade bombs. Such phenomena though take place when the national government is unwilling or too weak to assert control. Our so-called peacekeeping forces are limited by the individual policies of the governments which supply the soldiers which take precedence over United Nations policies, strategies or directives. All too frequently such interventions lack the mandate to carry out arrests or arraign the violent before courts of justice.

National governments claim the right to use force to maintain peace within their jurisdictions. It would take decades for Youth Maturity Institutes to achieve success in removing the aptitude toward violence from youth so that it is no longer acceptable in individuals. In the meantime ,and perhaps even then, the world needs an effective global government with a police force mandated to bring the violent, whoever they may be, ,to justice, and, equally pressing, to control or eliminate the production of industrial arms, from hand guns to nuclear bombs.

2012   Postscript

- The (UN) Arms Trade Treaty was tabled in August 2012 ad no teeth. State signatories were required to ensure that arms manufactured in their territory were not traded for immoral or illicit purposes and to provide an annual report to a yet to be created "implementation group". Despite this wishy washy text it was too much for the United States with its arms fetish to stomach and Russia was only too glad to follow in their opposition. Another blow to global government.
- Stiglitz, Joseph. *Making Globalization Work: The next steps to global justice.* London, Allen Lane, 3010
- Close to suicide, perhaps virtually the same, are thousands of young boys and girls who are recruited into guerrilla and sometimes national armies, indoctrinated with the fever of killing, and thrust into the front lines where they are most in danger. It is well documented that many, indeed the majority, have been kidnapped to serve as cannon fodder.[279] They are often in hysterical or drug-induced excitement, at the dangerous age of susceptibility. They take risks, voluntarily or under pressure, in which the likelihood of death or life-long injury, before or after episodes of looting and socially destructive seemingly inhuman acts, is high. They are removed from the world of normal society, pariahs to civilisation.
- New killing devices are crated all the time. One wonders at the moral turpitude of those engaged in creating and developing them. One of the latest is a smart bullet which zeroes in on body warmth, thus seeking out

soldiers hiding in forest or other vegetation (incidentally one of the strengths of the Taliban).

- International conventions to which most countries adhere make the use of chemical weapons illegal. This position emerges from the horrific use of mustard gas in World War I. Some governments maintain stock piles. Yet paradoxically new sorts of chemical weapons might make warfare more humane, if that is possible. Appropriate chemical or bacterial weapons could knock out opposing forces temporarily without killing them, enabling them to be taken prisoner. We are not told what happens if both sides use them simultaneously...... Perhaps demonstrating the futility of armed conflict – and the end of warfare????

- The obverse of armed conflict is peacemaking and reconciliation, of which restorative justice may be a part. The difficulties in the concept and practice of restorative justice were examined at a conference organized by the School of Law, New York University in November 2011. The organisers wrote: "All over the world controversies continue to beset the practice of peacebuilding. Peace versus justice. Religious versus secular. Individual versus structural justice. Forgiveness versus retribution. Overcoming these dilemmas requires more than reforming institutions but rather new thinking about the questions: what is justice? how is it related to the building of peace?"

- A curious but understandable phenomenon is that neighbouring societies tend to be suspicious of each other and to chronically consider armed conflict. This principle was driven home to me in my studies of traditional Melanesia where it was obvious that neighbouring mini-cultures were hostile to each other, but welcomed interaction with those at least one neighbour removed. Suspicion of potential land grabs is an obvious factor. A study of chronic hostility in the Horn of Africa reinforces the point.[280]

- David Fisher asks "Can war be morally justified?" He answers yes. To be justified war must be waged by a competent authority, benefits must outweigh the harm, with no deliberate attack on non-combatants, or in self-defence. Traditionally war can be justified to remedy a serious grievance when no other method will resolve the issue. From the perspective of this Manifesto Fisher's argument fails. It provides excuses for war in a world which lacks the institutions to criminalize it. If we determine as we should that war is in itself immoral and an indication of global dysfunction we will have the obligation, as we should, to create the institutional structures which will remove such an immorality.[281]

- A particularly nasty by-product of war is the use of children. Most obviously they have been abducted and made to serve in the front lines. Some have managed to escape and survive the trauma. The Lord's Liberation

Army in northern Uganda and neighbouring states, which is bur just one of several movements, has been notorious. It is interesting and disturbing to note that the world, although with a little mobilization against them, has not put together the size and type of military offensive which would destroy them, which would involve massive aerial force and jungle equipped superior numbers of ground troops. To do so is deemed to be less important than supporting the Libyan revolution. Outside Africa children have been used as human shields and their sufferings used as propaganda tools. This has not been common in past centuries. The use of children was endorsed by the Pope in the First (Children's) Crusade. The Manifesto also objects to the use of children in non-violent demonstrations, for children do not have the maturity to know the facts of the issues and are being exploited as a propaganda tool controlled by their parents.

- It has long been a popular and often academically supported opinion that the actual conduct of war is beset by bad, even ignorant, decisions and the operation of luck rather than skill. (Perhaps the recognition of this lies behind United States strategy which demands the use of overwhelming force against an enemy before an attack is authorised, thus covering up mistakes) The Afghan fighting has provided a rare opportunity for outside observers to document tactics and decisions[282]. I would add that it is ironic that Nato places such emphasis on the *training* of Afghan troops where Afghans have fought and honed their skills by centuries of combat in the difficult mountainous terrain, with results that Nato forces themselves should know about and use more effectively.

The Taliban achieve such success as they sometimes have without benefit of Western instructors........

- Despite the current prevalence of armed combat today t appears that we have made some progress in reducing the amount of casualties.[283] Pinker notes that conflict killings have markedly declined, especially as tribes reduced open fighting in favour of urbanisation and the hopes of family wealth. UN peacekeeping slows down the beginnings of combat and sometimes reduces its intensity.. With sexuality and territory being the primary indictors of individual and social identity it is not umpiring that nation states have found it difficult to rein in tribal hostilities or that they use territory in their ideologies. Nor indeed that honour killing has proven so difficult to stamp out.

- A century ago anthropologists introduced the idea that sport can be a substitute for warfare. In Melanesia there was traditionally a ritualistic element to the bravado of conflict ,and a death would often require serious compensation. Papua New Guinea is a classic case of sport replacing warfare, although unpopular results can create fisticuffs. Since independence there has been a massive growth in several forms of football. By contrast in the Solomon Islands team sport is weak and armed conflict erupts, leading to the imposition of Australian colonialist "peacekeepers". National teams and athletes can bring divided nations together at least for the time of international competition. Rugby performs this function in many Pacific islands, soccer does so throughout Africa, and cricket in Sri Lanka, Bangladesh and Pakistan. The lesson was not lost on non-democratic polities which classically made and make use of sport not only as a popular circus diverting passions away from societal crises but to enhance identity. Today take note of North Korea, Belarus and depressed Britain with the 2012 Olympics and the role of Ukraine in the soccer World Cup to which some statesmen refused to attend because of that country's perceived political persecutions.

XVIII – Creating True Global Government

The major, but not the only, causes of strife between states and armed struggle within them consist in a parcel of inequities which lead to competition for power. The excuse is to relieve the inequities. (I say "excuse" because it is by no means unknown for the leadership to be motivated as much by personal or ethnic aggrandisement.)

In past history the *creation and reinforcement* of inequities through imperialist and expansionist dominance was a major driving force. It was as though the struggle for survival required such dominance and aggression; otherwise the would-be aggressor would itself succumb to others. In the nineteenth century, architects of dominion defined powerful "civilised" states as those which could defend themselves against the assumed aggression of competitors. The aggression might in fact be turned against weaker peoples or against neighbours. The competitor saw that as jostling for dominance.

The Cold War may have been the last major vestige of such drives on a world scale, though suspicion and armed competition are still there. Relatively new states (Indonesia, the Balkans) have adopted similar imperialist methods and the United States has not yet learned to use its power in a non-domineering manner and the effects of the resurgence of Chinese dynamism have yet to be seen.

One inequity is that of sheer size. When coupled with wealth, size lends itself to a non-democratic imbalance of military and diplomatic power between peoples. In the absence of an effective global government, the United States today stands out alone, although China, India Brasil and the European Union may provide counter balances in almost every dimension except possibly for that of technological armaments. Its potential power is weakened by ambiguities in the will to pay the price of such responsibility and by foreign policies directed by the opinions and interests of the single country population (rather than the global one), especially but not only at election time. This is not global government; nor is it legitimized policing, especially since in many respects the United States refuses to ratify or observe some international laws and courts. It is possible that the United States will change, gaining confidence and experience as a global policeman, enforcing United Nations laws. In the immediate future that does not seem likely. Furthermore, the dominance of any one major power does not last forever.

Is that what we want for our world? To depend on one or more Powers for this function inevitably means the imposition of that Power's values and perspectives on others. Global stability might come, but at the cost of diversity and democracy.

I will later be arguing that desirable Global Government is better achieved through the association of societal units which are closer to being equal. A Global Government of a few elephants surrounded by jackals and midges will achieve decisions only at the cost of great resentment, angers, jealousies, and frustrations which lead to distrust and the ignoring of inconvenient policies. The United States has been a front runner in undermining the United Nations family, frequently condemningthe organisations for undoubted inefficiencies, trying to impose its own idea of efficiency, and at times withholding its legally agreed financial obligations without which the United Nations group of organisations cannot be effective.

Apart from the United Nations, what Global Government there is consists of a spider's web of thousands of international agreements. Some are brought together in a substantive global grouping, as with the World Trade Organisation, nuclear non-proliferation and the painfully growing Law of the Sea. Others are regional in scope, with greater or lesser binding arrangements, from the European Union, to NATO, ASEAN, NAFTA, and all the other diplomatic acronyms. They have evolved rapidly in the past fifty years, demonstrating that behind the sabre rattling that has been going on there is a trend towards settling differences by binding agreement.

In addition there are scores of multilateral contacts affecting the ways in which bureaucracies and professions evolve. As Anne-Marie Slaughter[284] has pointed out, the network of bureaucrats and experts continuously communicate and develop policies behind the scenes. Musical, bureaucratic, professional and academic international communication, conferences, exchange of data and views create global influences on national cultures and official behaviour. Note the representatives of national governments, elements in their populations which try to influence the policies, and international non-governmental organisations and multinational companies which have become lobbyists for their own positions, as well as acting in parallel with governments in the international sphere. Add in the United Nations family of organisations, and regional agreements, organisations, and laws.

This is a diverse, competitive "organisation" which in a different essay I hope to examine as the culture of *Wemovagla* – the name derived from an acronym for the Web of Moral Values Globally Approved. Wemovagla is a global tribe, an ethnos, which in the last two centuries has been struggling to find its identity through ethnogenesis.[285] Wemovagla strives to create a global system of values which comes in conflict with and struggles to amend local values in the interests of the world. It deals with such matters as women's and children's rights, labour codes, educational goals, corruption, liberty and human rights, nutritional standards.

The gross inequalities between states govern the power structure when it comes to decision making and action. The larger states are as self-serving as any and are no slouches when it comes to bullying the smaller or weaker, as the recent disgrace of the failure of the World Trade Organisation to remedy the effects of nationalist subsidies, tariffs and trade barriers on Africa, Latin America and Asia clearly demonstrates.[286] And of course the failure of the 2009 Copenhagen and 2012 Rio de Janeiro meetings on climate change.

Plans for a Global Government must take into account such realities and overcome them. They are its greatest challenge which the current United Nations is not equipped to handle effectively.

Why should there be Global Government at all? Most observers would agree that the United Nations has not fully lived up to expectations. The operative word is "fully". The United Nations was set up with the primary task of preventing further wars between states. Its key instrument is the Security Council which gives a veto to the main victors of World War II, with little reference to current power positions. There is no doubt that the Council, with its vetoes, clarified the relationships between those states even as they were embroiled in the Cold War, and was the locus and inspiration for diplomacy which prevented a further world war.

Since the *de facto* peace that has ended the Cold War, the role of the Security Council in *preventing* war between states has been diminished. The United States, with Britain, exercised their "right" to go to pre-emptive war against Iraq, an action which the United Nations charter forbids, save with Security Council authority. As many predicted, other signatories to the Charter may now feel justified in following suit – as with Israel's U.S-approved raid into Syria in 2003. The United Nations and, significantly NATO, brought peace to the Balkans after horrendous military action by the competitors; but it is NATO carrying the military burden in Afghanistan. Numerous other conflicts – Sri Lanka, Darfur, Syria, Mali, Congo – have been hampered by the limitations imposed on United Nations actions and resources.[287]

Through its Social and Economic Council and related bodies the United Nations has mounted vast campaigns of famine relief, refugee help and technical assistance with awe-inspiring success, both directly and through international NGOs. It resists nationalist strings being attached to such help, which endears it to recipient countries. As I have noted many donor countries, however, prefer bilateral aid which enables the donors to give contracts to their own citizens, whether or not such contracts are in the best interests of the recipients.

Failure is therefore not an accurate or acceptable word. Not doing everything its evolving mandates demand and achieving both dramatic and little known successes is a more just description.

603

When that happens,despite some of its administrative inadequacies, it is not the United Nations *per se* that is at fault. The United Nations is a creature of its member states. If they do not want it to work, it can't. Although the United States is by far the largest financial contributor and has been generous with voluntary contributions, it tries very hard to turn the organisation into a fief, even to the withholding of contractual or agreed contributions when it is miffed.

Even when the Security Council gives its mandate and direction, the co-operation of willing states is in fact usually voluntary. The United Nations has no permanent military force, which makes logistics, communication, and scheduling a nightmare with slow reaction times as each contributing state places its own unique interpretation on the role of each contingent in a peace-making operation.

Although it is the creature of states, whose responsibility it is for any of its defects, in theory it stands above them all.[288] It is the only available coordinated and authoritative body to speak *on behalf of the whole world community*. We may not like its resolutions or concordats, but, theoretically, the world community has spoken. In the context of the war and occupation of Iraq the United States, in its actions, did not share the concept, frequently treating the United Nations as an organisation in parallel, rather than a superior organisation, both morally and legally.

"Theoretically, the world community has spoken". In practice this is not so. The resolutions, whether of the Security Council or the General Assembly, are the result of negotiations *between states.* It is the states who are responsible for any deficiencies which occur, including chronic under funding.

An effective Global Government there simply has to be. We have to find a way to create a world order which will *dominate, discipline and co-ordinate states*, rather than the other way round, in the interests of the *peoples* of the world community. We must tease out the weaknesses, and create new instruments which will have the kind of strengths we need. This is not in order to sanctify Global Government. It is because if we do not have an effective Global Government the world remains at the mercy of selfish political interests. And then our desired society will be further away than ever.

First, here are some of the functions desperately needed for a Global Government to carry out for the world – not only as a futuristic dream, but as a pressing necessity. We need the recognition of the functions which will help to determine the new organisation and structure of Global Government.[289]

1. As is required by the existing Charter, to ensure world peace and security *(in all areas both internal and international)*.

2. To prevent **unilateral** armed action under *any* circumstances by *whatever* entity – nation state or part of such a state. A corollary to this function is to ensure the disarmament of states and all armies and militias.

3. To destroy all nuclear arsenals and other instruments of mass destruction.

4. In order to carry out 1 and 2 to establish its own rapid deployment force, occupation forces, and other military and naval units. These will be financed through a percentage charge on states calculated on the basis of their current expenditures on armed forces. Such Global forces will also be available to police sanctions and other laws established by the Global Government.

As an important aside, when Global Government is confident of its power and role, it will possible to replace lethal weaponry with incapacitating weaponry. Under present conditions there is disgust and abhorrence at the potential use of chemical and biological weapons. They are in crude states of development, subject to the vagaries of weather and designed to create swathes of horrific death. But research is capable of designing protective gear for the users, and forms of such weaponry which incapacitate quickly for say a twenty-four hour period without disfiguring or lasting side effects. This surely would be preferable to the use of powerful explosives with their high degree of collateral damage.

5. To outlaw arms, including small arms, within state boundaries. Unfortunately, this will not in itself stop mayhem, since one cannot outlaw machetes and knives. A partial remedy is better than none at all. It would also meet resistance in countries such as the United States. Youth Maturity Institutes will eventually help.

6. To establish a global register of arms producers, production and distribution, with each weapon coded for rapid identification. Once again this would not eradicate the production of weapons by small artisan manufacturers and roadside bombers, but would deal with the major weaponry[290] [291][292]

In those parts of the world which can least afford it, men women and children take up arms, financed out of desperation by drug and similar traffic, accompanied by brutal suppression, sympathisers cheering from the sidelines, and mystery. Attemptsto impose arms embargoes have been weak at best for so-called conventional and chemical-biological weaponry. For the latter, raw materials are not difficult to combine, and, like explosives themselves, not difficult to plant for individual or terrorist purposes. The hardware for their trajectory, however, is another matter; it is not necessarily different from other such weapons.

There is somewhat more success in controlling nuclear devices, and a great deal more determination. Whereas conventional weapons may blow up the combatants and far-away civilians, nuclear weapons, wherever they are directed, do damage to all of us, and are relatively limited in distribution.

Major industries support the arms trade. Its disappearance over night would create unemployment in producing countries, that is everywhere. Individual countries are in fierce competition to gain market share. While a few countries share the nuclear industry, income can be generated from peaceful power plants, and those countries with political power stand to gain financially from restriction.

Is this too cynical? I do not believe it is. In June 1995 the respected and sometimes iconoclastic *Economist* included one of its famous special surveys, this time on defence technology. The survey treated the armaments industry as an industry just like any other. From that premise the industry should be technologically and financially more efficient, as a contribution to its *growth*. There was no discussion of killing off an industry whose primary purpose is to sell devices which kill humans, destroy cities and cultural treasures, ravage the countryside, cause massive destitution and forced population movements, and a huge bill for the international community to clean up the mess. There is no will, and I can detect no movement, to suppress the trade in arms. Such suppression is supposed to be impractical.

To some degree it is. Small arms and some large ones can be manufactured in primitive conditions, and escape rigorous controls. In today's world, however, they have limited value for major group violence, especially if confronted with a united Global Government rapid deployment force.

When it comes to international action to stop the arms traffic, critics of the idea will point out how difficult it is to monitor the seas, the air, even forested land borders. Of course it is. But it is by no means impossible[293]
.

In the nineteenth century a few navies, operating under international treaties or their State's policies, succeeded in outlawing and reducing slavery to its minimum, despite the fact that slavery was economically significant, well financed, and well organised, with much public opinion on its side. Colonial governments, when they had the will, stopped it in Africa. Like smallpox later, it was almost eradicated.

If it had the will, Global Government could reduce the international arms traffic to a manageable minimum. I doubt if any state in the United Nations has the present will to initiate such a move, even though such a step does not in itself amount to world disarmament. The revised elected membership in the Global Government's legislature which I shall suggest would almost certainly be prepared to do so.

Such a step requires supplementing by requiring junior levels of government, such as States, to introduce full registration of firearms of all kinds, and to eliminate them except for those deemed to have a necessary and positive function outside of human aggression. (Survival hunting might be one such exception.)

It also requires State disarmament, and the accord of power to the Global Government, which I shall argue for below.

Similar controls need to be in place to put a stop to the use of children in armed units. Indeed, since everything cannot be done at once, strategically child armies, such as those creating havoc in northern Uganda, might be the priority target.[294]

In the present world it is too easy for those who use military force to escape international wrath.[295] There is no excuse, save for self-defence. To remove the need for self-defence, the Global Government itself needs the power the United Nations does not have. While the constitution of the United Nations forbids resort to arms, the constitution is seldom used to expel or discipline a member. Under a Global Government constitution, States would not be members of the Global Government directly; populations would. States which defied the Global Government on such a matter would be replaced in law, declared invalid and outlawed, and assured that any gains made by force of arms would not be recognised. I will later argue for the institution of a form of Trusteeship.

7. To define terrorism and piracy and to make the planning, financing and exercise of terrorism and piracy crimes subject to international law superseding state law.

8. To codify and clarify all international conventions and treaties which place obligations on governments, organisations and individuals, and to provide for their mandatory enforcement, *whether or not specific nations sign the relevant agreements,* through international courts and systems of policing.

9. To bring under its control and coordination the programmes of what is known as the United Nations family of organisations (UNESCO, FAO, ILO, WHO, WTO and the like) and other organisations established by global treaties (for example, fisheries, environment, airlines).

10. To establish, with the help of appropriate NGOs, including scientific and social scientific ones, long term dynamic development programmes with the aim of reducing global inequalities, expressing localised values, and enabling sustainable self-sufficiency in the context of world trade. The aim should not be the conservation of ways of life, though these should be respected for their positive contributions, but to balance and create equity of opportunity in the global division of labour.

11. To fold emergency relief actions into 9.

12. To smooth the way for refugees and economic migrants, taking into account that this implies social tension and change, and alterations in the demographic structure of the world.

13. To direct medical action and research to the types of programmes at present handled by WHO, creating a balance between the needs of tropical countries and others, and between "populist" demands (AIDS, cancer) and those which receive less press attention (malaria, the common cold, arthritis, macular degeneration). Where necessary create drug manufacture and research with the aim of distribution according to ability of societies to pay modified by the need for equality of service.

14. To enforce global environmental standards, and to compensate and assist those societies and states for which observance of the standards may create an initial industrial or other disruption. To make wilful or careless environmental damage an international crime.

15. To organise massive support for the training of teachers, therapists and others concerned with youth, and their distribution for enhanced primary and secondary education, and, better, Youth Maturity Institutes as described earlier.

16. To *require* states to observe conventions with regard to human rights, international courts, nuclear arms,

ethnocide, genocide, and the like, *whether or not* the states in question have signed on to them.

17. To establish a system of Trusteeship in which the Global Government would take in charge the administration of failed states, including states that continue to refuse to accept such international mandates as freedom of expression or the criminality of torture.

The concept of Global Trusteeship needs considerable clarification if it is not to be misunderstood. Near-trusteeship UN operations have been reasonably successful in Timor and Kampuchea, with the agreements of the populations involved, and partially successful in Kosovo. There are countries where the situations underline the difficulties in the application, such a Burundi, Sudan, Myanmar. But note that these difficulties stem partly from the *present* structure of the United Nations, which is a far cry from Global Government.

Global Trusteeship will be most effective when national disarmament takes place on a world scale, although there will be some instances when a Trusteeship will need to be imposed when a country refuses to disarm. The decision to undertake Global Trusteeship will be most effective when it is based upon a Global Statute of International Law, adopted by an assembly which is that of the people, rather than governments. Only then will it have clear moral and legal authority.

The administration of a Trusteeship requires a civilian executive who is policy oriented. One of the U.S. failures in Iraq was to make use of an Ambassador with colonial style powers, but no experience in policy making under such circumstances, and no global mandate. Rather the operation was an extension of U.S. culture in which corporate executive and military power values dominate.

Thus a Trusteeship executive must have a United Nations force *under his civilian authority.* The force should be prepared and equipped for police actions rather than for military occupation, though the latter may be necessary in parts of a given country. The Trusteeship executive should work entirely through localized political power, wherever possible, using its authority to educate and reinforce the political authority to take remedial steps. The executive may in the early stages, consult with a group of social scientists appointed by the International Social Science Council, as far as possible drawn from the country itself, plus outsiders specialising in the country's affairs; this to assist the Trusteeship executive in refining the problem issues and the approach to their resolution.

Apart from this, officials of the executive, drawn from Global Government resources, would, in principle, be stationed as advisers and monitors to ministries, regional authorities, and the like.

The duration of the Trusteeship would be finite, open to extension. Usually country-wide elections would be expected in a year. Western ideas of appropriate election procedures would not necessarily constitute criteria – there are other forms which might be more appropriate in the short run, and which might be used to create approximate representation to avoid delays in handing authority back to the country[296].

After such a return to country authority, monitoring would continue until such time as the Trusteeship executive, by now relieved of executive powers, aided by the group of social scientists, could certify to Global Government that the country has satisfactorily resolved, or near-resolved, the issues that caused a Trusteeship to be mandated in the first place.

18. To establish conditions under which political self-determination will lead to state "independence".[297] Currently the situation in such areas as Chechnya, West Papua, and Kurdistan are examples of a *prima facie* desire for such a change, amongst many others. The evolution of states from competitive powers into local authorities should remove some of the perceived problems in such moves.

19. To make torture, detention without trial, capital punishment and similar offences internationally and effectively punishable, whatever the jurisdiction of the offending system may say[298].

20. To create an entity which, on behalf of the world's population, will begin the centuries-long task of finding another earth to colonize as a home for humans

when the inevitable happens, and the forces of the universe turn this earth into blinding dust.

This is not intended to be an exhaustive list, for there are scores of other issues, from illiteracy eradication to maritime governance and rights of workers, embodied in the programmes of the United Nations family of organisation and in near-global treaties.

What is different about my proposal is two-fold. The first is the co-ordination of the work of Global Government and *all* the existing independent members of the United Nation family within *one* framework instead of a multiplicity. We shall see that the existing "organisation" is, almost, anti-Global Government. The principle requires major and far-reaching changes in the organisation itself. The second is giving Global Government strengthened legal and enforcing powers. This requires fundamental changes in the relationship between States and Global Government and between functional elements in the present United Nations system.

The biggest bugbear ever to get in the way of a decent peaceful world is the entrenched respect for the autonomy of states, to whom all organisations in the United Nations family of organisations genuflect. Slowly, very slowly, this is modifying. Worse still, any state can get away with almost anything if it simply declares "My asserted crime is my internal affair". Official torture, murder, rape, massacre, bloody internal war, ethnocide, political imprisonment of rather mild dissidents, exploitation of women and children, sexual slavery are blatantly occurring as I write, have occurred consistently throughout the full history of the United Nations, and will be occurring long after you have read this. Indeed such matters were not the primary *raison d'être* for the United Nation's creation. They will continue unless we have powerful, effective, Global Government.

The United Nations has achieved an enormous amount during its short life – half a century. The achievements go largely unnoticed because they are, in terms of the media, undramatic. They do not get attention up front. They seldom make front page headlines. They are based on hard, solid work, enormous diplomatic successes, carried out with minimal fuss and even fewer resources, and with enormously dedicated personnel. Refugee conventions and resettlement; protection of aid operations; development assistance; regional co-operation in research and development; arid land renewal; major successes in the near elimination of some disease; mass literacy programmes; mass self-help programmes; population control – one could in fact go on for volumes.

But the moment the United Nations comes up against determined State defiance, it is stuck. It can do almost nothing, except against the relatively weak. Its funds are with-held. Every single State has become an expert in using verbiage and hypocritical legalese to defy. The nose is thumbed.

Every single one of the numerous organisational weaknesses of the United Nations family is a result of the self-interest of states which have put their own power and autonomy first – from the national self-serving and inefficiently hypocritical staffing systems (despite the extraordinary dedication and frustrated competence of the best international civil servants), to the replication of services between organisations, to the costs of translation, to the use of obfuscating UN-ese as a distinct language, to restricting the capacity of peace-keepers; to the enormous costs of numerous and massive governing bodies, to the proportion of funds used for administration rather than programmes; to power-maintaining rivalries and competition between organisations; to programme unworkability because of lack of local support or international resources; to overlapping rivalries and destructive competition with bilateral aid agencies; to lack of effective use of and decentralisation to competent NGOs; to dependencies on a coterie of "experts" instead of available NGO experts (there are notable exceptions to this); and so on and on.

One could in each case point to speeches in governing bodies deploring such defects, pleas to correct them, funds with-held because they have not been corrected. And one could find the powerful legal resolutions of the governing bodies that override these concerns by *mandating* the Secretaries-General to do exactly what they are in fact doing however ineffective a specific proposal may be. Resources necessary for correction are not supplied. Frustrated reforms are contrary to the interests of some bloc, even of states which wish to "banish" incompetent civil servants in their own bureaucracies to one of the UN family of organisations, or to reward a time-server.

Privately, most states do not *want* the United Nations to be a Global Government. States mistakenly believe that the world can go on as it is, that the public will not rise up in anger at the way states are betraying the future of our grandchildren. States are trying to brainwash the public into believing that Global Government is a danger to their own independence and culture.

Consider one major phenomenon. The United Nations system consists of a *family* of organisations. It is literally forbidden for bureaucrats, consultants, or diplomats related to any of them to refer to UNESCO or WHO or FAO or the World Trade Organisation as in any way implying that they are part of, or subject to, UNO, the United Nations Organisation in New York. Forget a governing world system. Instead there is a getting together of grown up independent career-oriented rivalrous siblings.

Result. While some of the organisations are indeed children of one of the foundation organisations and maintain umbilical cords, and while some are not accorded full sovereign status, the primary ones do have that status. Around *each* of them is a separate panoply of Ambassadors from the Member States. While there may be smaller executive councils with restrictive powers (of which the primary one is the U.N. Security Council), sovereignty is vested in *each* of their General Assemblies. Every single one has something of that kind, and most of them bring together full delegations (separate from the Ambassadors) from all the member states once every two or three years. UNESCO's can last up to two months, divided into large sectoral segments meeting simultaneously – and therefore requiringlarge delegations, to cover each segment, from each of the countries (which many countries cannot afford but do anyway) – as well as committees and negotiations in the corridors and at restaurants.

Add this up financially – the cost of delegations to expensive capitals for the General Assemblies; the cost of Ambassadors and liaison officers in the same capitals (different Ambassadors for almost every organisation); the cost in time and travel to the organisations themselves for liaison meetings – and with almost the same money you could possibly create a permanent peace-keeping force, reasonably equipped, or triple the amount spent on development aid. Of course a few highly paid, hubris-creating, Ambassadorial perks would be lost......

Aha, say the critics, including politicians who are resisting paying up their countries' assessments, massive waste. Cut back the finances until they get their house in order.

Such remarks, unfortunately typically snide, ignore the fact that every single one of these major wastages, and others such as appointment of staff on the basis of geographical and national quotas instead of ability, derive from binding resolutions of the General Assemblies (composed of representatives of the states themselves) of the organisations, or from equally directive decisions of their Executive Boards of the organisations. The wastage in the United Nations family is not a result of international servants' decisions: it is the result of decisions by the Member States in the governing bodies – who often act as if they did not *want* the United Nations to work.

The actions of the United Nations with respect to Global Policy are, by constitution, limited and over-ruled by the reserved powers of states which they arrogate to themselves. The United Nations and associated organisations have massive bureaucracies for the implementation of policy, bureaucracies which sometimes, it is true, run away with their own hubris, especially since legislative control is so unwieldy. That leads the public to think of them as having strong executive governing powers.

This is quite wrong. The bodies are much more like associations of states whose resolutions are more like treaties than like legislated laws. States adhere to agreements, or refuse to do so. Many policies are in place only for a minority of ratifying states, lacking global force since a ratification quorum may not be achieved. Important policies, such as the cultural heritage policies of UNESCO, or UN peace-keeping, are primarily paid for by

621

contributions to special funds outside the restricted and be-ruled general budget. Some such contributions are entirely voluntary; some are governed by principles of payment, which, however, contributors can and do ignore.

Originally, there was some sense to the arrangements. The organisations were small, brilliantly staffed, well focused, a coming together of allies after a devastating war, gradually admitting everybody else who wanted to join. It was thought of less as Global Government – anathema to the peace-time allies – but as a safety valve putting a limit on international snarling, and finding useful international things to do to improve humanity's lot. Even the last function was in competition with bilateral programmes, which served state interests more directly.

This sort of self-serving statehood is damaging and is standing *in the way* of achieving global policies that are urgently and desperately needed. *Major policies can only be resolved, can only function properly, as global ones.* Peace, world trade, the relief of disaster and poverty, violence, everything to do with eco-systems, the oceans, the high mountains, desertification, migration, the control of disease and its spread, nuclear policy – make your own list.

The functions of states and Regional Confederations in the global order are to ensure that communes, states or provinces, city governments, and so on, effectively express their local character, administer global laws and understandings in terms of that local character, and make sure that the populations they represent have effective mechanisms for placing their ideas, their point of view, their concerns, before the global policy makers. It is essential, for the world I am conceiving, that the lower levels of government (a) be sanctioned effectively for major and damaging breaches of world policy, and (b), equally significantly, have rights and obligations which enable them to vary appropriate details of global policy to conform with local cultures and conditions.

Let us approach the structure of the Global Government on the basis of what we know of the present.[299]

If you were to draw up an organisation chart for a state government, would you do the following? Would you divide up the operational tasks into the equivalent of government departments, to deal, for example, with agriculture and fisheries, with health, with labour, with education, with science, with trade, with culture, and so on? I imagine you would. You would also though ensure that *each* department had an effective Director in charge, and an efficient staff to analyse and implement.

Would you then say that each department should have its own elected legislature, independent of whatever there was of central government, and without any obligation to create its rules and regulations to harmonise with other departmental legislatures? That the Ministers in charge should each be a kind of Prime Minister appointed by and responsible to a *different* legislature from any of the others?

This in effect is how world government is organised at present – a range of subject and policy areas, each with its own independent parliament. You might well say that Nation States are perpetuating a divide and rule system in order to *prevent* Global Government from being effective, or being in fact a government at all. It is against their short-sighted interests. They are not ready for it. They must be at some time, pretty soon. We need them to start moving!.

So the first major reforms for Global Government would be to:

1. Turn each one of the "family" of United Nations organisations into a *department* of the Global Government, e.g. for global security, military affairs, education, agriculture and fisheries, migration and refugees, culture and science, health, industrial and labour organisation, financial organisations, human rights, and so forth.

2. Change the rank of Directors-General to Directors, except for the *one* over-all position.

3. Terminate the General Assemblies or equivalents, except that for the Global Government (once the United Nations) itself.

624

4. Allow the creation of strictly advisory global consultative Committees of Experts, small in size, a-political, and "representative" *informally* of relevant sub-global differences (depending on subject matter the differences could be, for example, geographical regions, the nature of trade, cultural emphases).

5. Restructure the bureaucracy so that it reflects ability alone, administered by an independent tribunal, without reference to group identity, using global examinations to sort entry-level candidates.[300]

6. Vest the General Assembly of the Global Government with legislative powers *in all substantive* domains including those of the specialised departments.

7. The General Assembly to elect cabinet members for limited terms to oversee the departments mentioned in paragraph 1. They would constitute the executive and policy referral cabinet, chaired by a rotating President. The Swiss model might be considered.[301]

8. Laws to be enforceable on states and individuals, through World and Regional courts, appropriately supported, without treaty or ratification.

9. The Global Government to become the *sole* repository of military forces anywhere. The Global Government would be the sole authority permitted to have armed forces. It would have its own military command structure and permanent military units, including rapid

deployment forces, to contain and eliminate violent flare-ups, aggression between states or their internal units, genocide and the like. *No units would be subject to nation state policies.* The military command would probably also be a police force to supplement state activity directed against such phenomena as piracy and contraband traffic (drugs, slaves, endangered species, cultural artefacts).

10. The division of the political world into electoral Districts. Each large state would be divided into Districts of, say, 10 million people. States between 5 and 10 million population would constitute one District. States with less than 5 million population would combine to create Districts of up to five million. This is an example only.

Whatever the solution, one person one vote will bring about a major shift in power as between peoples. Instead of, according to substantial myth, the values of Western capitalism pervading political and cultural areas from music to computing, that influence would be to some extent modified by the views of major population blocs. We can envisage North America and Europe being counter-balanced by China, India, Brasil, Hispanic America, South East Asia with Indonesia Nigeria, Arabia and Africa South of the Sahara. Some in the now dominant parts of the world may find this frightening. I would welcome it, provided the elections were free of national governmental control. I trust the common human, but less so their competitive and power hungry rulers.

11. Election to the General Assembly would be on the basis of, say, two Delegates per District.

12. Enumeration for the above purpose would be by *residence* rather than by restrictive definitions such as citizenship.

13. States would be entitled to have *one* Ambassador each to the Global Government.

14. The General Assembly (or global parliament) would elect the Ministerial Cabinet.

15. The Ministerial Cabinet would appoint a Civil Service Commission which would then make *all* appointments to the bureaucracy in accordance with the budget.

16. The General Assembly would approve and amend budgets, preferably with a five year forecast.

17. Income would be based on an assessment to each state, linked to that state's GDP. States would be responsible for the transfer of that assessment to the Global Government within a fixed time period, delays in payment being subject to a penalty, the whole being subject to an "ability to pay" rule set by the Ministry of Finance with General Assembly approval.[302]

18. The operations of the armed forces would be controlled by a Minister, subject to Cabinet directives which would be ratified by the General Assembly.

19. There are to be no vetoes, statutory or otherwise

20. There will be instances, as there are now, where individual states will be incapable of administering their own society. There need to be reasonably clear criteria which could be used to define such a condition, avoiding the danger of cross-cultural misunderstanding. This having been done, Global Government needs to re-institute the category of Global Trusteeship. The General Assembly would then ratify recommendations from the Cabinet to create or terminate a given condition of Trusteeship.[303]

The listing of such principles and reforms is indicative of the major challenges facing reformers of Global Government. Vested interests already built into the system have prevented or stalled the application of timid, try-to-please-everyone changes that blue ribbon and other committees have recommended over the years, including in 2005. It might well be that only a global cataclysm or its imminent threat will force those governments that have the power to change to face reality and act accordingly and in concert. This is not our wish. Or, better, a general movement at the grass roots to say "enough is enough" and to mobilise a public opinion fed up with global chaos, sufficiently powerful to wake up state governments to the reality that to continue to obfuscate and defend their powers is to undermine, perhaps destroy, the well-being of the world, including themselves. This kind of road block will lead me to explore an alternative mechanism in my final chapter.

Such a re-organisation rests on the premises that inequities in size between voting units should be reduced, and that states should be the in the middle rank of global political structure, representing their people in their internal affairs and administering policies on behalf of Global Government. In other words, states should be as to Global Government as provinces, *lande,* cantons and states are to nation states. It may well be that between states and Global Government are regional tiers of voluntary agreement.

The fate of human survival, let alone a desirable world, depends on the success with which such reforms can be accomplished, and the effectiveness with which the reformed instrument tackles the issues.

Global Government consists of an organisation to create and carryout policies. Our goal will be reached if the policies are in conformity with more general civilized world values. Writing about a re-organisation will not secure this. We have to set out what we believe in, and, as in every other domain of life, exert whatever tiny influence we may have to improve the lot of the generations who follow; to make it a little easier for them

629

to move the next goal on the foundation of such an achievement.

Any global government must balance the global "civilized" values it expresses with the justified requirement that peoples – not States – have their own systemic values they wish to preserve. Not only that, but there may be clashes between the local values and the global ones. Any attempt to impose, internationally, a particular moral code must do so, not simply by expressing a law in an international convention or legislation of the General Assembly, but by intimate and close analysis of the effects of such changes in particular cultures. What does the abolition of *de facto* slavery do? What are the implications of female circumcision or death by stoning for attitudes towards women (who then may be regarded as potential whores), the structure of the family, and the moral system, which may indicate a need for further action in other aspects of culture? Thus the law makers must have more than the law itself in mind, but consequent actions to help restore the functioning of society in new forms. This is not an undertaking to be treated lightly, and may require socio-cultural advisory commissions to pronounce on the implications of each piece of legislation before it becomes law.[304]

Reference to the issues of human rights illustrates the complexities with which Global Government will have to deal.

The definition of civil liberties, of freedom itself, which seems so natural to those who live them, is not self-evident to others. It must always be argued for, defined, with passion and clarity and always against the erroneous perspective that civil rights conflict with security. When a Global Government is achieved, it will, I think, reach fruition because of a greater consensus about civilised values and freedoms and responsibilities, based on holistic information, analysis and debate. If this is not so, Global Government will have an uphill task to establish itself or to be relevant in the ways we hope for.

While it is relatively easy to define genocide as the physical destruction of members of a specific group,[305] most of the time attacks against groups fall short of this. Attacks against indigenous peoples, minorities, and so forth are designed to strip them of property, prevent them from achieving a secure life-style, force them by social, political, and material pressure to conform to the culture of those in power (not always the majority).

Difficulties in definition arise for various reasons. Ethnocide is held to be the forceful destruction of an ethnos, or traditional culture, whereas attacks against other groups, such as religious cults or followers of alternative lifestyles, are handled separately in a different way. They must be, or else brought together analytically, for they are all cultural variants. Again, some instruments of social pressure are regarded by some as not reprehensible, even good. Religious proselytisation is a major issue of contention in some parts of the world,

631

although its proponents are driven to it by their faiths. Education is a major changer of culture, bearing down on children whose only "defence" is that of their parents, who may be excoriated for resisting a "proper" influence. The Japanese argue that they want a homogeneous society, not one with ethnic variation (although they have religious and other significant disparities). Is the destruction of such attitudes ethnocidal?

We cannot realistically interpret ethnocide as meaning no change whatsoever in cultural groups. Everything, from TV to the Internet, from pop music to universities, promotes change, and does so unequally. It is therefore necessary to be explicit for a Global Government to be able to face such a problem.

Face it, it must. The extreme cases are patently obvious. Rwanda, Burundi, former Armenians, Kurdistan, the Balkans, Brazil, Paraguay, Myanmar, Kashmir. There are troublesome middle cases: Mexico, First Nations of North America, Nigeria, Indian "tribals" and untouchables, and many others.

At least the extreme cases require intervention. At present interference is weak, devoted to human aid, but not facing the certainty that resolution cannot or will not always be achieved by state governments in power. The new government of Rwanda is trying to achieve a just society. If so, it deserves very much more support than the world is giving it. If that support is given, and it were to turn its back on such a goal, the world is justified in dismissing such a government.

I use the term advisedly. State governments do *NOT* have a God-given right to be in power. Power has to rest in the people. God does not ensure this either. The people have to achieve their powers, governments to earn them. We want both factors to prevail. But they will not arrive automatically.

In some parts of the world there is no sign of movement in that direction. Again, I do not advocate intervention in marginal cases. But I do most certainly advocate intervention, and strongly, in those instances where governments have over the years shown themselves to be so incompetent as to destroy a reasonable viability of the country, a functional society, or a minimum material base of life.

The subjects that I have used to exemplify policy concerns for Global Government imply decision-making, adjudication, and the power to impose sanctions. Adjudication implies a structure of international courts. These are almost useless without the power to enforce court decisions against states if necessary. Ultimately, that implies power.

Global Government will require military force to bring equity and justice about. There is little doubt that in the first stages it would have to use every kind of pressure, with the threat of force, to induce recalcitrant states (and other organisations, for those there will be) to disarm. Threats are useless unless they are known to be real, as United Nations history has shown.

Global Government will not be cheap. How can we afford it? It is not enough to say, we cannot **not** afford it. We are at liberty to choose ultimate cataclysm for our descendants, to refuse to pay the price for achieving not only what we want but what is necessary for survival. I have proposed a complete restructuring of state fiscal systems, which will simplify national and international public finances. The removal of state military budgets will go a long way to help.

The challenges are huge, and only partly expressed here. Each one, considered in relation to the others, links to a coordinated march forward, offers hope to populations which may otherwise be cynical about or helpless in the face of the short-term, self-serving, futureless state political systems that so often seem to stand in the way of progress.

We desperately need Global Government. Let's get on with it. How?

2012Postscript

- A major issue to be resolved will be that of the organisation and accountability of the institutions which uphold the rule of global law.[306] [307]

Manifesto for the New Age

XVII – How to Get There

WE MUST just do it !!! YES

WE WILL !

Youths of the World UNITE !

Arise ye Citizens of the World!!!!!

Slogans by themselves do not work. They must be attached to hard focussed work.

It is YOUR world. The mass demonstrations of the early 21st century have shown that the youth and citizenry can overcome state governmental negligence. Egypt shows that there must be strong vigilance to prevent changes from being undermined. And Syria has shown that religious ideology and traditional hostilities can stand destroy hope.

It is now the time for other countries to put aside state nationalism and create a civilized *world.*

Demonstrations are awakening tools but are not in themselves democratic or necessarily an indicator of public opinion. They are a starting point demanding attention. The Occupy movement lacked coherent goal of change or a clear political aim. They often by themselves give participants a false sense of doing something, of giving vent to their feelings and there is a sense of depression and anger when there is no follow up. It does give authority a notice that all is not well.

It is predominantly youth who can establish a long term vision. I do not mean teenagers who rightly work with simplified emotions, and must be involved, but the youth of their next twenty years or so.

What is then missing is organised and functional experience. I suggest that this is to be fund in the major international non-governmental organisations. By definition their work is an indicator of the weakness and unsuitability of national governments in putting the world to rights. In their work they come up against the dysfunctionality of those governments to the real misery of the world's populations. Think Médecins sans frontièrs, Journalism without Borders, Amnesty International, the Red Cross and Red Crescent, the International Social Science Council and many others of a like kind.

Most such organisations are forbidden in their statutes from engaging in political activities and in some countries would lose taxation privileges and subsidies if they did so. Yet what is needed is for them to use their expertise and skills for direct political action as we shall propose. Youth demonstrations need to target such inhibitors for what is required is political action on a coordinated global scale. Demonstrations are needed to help NGOs to take the plunge.

It is all very well setting out a personal view of where to go in the 21st Century. After all, I won't be there to see it. But brave words are not enough. If I believe we can reach our goal, it is up to me to suggest how to reach it.

I cannot imagine that your view of the desired result will be the same as mine in all respects. Perhaps you reject the totality of what I have said. You may by your arguments change my view of many things, although I am rather stubborn.

On one matter, however, you are almost certain to be in agreement. We are racing ever and ever faster into the future. Although there are many who attempt to predict the future, and others who discuss ethical and policy issues based upon such predictions, there is considerably less discussion of where we **want** to arrive. In my view this is disturbing because it implies that the future is a natural outcome of present dynamics whereas it surely behoves us to *take control* of our destiny consciously and conscientiously.

Perhaps you also agree with me that, especially since change is happening so fast, we should be trying to mobilise public opinion to discuss our goals, and to devise ways of influencing our directions. We are not going to agree about everything. So that underlying the effort must be the principle of assessing the compatibility of our differences within one world, non-confrontationally. If they are incompatible for individuals living in one location, they may not be for individuals living elsewhere, and but can still be functional. There will be incompatibilities in the long run that are cause for distrust, violence, vilification. These must not continue in that confrontational form in a our new global society. We will have to devise means for recognising the limits, and resolving the issues so that we can live together in respect and peace, if not in total harmony. I hope we will not discourage difference, which is essential to civilised movement and adjustment; but it is essential over time to remove violence and to turn distrust and vilification into respect.

If you are agreed on this one principle, that it is desirable for all of us in the world to take control of our destiny, that is enough to begin with and to work toward.

There are of course the nay-sayers, those individuals who regard such determinations as an impracticable dream. Their objections are in my opinion simply a refusal to take responsibility, or an inhibited fear of doing something positive because one is afraid of change. It is easier to let matters and life go by, taking the pain or dysfunction as inevitable.

We can identify several of the excuses. "But human nature will never change" is the canard that was thrust against my ideological idealism when I was young, and it's still there. Humans will always be selfish, egotistical, prone to violence. What rubbish! What an excuse for laziness and inaction! There are quite enough people right now who are unselfish, caring and peaceable to constitute a major potential force in world society.

"Human nature", the concept, is an agglomeration of individuals. Individuals, locally and globally, are enormously differentiated. It takes only a few shifts in the *nature of individuals* to change the statistical profile of "human" nature. That is happening all the time. Human nature is highly malleable and highly dynamic. We have control over it. It is up to us to put it right, and not use weasel words to escape responsibility.

Or, "we can't make a change – it's the system". This one has more force. Yes, we as individuals are caught up in systems. Whistle blowers are sacked. Managements, private and public, treat non-conformists with suspicion. The "system" is that great big amorphous nonentity of an organisation in which we poor cogs drive the wheels. Again, this is sheer laziness and defeatism. It is the excuse with which employees at the bottom of the rung give you when your complaints or objections hit the stone walls of organisational stasis. "It's not our policy". OK, get that policy changed.

Or, "we don't have power". Tell that to the people of Georgia and the Ukraine, Iraq Palestine and Afghanistan. For the world's sake, *take the power*. Just taking power won't solve the problems, but it will remove the excuses. And it is much more than simply accepting some version of democracy, which can have dull, corrupt, conservative and banal results. It is a matter of all of us - each one of us - exercising and manifesting will, despite what officialdom, bureaucracy, managers and politicians have to say, and not just at election time.

Just the same, why bother? Humanity has muddled through enormous cataclysms in its brief history, embarking on self-destructive activities like no other species (except lemmings). There are numerous other self-induced threats to our existence, from environmental disaster to national aggrandisement and terrorism, from reproductive disaster to the failure to contain pandemics, from the exhaustion of energy sources to religious myopia. Each of these needs the kinds of resolution that are contained in this analysis. And many of the champions of reform use the theme "If we don't do this, then humanity will disappear"

That's no good. Fear begets more fear, creates disruptive anxiety and strife. This is dysfunctional and it inhibits clear thinking and global rational action. To succeed we need to be positive, set positive goals, abjure the negative. And indeed ask yet again, why bother? Why waste time abetting the continuity and well-being of humanity? To answer such a question we need to have some kind of an answer to the question, what is the purpose of life, of living?

If your answer is that it is to secure a better place in the Hereafter, then forget this task. The worldly future doesn't matter, and is not worth the effort, since, although "being good" will no doubt count, all rewards are lying fundamentally outside the realm of the defective present.[308]

Insofar as human living has a purpose, in my view it is to improve human living and humanity itself. It is in a way a vortex, each state of life creating a new set of hopes and desires. That is why each of us is here. There is nothing static about it; it is ever moving. It is a secular, a natural, purpose, not a transcendental or religious one. It is down to earth, not airy-fairy. It is of the here and now and also of future millennia. The theme may be expressed in the upbringing of children, in love, in creativity, in the wholesome and infectious joy of life itself, in improving wealth in non material as well as material ways, in everything else we do and experience.

As I mentioned as long ago as the *Point of View* Manifesto beginning, the classic argument between the primacy of duty and the primacy of consequences is resolved if we assert that our duty is to humankind, rather than to any individual or part of it, except insofar as the latter contributes to the well being of humankind (as it does for example in a warm and open relationship between a man and a woman). And the consideration of consequences is subject to a time dimension: immediately beneficial consequences may be deadly in terms of the future 21st and 22nd century achievements.[309]

That is why we need to achieve the new world – to give expression to the very purpose of being alive. That is why each one of us must find a way, however modestly, to do his or her little bit. While we may set our goals in terms of what we can achieve in the 21st century, that will not be the end of it. We will simply have learned how to control our destiny, and after the end of the 21st century there will be more challenges, yet other objectives for life which we cannot imagine now. What fun! I wish I could be floating around in the atmosphere somewhere with the capacity to see it and understand it all, not as some experts on heaven suggest, to be separate and rejecting interest in it.

Then let us set about doing it. Every single one of us has responsibility and is in a position to exercise some part of it. At a perfect dinner my friend brought up, as she often does, the huge gap between what we were doing, having dinner, and the pain in, for example, Syrian refugee camps. Should we therefore not have dinner? That by itself does nothing for anyone else, and if adopted universally would mean destroying a valued creative art, to say nothing of restaurant employment. If we were able to turn the cost of the dinner toward a charitable relief, there might be some point. Otherwise it is guilty self-flagellation. And we do not want to **reduce** the quality of life, but to **improve** and expand it. Where there is an absence of life's qualities we must think of helping, not of destroying what some already have.

No. The aims of world improvement may sometimes be helped by the temporary reduction in our own satisfaction. Rich countries will at times have to reduce their riches to meet particular crises, as indeed they do rather miserably now. They devote a proportion of their riches, a tiny proportion, to such needs as charitable responses and peace keeping, and to aid projects that, sometimes, improve the dynamics and viability of poorer countries. They must do better.

It will not improve healthily on the basis of guilt. Guilt is an excuse, not a helpful activity. We are not guilty because of what our forebears may or may not have done during the bloody and gruesome history of the world. The past was a faltering step to the present, and hence a step towards our goals. If we accept guilt because ideologists, frustrated by their lack of progress or power, escape their own responsibility by laying the guilt on us, we will not think or act clearly, and are likely to do as much damage as we wish to repair. Guilt, if there, must be related to a concrete situation for which we have been clearly and consciously responsible, not generalised to everything our civilisation does or has done.

The way we move forward, for those of us who are ordinary citizens, is to exercise our individual creativity and skills toward the common purpose. One of my friends is a teacher. A part of her contribution to the arrival of the new world is to teach well, and, perhaps within the framework of her discipline, if appropriate, even to discuss the kind of goals set out in this book and how we get to them. Then as citizen, in social contacts to talk about where we are going. That is enough for many an individual person.

Others will try to amend their personal lives, more consciously asking, is this consistent with a movement toward future world goals? (The world being and amalgam of individuals.) Personal relationships, abandonment of jealousies, understanding of others, political action.

Others will go further. They may bring the issues I have raised out into the forum of public discussion, and amend them or add other issues to them. At present there are many forums, nearly all around specific, mostly localised, concerns: abortion, euthanasia, logging and fishing practices, peace-keeping, gun control, sexual harassment, substance abuse, child abuse, crime and punishment, the protection of privacy. Nearly all strike me not only as localised in their programmes, as they must be to be effective, but as dealing with the relatively immediate. Nevertheless the immediate relates to long term values -- environmental issues to the health of ecosystems; abuse to the health and welfare of citizens; peace-keeping to world order. And by influencing each immediate outcome as it arises, one pushes, however minutely, global society in a specific direction. It is best if that direction be conscious and chosen. Peace keeping as a step toward the global removal of violence, for example. Again, removing jealousy as a step towards both more wholesome lives and reduction in crime and violence, for example.

The point of my argument is to try to bring the *long-term* issues to the fore, to make them more open to discussion and resolution, to move toward the principles that most of us can agree on as representing world values and practices. We must argue about such visions before we can share them.

It should become normal practice for every decision to be conceived, specifically and consciously, in the context of the long term goals, as identified at the time.

To the extent that this is done, the local and immediate concerns become steps on the way to the finer future, a consciously defined future. They are seen as part of a grander movement toward a state of civilised living that is within reach, that can be made real. When your politicians, city councillors and others make a proposal to solve an immediate problem, always challenge them. How does your solution contribute to more fundamental goals?

So that is what I ask of you, the reader. I ask that where you disagree with the vision I have set out, that you work out in your own mind, or with others, the implications of your disagreement. Don't just say I disagree for this or that reason. In addition, trace through the ramifications of the disagreement for the world you desire for your descendants. Treat what I have written as a draft. Re-write it from your own point of view.[310]

Let the draft be re-drafted many times progressively. If I am up to it, I may do exactly that in a few years time. For in those years many things will have changed, many elements of knowledge will have become clearer, perhaps my views will have been debated in ways that I for one can learn from. Let others do it also, from their perspectives.

What I am advocating is not as sharply focussed, is more diffuse, and is more open-ended in its objectives than an ideology. It requires study, thought, exchange of opinions. The mode of action is through personal example, and by persuading sources of power, influence and authority, toward the point of view that innovations should be oriented toward the long-term goal of Utopia, that achieving Utopia must be in the forefront of our strategies.

If this book is to be any use in that process, it *global* well being thought of as a framework for arriving at socio-political goals that create a fine world not for us but for our descendants. New beams can be added to the framework, since there are enormous subjects I have not discussed fully, or where my point of view is inadequately informed.

Furthermore it is open for any citizen to take elements in the framework, replacing them with better materials and design. Such changes will be responses to new knowledge, to differing ideas as to what the structure represents, and to improved concepts as to how the beams hold together -- what their relationship is to each other. But the building must hold together.

It *is* a structure. So that if you redesign part of the building, work through, to the extent it is desirable, resultant modifications elsewhere in it. Let there be, over time, revised and alternative answers to the question, **What is our ultimate goal?** Don't let the question remain unanswered, shoved aside, forgotten.

When smaller issues arise, however emotionally charged or intellectually important, say out loud how they fit with your view of the ultimate goal, how they represent, if done correctly, steps along the way, how they must be judged in those terms. Introduce the long view. Don't let it drop out of sight.

In matters of public policy, or politics at whatever level, more dramatic opportunities exist. The nature of the new world has to be brought to the forefront. The programmes of political parties for the next five years, if elected, must be related to the ultimate goals. To what extent do those five year plans, or whatever, those massive volumes of legislation, help us to arrive - or indeed, do they stand in the way? There are indeed usually long term philosophies at work, but they are often inferred or piecemeal. Individual initiative may be lauded to the skies; but for itself, not because it fits into the grand scheme of a world in which it links up with other significant principles. "We must work toward full employment; and at the same time we must reduce the work force." Such statements are not merely illogical, but indicate nothing about what we *want* life to be like. This, surely, must be the criterion against which policy should be judged -- where does it lead us? Toward a desired quality of life?

It is time to bring the point to the forefront, to return vision to political agendas. At no time in world history has a global Utopia been within reach to the extent that it is coming to be in reach now. It is not around the next corner. The trail is much longer and more difficult in many countries than it is in others. But, because of the present state of the world, the steps that have to be taken can now be set out with reasonable realism, as being within our power to accomplish.

Governments, as they are structured now, will not do it of themselves. Many changes do not require governmental action. Many do. This is a potential road block, because governments are typically behind, not in front of, the people's will. Thus it requires intense public mobilisation, with populist pressure, to influence and persuade governments that this or that long term goal is within their reach, and will provide them with political dividends. To establish Youth Maturity Institutes for example or to change the interplay between the administration of the law and health services. I have already referred to the need for international non-governmental organisations to mobilise public opinion to make global government modern and equitable[311].

In fact international NGOs constitute the strongest institutional apparatus available to advance thinking and action along these lines. They exist to link activists and professionals in every field you can think of, from education to hydrology, from charity to global IT improvement, from commerce to UN affairs. To some extent they are rivalrous, establishing competitive boundaries and tapping similar sources of funds both governmental and private. They are naturally and properly focused on their own individual mandates.

My point links with the concept of the power of *civil society.* This consists of movements outside the formal political structure. James Walter and Andrew Thomson[312] have examined the scope and influence of civil society movements, including formal NGOs, on public policy. There have been movements which have altered the political course of countries (most notably, recently, Ukraine and Georgia) though with agendas that are localised and limited in effect, rather than with *global* issues in mind.

This is where I place great hope on students in places of higher education and in due course those from Youth Maturity Institutes. Every one of them is aiming for a full adult life. Every one of them is in an educational system which requires them to choose a major subject or two of interest. Every one of those subjects has an organisation, an association, which has as its aim the furthering of the professional interests and bases of knowledge of its adherents. And most of those are linked in a form of international federation which is indeed a Non-Governmental (academic, professional or policy oriented) Organisation.

So here is my challenge to the student reader. Join with your fellows and discuss with your mentors the nature of those organisations which otherwise be hidden from you. Some of your mentors may not even be aware that the national organisation is a part of an international one. Get the relationship out in the open. Then exert pressure, with students from other campuses. To have those bodies seriously address issues of the world which are relevant to their interests. Let the international NGOs understand that their members want a better world, and that the NGO is in a position to forward at least part of it. This will almost be on the basis of a fusion of religion and science, in the sense in which I have earlier used the terms – science, because rooted in questioning knowledge; faith, because of the belief that our desired world is possible in the 21st century.

Just one example. Anthropologists have their own national associations in many countries. Most of these elect delegations to the International Union of Anthropological and Ethnological Sciences. That body in turn (almost uniquely) is a member of three over-riding major power centres – the International Scientific Union, the International Social Science Council, and the International Council for Philosophy and the Humanities. Through these and also directly it has admittedly tenuous links with UNESCO and the social development arms of the United Nations.

Similar links are in every field – education, law, psychology, chemistry, social work, demography, planning, political science, physics, astronomy, economics, branches of medicine and all the others.

If there has been a sub-text in this book, it is to assert that the issues are interdependent, that we are faced with systemic, not atomised, challenges. "Interdisciplinarity" has been a watchword, often used in vain, within some of the NGOs. In academic life it is difficult to achieve.

Nevertheless, we must try harder, especially in applications of knowledge to empirical issues.

As a first move I would hope that some of the main NGOs would take the step of creating a World Council of NGOs.[313] The prime first task of such an organisation would be specific. It would be to define and advocate the goal of Global Government to be achieved within the 21st century. It would be to prepare position papers on relevant topics, perhaps along the lines of the topics of this book. It would mobilise debate in each country where the NGOs have national affiliates. Imagine the effect of debates going on in your country within the affiliates of scores of NGOs.......

This proposal is also in the direct interest of the NGOs themselves. Most are affiliated one way or another with the United Nations family, and are critically aware of the defects of the world system in their fields of work. To strive for fundamental long term reforms in a coordinated way can only be of benefit to them.

There may be psychological resistance. This is where the popular will must show itself. This is why I call for a global spring, mass movements to enhance the persistence of the NGOs.

Then comes the next powerful step. Once the parameters of a global policy on the topic are opened up no doubt with many a regional variation, the power of the united NGOs would be unleashed. This of course would be especially important in designing and implementing Global Government by peoples instead of by states.

The message would in essence by quite simple. "Enough is enough – we the people are tired of myopic views, of petty tinkering with life's challenges. We demand change, and this is what we want. In country after country, until we have what we want. And as governments are unwilling or unable to do it, we will find an alternative in the strengths of expert organisations which think of people and beyond the limits of nation states".

It may well be that yet a further step will be necessary. States will not give up their control of the United Nations very easily. Indeed it may be necessary to set up the true Global Government outside that organisation rather than reforming it. In whatever way, the International Council for NGOs will have to take the initiative in actually setting it up, designing its charter, funding, and inaugural activities.[314]

If the NGOs are to take the lead they will need not only a stimulus but additional professionals and volunteers since they must not be distracted from their primary purposes but use this movement to support them. Here I speculate that the activists who created Occupy Wall Street[315] and the generation following them might take those elements of the Manifesto which they can handle, support the NGOs, and help carry the globe into its future.

This is the time, but let us not expect hasty miracles. I have pointed out that the effects of Youth Maturity Institutes will not be felt fully for maybe fifty years after their introduction. The adoption of other systemic reforms require debate, much more analytic and practical thought, and deliberate implementation, often hesitant, and subject to the criticism of those for whom immediate results take precedence over long term solutions.

We must begin or it will never happen, and that is too disastrous to contemplate. This is the time to begin. This is our opportunity. Let us start deliberately, no longer feeling like small insignificant cogs rotating helplessly, but rather knowing that we have the power -- and responsibility -- each one of us, to make decisions. And, when we have the courage to do so, to live our beliefs --

Let a Global Spring create the Rainbow Revolution !

Just Do it   !!!

NOTES

---

[1] I first made this point in my *Conditions of Social Performance; an exploratory theory.* London Routledge 1970 and 1998.

[2] Also originally expressed op. cit.

[3] This comment has become even more relevant after the Arab Spring and the growth of political manifestations throughout the · world.

[4] In fact the draft of two chapters, on education and on global government, received the 2004-5 World Utopian Championship. Cf http://www.soc.nu/utopian

[5] And sometimes creating reactionary backlashes.

[6] Amartya Sen, *The Argumentative Indian*, London, Allen Lane, 2005; and the *Bhagavad Gita.*

[7] See my *The Sorcerer's Apprentice: an anthropology of public policy*, Oxford, Pergamon Press, 1976

[8] Broad, Eli, *the Art of Being Unreasonable: Lessons in*

---

unconventional thinking. London, Wiley, 2012

[9] My theory of innovation was foreshadowed in my doctoral thesis but primarily elaborated in *The Conditions of Social Performance: An exploratory theory* London, Routledge, 1970 and 1998.

[10] See my *Traditional Exchange and Modern Markets*, Englewood Cliffs, Prentice-Hall,, 1965

[11] Many people especially creators, embrace tension, finding it a pleasurable source of new ideas.

[12] This truism is the devil in the detail of international technical assistance. I observed agriculturalists in the Solomon Islands rejecting the use of the spade. Traditional digging sticks made smaller and less wasteful holes and spades required the use of muscles and actions which were not habitual.

[13] There are theoretical though difficult in practice, ways of getting around this by applying the notion of elasticity of demand for time. See my *Conditions of Social Performance, op.cit.* and "The identification of values in anthropology" in *How do we Know?* Webzines of Vancouver, 2011.

[14] Pope, Rob. *Creativity – Theory, History, Practice.* Abingdon, Routledge, 2005. The book contains an extensive bibliography.

---

[15] There is one attempt, quoted from Henry Petrovski, *Invention by Design* on page 267 with hints towards a generalisation.

[16] An early draft of this chapter was part of the winning entry for the World Utopian Championship in 2005. That draft has been published in *From Youth Maturity to Global Government the Utopian tapestry.* Stockholm, Raketa Press,2011 and in my *How do we Know.* Vancouver, Webzines 2011.

[17] Despite sentences of this kind it is not my intention to imply certainty about future trends.

[18] The role of prisons in recruiting alienated youth into gangs is well documented, See also Chetterburg, Michael *Young Thugs.* Toronto, Harper Collins 2007 and 2008 for an in depth study of the formation and operation of youth gangs, and Collins, Randall. *Violence: a micro sociological theory.* Princeton, Princeton university Press 2008, which is a profound examination of the roots of violence and their dynamics in behaviour and culture.

[19] In the late 'forties I had the experience of conducting research amongst units of the British armed forces. The then government was determined to change the culture of the by now professional officer corps. Young officers were indoctrinated with the new ideas, but as they were posted one by one to their regiments or squadrons they rapidly succumbed to the values and culture of the officers' mess.

---

²⁰ Other institutions such as churches, sports associations and so on normally deal with segments of society, whereas schools, one way or another, penetrate all corners.

²¹ This is not to say that authoritarian regimes cannot achieve amazing results in limited highly concentrated teaching, usually in technical areas. In Soviet Moscow I was astounded at the ability of a seven year old attending an elite language school to converse easily in English.

²² Pennac, Daniel in *School Blues* Maclehose Press, 2011, argues that French schools are too quick to identify "dunces" with insufficient empathy for what may be well known learning disabilities which could be treated with more understanding..

²³ In a recent visit to New Zealand I was impressed by the groups of high school boys and girls in smart uniforms. They are also common in most of the once colonial world.

²⁴ I exempt the banning of face veils from this judgement; facial expression is an integral part of communication, which is an essential characteristic of good schools.

²⁵ See Chapters X and XI. Our desired world will have less mandatory employment, more non-employed activity.

²⁶ How many school career counsellors even imagine the

possibility of anthropology as a career, even if they know what the word means?

27 Among the publications note the revealing titles of the following: Cross, Gary. *Men to Boys: the making of modern immaturity.* New York, Columbia University Press; Coté, *Arrested Adulthood: the changing nature of maturity and identity.* New York, New York University Press, 2000.

28 Did – do - schools in Rwanda teach knowledge of and respect for the two competing social groups? How much do northern Sudanese schools teach positively about their southern or their Darfur co--citizens? They don't and they are neither mandated nor equipped to do so. How many Christian schools fail to each Islam or Judaism positively, and vice versa?

29 Note the following by E. M. Foster: "Tolerance is a very dull virtue. It is boring. Unlike love, it has always had a bad press. It is negative. It merely means putting up with people, being able to stand things." Quoted in the *Globe and Mail* July 5th 2005.

30 Laziness was what they and I thought. In fact I had a disability, namely a total inability to use rote memory, whether in music, mathematical functions or poetry.

31 Fortunately I am not alone in my thinking. On 23rd May 2006 the Sex Education Forum associated with the Department of education in Britain issued a report asserting that the subject was treated over-biologically in schools.

[32] Cf. Lloyd, Charlotte A., *The Case of the Female Orgasm: Bias in the Science of Evolution*, Cambridge, Harvard University Press, 2005 and also Margolis, Jonathan, *O: The Intimate History the Orgasm* London, Arrow Books, 2005

[33] I am indebted to E. S. Turner's review of Francis Wheen, *How Mumbo-jumbo Conquered the World, a short history of modern delusions* Fourth Estate, 2004 in the *Times Literary Supplement* Feb 14th 2004 p. 36 for the choice of epithets.

[34]See my *Towers Besieged: The Dilemma of the Creative University*, Toronto, McClelland and Stewart, 1974 for a fuller discussion. To be republished by Webzines of Vancouver, distributed at Lulu.com in 2010.

[35] I will be showing in Chapter **XI** that this is likely to continue, and that, *properly handled*, our new world should value it, not reject it.

[36] This point is expanded in Chapter VI, Community and Diversity and has been foreshadowed in out discussion of innovation.

[37] In late 2005 the press reported that the United Kingdom government is planning to remove schools from Local Council jurisdictions, giving them greater control over their curricula, philosophies and operations. It has been interpreted as moving the principles of the public = private schools into the state sector and giving more weight to independent religious schools. This is a step in

the direction toward Youth Maturity Institutes but I have not seen reference to any required element of material such as risk taking, elimination of violence, or the integration of therapy professionals into the system. We do not expect the full implementation of Youth Maturity Institutes to be achieved over night.

[38] And it would have an effect on the role of and support for such groups

[39] This relates to the reform of the "justice" system in the next Chapter

[40] There is a model to be studied for possible insights – that of the efficient hospital. Diagnosis reveals an issue which, when being treated, displays other dimensions of concern resulting in a coordinated team of expert professionals.

[41] There is a thirty year study of this matter by S.A. Mednick, W.F. Gabrielli and B. Hutchings "Genetic influences in Criminal Convictions: Evidence from an Adoption Court" in *Science* vol. 224. no. 79, 1984 which traces the behaviour of those with the gene. Quoted in Jane Walfogel, *What Children Need* Cambridge, Harvard University Press, 2006,

[42] For the attitude of legal authorities to "precautionary risk" see Sunstein, Cass R. *Laws of Fear*. Cambridge and New York, Cambridge University Press, , 2005

---

[43] The latest, and bound to be classical, work on global kinship relationships is the brilliant treatise of Maurice Godelier, *Métamorphoses de la parenté,* Paris, Fayard, 2004 which I believe has unfortunately not yet appeared in English.

[44] Anthropologists, discovering varieties of norms, translated indigenous words as "marriage". Usually the primary criterion was cohabitation though the household might include others. But in some societies men live in common houses without females or their wives. Then the criterion had to move to that of sexual monopoly. But then there are instances in which young men have secret but permitted access to polygynous wives......

[45] In journalism and popular talk the work "polygamy" is bandied about. Technically it means a man taking multiple wives, *and* a woman taking multiple husbands – I do not know of such a state, though it would balance the sexes. For a man taking multiple wives the term is *polygyny.* For a woman taking multiple husbands, the term is *polyandry.* Julian Wake informs me of a Sherpa who had five husbands (brothers).

[46] This does NOT equate with 75% of the human population.

[47] Cf. Jacobson, Cardell K., and Lara Burtib, eds., *Modern Polygamy in the United States: Historical, cultural and legal issues.* 2011

[48] Sometimes it seems that property developers are dictating household trends.

49   A census report by Statistics Canada in 2012 revealed a sharp rise in the proportion of households consisting of a single person.

50   For those interested in the variations in family structure, and their implications for the modern world, I recommend the classic treatise of Maurice Godelier, *Métamorphoses de la Parenté*, Paris, Fayard, 2004.

51   Maurice Godelier *Métamorphoses de la parenté.* Paris, Fayard, 2004, p.564.

52   Under existing mores there is also a predatory behaviour dubbed "mate poaching" in which the initiator deliberately tries to move the affections of another person from his or her mate. This is almost deliberately hurtful and bears little resemblance to consensual multiple partnerships. See D. P. Schmidt, "Patterns and universals of mate poaching across 53 nations: The effects of sex, culture, and personality on romantically attracting another person's partner," *Journal of Personality and Social Psychology*, vol. 86 no 4 (April 2004), pp.560-584.

53   I am well aware that these assertions will be emotionally abhorrent to many. That fact does not remove the necessity to face up to their illogicality, and the ways in which the issue puts poison into other aspects of Utopian life. If in the long run I am wrong, then other aspects of Utopia will require amendment.

[54] Anato, Paul R., Alan Booth. David R. Johnson, and Stacey J. Rogers, *Alone Together: How Marriage in America is Changing.* Cambridge, Harvard University Press, 2007. Also a discussion of the postponement of formal marriage.

[55] The increased popularity of high rise condominiums, encouraged for its saving of land areas, can provide an easy and convenient practical answer. It enables partners to have two small area apartments in close proximity. Census statistics do not identify such formats.

[56] This has by no means always been the case. Muslim laws no doubt still have views on cohabitation without marriage. Such laws are still on the books of some U. S. States – in 2005 a woman is being prosecuted under an 1808 statue for cohabiting without marriage. And the European habit of requiring identification from both clients seeking a matrimonial room, and refusing such rooms to the unmarried, gave way only in the late 20th century. The illegality of homosexual interactions and sex is only just disappearing and is not yet global.

[57] The possibility of *in vitro* conception and other procedures modify this argument.

[58] Some relevant references: Lundy, Liza. *Everything Conceivable.* New York, Alfred Knopf, 2007; Almond, Brenda. *The Babies in the Twentyfirst Century* New York, Strauss and Giroux 2007; ditto *Engineering Family.* Oxford, Clarendon Press, 2006.

665

---

[59] Cloning from stem cells is on the horizon though it has so far failed in mice. While most countries seem to be disinclined to permit human cloning, in the absence of effective global government there is bound to be some place on earth where it will b e permitted. Buying babies is rampant, in addition to normal adoption, another way of creating a family. Des

[60] If you doubt this, read Charles Dickens.

[61] Quoted by Gillian Shaw in the *Vancouver Sun* December 2009

[62] Dustin Wax on the Anthro-L List Serv, September 13[th,] 2005.

[63] In some so-called "primitive" cultures such behaviour equivalents are absent, unless directed at neighbour villages as enemies. In others the brazen stance is adopted by older gangs who become role models.

[64] One does not neglect the negative sides of honour killing, and the frequent stress experienced by young people who must reject oppressive family ties to be creative in the wider world.

[65] However, it is to be hoped that Youth Maturity Institutes will in time reduce the frequency of boredom in the elderly.

[66]   I know of course of 75 year old Canadians biking in Jordan, France, Morocco and hiking in Peru, on their own, not in an organised group.

[67]   But we rejoice at the smiles, the extraordinary good will and calm support, of hospital professionals from doctors to nursing assistants.

[68]   Hvistedahl, Mara. *Unnatural Selection; Choosing boys over girls and the consequences of a world full of men.* London Public Affairs 2011.

[69]   Abott, Elizabeth ,"To the Exclusion of All Others: In a liberal society is polygamy still intolerable?" in *Walrus* May 2011 pp30-2

[70]   Lampinen, James and Cathy Secton-Radek, eds. *Protecting Children from violence: Evidence based interventions.* London, Psychology Press, 2010

[71] In November 2011 jobless rate in South Africa was 25%, 10.2% in the Euro zone, 8.3% in the U K, 9% in the U.S., and 7.3% in Canada. Rates would probably higher if those who have given up looking were included. Disproportionally high amongst youth entering the market. Note Spam, Italy, Greece, Japan.

[72]   The Arab spring raised huge expectations not just for freedom but for an immediate improvement in living conditions. The *Times Literary Supplement* of August 17 and 23 2012, page 13 reviewed the following books which I have not been able to consult: Lynch, Marc. *The Arab Uprising: The unfinished revolutions of the new Middle East.* Public Affairs Books. Bradley, John R. *After the Arab Spring: How Islamists hijacked the Middle East revolts.* Macmillan.   Dabashi, Hamid. *The Arab   Spring The end of post-colonialism.* Zed Books. Smin, Magdi *et al After the Spring: Economic Transitions in the Arab World.* Oxford University Press Weddady, Nasser and Sohrab Ahmari, eds. *Arab Spring Dreams: The next generation speaks out for freedom.* Palgrave Macmillan..

[73]   Cf. Graeber, David and Gustaaf Houtman "The Occupy Movement and Debt" in *Anthropology Today* vol. 28 no. 3 October 2012 pp. 17-18.

[74]   Cf. Smith, Christian *et al. Lost in Transition: The dark side of emerging adulthood. Oxford. Oxford University Press.*

[76] See Chapter III – Reformed Education is Imperative

[77] Check Chapter XI - Fiscal Balance – Paying for Reforms

---

[78] Another argument for morphing schools into Youth Maturity Institutes.

[80] It can be argued that the Israeli-Palestinian issue and many other contemporary military crimes will not be resolved until the combatants formally abandon that part of their religion or beliefs which requires the enforced removal of "an eye for an eye and a tooth for a tooth".

[81] Cf. Kamin. F.M. *Intricate Ethics: Rights, Responsibilities and Permissible Harm* .oxford, Oxford University Press, 2007. A somewhat doubtful use of the term "non-consequential ethics".

[82] Full graduation from a Youth Maturity Institute could be one element in such tests and ceremonies.

[83] See *Bumps on a Long Road: Essays from an Anthropologist's Memory, Volume II.* Vancouver, Webzines and Lulu.com, 2009

[84] There are of course a few charitable and some official organisations which endeavour to mitigate such problems.

---

[85] For example homosexuality, or if a man and a woman, unmarried, booked into a hotel.

[86] The physical abuses of Abu Ghaira and Guantanamo Bay are *not* an aberration. They are part of the hidden culture of United States hard-core prisons.

[87] Such policies justify citizens of other countries heaping scorn on what they can see as hypocritical bafflegab as US officials call on other countries to observe the rule of law and of international standards of just procedures. There is an extraordinary lack of a sense of irony when President Obama or Hillary Clinton pontificate on such matters. No wonder the United States will not sign onto the International Court of Justice.

[88] Michael Tonry *Thinking about Crime: Sense and Sensibility in American Penal Culture*, New York, Oxford University Press, 2004.

[89] The never-ending belief almost in the sacred pursuit of revenge between tribes in Libya and Afghanistan confuses those Western advisors and commentators who preach the merits of one man one vote. Syria is building up a huge library of revenge for which the only practical answer, and that still dangerous, may be the partition of the country.

[90] Unfortunately, this is *not* typical of the way authorities handle such trauma.

---

[91] The jurisprudence of Western criminal law

[92] Of course in some cases it is indeed the state which has been hurt, which is the victim.

[93] Mixing the discussion of youths and adults, note Griswwold, Charles E. *Forgiveness: a Philosophical Exploration.* Cambridge, Cambridge University Press, 2007.

[94] I am completely sceptical of this concept. Personally I do not believe that complete closure in the form of almost denial is practical or a likely achievement.

[95] See Heyman, Gene M. *A Disorder of Choice.* Cambridge, Harvard University Press, 2009

[96] "The no-computer virus" *The Economist* April 30th 2005, pp 65-7.

[97] Unfortunately both have closed for lack of funding. But another has opened.

[98] Think of the world's reaction to the plague, to the Black Death, even to modern influenza epidemics or Ebola.

---

[99] Source: Workers Compensation Board of British Columbia.

[100] Chatterburgh, Michael. *Gladiator School, Life inside Canadian Prisons.* Toronto, Harper Collins to appear in 2011. Chatterburgh has written perceptively in other works of youth ad gangs.

[101] We must be wary of this generalisation. Emergent studies of autism demonstrate that non-sociable individuals frequently have enormously creative intellectual capacities, and most modern creative philosophers have had social differences from the norm, and psychological pains.

[102] The destruction of the legal state of British Commonwealth citizen leads to the ambition that in its place there be such a status as Global Citizen.

[103] Cf. Bloomraad, Irene *Becoming a Citizen: Incorporating Immigrants and Refugees in the United States and Canada.* Berkeley, University of California Press, 2006.

[104] There are practical reasons for resisting the use of the complete head scarf. In modern society it is necessary on official occasions to be able to interpret facial expression.

[105] I believe it is insufficiently studied in present day

anthropology.

[106] The term, referring to the creation of a new culture, was invented by Yulian Bromley, director of a major institute of ethnology, which earned him the rank of Candidate in the USSR Academy of Sciences.

[107] Perhaps it is not accidental that the high density of adoption of smart phones in some parts of Africa is related to the upsurge in entrepreneurial activity and social activism.

[108] Urban residents the world over are increasingly embracing the foods of other cultures. Pop music, British, Canadian, Scandinavian as well as from the U.S., has an almost universal spread.

[109] Though extraordinarily fast changes are taking place. In 2009 major cables linked Africa to the internet via India and thence the wide world, in the process reducing costs. I have mentioned Uganda's use of the internet to improve medical efficiencies. Rwanda has embarked on an ambitious programme to provide a country wide internet system in which all school children will have a laptop. India is using a variety of innovative technical de vices to provide power and linkages to villages.

[110] The renaissance is by no means uniform. There is also still destitution, depression and suicide. So far positive First Nations do not help those which are lost in poverty, both material and psychological.

[111]   But note the incipient violence of gangs and often the difficulty of escaping them.

[112]   His paper is on line at the site of the Championship at http://www.soc.nu/utopian

[113]   Grewal, David Singh, *Network Power : The Social Dynamics of Globalisation.* New Haven, Yale University Press, 2008.

[114]   see, for example, André Weckmann *La Roue du Paon.* Strasbourg, bf éditions, 1988, originally published as *Odil eoder das Magiische Dreieck.* Kehl, Morstadt, 1986.

[115]   Cf. Cairns, Ed and Michael D. Roe (eds) *The Role of Memory in Ethnic Conflict.* Basingstoke and New York, 2003

[116]   This may be changing as the Hispanic population asserts its own identity.

[117] The very concept of "curry" was a British invention arising out of the need to feed sepoys. The popular Indian dish vindaloo was created by the ladies of the Portuguese in Goa as a highly spiced version of Portuguese stew – chilli had arrive d in Portugal and was now thriving in the part of India.

[118] Frequently welcomed by feudally-oppressed peasantry.

[119] Sen, Armartya *Identity and Violence: The Illusion of Destiny.* New York W.W .Norton, 2006. How distorted views of history, reality and culture can transform activity into violence.

[120] Lamey, Andy *Frontier Justice: The Global refugee Crisis and What to do about it.* Toronto Doubleday 2011. Zaiotti, Ruben *Cultures of Border Controls: Shengen and the Evolution of European Frontiers.* Chicago, University of Chicago Press, 3011. Saunders, Doug. *The Rights of Refugees.* In *Literary Review of Canada* May/August 2011 pp.3-4. Discuss refugees. 1951 U N Refugee Convention. Sovereignty v human rights, both universal.

[121] Nightingale, Carl. *Segregation: a global history of divided cities.* Chicago, University of Chicago Press, 2012

[122] In December 2012 a conference under the auspices of the All Indian Rights Organisation (AIRO) the Indian Association of Social Scientists (IAOSS) on the topic *The Future of Human Rights, Humanity and Culture in Emerging Globalized World* to be held in Lucknow

[123] In August 2012 the LSE held a Research Workshop on Business and Human Rights

[124] The phrase "natural world" is redundant, for the total world is natural. However the phrase indicates a way of thinking about that world.

[125] Clive Bell, *Civilization* Harmondsworth, Penguin, 1928.

[126] Martin Cruz Smith, *Wolves Eat Dogs*, New York etc., Simon and Schuster, 2004.

[127] Reice, Seth R. *The Silver Lining: the benefits of Natural Disasters*. Princeton, Princeton University Press, 2009.

[128] Rolf Philipona quoted by Richard Black on the BBC News website 12 November 2005.

[129] A study undertaken by scholars at five North American universities concluded that the arctic was warming at a rate faster than has been the case in 200.000 years. Californian scientist have pointed out that one effect of the warming is that sea life will migrate between the Atlantic and Pacific oceans.

[130] Reported by Jonathan Amos in BBC News Service 8 Sept. 2005.

[131] CarboEurope has established a number of towers across

Europe which monitor carbon conditions. They also refer to data from satellite instruments and records of plant growth, including forests.

[132] *Economist* 14 April 2009. The findings were reported to the BBC in September 2005.

[133] *Economist* 8 April 3009.

[134] Over-fishing here, spurred by the decline of stocks elsewhere, is the culprit.

[135] Oxfam report released 28 August 2009.

[136] The evidence is partly from tree rings supported by historical though irregular data. United States National Research council report published after release by the National Academies Press. In addition specific locations have had warmer periods from time to time. On the other hand historical data also indicate a cold spell in northern Europe.

[137] In January 2010 the United nations group on climate change was forced to admit that it prediction that Himalayan glaciers would shortly become extinct, with devastating results on major South Asian river flows, was erroneous. There was even a whiff of a corruption scandal.

---

[138] For example a meeting of sceptics was convened in London on 27 January 2005 to counter the findings of the Hedley Centre of the British Meteorological Office.

[139] This is the opinion of the Global Humanitarian Forum which is administered by Kofi Annan. In May 2009. The forum points out that estimates of rising ocean waters are highly varied.

[140] The U.K. Environmental Audit Committee says biofuels are ineffective at cutting greenhouse gases and can be expensive[140] European Union targets for 2010 unrealistic and too costly.

[141] Grant Ferrett in BBC News 17 Oct 2007

[142] Reported in BBC News 29 June 2007

[143] BBC News 13 June 2007

[144] A discussion group of the royal society of Great Britain and Ireland in April 2005 sounded an alarm and called for increased research on the modification of crops to withstand the effects of climate change. The Royal Society published the report in June 2005. It was thought that there were major benefits from the effects of CO_2 in the atmosphere, but this is less than was thought. Some crops will have their yields reduced by 30% as a result of near surface ozone.

[145] See "Lost Property: The world's fisheries are in an even worse state than previously feared." *Economist* 25 February 2012 pp.71-2

[146] Médecins sans frontiers 2011

[147] Devleena Ghosh, Heather Goodall, Stephanie Hemelryk Donald, eds. *Water, Sovereignty and Borders in Asia and Oceania.* Routledge Studies in Physical Geography and Environment Series. New York Routledge, 2009.

[148] Cf Dorothee Brantz, ed. Beastly Natures: Animals, Humans, and the Study of History. Charlottesville University of Virginia Press, 2010.

[149] BBC report in 2012.

[150] *Economist* 3 December 2011

[151] BBC 26 December 2011

[152] "*Chilling out in the winter sun*" *Economist* October 15th 2011 p.91

[153] *Economist* October 15th 2011 *p.75-6*

[154] Mainwaring, A. Bruce *et al Climate Crises in Society Human History.* American Philosophical Society 2011

[155] Yergin, Daniel *The Quest, Energy. Security, and the Remaking of the Modern World.* Penguin Press 2011.

[156] *Click* BBC World August 29 21

[157] [157] Note Michio *Physics of the Future: How science will shape human destiny and our daily lives by 2100* London Allen Lane and New York Doubleday 2011.

[158] January 30 2010.

[159] "PLOS" stands for "Public Library of Science"

[160] Much of what follows I initially treated in my book *Towers Besieged: The dilemmas of the creative university.* Routledge 1970

[161] This statement anticipates my argument about guaranteed basic income in chapters XI and XII.

---

[162] *The Economist* has frequently made similar points even more vigorously. See for example the issue of January 12th 2005 p.28. The number of on line Open Access scientific journals is expanding day by day. (I edit one of them called AnthroGlobe which is multilingual and multimedia, impossible in print.) And the Google search engine attempts to separate the gold from the dross by operating special searches which go to the original scientific documents.

[163] As I write the new e-book readers have limitations which will surely be overcome. For the many readers, especially the elderly, who have poor eyesight as with increasing macular degeneration, larger screens are desirable. For serious reading there should be an ability to take notes, verbally or by writing. I do not know of any universal catalogue of e-books similar to the printed *books in Print*, so that those interested may not find the catalogue which has the kind of book they are looking for. Rather there is an increasing number of individual lists.

[164] It is true that the price of e-books is tiny by comparison with printed, and thus royalties per copy are also tiny. But this is a market which would not otherwise exist.

[165] Some participants did not receive the news and turned up. A strong contingent of Israelis defied the ban, arrived by bus, and held their own scientific sessions.

[166] In 2012 a consortium of Arab *and Israeli* institutions announced governmental support for the creation of a centrifuge and its associated research. Arab scholars have contributed to a journal of desertification edited from Ben Gurian University near Tel Aviv and participate in joint meetings in "neutral" countries..

---

[167] In the years since I first drafted this paragraph there have been revolutionary changes in the techniques of enquiry and the resultant knowledge of the brain.

[168] Note recent advances in detecting responses and thought in persons who are unable to communicate directly.

[169] I read recently an account of voids in the universe. Observations were discovering that there was activity within the voids even though by definition they are empty of matter. Under such circumstances I find it difficult to understand how voids can in fact be empty. Activity implies energy and energy is a something. I this last sentence is to have meaning then voids are not empty and the concept of emptiness is physically meaningless.

[170] For example NASA's Near Earth Programme is directed to the interception of asteroids and there is a plan by the British firm EADS Atrium to develop a gravity tractor to interfere with the advance of asteroids.

[171] It strikes me that the identification of an eco-system is a little like the identification of a society -- an arbitrary creation of a boundary within which a system can be abstracted by leaving out of consideration external factors. Thus a neighbourhood as a social system, an ethnic community as a society, a country is one. The only true society that corresponds with nature, the only true eco-system that corresponds with nature, is global. And even that, particularly with nature, can be extended to include extra-terrestrial events.

[172] Norway is working on an Arctic vault intended to preserve the seeds of all known crops.

[173] Byers, William. *The Blind Spot: Science and the Crisis of Uncertainty.* Princeton, Princeton University Press, 2011

[174] *Economist* 31 Dec 2011 p. 63

[175] Basen, Ira *"Economics has met the enemy and the enemy is economics".* *Globe and Mail* October 15, 2011 pp F1, 6-7

[176] Goldacre, Ben *Bad Science.* London, Fourth Estate, 2009. A well documented account of bad science and scientific reporting including the misuse of statistics, A warning not to take reports of "scientific" conclusions at face value without assessing the procedures used.

[177] Basen, Ira *"Economics has met the enemy and the enemy is economics".* *Globe and Mail* October 15, 2011 pp F1, 6-7

[178] Georg3 Dyson quoted by Dens Overbye in the New York Times Science Times of June 5th 2012.

[179] When I pointed this out during the discussion (which could hardly be called a debate) I was almost booed and the President of the session appeared to take pains to ignore my later requests for the floor.

683

[180] Only one of the economics Nobel prize winners still specialised in matters of choice: Kenneth Arrow. I gave up reading the Journal of the Royal Economics Society in the 1940's when mathematics started to dominate their articles.

[181] *Click* BBC World 29 August 211

[183] See Bernard Lewis, *The Assassins, a radical sect in Islam*, London, Weidenfeld and Nicholson, 1967.

[184] See Nevin Halici, *Sufi Cuisine*. London, Saqi, 2005.

[185] Cf. Ledwidge, Frank. *Losing Small Wars: British military failure in Iraq and Afghanistan.* New Haven, Yale University Press, 2012

[186] Political or religious murder has been with us from early days. It was used in the Greco-Roman world. But its use coupled with propaganda and threats, true deliberate terrorism, seems to have begun with the Assassins, a breakaway Shi'a-Ismaili sect, and there are passages in the Q'ran which terrorists can use to justify the removal of an unjust ruler by such means. There is a direct ideological link between today's Middle Eastern terrorists and the movements of centuries ago, although no one these days would like

Ismaili with the branches of Shi'a which rely on such thoughts. Nineteenth-twentieth century Anarchists often held such views. See the excellent summary in Chapter 6 of Lewis, Bernard, *The Assassins* London, Wiedenfeld and Nicholson, 1967. However a major difference between Assassins and Anarchists on the one hand and modern Islamist terrorists, on the other is that the latter target civilians, for which there is clearly no justification in the Q'ran.

[187] One segment of the Taliban has issued a code of conduct in which it eschews violence and the harming of civilians.

[188] My views about Islam have been enhanced by accessing debates in the Sociology of Islam internet discussion group, where all aspects of Muslim religion interpretations and also public policy are clearly and vehemently discussed.

[189] For the shameful tragedy in Darfur, which once again demonstrates the self-seeking stance of nation states which I will examine in a later chapter, see Prunier, Gérard, *Darfur: The Ambiguous Genocide* Ithaca, Cornell University Press, 2005.

[190] For those readers interested in the dynamics and genesis of ideological violence, I recommend the papers contributed to the internet journal *Ideologies of War and Terror* which go well beyond current events at http://www.ideologiesofwarandterror.com

[191] A vivid account of the claustrophobic world of Palestine and its relationship to the *intifada* and terrorism is given in Anne-Marie Olivfier and Paul Feinberg, *The Road to Martyrs' Square: a*

journey into the world of the suicide bomber, Oxford, Oxford University Press, 2005.

[192]   In my *The Sorcerer's Apprentice: an anthropology of public policy,* New York etc. Pergamon.

[193]   Anne-Marie Olivier and Paul Feinberg op.cit.

[194]   As in 2012 Northern Mali where a movement with the same name is preaching more secular and popular messages, quite different from the more radical movement of Yemen.

[195]   Some support for my thesis may be found in   Mai Ghoussoub and   Emma Sinclair-Webb, eds. Imag*ined Masculinities: Modernity and Culture in the Modern Middle East,* London, Saqi Books, 2000.   Note also Lahouzine   Ouzgane, ed. *Islamic Masculinities,* London, Zed Books, 2006

[196] The situation is different for women. Women terrorists seem to be mostly well educated in both secular and religious matters. Here I see them excluded from recognition in society: supporting political movements, including terrorism, provides a route to recognition with martyrdom the apogee.

[197] In Lahoucine Ouzgane, *op. cit.*

[198] For Irian Jaya (West Papua) see the *Economist* June 30th

Manifesto for the New Age

2012 p.46

[199] The inaugural edition of the *Journal of International Relations Research* in 2012 *was* devoted to the theme "Terrorism and Violence" with the comment in its 2011 call for papers "The human fascination with violence and terrorism is evident in the wealth of multimedia news reporting as well as academic and popular writing on the subject. But how does this reflect on society and the subject matter at hand? Are contemporary narratives, explanations and analysis providing fruitful or even sufficient representations of the realities?

[200] Cabanssu G, William T. *The Myth of Religious Violence.* London and New York Oxford University Press 2010 stresses hat religious violence can be the surface of deeper political family and secular expansionist interests. Toscano, Alberto. *Fanaticism; On the uses of an idea.* London, Verso, 2010 Religion is a social unifying force organising other objectives. The   For the nature and ramifications of fear in societies see Gardner, Daniel *The Science of Fear: How we fear things we shouldn't – and put ourselves in greater danger.* New York, Dutton, 2008. Discussions on the War on Terror are offered in books listed in *The Economist* Sept 3 2011 as Gerges, Franz. *The Rise and Fall of Al Qaeda* Oxford University Press; Wright, Robin. *Rock the Casbah, Rage and rebellion across the Arab World* Simon and Schuster 2011; Cowper-Coles, Sherard. *Cables from Kabul, The inside story of the West/s Afghanistan Campaign* Harper Press 2011; Burke, Jason. *The 9/11 Wars* Penguin Global, 2011. Note also: Rashid, Ahmed. *Descent into Chaos: The World's most unstable region and the threat to global security.* Penguin 2009; Crews Robert D and Amin Trazi, eds. *The Taliban and the Crisis of Afghanistan.* Harvard University Press 2009; Tanner, Stephen. *Afghanistan; A military history from Alexander the Great to the war against the Taliban.* Da Capo Press, 2009.   A history of tribal leaders who asserted power through warfare and resistance to so

called superior administration, like Mongol tribal leaders. Taliban an uncentralised alliance. Northern Tajiks and Uzbeks who resent the theoretical loss of power to the centre; Pashtun who dominate the Taliban. Shi'a Hazaras who are resentful of the Pashtun. (Pathans?) Tendency to accuse local rivals as Taliban.

[201] Roach, Kent *The 9-11 Effect: Comparative Counter-terrorism.* Cambridge, Cambridge University Press, 2011

[202] Cf. De Botton, Alain. *The Pleasures and Sorrows of Work*, London, Hamish Hamilton, 2008. An ironic survey.

[203] On 13 February 2010 the New Economics Foundation called for a 21 hour work week which it claimed would boost the economy – BBC News

[204] The young, leaving high school, are increasingly aware of this opportunity, taking time off to backpack around the world before going on to higher education or employment.

[205] And only too often the validatory myth honours ruthless competition with an objective of squishing the rivals.

[206] Mount, Ferdinand. *The New Few: Or a very British oligarchy: Power and inequality in Britain now.* London, Simon and Schuster 2012

[207] Paperny, Anna Mehler and Tavia Grant "How Paying People's Way out of Poverty can Improve all our Pocketbooks:

[208] Andersen, Erin. *To end poverty guarantee everyone in Canada $20,000 a year.* *Globe and Mail* November 20 2010 pp F1 *et seq.*

[209] Note the persuasive analysis by James Hughes "Why we can't afford poverty" *Literary Review of Canada* vol. 20 no.3 April 2012 pp. 3-5.

[210] *Economist* 26 March 2011

[211] Al Jazeera 24 November 2011

[212] Note however Bauman, Zygmunt. *Collateral Damage: Social inequality in a global age.* Polity Press, 2011

[213] de Wolff, Alice. *Working Without Commitment: The Health effects of Precarious Employment.* Toronto, McGill Queens University Press, 2006

[214] Although I will be challenging the ideology of unrestrained growth in the next chapter.

[215] Many of which still have to be argued for in later chapters.

[216] Flat tax introduced in Estonia (26% personal and corporate, no deductions) Latvia, Lithuania, Russia (13% personal), Slovakia (19% personal and corporate), Poland leaning in the direction.

[217] Cf. My *The Conditions of Social Performance op.cit.*

[218] Compare Barbera. Robert *The Cost of Capitalism: Understanding Market Mayhem and Stabilising our Economic Future.* New York, McGraw Hill 2009 and Elliott, Larry and Dan Atkinson *The gods that Failed: How Blind Faith in Markets has cost us our Future.* New York Nation Books 2009

[219] In some countries, such as Thailand, the military directly own and operate firms.

[220] I am not sufficiently informed as to how Muslim banking handles these issues. In Britain Shari 'a banks lend by taking a share in the profits of the recipient company.

[221] Cf. *The Economist* 26 Sept 2009 for a critique of business

schools, though not along these lines.

222 The 2008-10 financial crisis cut off the *supply* of capital though the *demand* remained high. And would have been higher if consumption has been supported.

223 The golf course, the membership club. Yachts, dining parties and the now common institution of networking, prove to be crucial institutions for the creation of partnerships and access to money.

224 Business newspapers often put "financial" in their titles and almost always devote the major part of their copy to the discussion of stock prices, the financial aspect of company takeovers, profit and loss, with far lee space given to the nature of the product. Perhaps the rise of digital technology at the present speed does give an impetus to informing readers about some technical advance. What workers think of the company is hardly even mentioned, except in lists of "best employers".

225 Ideas and studies are appearing almost monthly. E.g. Bair, Sheila, *Bull by the Horns: Fighting to Save Main Street from Wall Street and Wall Street from itself.* New York Simon and Schuster, 2o1;

226 I set out the variables which need to be measured in *The Conditions of Social Performance, op. cit.*

[227] www.ihdp.unu.edu/article/iwr June 17 2011 to be published by Cambridge University Press. Though the unit of comparison is the country, similar considerations apply to organisations.

[228] an interview with Immanuel Wallerstein Thanks to John McCrery.

[229] Das, Sanjit. *Extreme Money; Masters of the Universe and the Cult of Risk.*. New York, Prentice Hall 2011.

[230] "Cut or Lose: History suggests that austerity and growth don't Mix." In *Economist* July 16th 2011 p.79.

[231] *Globe and Mail* 23 August 2012 p.1.

[232] I noticed this in the approaches to Lima. On my first visit the shacks beside the river on the way in from the airport were built of cardboard and flattened tins. Later, slowly, more durable materials supplanted these. Then came upper stories and TV antennas.

[233] I have an account of the webs of reciprocity related to marriage and other events in my *Under the Ivi Tree: Social and Economic Growth in Rural Fiji*. London Routledge and Kegan Paul, 1964 Reprinted in 2004 in Routledge Library Editions.

234   I give some European examples and examine the technical issues involved in my *The Conditions of Social Performance: an exploratory theory.* London, Routledge and Kegan Paul, 1969. Reprinted in the International Library of Sociology: Theory and Methods, Routledge, 1996.

235 The 2005 Report on the State of World Population of the United Nations Population Fund at http://www.unfpa.org/swp/2005/pdf/en_swp05.pdf singles out gender inequality and reproductive health as the two major factors hindering the ability of populations to take advantage of measures of societal progress.

236 And we must beware a tendency for a few crisis-managing NGOs to perpetuate themselves and become businesses in their own right.

237 *A Critical Analysis of Community Development as an Economic, Social and Administrative Process.* Mimeograph paper for an ad hoc group of experts, Bureau of Social Affairs, United Nations, 1962.

238   *Under the Ivi Tree: Society and Economic Growth in Rural Fiji,* London, Routledge and Kegan Paul, 1964. Reissued 2004.

239 When the Community Development movement in India moved from spontaneity to becoming a department of government

240 This is not unknown in the richer world. I was once called in to report on dysfunctional rivalries in the British Columbia cooperative movement. The C.D. officers were given targets of results to meet, which subverted the underlying principle that the goals of the programmes should precisely reflect the goals of the people.

241 See Jim Igoe and Tim Kensall, *Between a Rock and a Hard Place: African NGOs, Donors and the State.* Durham, University of Carolina Press, 2005, for good case studies and analysis.

242 See my 'Evaluation of Technical Assistance as a Contribution to Development', *International Development Review*, June 1966 vol. VIII, no 3.

243 There are unfortunately some NGOs whose purpose is distorted by ideological or proselytizing goals.

244 Jeffrey Sachs, *The End of Poverty: How we can make it happen in our time.* London, Penguin, 2005.

245 See the work of the Kenyan anthropologist A.B.C. Ocholla-Ayoyo.

246 Sometimes such questions are genuinely explored and sometimes they are then abandoned as being beyond the mandate or

the resources of the aid agent.

[247]Cf. my "Evaluation of Technical Assistance as a Contribution to Development", *International Development Review* vol. viii, no 2, pp 2-6 and 23, 1966.

[248] The shocking slum bulldozing in Zimbabwe in 2005 is but one example, which hit the headlines because it is Zimbabwe. It has also happened in Malawi.

[249] See Norenna Herttz, *The Debt Threat: How Debt is Destroying the Developing World.* New York, Harper Collins 2005.

[250] In October 2005 African Ministers of Science and Technology committed to integrate science, technology and innovation into their development plans. This is a very small part of the issue for countries without natural resources.

[251] Popular music has led the way in many poorer and poorest countries. A number of great architects have emerged on the international scene from Brasil and the Middle East. India has dramatically entered the IT world.

[252] The production of ethanol from other sources, such as maize, has major problems resulting from the overuse of lands and the extension of crops in deforested lands. My thought is directed to the conversion of *existing* sugar producing lands.

[253]   Mishkin, Frederick S. *The Nest great Globalization: How disadvantaged nations can harness their financial systems to get rich.* Princeton, Princeton University Press, 2010

[254]   Nutt, Samantha *Damned Nations: Greed, Guns, Armies and Aid*   Oxford, Signal, 2011

[255]   Smillie, Ian *Blood on the Stone: Greed. Corruption and war in the global diamond trade.* Anthenm Press, 2010

[256] *Economist* September 24 2011 pp 72 *et seq.*

[257] Salzman, Philip, *Culture and Conflict in the Middle East.* New York, Humanity Books, 2008. Salzman's Middle East stretched from Iran to Morocco.

[258] Kublai Khan's claims were disputed because he was too "Chinese" and turned his back on nomadic roots.   Much later Tamerlane though the undisputed master of armies which he held together from Russia through pillage, refused the claim the Great Khanate for lack of genealogical legitimacy. He appointed puppets from   those   who   claimed Ghengis as their ancestors.

---

[259] Salzman, Philip, *op.cit.*

[260] A religion centred on a tribe.

[261] The holistic principle which I am using links this situation directly with issues relating to global government and to the analysis of the desirable position of the state itself.

[262] Interestingly by contrast, United Nation influenced policy in Somalia as Mogadishu was regaining control, legitimized constitutional decisions through an assembly of tribal "elders".

[263] The late Mongol leader Tamerlane took care not to name himself Khan for he lacked the genealogical legitimacy.

[264] Al-Jazeera English 22 August 2012

[265] A view of the place of States in the world order, consistent with and perhaps reinforcing this argument, is presented in Robert Cooper, *The Breaking of Nations: Order and Chaos in the 21st Century*. London, Atlantic Books, 2003.

[266] Although I am in favour of using abstract theory when the propositions are testable, I am not enamoured of the approach of Patrick Carroll in *Science, Culture and Modern State Formation*

Berkeley, University of California Press,, 2006, which appear to me to be a pretty fantasy devoid of reality and containing untestable generalizations.

[267] There is a need for a glob organisation of copyrights and patents

[268] I have explored the methodological implications of this perspective in my *The Conditions of Social Performance, op.cit.* The unpublished study compares Canada and the Swiss Romande.

[269] This is why, if my first responder does not handle my issue appropriately I now ignore the middle ranks an immediately go directly to the Minister pr the CEO.

[270] At present unpublished.

[271] Contemporary Swiss labour law and practice, for example, is a result of the horror of the population at the violence and disruption caused by labour disruption during the Great Depression.

[272] The homogeneity is on the way out. Feigners lead large Japanese corporations. Foreign workers are imported and demanding recognition and equal rights.

[273] Clear differences in political opinion exist from state to state, and in the 2012 presidential election the media placed major emphasis on black v. Whit v. Latino opinions, rooted in differences in

---

way of life.

[274] Vancouver city announcements are regularly provided in translation for such languages. Despite the high Germanic population, German speakers are expected to be natural in English.

[275] There are many who disagree with my thesis. Two such are Alexander Gray and Adam Tomkins, *How We Should Rule Ourselves*, Edinburgh, Canongate, 2005. Writing of Scotland, they do not face up to the problem that democracies, as in the Weimar Republic, can go horribly wrong – and then what?

[276] An exception is perhaps Thailand, a country of past coups and coup threats. Even here though, the reverence with which the public holds the royal family enables the King to intervene more directly than would normally be the case.

[277] See the final chapter.

[278] Note: Acemoglu, Daron and James A. Robinson. *Why Nations Fail: The origins of power, prosperity and poverty*. Chicago, University of Chicago Press, 2012.

[279] See Chapter IX for further reference to this subject.

[280] Cyril Belshaw *Changing Melanesia* Melbourne Oxford University Press, 1954. Reid, Richard J. *Frontiers of Violence in North-East Africa: Genealogies of conflict since c.1800* Oxford, Oxford University Press, 2011

[281] Fisher, David. *Morality and War: Can war be just in the twenty-first century?* London, Oxford University Press, 2011

[282] Cowper-Coles, Sherard. *Cables from Kabul: The inside story of the West's Afghanistan campaign."*London, Harper, 2011. Shaffer, Antony. *Operation Dark Heart: Spycraft and Special Operations on the front lines of Afghanistan."*. Mainstream Press, 2011. Bird, Tim and Alex Marshall. *"Afghanistan: How the West lost its way."* New Haven, Yale University Press, 2011. Tomsen, Peter. *The Wars of Afghanistan: Messianic terrorism, tribal conflicts, and the failures of the Great Powers."* Public Affairs, 2011

[283] Pinker, Steven. *The Better Aspects of our Nature: How violence has declined,* New York Viking 2011. Munchem, Robert. *A History of Violence: From the end of the Middle Ages to the present.* London, Polity, 2011

[284] Anne-Marie Slaughter, *A New World Order*, Princeton and Oxford, Princeton University Press, 2004. See also Drezner, Daniel. *All Politics is Global: Explaining International Regulatory Regime.* Princeton, Princeton University Press 2007 which includes case studies and his *Locating the Proper Authorities, the interaction between domestic and international institutions.* University of Michigan Press 2006 which contains a collection of essays

demonstrating the interweaving.

[285] The evolving draft may be checked for input at http://www.anthropologising.ca/writing/wemovagla.htm

[286] Whether this will change as a result of the 2005 G8 summit remains to be seen.

[287] Armstrong, Paddy *swords into Ploughshares: Bringing Peace to the 21st Century* London, Weidenfeld and Nicholson, 2007 is a case study of Bosnia where he was the United Nations administrator. Also Reed, Charles and David Ryan *The Price of Peace: Just War in the 21st Century.* Cambridge, Cambridge University Press 2007 which is a Christian view of the just war and is relevant for the Global Government interventions I advocate.

[288] President George W. Bush either does not understand or will not recognize this jural position. He gives the impression that his conception of the United Nations is that of just another country to be used or ignored at his will. The United States does not subject its policies to the oversight of the United Nations, but feels free to accept or reject that oversight as it suits. It is not the only country to do so, but it is the most obvious one, and its example encourages others to do likewise.

[289] As I prepare this text, *The Independent* carries a story indicating that the new US Ambassador to the United Nations is seeking to roll back proposed UN commitments on aid to developing countries, combating global warming and nuclear disarmament. This strengthens my proposition below that States are incapable of

701

objectively operating a world government.

[290] Small Arms Survey Project reports that 640 million small arms and light weapons are responsible for at least 300,000 deaths annually. Graduate Institute for International Studies, Geneva. Oxford, Oxford University Press, 2004.

[291] The Harry Frank Guggenheim Foundation is supporting research in these matters and is considering the possibility of the establishment of a consortium for the coordination of such research. Papers on the subject and the proposal are contained in the Foundation's *HFG Review,* 2005, "Small Arms and Light Weapons". The material is also available at http://www.temple.edu'cenfad/small

[292] Brian Wood in *Le Monde Diplomatique* June 2006 urges tough controls over the arms trade.

[293] The success of ocean piracy off the east coast of Africa, in the Indian ocean and in the straits of Malacca may be adduced in favour of the idea of impracticality. Although French and Chinese navies have achieved success, the combination of revised laws of the sea and escorted groups of ships un der Global Government control could be substantially more effective. The *effective* Global Government I shall advocate would be able to authorise and deploy rapid military action against such havens as the Somali pirate settlements without fear of one power veto.

[294] P. W Singer, *Children at War*. New York, Pantheon, 2005 and Lynn Jones, *Then they started shooting: Growing up in Wartime Bosnia.* Cambridge, Harvard University Press, 2005.

---

[295] There are two excellent and well written books on the history of warfare up to the present emergence of "industrial warfare". Both, in their conclusions, accept the power of nation states to conduct warfare, which is the antithesis of my argument. Rupert Smith, in *The Utility of Force: the art of war in the modern world* London, Allen Lane, 2005, indeed accepts war as a fact of life and confines his reforms to applying reason to a decision to embark on war, thus making States more cautious. Dwayne Dyer, in *War* (new edition) Toronto, Viking Canada 2005 concludes with a chapter "The End of War" which in fact sees no end. These two approaches, though cries of despair, give up far too easily.

[296] A major defect in the Western approach to Afghanistan political reform has been to use a Western model of "democracy" as the goal without adapting and building upon traditional local procedures.

[297] I put independence in inverted commas because, clearly, Utopian Global Government implies the transfer of many State powers to the global entity, as is, of course, already the case.

[298] The failure of the United States to accept that the holding of prisoners in Guantanamo bay a and their reception by countries under the same conditions, without trial or sufficient evidence to lead to a trial, is contrary to this sort of proposition.

[299] See T. G. Otte's review of George Monbiot's, *The Age of Consent: A Manifesto for a new world order.* in the *Times Literary Supplement,* Sept. 26, 2003 and found his book which is: George Monbiot, *The Age of Consent.* London Flamingo, 2003. Monbiot's scheme for the democratization of the United Nations has something in common with my own. To that extent the heading "Lonely on a Cold Mountain" and the condescending assertion that "even"

703

Monbiot accedes that his ideas are impractical are disproven by the fact that he and I come to similar conclusions independently. In other words, individuals are moving their thoughts in similar directions. However, in my view Monbiot is so scared of his own ideas he weakens them. He acknowledges the cost of a world parliament as overwhelming – but it would be far less than the combined General Assemblies of the total United Nations family with which I would do away.

[300] Note that I have been emphasizing the importance of higher education in poorer countries.

[301] The small Swiss Cabinet consists of members of the main political parties in the legislature, not just a majority party. It is chaired by a President, an office which rotate through the cabinet each New Year.

[302] The case for present day global taxation is forcibly made in articles to appear in *The Journal of Applied Philosophy* in 2013.

[303] Examples of appropriate conditions might be: failure to maintain a level of living over a given number of years; internal massacres; breaches of human rights, failure to operate an educational system. Trusteeship could be a tool to back up the rapid deployment force (Rwanda) and could have been used to handle post-war Iraq pending the establishment of security and self-government. In a sense something like it has been used for Bosnia and Kosovo.

[304] I am in the process of studying and analysing the

relationship between the "Web of Moral Values Globally Approved" and local cultures (from the United States to Papua New Guinea). A very preliminary draft may be viewed at http://www.anthropologising.ca./writing/wemovagla.doc.

[305] As originally proposed, "genocide" included what we now call "ethnocide" but this broad definition was not internationally adopted so that internationally ethnocide without the physical destruction of populations, come under the heading of the right to cultural survival.

[306] In September 2012 the department of political science in the University of St Gallen held a conference on the topic *Justice and Legitimacy in Global Governance* at which papers on the following topics were presented: *'What Democracy Requires': 'Justice and Accountability in the Global Order': 'Internationalist Agenda, Transnational Political Action': 'Human Rights, Sovereignty and the Legitimacy of International Law' :'Today's Deep Global (Mis-) Governance'* http://www.gdg-hsg.ch/index-workshops-2012justice.html

[307] Khabba, Parag. *How to Run the World; Charting a course to the Next Renaissance.* New York, Random House, 2011 Attempts to make a case for global NGOs to democratise and influence world government

---

[308] It is ironic that highly religious movements, believing in a hereafter of Paradise, frequently attempt to achieve paradise on earth through mystical means.

[309] Amartya Sen, *The Argumentative Indian*, London, Allen Lane, 2005, and the *Bhagavad Gita* again.

[311] Khabba, Parag. *How to Run the World; Charting a course to the Next Renaissance.* New York, Random House, 2011 Attempts to make a case for global NGOs to democratise and influence world government.

[312] Walker, James W. St. G., and Andrew S. Thomson *Critical Mass The Emergence of Global civil society* Waterloo, Ontario, Wilfred Laurier University Press 2008.

[313] The name may have to be adjusted. A quick Internet search brings up an International Council of Voluntary Agencies (concerned with volunteerism), a Council of International NGOs (concerned with Kosovo), World Volunteers for Africa. There is a World Movement for Non-Violence based in southern Brasil which proposes in its constitution a World Council of NGOs.

---

[314] Per Nor beck, who joined me on the podium as a winner in the 2004-2005 World Utopian Championship, received accolades for a limited but creative and practical initiative. In his home town of Vallentuna, Sweden, he mobilised high school students and other young people to discuss city issues via the Internet. The response was electric, so much so that a non-partisan political party formed and elected a member to the city council, and influenced its policies. Apply such a technique and principle to the national and global stage.

[315] Which at its inception lacked a strategic focus.

www.ingramcontent.com/pod-product-compliance
Lightning Source LLC
Chambersburg PA
CBHW031300310326
41914CB00116B/1737/J